# Also in Plains Histories

# Women on the North American Plains

# Women on the North American Plains

Edited by **Renee M. Laegreid**
and **Sandra K. Mathews**

Foreword by Joan M. Jensen

Texas Tech University Press

This book is typeset in Minion. The paper used in this book meets the minimum requirements of ANSI/NISO Z39.48–1992 (R1997). ∞

Designed by Kasey McBeath

Library of Congress Cataloging-in-Publication Data

Women on the North American Plains / edited by Renee M. Laegreid and Sandra K. Mathews ; foreword by Joan M. Jensen.
        p. cm. — (Plains histories)
    Includes bibliographical references and index.
    Summary: "The first comprehensive work highlighting the diversity of women's experiences on the North American Plains; twelve essays present women's perspectives from prehistory to the present, across the northern, central, and southern plains"—Provided by publisher.
        ISBN 978-0-89672-733-5 (hardcover : alk. paper) — ISBN 978-0-89672-728-1 (pbk. : alk. paper) 1. Women—Great Plains—History. 2. Women—Great Plains—Social conditions. 3. Sex role—Great Plains—History. 4. Frontier and pioneer life—Great Plains. I. Laegreid, Renee M. II. Mathews, Sandra K., 1963-
        HQ1410.W66 2011
        305.40978—dc23                                          2011024876

Printed in the United States of America
11 12 13 14 15 16 17 18 19 / 9 8 7 6 5 4 3 2 1

Texas Tech University Press
Box 41037 I Lubbock, Texas 79409–1037 USA
800.832.4042 I ttup@ttu.edu I www.ttupress.org

To the memory of my grandmother, Italia
Evelina Presutti Martini Drommond, who
never shied away from an adventure

Renee M. Laegreid

To my eternally supportive parents, M. Jack
and Dorothy J. Mathews; my loving husband,
Dale M. Benham; and my four-legged sidekick,
Dulcinea

Sandra K. Mathews

# Contents

# Part III

# Illustrations and Maps

# Acknowledgments

Creating this anthology has been an amazing adventure, from the initial conceptualization of the project onward, and we are deeply indebted to the many people who helped bring it to fruition. First and foremost we thank the talented group of authors who contributed to this volume; their words bring to life the diversity of women and their roles throughout the Great Plains.

Several colleagues provided comments on the manuscript at various stages, and their thoughtful criticisms and suggestions have been immensely helpful in constructing the final version. Many thanks to Susan Armitage, Michael Lansing, and Todd Kerstetter, as well as the anonymous reviewers, for providing valuable critiques and guidance. We have had the good fortune to work with colleagues at our respective institutions that have made our jobs easier. Meg Goodenburger, Hastings College librarian, is nothing short of a magician for obtaining obscure interlibrary loan requests; Connie Gerhardt, administrative assistant in the History Department, provided assistance-on-demand and good cheer, as have the undergraduate history assistants over the years: Marie Pylypczuk, Rebecca Burgess, Carrie Moore, and Heidi Hullinger. To Carl Laegreid, HC alumnus, we owe a debt of thanks for supplying the maps. Colleagues at Nebraska Wesleyan University who deserve special recognition include Maxine Fawcett-Yeske, Sara Jane Dietzman, and Rachel Pokora, as well as Daniel P. Aragón, currently of the State Department in Brazil.

We owe sincere thanks to two individuals. John Wunder, editor for the Texas Tech University Press Plains Histories series, suggested the idea for this volume and has generously given advice and support as the project unfolded. Our wonderful editor, Judith Keeling, truly understood the nature of this undertaking. She encouraged us throughout with unfailing patience, guidance, good humor, and faith that we would, indeed, reach the end of the tunnel.

# In the Absence of Trees and Women's Voices

## A Plainsword

*Women on the North American Plains* amplifies the voices of women so that they rise above the sound of the wind coming off those treeless places. They become a part of our journeys throughout that wide swath that separates east from west, that runs in a crescent of grasslands north and south.

I look at the map of the Great Plains and am awash in personal memories of this inland sea of grass, this fertile desert, as it has sometimes been called. I try to make order of my memories of crossing the plains, for I have never paused to live there. My points of reference are the northern Midwest where I was born, just east of the Mississippi, and the Southwest where I grew up and have lived most of my life.

I now live in the Mesilla Valley, New Mexico, just west of the most southern outcropping of the Rocky Mountains. From this valley, at the tail end of the Rockies, I must drive east and north, across the plains, to get to most places I want to go. Sometimes I have been a part of the fly-over, that term coined in reference to those who pass above the plains and never experience it. Mostly, however, I have driven across. When I drive east, my favorite route is out over the Organ and Sacramento Mountains across the New Mexico plains through Clovis with its smell of roasting peanuts. I head for Amarillo, which seems comfortable smack dab in the middle of the southern plains. Other cities cling to the margins of the plains. San Antonio, at the southern edge, looks northwest. Calgary, Saskatchewan, at the northern edge, looks southeast. Denver, with its back to the Rockies, looks out at what folks there call the Front Range. People to the east, in Lincoln, Nebraska, say they live at the eastern edge of the plains. All this hints at a sort of dread—perhaps a disenfranchisement—of the plains, which may be why we seldom hear the voices of the women who lived there.

I try to fit my experiences into this new frame where women speak up and form a chorus for the landscape. I remember a side trip from Amarillo to Palo Duro Canyon, encased in so much foggy morning light that it did no good to leave the car for I could not see past the guardrail. Then there was the small motel, one of the last in the hinterlands of Amarillo, where the owner insisted I try "her" breakfast gravy. To me gravy was brown, not white, so I refused. She persisted. I ate. Her pride as a cook, and that extraordinarily delicious gravy, still lingers in memory. Once, when I crossed the plains heading toward Amarillo, both roadsides of Interstate 40 were blanketed in yellow wildflowers as far as I could see. Another time, rime etched each blade of grass. I usually turned north at Oklahoma City and left what I knew as the eastern edge of my West.

There were two visits to Lubbock, Texas, too. Like Amarillo to its north, it sprawls across the southern plains. I arrived in the 1990s to a booming city, mingling its profits from ranching and oil. I could not match it to the raw and barren small town of the 1950s, where I had visited from Southern California for my brother's wedding. He was an air force officer training at Reece Air Force Base and the small town then seemed to meld uneasily its southern attitudes with the more international views of its airmen temporarily resident there. Then I was a shy high school student; now I was an established historian of women. I had been asked to speak on rural Texas women, and I did. But women at the university also introduced me to that rather surprising way Texas ranch women had collected art. The Diamond M fine arts collection had just arrived on campus a few years earlier, and I learned how Evelyn Claire Littleton McLaughlin, a Tennessee schoolteacher, now ranch and oil baroness, had started collecting art with her husband in 1921 and added to it until her death in 1971. How could one landscape and one history contain these extremes of wealth and poverty: the women who labored in the cotton fields and the ranch women who presided over the households, if not the fields, of these vast holdings of rangeland dotted with oil wells?

When my research road trips took me north, I headed northeast through Raton, New Mexico, and out onto the plains at Trinidad, Colorado, for the journey toward the eastern border of Colorado. I passed through the Comanche National Grasslands, then north through land now irrigated with pivot sprinklers. One lucky day, I saw fields of sunflowers turned toward me in the morning sun. Just south of the Kansas border, I would join Interstate 70 and head east to Kansas City.

One year I continued north through the grasslands of western Nebraska. A small figure appeared on the horizon. As we drew closer, it turned out to be a flag woman, who motioned us to stop. There was not a house, or car, or another person, just two of us in the car, and the wind blowing past this solitary woman. I rolled down the window to chat. "Beautiful," I remarked. "Is it always so windy?" I asked. "Always," she replied with a frown. A few minutes later, in response to her walkie-talkie, she motioned me on through. I left her there on the plains like some modern version of that 1917 photograph by Laura Gilpin, the one where a woman, a long skirt billowing around her, gazes across the flat grasslands. I took the small roads that year and clocked only forty miles on the interstate highways between Trinidad, Colorado, and Mankato, Minnesota.

On yet another trip, I found my aunt's grave on a hill west of Regina, Saskatchewan. I never could find her farmstead, lost as it was to view among the oil wells and the unmarked squares of farmland around them. I used to wonder as a child how letters addressed simply to Browning, Saskatchewan, could possibly reach her. I have a photo of me, aged three, atop one of their giant workhorses. And I remember her stories of her hard life there on the plains.

I travel south to north as did the Hispania Patricia de la Garza de León, the rancher described in one essay—as Mexican women still travel, though with increasing difficulty. As I travel north, it is not only the land that echoes with these women's stories but the expressive cultures that they left behind. Everywhere we look, when we really look, we see their material legacy. In the Southwest, we see their aesthetic traditions in paper and textiles. Paper flowers still decorate their graves—though more likely women now use plastic rather than paper. They still create family *altarcitos* (little altars) and temporary ones for the Day of the Dead. *Nichos*, with statues of saints, still dot some yards. *Colchas* (embroideries) and quilts are preserved in museums as well as in family collections. Hispanias brought many of their traditions onto the southern plains.

Catholic nuns taught embroidery skills to Hispanic and Native women alike. Protestant missionary women brought quilting west, then taught it to Kiowa and Crow women. Native women were willing to listen to these women preachers to get their hands on calico and to learn piecing techniques. The geometry of piecing was especially compatible with the aesthetic traditions of the Sioux women who adopted the Star quilt pattern to their own cultural traditions. Everywhere that fabric and beads became commercially available, women of the plains created art to embellish dwelling places and the bodies of people and horses. From the South, through Oklahoma, women brought quilt traditions shared by African and Anglo American women alike. While dealing creatively with climate, patrons, patriarchs, government officials, wind and snow, heat and drought, women drew strength from singing and feasting, and from fashioning material goods into objects of beauty.

Some years ago, I arrived in Cody, Wyoming, near the northwest corner of the plains. It was July and a dry wind had bedeviled us all the way from Raton on the southwest plains. We parked our RV at the edge of a ravine and huddled there as a blizzard shook our tin-walled vehicle. We made an emergency trip to a local store for an auxiliary heater, and coped. The next day I went to see the Plains Indian Museum. As I entered, I took a mimeographed leaflet that explained that three-quarters of the objects displayed were made by women—the wall of moccasins, the elaborately quilled and beaded clothing, the horse equipage. I remember the wind, but even more the beauty that women created on these plains.

I have haunted museums and archives, I admit, looking for the history of women. The bits and pieces of their history usually lie scattered about, casually, isolated in time and space. In this book, these bits and pieces are gathered together, examined carefully, and placed within this vast landscape we call The Plains. While certainly not a complete chorus, the voices of the women are here more amplified than anywhere else. These stories invite us to listen and watch more carefully as we cross the plains from south to north, and north to south. As newcomers to the plains seek the security of jobs in the north and warmth in retirement in the south, these stories should be a part of their grounding in new places. The plains may still be treeless, but the voices of women now rise more clearly from this windswept landscape. Just as the objects they left behind echo the voices of women who peopled the plains, the stories in this book mark the passage of women through the grasslands. Here are the cultures women created and left behind for us to wonder at.

JOAN M. JENSEN

# Introduction to the Collection

RENEE M. LAEGREID

ODD AS IT MAY SEEM, it is hard to begin a book about women on the Great Plains without mentioning Walter Prescott Webb. In his classic study, *The Great Plains* (1931), he is perhaps as famous among women historians for what he did do—introduce the idea of region into the study of the West—as what he did not, which is to say much about the women who lived on the plains. In the final pages of the last chapter, "The Mysteries of the Great Plains in American Life," the subject of women garners only two pages, and this brief description, concluding with the sentiment that the plains "seemed to overwhelm the women with a sense of desolation, insecurity, and futility," is hardly encouraging.[1] Whether or not Webb knew the old adage, popular in his state, that "Texas is a heaven for men and dogs, but a hell for women and oxen," his discussion on women's lives expanded that sentiment to encompass the entirety of the Great Plains.[2] And like the old adage, Webb's analysis not only overlooked women's opinions on the subject but also implicitly ignored the existence of non-Anglo women as well.

Although it took a while, Webb's casual neglect ultimately helped inspire scholars to challenge this narrow view of women's role on the Great Plains and to bring women's voices into the story of the region. Since the 1970s, in line with a larger movement to bring women into the national historical landscape, diaries, biographies, and studies on plains women associated with particular states have proliferated, adding a much-needed perspective to the history of the region.[3] This book adds to that growing body of research. Rather than focusing on a single person, place, or era, this volume provides an overview that encompasses the lives of many women, some famous, most not,

Map of the Great Plains. Copyright (c) 2011 by Carl Laegreid

throughout the entire region. Striving for comprehension and diversity rather than specificity, the following essays illustrate the richness, variety, and complexity of women's experiences on the North American plains.

The essays in this collection explore various combinations of place, space, and people that created specific experiences on the plains. As a place, the Great

Plains have been both stage and actor in the relationships that have been "produced, lived, and represented."[4] The place played a significant role in the lives of women who, from the earliest inhabitants to the present, moved to, through, or within the plains, carrying cultural ideas and patterns with them as they adjusted to the specifics of the environment, either temporarily or on a more permanent basis. For some women the plains had been their home for generations: Native women learned to interact with the particular rigors of the land, adjusting as the introduction of new peoples and animals created significant changes to their traditional ways of life. Some women traversed the plains on their way to other places, for example, Native women forced to relocate, or Euro-American women moving for economic reasons to the Far West, or for religious reasons as part of the Mormon migration. Others came to the plains for a short time—military wives, laundresses, or activists, for example—while still other women came with the intention of building permanent homes and re-creating the societies they had left behind. Whatever their motivations, the environmental conditions on the Great Plains created new challenges to performing traditionally female tasks, such as cooking, caring for children, contributing to the family economy, as well as developing a sense of community. In one sense, it would seem that women shared a commonality in their efforts to succeed in the often harsh and unfamiliar environment. Yet even an experience as seemingly universal as caring for a family could be shaped by differences based on socially constructed attitudes of race, class, gender, religion, and ethnicity. So, too, could the types of activities women engaged in to contribute to their family's economy—working in the fur trade, or leading labor activism, or starting a homestead. The shared fact of their biological sex, moreover, did not mean that women would necessarily consider themselves equals. The personal "spaces" women created among themselves as they negotiated interactions with one another or with people outside their own social group often serves to highlight these differences within the larger "place" of the Great Plains.[5] This combination of difference and unity, of spaces within place, is what makes this region so rich for study. To date, no published work exists that attempts to show such a comprehensive view of women on the Great Plains.[6]

The ideological foundation for this book is based on the field of western women's history. The imperative to challenge the masculine, heroic, individualistic, and mostly all-white perception of the West began in the 1970s; in a conference held in 1983, at Sun Valley, Idaho, western women's history officially emerged as a distinct field of historical study. The enthusiasm for placing women's voices into the story of the West inspired a growing number of historians to rethink the theories and methodology useful for understanding the complex relationship of women to the West. In the nearly thirty years since the field of women's western history began, the focus of study has expanded past the experiences of Euro-American women on the frontier to the "countless combinations of race, ethnicity, class, gender, age, religion," that reflect the everyday experiences of women in the West.[7] Western women's history, of which Great Plains history is a part, has an imperative to be as inclusive as possible. Not only does inclusiveness help dismantle monolithic stereotypes of women, but it also reminds us of the intricate web of relations that, in both obvious and subtle ways, weave the people and the history of this region together.

The essays in this collection build on the framework of inclusiveness and, in doing so, draw upon some of the most innovative theoretical and methodological approaches in current historical research. For example, themes that include a growing understanding of gender/transgender studies and of the decolonization of Native peoples are explored, and archival research as well as oral histories help show the connection of women to place. But the essays also place women into a larger social and political context. Regional studies, such as this volume, play an important role connecting specific people and locations to a larger picture, providing a more comprehensive view of American history. "It has become clear that regionalism is more than just nostalgic 'local color,'" David Jordan writes. "It composes a dynamic interplay of political, cultural, and psychological forces."[8] While the essays recognize the importance of the Great Plains in the lives of women, they also take care to place the women into the context of larger social, economic, and political trends. Connecting them to a wider national and international context enriches our understanding of women's lives in this particular region.[9]

Since regionalism is based on the concept of difference it is useful to have a clear understanding of the characteristics that set the Great Plains region apart from other places. Webb defined the Great Plains as being flat, treeless, and arid. Although admitting to the varying degrees of these three characteristics found in any one space, he argued that the unity of the three dominant characteristics "has from the beginning worked its inexorable effect on nature's children . . . bent and molded Anglo-American life, have destroyed traditions, and have influenced institutions in a most singular manner."[10] Webb was consistent in his masculine, expansionist, Anglo-Saxon view. More recently, David Wishart, editor of *The Encyclopedia of the Great Plains* (2003), took on the challenge of redefining the region and rethinking its raison d'être in a way that acknowledged the diversity within its borders. He began by examining the fifty or so published boundaries that had been used to define the Great Plains since Zebulon Pike and Stephen Long first claimed the plains a region, and he simplified the scrawl of overlapping boundaries into one clear, crisp line.[11] Wishart broadened Webb's three defining characteristics to include the transitional character of the physical environment, distance, sparse population, absence of features, magnet for settlers (beginning with Paleo-Indians), impact of railroads, and extractive industries. This expanded combination of criteria acknowledged "great diversity" within the region, while still exhibiting environment and cultural characteristics "sufficiently distinctive from surrounding areas to merit separate identification" in the area of North America recognized as the Great Plains.[12]

Having an overarching definition of the Great Plains is useful and necessary. It did not take long, however, to recognize that in order to gain a more comprehensive view of women's experiences it would be necessary to refine our angle of analysis. Experiences are shaped by a combination of distinct variations in the environment and the diverse social, political, and economic relationships that in turn arise from environmental particularities. For this reason the book is organized into three subregions. Maintaining Wishart's east-west boundaries, our northern plains subregion encompasses the Parkland Belt region in the north and extends south to the Niobrara River in Nebraska. The central plains subregion includes the Niobrara River south to what eventually became the Kansas-Oklahoma border. We defined the southern plains area from roughly this border to the Balconeo Escarpment. Each of these subregions exhibits similarities with the overall Great Plains region—sharing what Elliot West describes as "varied people of unequal power [who] have adapted in their own ways while contesting with each other for shrinking resources within diverse and changing environments shaped by an erratic climate."[13] And yet while specific differences based on geographic and geopolitical factors warrant the distinction into these subregions, our internal boundaries are not hard and fast lines; they tend to be a bit "smudgy" to allow for the less-than-tidy transitions found in both geography and culture—the interaction of people and places across time and space.

Considering environmental differences within the region is one way to understand the diversity of women's experiences, but time matters, too. The three major subregions of this volume are arranged chronologically into four periods that highlight changes within or between groups and further enhance the examples of difference, contested power, and dynamics in the region. The first period, which leads up to the Louisiana Purchase in 1803, explores the lives of precontact Native women, then shifts to accommodate the contests over power and territory that developed as increasing numbers of Europeans entered and remained in the territory. The 1803–1862 period involves public decisions, such as the US-Mexico War, Indian Removal, or the passage of the Transcontinental Railroad Act that affected the lives of women of all ethnic, racial, and class groups. During the period 1862–1930, the essays center on the dynamic clashes of race, religion, and ethnicity. With the influx of Euro-Americans moving through or onto the plains, this era presented opportunity for some women but devastating change for others. The final period, 1930 to the present, opens with the twin disasters of the Great Depression and the Dust Bowl. These economic and environmental disasters affected women unevenly throughout the Great Plains, depending on their geographical proximity to the centers of disaster, rural versus urban location, as well as along class, ethnic, and racial lines. The essays continue by discussing the challenges faced by women on the plains up to the present.

Since this introduction began by mentioning Walter Prescott Webb, perhaps it is fitting to end with him, or rather, to reinforce the idea that his view of women's experiences on the Great Plains is well past its end. Western women's history is a dynamic and thriving discipline, and this volume is one more contribution to the growing body of work that seeks to integrate the lives of women on the Great Plains into the scholarship of the region, the West, and the larger record of North American history. Despite its aim for inclusiveness, it is certainly not a complete view—our focus on rural women will hopefully inspire others to explore the experiences of urban women—and while building on the work of earlier women's historians, this volume is not the final word. It is, we hope, another step along the way of exploring the diverse lives of the women who were—and who continue to be—an integral part of life on the Great Plains.

Part I
# The Northern Plains

Amy MacLennan, *Sacagawea-obliquated* (2010). Courtesy Amy MacLennan

# Sacagawea, a Vignette

RENEE M. LAEGREID

THE IMAGE OF SACAGAWEA IS AS FAMILIAR TO MOST AMERICANS as it is a fabrication. This northern plains woman is arguably one of the most well-known women in United States history, represented in paintings, illustrations, and even currency. Yet since no recorded likeness of her image exists, the numerous images that have been created project what the artists think she would—or should—have looked like. Details of her life are missing, as well: simple things like how to pronounce her name or names (it is likely she had several), or the name by which she preferred to be known.

To be sure, the basic outline of her life has become woven into the fabric of our nation's consciousness: a Shoshone from the Wind River Basin, she had been abducted by an enemy tribe and traded to the Hidatsas as a child. She became the wife of a French trader, and at age sixteen she met Meriwether Lewis and William Clark when they wintered at the Hidatsa village. She bore a child that winter, and in the spring she began the journey across half a continent to the Pacific Ocean and back, caring for her child, helping the expedition, and serving as mediator to the Native groups they met along the way. That much can be documented from the explorers' journals. But their interest in a Native American woman, deeply colored by their Anglo-American views of superiority in terms of both civilization and gender, did not encourage them to record her perspective on any number of subjects that would interest future scholars. And so the details of her life, her thoughts, her experiences, her motivations, and her concerns for family, kin, and tribe remain part of the mystery that continues to surround her life.

Obscurity, though, did make it easier to construct myths about her life. Sacagawea's role in the transcontinental journey elevated her to national fame in the late 1800s. Encouraged by a lack of actual knowledge, writers ascribed virtuous characteristics to her role with the Corps of Discovery that fit neatly within ideological causes of their times. She was depicted as a guide for the Corps, a metaphor for Manifest Destiny, an example for emancipated women, a showcase for Indian Princess-helper-in-the-wilderness, and a model for American womanhood. Sacagawea developed this impressive résumé based on the fact that no extant evidence provided her view of the journey, her view of the participants, or how this experience fit into the larger picture of her life.[1]

This imperfect understanding of a Native woman is not unique to Sacagawea, of course; her historic visibility, though, serves to highlight problems that arise when Euro-Americans impose their own cultural definitions and meaning onto Native women. Despite the myths that surround her—or maybe because of them—she remains a compelling figure. As a result, we want to know more about Sacagawea, the woman behind those myths. To move beyond the few basic facts left in the explorers' diaries, researchers have had to learn to look for evidence in unexpected ways, in unusual places, by listening to stories that had gone unnoticed, and by piecing together fragments of evidence.[2] As far as learning more conclusive information about Sacagawea, time and lack of primary sources work against that goal. In the end, learning to rethink ways to find the real Sacagawea may be her most enduring legacy.

# Introduction to the Northern Plains

ELAINE LINDGREN

FOR MANY, mention of the northern plains immediately brings to mind visions of blizzards, prairie fires, and drought, of big skies and emptiness. It is a place, plains author Kathleen Norris writes, where "our odd, tortured landscape terrifies many people. Some think it is as barren as the moon, but others are possessed by it."[1] Throughout history, much of the writing related to the importance of women's lives in this challenging environment has concentrated on women of European descent, generally ignoring indigenous peoples, such as the Crows, Assiniboines, Gros Ventres, and Arapahos, to name a few, who had exploited the environmental possibilities to create their livelihoods and vibrant cultures. The lives of European women, when discussed, were portrayed in narrow and often biased descriptions, and the women themselves as passive, reluctant, lonely, degraded, and, in general, uninteresting and unimportant.

These images, originating in the observer bias of European explorers, trappers, and settlers, inhibited our understanding of the complex and diverse roles women held in this formidable yet compelling region. The northern border is formed between the Parkland Belt of mixed woodland and grassland and the boreal forest of the north found in the Canadian provinces of Alberta and Saskatchewan. The western boundary is perhaps the most clearly defined, extending across the US-Canadian border as it follows the foothills of the Rocky Mountains. The eastern boundary encompasses southern Manitoba, including the city of Winnipeg, and follows the eastern boundaries of the states of North Dakota and South Dakota. The southern boundary follows the southern border of the state of South Dakota and includes the northeast corner of Wyoming. As with the Great Plains region in general, the moisture level drops significantly moving from east to west. Vast distances characterize this area, as do its constant winds, sparse population, relatively few trees, and

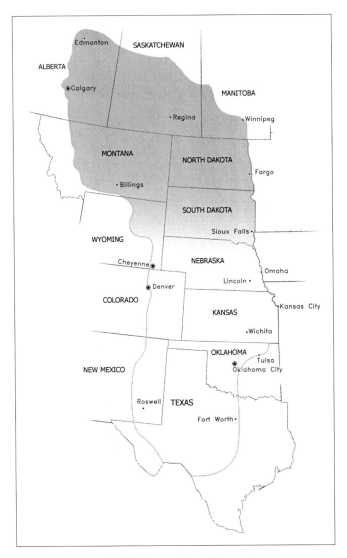

Map highlighting northern plains region.
Copyright (c) 2011 by Carl Laegreid

an expansive sky.[2] In this great openness, Norris reflects, we learn to appreciate "the possibilities inherent in emptiness."[3]

Beginning in the 1970s, research began to provide a much more realistic
picture of the possibilities women embraced. The work of plains archaeologists and anthropologists, such as Alice B. Kehoe and Katherine Weist, brought
to light the range of women's roles during the pre- and protocontact era. Con-
trary to earlier stereotypes, research on Native women showed they had active

roles in war parties, trade, and the use of ritual sexuality as a means of under-standing and sharing cultural knowledge of "outsiders."[4] Silvia Van Kirk's trailblazing work brought to light the impact of late-sixteenth-century French and British explorers and fur traders in the region as they established relations with the native populations. Scholarship on European women also challenged earlier historical biases of women's roles; only with the completion of the rail-roads in the 1880s did European immigrant families begin to rapidly settle in the region, seeking their own economic possibilities in ranching or planting crops that would withstand the short, dry growing season. This recent re-search, as the examples below indicate, provides a much more realistic picture of the diversity of women in this region and the possibilities they embraced.

In 1902, at the age of nine, Olava Holland emigrated from Norway to North Dakota with her mother and younger sister. They joined her father, who was living in a sod house and had been farming on the prairies for about five years. By the time she was twelve, Olava had helped her father break the sod with a walking plow hitched behind four horses. Later she spent time working in her father's blacksmith shop fixing horseshoes and even learning to sharpen the plow. In a 1983 interview, Olava recollected,

> Oh, yes, I could do anything the men folks could do, and they would say, "Ya know, she can do anything but one thing, she can't ride the stallion." I knew I couldn't. That bothered me. So Ma and Pa went to town one time and there was just a young kid there, and I thought today is the day for me to ride that horse. And he said, "You can't do it. . . . [H]e will kill you." I said, "I don't care." I went and got on the horse all right and my little feet . . . stuck straight out, big horse. . . . When I got to [the pas-ture] he saw the other horses and you can guess what happened. He went wild and there I sat and hung on to the mane. And I thought, "This is the end of me." . . . I got home and as luck would have it he ran right for the barn and that boy was there and he caught him. And I said to him, "Don't you dare tell Pa and Ma that I rode him."[5]

In *Wheat & Women*, Georgina Binnie-Clark, a journalist from England, chronicles her three years of farming in Saskatchewan, Canada (1905–1908). This was an unlikely endeavor, especially for a woman of her status. She was told it would be impossible for her to be successful. She succeeded in spite of the fact that she had to purchase the land. In Canada, single women were not eligible to apply for homestead land.[6]

Today, the women in these studies would be considered "movers and shakers." In many ways, they mirror contemporary women. Their schedules were demanding, requiring flexibility, ingenuity, and endurance. Many were instrumental in building churches, schools, and other community institutions. They juggled their time among responsibilities on the homestead with work for pay wherever they could find it, community activities, and their personal commitment to art, music, literature, and even poetry. In spite of their complicated schedules, they found time to enjoy themselves and have fun, and it is obvious that humor played an important part in shaping their outlook on life.[7] Although this research on European women showed the lighter side of life on the northern plains, it also established the importance of these women in building their communities. While accounts of their lives show a fascinating combination of domestic activities coupled with activities that tended to be considered the prerogative of males, this observation can be applied to women of all races and ethnicities, as the authors in the following chapters demonstrate. Throughout history, the importance of women's activities and the cooperative nature of men and women's work has been underestimated, often described in terms of observer bias. The following essays broaden our understanding of the diversity of women and women's roles on the northern plains and indicate we still have much to learn.

"Living with the Land: Women on the Northern Plains to 1803," by Sandra K. Mathews and Renee M. Laegreid, combines Native origin stories and archaeological information to examine the livelihoods and gender roles of Native peoples from the earliest inhabitants on the North American continent through the Lewis and Clark Expedition. This essay challenges Eurocentric views of the roles and positions of Native women in their societies. Native oral histories and ethnohistorical evidence illustrate the complementary nature of gender roles required for survival, as well as show how rituals and beliefs connected individual tribes to their environment and spiritual traditions.

In "Glimpsing the Lives of Women on the Northern Great Plains, 1803–1862: Sources and Perspectives," Gretchen A. Albers discusses the sources available for the study of women on the northern plains, including documents written by missionaries, historians, fur traders, anthropologists, and ethnographers. The importance of understanding author bias is a fundamental theme in this essay. Albers's discussions on Hidatsa, Mandan, and Arikara women as active participants in the fur trade help break the narrow and biased image of women in the region. Fur traders themselves recorded that it was Native women who made their moccasins, processed their meat, gathered supplementary food, dressed furs, served as interpreters, and helped to make and also operate the birch bark canoes. The evidence presented through her sources contradicts those that portrayed Native women's lives as degraded and unimportant.

"'Willing Challengers': Women's Experiences on the Northern Plains, 1862–1930," by Andrea G. Radke-Moss, utilizes the framework of nineteenth-century domesticity. She explores the writings of women authors to dispel the idea of frontier life as a singularly unfulfilling experience. She points out the significance of works by northern plains authors Laura Ingalls Wilder, Nellie McClung, Willa Cather, and Mari Sandoz, who suggest the plains did not offer an oppressive environment but rather one of "deep physical and spiritual connectedness to their plains environment and culture." The framework of domesticity is also used to explore the role of frontier women as active agents of American imperialist expansion. While men sought conquest of the land and indigenous peoples in the "public" domain, women applied their domestic skills to "civilizing" Native women and children. By using Native women's oral histories, Radke-Moss provides insights into the difficult transformation and adaptation Native women faced as increasing contact with settlers impacted their lives.

Sarah R. Payne takes a transnational approach in her chapter, "Place, Gender, Ethnicity, and the Role of the Nation in the Lives of Northern Plains Women." Payne uses autobiographical writings of African Canadian and African American women, World War II war brides, and Native women to both link and contrast the experience of women who live across the political border that bisects this region. By showing how gender operates and intersects with ethnicity and place, the women in Payne's essay dispel earlier, negative views of women's experiences while bringing to light women whose lives have largely been neglected by scholars.

The information presented in these essays provides a basis for greater understanding of the complex nature of gender roles on the northern plains. The authors provide a much-needed challenge to the perceptions of women in this region that originated so long ago. As their essays demonstrate, the old stereotypes are no longer adequate.

# 1

# Living with the Land

## Women on the Northern Plains to 1803

SANDRA K. MATHEWS AND RENEE M. LAEGREID

The story of women on the plains begins in the north. From the first people who migrated across the land bridge onto the North American continent and found their way into this region, women adapted to and interacted with the environment as they worked to establish tribal bonds, intricate spiritual systems, and extensive trade networks. Over the millennia, social organization, technologies, and territorial affiliations changed—the result of transformations in the climate, the land, and interaction with new people—and women's responsibilities changed as well. Life experiences for individual women on the northern plains varied, of course, depending on factors such as whether her tribe's subsistence base was nomadic, semisedentary, or sedentary, and the position of each woman within her tribe. No matter the diversity, though, women held roles integral to the survival of their tribes, earning respect and prestige as givers of life, producers and traders, keepers of tradition and the home, healers, storytellers, and even defenders.

Knowledge of women's valued position within their tribes stretches back across time, integrated into origin stories and oral traditions.[1] One of the most important stories told by tribal elders was their origin story. While it may be cliché, every origin story is unique, developed from a shared narrative and understanding of the past, and grounded in the history and spirituality of each tribe. These stories help explain how indigenous people came to inhabit the northern plains, setting their presence firmly within their environment. Native American scholar Angela Cavender Wilson explains that Native stories "often incorporate the experiences of both human and non-human beings," and importantly, are "transmissions of culture upon which our survival as a people depends."[2] Plants and animals figure into the stories, as do relationships with specific geographic or environmental features of their land. Origin stories are often centered on a trickster or creator figure who takes the form of an animal, and many stories share a theme of an "earth diver," who dove far under the waters to bring mud up to form land.[3] Not only do origin stories serve to remind tribal members of the dynamic history they share and the basis for their existence, but they also provide a framework to help guide them in a changing world.[4]

The common denominator in these diverse stories is the interconnectedness between humanity and the specific characteristics of each tribe's natural world. Equally important, creation stories instruct tribal members about the natural or initial order of things, providing "a basic statement about their relationship with nature and about their perception of the source of power in the universe." As a means for understanding gender roles, creation stories explain each tribe's relationship to the natural world and "holds the key for understanding sexual identities and corresponding roles."[5] The codependence between men and women is an idea that flows seamlessly in the natural order of the universe.

Many of the northern plains origin stories feature both male and female protagonists. A well-known Arikara story indicates that a woman played a key role in the origin of the tribe. This story explained that their people originally came from the east. As they traveled they encountered many difficulties and obstacles, but they never deviated from their direction toward the setting sun. When they finally stopped, they found themselves at a "beautiful place where Corn Mother taught them how to live and work."[6] This beautiful place lay along the Loup River; eventually they found themselves living further north, along the Missouri River. For the Arikaras, a woman provided the essential knowledge for survival, telling them where to stop and create their homeland—a place where women would continue to plant, tend, and own the produce of their labors. Among the Arikaras and other northern plains horticultural societies, archaeologist Preston Holder notes, "basic concepts which reveal high status and a position of authority for women as well as high prestige for the female role in general" were woven into their religion and rituals.[7]

While in some origin stories a male character figures as the creator of the tribe, generally a female counterpart appears soon thereafter. The relationship between the male and female superhuman beings served as an example for ordinary people within the tribe. As historian Colin Calloway writes, among the Blackfeet, Old Man, or Napi, "whose father was the Sun and mother the Moon, 'came from the south, making the mountains, the prairies, and the forests as he passed along . . . arranging the world as we see it today.'"⁸ After creating birds and animals, he covered the plains with grass, then made a woman and child and said, "You must be people."⁹ Another Blackfeet story highlights the benefits that come when women and men work together. "Order of Life and Death" begins this way: "There was once a time when there were but two persons in the world, Old Man and Old Woman." In the story they come to an agreement on how they would decide the way in which people would live. Old Man said, "'I shall have the first say in everything.' To this Old Woman agreed, provided she had the second say." As Old Man covered everything that people would need to live, to the placement of genitals to whether or not people should live forever, Old Woman considered his ideas, then explained why they should be modified. Since she had second say, her modifications became the final word. Because of their mutual respect and willingness to work together, the final result turned out better than if either one had complete control over the decision-making process.¹⁰

The complementary nature of women's and men's roles extended into the spiritual traditions of Plains tribes as well. An example of the importance of women in the realm of Native understanding is the story of White Buffalo Calf (or Cow) Woman. Among the Lakota tribe, the story of White Buffalo Calf Woman has long endured and continues to give hope to the Lakota and many other tribes. While the story varies slightly in the telling, the message remains the same across languages and tribes, not just on the plains but throughout Indian America.

As the story goes, one day the Lakota sent a group to go east to find the power that gave life. On their return home, just as they crossed the Missouri River, two of the men who had been sent out to hunt came across a white buffalo calf running across the grasses of the plains. As they looked, the buffalo calf turned into a *wakan* (sacred being), a woman dressed in buckskins. She told them that she had a message to give to their tribe and that they should return to camp and prepare for her.

One of the hunters saw her beauty and began thinking about her in an inappropriate way—as a man seeing a beautiful woman might do. Announcing that he would approach her, she welcomed him; but when he reached out to touch her, he was enveloped by a dark cloud. Then the dust began to swirl. When the dust cloud subsided, all that remained was dust and bones being devoured by a snake. The other warrior feared for his life and returned to camp to prepare his people.

She arrived four days later, where the tribe greeted her. She thanked them and told them that she was the child of the Sun and the Moon. For four days she stayed among them, teaching them the seven sacred ceremonies and explaining the sacred pipe. Its red stone bowl, with the head of the buffalo calf carved at the center, represented all of those who lived upon Mother Earth, the two- and four-leggeds. The pipe's wooden stem represented all plants. The feathers that hung from the stem represented those things that flew. When they smoked the pipe, all of these things would join together and their words would be carried to the Great Spirit. Equally important, she gave them a red stone that had seven circles, representing the seven sacred ceremonies. After smoking the pipe, she told them that the pipe represented peace and truth. She told them to make sure that they cared for the pipe and that every generation that followed understood the pipe and what it stood for. She warned that she would return for it sometime in the future and that the sign of her coming would be a white buffalo calf.

She met with the children, then with all the members of the tribe, expressing to them that they should love and care for the animals. She explained that all of living creation was intertwined and connected and that their health and survival depended on the balance between them. To the hunters, she taught how they must conduct themselves with the hunt. That which they hunted was their brother, after all, and the earth was the mother of *all* creation—not just of humans. Giving thanks to the Creator and keeping the balance that the Creator had made was important.

The following day she taught them about the seven sacred ceremonies, and chose holy men among their elders who would learn the sacred ceremonies so that they could talk directly with the Great Spirit. She taught them how to use the pipe for seven different rites: *Inipi* ("purification"), *Tapa Wanka Yap* ("throwing of the ball," the drive for knowledge of the Great Spirit), *Ishna Ta Awi cha Lowan* ("preparing a girl for womanhood"), *Hanblecheyapi* ("crying for a vision"), *Hunkapi* ("making of relatives"), *Wana'gi Yuahapi* ("keeping and releasing the soul"), and *Wiwanyag Wachipi* ("Sun Dance").[11] After they had learned proper reverence for the Great Spirit, the ceremonies, and the earth's balance, she left, promising to return. Through a great woman spirit, or *wakan*, the Lakota learned their most important spiritual ceremonies. In the hopes that she would return, the Lakota have continued to pass down the seven sacred ceremonies and the sacred pipe for more than nineteen generations.[12]

From stories like the White Buffalo Calf Woman it becomes apparent that the idea of interconnectedness and respect for the natural world, family, and village permeated Native society. Tribes functioned best, or perhaps only, when each member of the community worked together for the benefit of the whole. Origin stories and other oral traditions that have survived the on-slaught of white westward migration provide traditional Native views on their emergence onto the northern plains and show the interdependence of men and women that allowed tribes to survive for millennia.[13]

Archaeologists, on the other hand, have taken a different approach to ex-plaining the origins of Native people into this region. Instead of stories, they search the landscape for physical clues to learn when human habitation first occurred. Over the course of the earth's history, extended warm and cold pe-riods have occurred. During one of the long cold periods, an ice age that last-ed from 25,000 to 12,000 BCE, the Bering Strait dropped about 300 feet, al-lowing a 1,000-mile-wide Beringia, or land bridge, to emerge.[14] With the appearance of this passageway, humans, animals, and plants migrated across the vast region, continuing until warmer temperatures returned and the level of the Bering Sea rose, resubmerging the land bridge and isolating the North American continent once again. Animals and humans that crossed Beringia headed south, some traveling to the furthest points of South America, some turning eastward toward the Atlantic coast, others west along the California coast. According to anthropologists' theories, the northern plains served as a migratory route for some of the earliest peoples as they followed one of the migration paths along the eastern side of the Rocky Mountains.[15]

The last cold period saw the development of the Laurentide Ice Shield, a layer of glacial ice more than one mile thick, extending across portions of North America. The ice began receding around 14,500 BCE. As the northern plains slowly emerged from under the ice field, new opportunities for hunt-ing, fishing, and gathering of wild berries, tubers, and other food sources de-veloped.[16] Archaeological evidence suggests that hunters and gatherers moved onto the northern plains to take advantage of the abundant resources as early as 10,000 BCE, approximately when the ice had completely melted from the area that is now in the United States.[17]

Trying to reconstruct the lives of these early people is difficult. Artifacts and the types of building materials utilized by the northern plains peoples did not survive the ravages of time, climate, and weather, leaving precious little material culture for archaeologists to study. Yet some key pieces of evidence have been found, such as projectile points fashioned at the end of spears, sim-ilar to those discovered in Folsom, New Mexico. Fluted points discovered shortly thereafter in nearby Clovis, New Mexico, were located near mammoth bones and other items associated with continuous human occupation. This evidence indicates that ten thousand to thirteen thousand years ago hunters followed eohippus, an early form of horse, and larger animals—mastodons, mammoths, and camels.[18]

In such a demanding environment, the day-to-day struggle for survival required that every member of the group contribute to their collective welfare in whatever way necessary. Over time, though, gender-specific roles became more clearly discernable. When the men succeeded in a hunt, women prepared the skins for use as shelter, clothing, and tools, the meat for food, the sinew for sewing, the brains and fat for softening and preparing the skins for clothing, and the bones for tools. Women acquired other resources from their environment as well, such as plant-based food items and bones and stones for tanning tools. Survival, then, required an intimate knowledge of the land and a continual process of adaptation to changes in the environment, climate, and available resources.

One key adaptation made during the Early Archaic Period on the northern plains (8000 to 5000 BCE) included their understanding of how to use the environment itself for hunting: groups of people began coordinated efforts to run animals off a cliff or other precipice. Archaeologists have located surround and jump-kill sites at the bases of cliffs or high hills with steep drop-offs. Paleo-Indians would have gathered to scare herds of animals toward a cliff, causing them to fall to the depths—and their deaths—below. The 6,500-year-old jump-kill site used for bison in northeast Wyoming is an example of this common method of hunting.[19] At the base of the cliff early Paleo-Indians butchered the animals, then shared them among the tribe, or perhaps with neighboring tribes (most likely extended family groups) who had participated in this labor-intensive activity. The emergence of surround and jump-kill sites indicates that the populations of these early peoples had learned to organize their efforts and work collaboratively to feed their growing numbers.

With the surplus generated by these jump-kill sites, and encouraged by their travel to find adequate sources of game and salt for curing, northern plains people entered into the extensive trade networks developing across the continent. Continuing their role as essential contributors to their tribe's survival by preparing food and robes, women found their responsibilities within their tribes increased as social and trade networks developed. Through interaction with diverse peoples, northern plains women learned of new food sources, medicinal uses of plants, and different technologies. They were introduced to decorative items or spiritual materials or objects from outside their own region, such as pipestone from southwestern Minnesota's sacred pipestone quarry. And while given scant scholarly attention, games of chance likely played a significant role in diffusing goods across the continent. In the "archeological accounts of exchange and gender," games of chance, primarily dice games played by women, have been strongly linked to the movement of goods.[20] While small-stakes betting would most likely have been the norm within a tribe, as historian Warren R. DeBoer notes, "gambling, like marriage, war or exchange in general was outward directed," helping to promote a transfer of goods that "permeated regional landscapes," as early as the Archaic era.[21]

Northern plains Archaic era differed somewhat from the central and southern plains chronology; here the Middle Plains Archaic lasted until approximately 5500 to 3000 BCE, the Late Plains Archaic roughly until 3000 to 1500 BCE.[22] During the Archaic era, Indian peoples continued to study their world for clues as to recurring seasons and attempted to influence natural events such as rain or storms, wind, snow, sunshine, and animal and bird migrations. They also began to establish recognizable cultural and linguistic groups, refine gender roles, construct identifiable communities, and create more elaborate artwork, architectural styles, and spiritual systems. Some tribes developed highly stratified societies based on skill in the hunt, which gave individuals who excelled at the hunt credibility as leaders. Warrior status became highly respected, and women sought bonds with men who could best protect and feed their family. The importance placed on hunting and warrior skills did not diminish the respect and equality between the sexes, though. In an environment where survival depended on cooperation and mutual assistance, men sought the hardiest and most skilled women for their mates, women who had earned recognition for their industry—the ability to prepare meals, fashion skins into lodges, and make clothing.[23]

By the end of the Late Archaic period of 3000 to 1500 BCE, small, hunter-gatherer bands and family groups grew into larger, more organized communities, and stratified systems of organization developed. Social organization, security networks in an insecure and unpredictable environment, became formalized along kinship lines. The tribes that early explorers and trappers recognized as the Crows, Plains Ojibwas, Lakota, Hidatsas, and Mandans developed matrilineal societies. In these societies, children inherited the clan of their mother, who, along with maternal aunts and uncles, taught children the stories and ceremonies specific to her clan. In patrilineal clans, children inherited the clan of their father, and in bilateral descent structure, children claimed their heritage equally from their mother's and father's families.[24]

As they continued to transmit knowledge in the form of stories and learned from their elders, the knowledge became more organized and ritual-ized; elements of the sacred began to infuse into their world "knowings." Some stories became gender specific, to be shared only among women. During a Lakota woman's menstrual cycle, for example, she would go to a small lodge set apart from the rest of the community. Since they believed that menstrual blood gave women a temporary power that clashed with the *wakan* power of men, the women remained isolated from the rest of the tribe. In their lodge, they shared stories that taught lessons about menstruation and childbirth. During a Lakota girl's first cycle, she participated in the *Ishna Ta Awi Cha Lowan*, or "Her Alone the Sing Over," ceremony given to the Lakota by White Buffalo Calf Woman. A female elder would instruct the girl in things that ev-ery woman should understand. The elder had to be a "good and holy person, for at this time her virtues and habits passed into the young girl whom she was purifying. Before she was permitted to return to her family . . . the young girl had to be further purified in the *Inipi* lodge."[25] This ritual announced to the tribe the important role the young girl would now have among them; her success in learning skills from her elders would contributed to the overall suc-cess of the tribe.[26]

The diversity of rituals among the northern plains tribes, as with histories, languages, religious systems, and cultural norms, rests on the fact that, as an-thropologist and northern plains scholar Loretta Fowler wrote, "the history of the native peoples of the Great Plains is a dynamic one, in which there has been a great deal of social flux."[27] People moved across the plains for a variety of reasons: to follow resources, to participate as members of allied tribes, to trade, and as a result of intermarriage or captivity. Tribal movement in and around the northern plains continued, depending on climate, availability of food sources, and interactions with other peoples. Tribes known to frequent the northern plains in the area that is now Canada included the Assiniboine, Cree, Blackfeet, and Gros Ventres. Further south, in what would become the United States, the region became home to the Shoshone, Crow, Arapaho, Ki-owa, Hidatsa, Mandan, Arikara, and Santee Dakota.[28]

In addition to movement onto and off of the plains, a great deal of internal movement existed as well. Nomadic tribes moved often. The stress placed on the land, from normal living activities to the need to dispose of human waste, compelled them to move to areas with fresh resources. This relocation to a new site meant a great deal of work for women. They carefully untied the hides from the lodge poles, wrapped their belongings in the hides—pots, bas-kets, blankets, and other tools related to women's tasks—and fastened them to the lodge poles. The poles would be harnessed to dogs, forming a travois, and dragged to their next camp. After the women packed up all their belongings the tribe generally began to move as a unit, with scouts ahead and behind for protection. Once settled at the new site, the women organized and set up the camp. Since women owned the lodges, they took great pride in the quality of their work, their lodges a "constant mute witness to women's capabilities," earning them prestige and honor.[29]

While significant variation existed between tribes—language, origin, belief systems—the harshness and unpredictability of the climate encouraged the development of similar subsistence strategies based on a mixed economy. The buffalo hunt could involve all members of the tribe, but men generally hunted wild game while women gathered edibles—wild fruits, berries, and tubers.[30] For generations, women handed down their knowledge of which edibles to gather, different ways of preparing and storing game for food, and techniques for processing skins for clothing and shelter to younger women in their clans.

Women played an integral role in the spiritual continuity of the tribe as well, through their own rituals and societies and through their support of and participation in community ceremonials and rituals. And, of course, women raised and cared for children and tended to the needs of the elders. An Oglala elder who lived on the plains before the reservation era explained the reciprocal nature of gender relations, saying, "It is well to be good to women in the strength of our manhood because we must sit under their hands at both ends of our lives."[31] For all their contributions to the welfare of the tribe, women earned appreciation, respect, and prestige.

As early as 900 CE, some tribes developed more sedentary lifestyles along stream and river banks and began to practice periodic and rudimentary farming.[32] By about 1100 CE, the Mandans, Hidatsas, and Arikaras had settled on the northern plains, establishing agricultural villages along the northern Missouri River valley.[33] Here they engaged in a lifestyle "characterized by a cultural adaptation to two separate but adjacent ecosystems in the Great Plains environment—raising domesticated plants in garden plots along the fertile bottomlands of the Missouri River, and hunting bison and other animals— large and small—in the wooded river valleys and on the prairie uplands."[34] Women built and owned the round earth lodges on terraces above the floodplains. They had full responsibility for growing corn, beans, squash, and sunflowers and for developing varieties of corn resistant to cold, wind, and drought.[35] Women of all ages tended the gardens: adults cleared, planted, and weeded, while young girls helped by protecting the crops. Other than occasional assistance from elderly men in the tribe, or help transporting harvested crops from the garden to the village, women controlled all aspects of food production, from preparing the fields through trading.[36]

As labor intensive as gardening undoubtedly was, women owned what they produced and determined what to keep for family use and what to trade, a practice that continued well into the nineteenth century. In 1807, explorer Manuel Lisa noted that the women from an Arikara village met his boat "with bags of corn to trade, just as they might have greeted Lakota or Assiniboine women in earlier decades."[37] During the 1850s, US surveyor Ferdinand. V. Hayden reported "although the women perform all the labor [of growing crops], they are compensated by having their full share of the profits."[38] But for centuries before the arrival of Europeans, women along the Missouri River "offered corn, squash, beans, and pumpkins—all grown by women—for the dried buffalo meat, dressed hides, and clothing—items processed or made by women—of the nomadic tribes."[39] The importance of their crops for subsistence and religious purposes, combined with their position as traders, gave women power and status within their tribe.

As mentioned earlier, in matrilineal societies children became members of the clans of their mothers; all the women—mothers, grandmothers, and aunts—shared child-rearing responsibilities for all the children in their group, teaching children the stories, traditions, knowledge, and skills of their clan. Even though children as young as five years of age had great freedom, that freedom came with responsibilities and consequences.[40] Parents and kin used stories as examples of proper behavior, to teach respect to one's kin and the natural world and the need to obey rules to prevent harm to themselves or to the tribe. Not obeying rules might result in serious injury, or worse, and a well-instructed child would feel shame for disobedience that had upset the natural balance of life.[41] Adults also used stories to scare their children into behaving: enemies lurking over the hill, for example, would take children away and enslave them if they strayed too far from camp. In her memoir, Waheenee, a Hidatsa, recalled hearing the admonishment "The owl will get you!" as a way to scare children into behaving. One of her mothers explained why this was so:

> Thousands and thousands of years ago, there lived a great owl. He was strong and had magic power, but he was a bad bird. When the hunters killed buffaloes, the owl would turn all the meat bitter, so that the Indians could not eat it, and so they were always hungry. On this earth there lived a young man called the Sun's Child; for the sun was his father. He heard how the Indians were made hungry, and he came to help them.

The owl lived in a hollow tree that had a hole high up in its trunk. The Sun's Child climbed the tree, and when the owl put his head out of the hole, he caught the bird by the neck. "Do not let the Sun's Child kill me!" the owl cried to the Indians. "I have been a bad bird; now I will be good and I will help your children." As soon as a child is old enough to understand you when you speak to him, cut his hair with two tufts like my own. Do this to make him look like an owl; and I will remember and make the child grow strong and healthy. If a child weeps or will not obey, say to him, "The owl will get you!" This will frighten him, so that he will obey you.[42]

Through the everyday practice of storytelling, children like Waheenee learned to connect themselves to the natural world around them and to understand the rules and mores of the tribe.

In preparation for adulthood, children learned what would be expected of them through "play" activities. Real contributions to helping their mothers began when girls were about five years of age by babysitting, helping prepare meals, and packing the camp for moves. Boys of the same age began playing games of physical dexterity, building their athletic prowess for the skills required later in life for survival: strength and speed. From a very early age girls learned to praise and encourage their brothers as the boys learned hunting and warrior skills; boys were taught to protect and provide for their sisters. In a gentle and consistent manner children of both genders developed the respect and reliance on one another that would sustain them as they grew to adulthood and had their own families.[43]

As young girls grew out of childhood tribal mores encouraged them to separate themselves from the boys. Chaperoned by women, girls learned the arts of quilling, beading, and tanning hides under the watchful gaze of their kin. Becoming initiated into female society was critical, as historian Katherine Weist notes, for "in all societies women's closest associations were with other women. They assisted each other with the laborious tasks of moving camps, setting up the lodges, with midwifery."[44] Separation from the boys was also important in order to maintain a girl's reputation as chaste, a reputation closely tied to the honor of her family. Among the Sioux, a young girl's brothers would guard her, "protecting her from the advances of other men."[45] In Cheyenne, Arapahoe, and Crow tribes, unmarried girls often wore chastity belts; among these and other northern plains tribes, the community publicly honored and rewarded premarital chastity.[46]

Since young women generally had little contact with the young men in their tribes, the selection process to find a mate could follow several paths.[47] A father might choose a young man from the tribe to become his son-in-law, or a young man might take the initiative and choose his own bride; these events could happen without the young woman's consent. Sometimes Indian youth fell in love and chose each other. In these last two cases, the hopeful bridegroom approached the young woman's father to ask for permission to marry. The higher the status of the young woman and her family, the greater the number of gifts the young man would feel obliged to offer. Blankets, tools, or perhaps the promise of meat for her family from his kills for up to a year would be offered; after the mid-1700s, horses became particularly valuable gifts. In part, the gifts served to compensate her family for the loss of her labors when she married. Anglo-Americans mistakenly considered the young man's offerings as a bride price, when, in fact, his gifts were only "one facet of a set of exchanges between the relatives of the groom, or the groom himself, and the family of the bride."[48] After the marriage the groom's family would present additional gifts to the new bride—seeds, baskets, bead or quill work, meat, hides, or fine buckskins—as a sign of reverence for her value as a new member of their family.[49]

Once engaged, the couple and their families followed strict protocols. To ensure the young woman's reputation, families closely monitored interaction between the engaged couple. "Young men did not walk with their sweethearts in the daytime," recalled Waheenee, "We would have thought that foolish."[50] After the marriage, too, the newlyweds followed tribal protocols and adhered to social mores or taboos. Depending on the arrangements, and whether a tribe was matrilocal or patrilocal, the couple might live next to her or his parents or temporarily share a lodge with one set of parents. Among some plains tribes the husband could not speak to his married sister-in-law, nor could she speak to him; any information passed between them had to be sent by the wife's brother even if they shared a lodge. In some cases the husband and his mother-in-law could not speak to each other, nor could they sit in the same lodge.[51] Should the marriage fail, divorce could easily be initiated by either the husband or the wife. Since women owned the lodges, placing a husband's possessions outside the front door provided an effective means of announcing the end of a union.

Long before the first Europeans arrived on the plains, then, Native women had fully shared the burden of responsibility—and rewards—as they worked, cared for family, and participated in kin and trade ties that extended beyond their own communities. The gradual formation of gender-specific roles acknowledged the codependent nature of survival. Men and women recognized the importance of each other's roles, and they awarded respect to each other's contributions to the success of the tribe. Codependency and complementary roles, however, do not mean a rigid concept of gender roles. Their cultures allowed the flexibility for men to engage in female roles (berdache) and for women to engage in male roles, either from necessity or by choice.[52] Aside from the obvious need to protect themselves, their children, and elders from enemy attack when men were away from camp, women could join hunting and raiding parties.[53] To aspire to become a warrior was "one of several culturally accepted positions which accorded women power and prestige."[54] Cheyenne, Crow, and Gros Ventre women, in particular, earned widespread recognition as fighters and raiders. Pretty-Shield, a Crow woman, recalled watching a woman warrior from her tribe: "I saw Strikes-two, a woman sixty years old, riding around camp on a gray horse. She carried only her root-digger, and she was singing her medicine song, as though Lacota [sic] bullets and arrows were not flying around her. . . . I saw her, I heard her, and my heart swelled because she was a woman."[55]

But if codependency does not mean firm concept of gender roles, neither did it mean total equality. Husbands expected women to remain faithful, while men "sought to seduce the chaste wives of other men," says Weist.[56] Women could suffer physical abuse or violent actions against them for adultery, yet their only recourse for an unfaithful husband was divorce.[57] And while gambling away a wife was a theme repeated in tales and myths, no accounts have come to light of a wife wagering her husband.[58] Nevertheless, the gender system that Native peoples developed over the course of millennia had served them well and would likely have continued, adapting as circumstances required, if not for the intrusion of non-Indians. While gender roles have changed over time, as Devon Mihesuah observes, "Europeans were among the catalysts of change," which profoundly influenced the lives of northern plains women.[59]

Generally speaking, Europeans who arrived on the North American continent had a disruptive effect on all Native peoples, and bringing Native tribes into the fur trade set off a chain of events that reached into the Great Plains. Competition over access to trapping and trade in the east pushed some tribes west. The Lakota and Cheyenne, for example, arrived on the northeastern edge of the plains from the region west of the Great Lakes around the mid- to late 1700s.[60] Some of the first non-Indians to enter the northern plains included the French, who arrived in the Saint Lawrence River region by the mid-1530s. The westward expansion of French allies, as well as the appearance of *coureurs des bois*, or French fur traders, on the upper Red River between Minnesota and the Dakotas, brought French influence into the northern plains region. With the French traders came new trade partners and goods, as well as diseases to which Native peoples had no immunity.[61]

Starting in the early 1600s, the French engaged the Montagnais and other Algonkin-speaking tribes in the Saint Lawrence region in the fur trade industry. Also in the early 1600s, bands of Huron had trapped out their traditional homeland in the Saint Lawrence River valley and headed west to help quench France's insatiable thirst for furs. Samuel de Champlain sent Jean Nicollet to establish relations with western tribes and to bring them into the fur trade. He encountered the Ho-Chunk Nation (Winnebago), and even though he was the first European to see Lake Michigan, he would not be the only Frenchman to encounter Indians in the western Great Lakes and northern plains regions. The Jesuits, an order of Catholic priests who dedicated themselves to living among the tribes in the Americas, had traveled up the Saint Lawrence River and found themselves west of the Great Lakes.[62]

By the mid-1600s, the French had established outposts as far west as Saint Francois Xavier on the western end of Lake Michigan, and Chequamegon and Saint Esprit on the southwestern edge of Lake Superior. From those bases, as well as from their presence near the Red River, the French expanded their trade onto the northern plains. Perhaps the first recorded interaction between a Frenchman and northern plains Indians occurred in 1660, when Pierre-Esprit Radisson participated in a meeting with Lakotas not far from the Red River. He noted that the women arrived in advance of the men, setting up their skin lodges in less than a half hour—an example of their dexterity and ability, their responsibility for spatial organization of the camp, and their ownership of the lodges. The Lakota men appeared later to make speeches and give gifts in promise of being steadfast allies. Having witnessed gendered protocols of the meeting, the Frenchman recognized the importance the women in trade proceedings as well their value to their community as a whole.[63]

By the 1660s, the French government had declared the territory of New France a "royal colony," thereby taking over the administration from the private companies who held monopolies in the fur trade. The French government actively discouraged French women from accompanying their husbands into the interior, perpetuating the already heavily skewed gender ratio among the French. Aside from the new regulations, the expense of passage from France and the risks of bringing women into this remote region contributed to their low numbers in the colony.[64] Of the few women who made the journey to New France, some remained in Quebec with their administrator husbands while others moved onto farms contracted with French ventures, such as the Company of 100 Associates, to produce food for the colony.

The scarcity of white women in New France led to men commonly engaged in relationships with Indian women from various tribes for companionship, assistance, and political prestige—a practice that fur company officials unofficially sanctioned, both around the fort and as trappers moved deeper into new territories.[65] By 1678, at least one enterprising Frenchman set out to explore the region inhabited by the Sioux and Assiniboines; by 1689, the French had laid claim to everything in the Saint Lawrence watershed and as far west as the Rocky Mountains in Canada.[66] As the *coureurs des bois* moved farther into the wilderness they integrated themselves into the fur economy of local tribes by marrying high-ranking Native women. Although Jesuits admonished the men who vanished into the western wilderness, taking up the habits and dress of the Indian and engaging in relationships with Indian women, these relationships helped to establish strong ties between the *coureur de bois* and tribes.[67]

For their part, Native women who chose to engage in relationships with French traders "acted from motives that were determined by their own cultures," writes Sara Sue Kidwell. Interracial relationships allowed Native women to learn about the ways of the non-Natives who had entered their world; they became cultural mediators, creating "sustained and enduring contacts with new cultural ways, and giving their men entrée into the cultures and communities of their own people."[68] While a woman's role in the relationship involved the tasks of food production and hide processing she had practiced since childhood, marriage to a trader provided her with access to European trade goods. Within the context of liaisons and intermarriage, women gained status with the French and their own kin for their roles as mediators, "companions, producers, and consumers—all in the context of liaisons and intermarriage."[69] They gained economic leverage from the relationships, as they sought social and economic benefits of trade.

No fixed pattern of longevity for interracial relationships existed between Indian women and their French husbands. Some lasted for many years, ending only with the death of a partner. While a small number of trappers took their wives back to their homes when they left trapping, a large number of French traders who married Indian women on the peripheries never returned to French settlements, instead using middlemen to take their furs to Quebec and beyond. These *coureurs des bois* had assimilated into Indian society where kinship ties proved stronger than royal law, and they chose to remain with their Indian families. Other marriages lasted only briefly, for example, when a trapper left for new territory or realized the obligation of providing for his wife extended to her kin as well. Native women used their traditional prerogative to end a marriage if their husband became abusive, or when the "cultural tensions inherent to interracial marriage," as historian Michael Lansing describes it, proved too difficult.[70] Women left to return to the familiarity of tribal concepts of marriage and kin, where children belonged to their clan rather than to the husband, women owned and controlled their own property, and making rules did not fall within the exclusive province of men.[71]

After the first two generations of contact, the offspring of Native women and the French traders, Métis, became the preferred choice of mates for the *coureur de bois*. This generation of women straddled the Indian and white worlds, providing French men with wives that had access to Native resources yet spoke their language and fit more easily into their view of "civilized" wives. By the mid-1700s, as the French colonies developed more comfortable amenities, Frenchmen began bringing their European wives to the colonies. As the number of non-Indian women in New France increased, French men increasingly shunned mixed-blood women as their mates. Now both Métis and full-blooded Native women faced marginalization from the French.[72]

During the mid-1700s, Native women also faced a decline of status among their own tribes, due to the introduction of horses onto the northern plains. Initially brought to Central America and the Caribbean in the early 1500s, horse culture entered the southern plains during the late seventeenth century and the central plains during the early eighteenth century. A "trade chain" brought horses and the knowledge of how to use and train them onto the northern plains—first to the Shoshones by 1700, then to the Blackfeet and Crows by 1740. Within the next decade and a half, horse culture spread throughout the northern plains region.[73]

While horses allowed for greater freedom of movement and lightened the workload for women as they moved camp, the animals proved a mixed blessing. Ethnohistorian Colin Calloway argues that the acquisition of horses played a significant role in the decline of Native women's status, allowing an "individualistic, male-dominated herding and equestrian hunting culture to develop, especially as it became linked to the European hide trade."[74] Horses encouraged a new mode of production that both favored men and shifted away from traditional communal-based society.[75] With the men mounted on horses, which they owned and controlled, hunting and raiding became exclusively a male domain, leading to a conspicuous "absence of women from the 19th century hunt."[76] This shifted women from their traditional role from participants in the hunt into a subordinate and less respected role as producers in the hide trade. Not only did this change highlight a reversal in age-old subsistence strategies—women no longer had a part in the bison hunt—but more importantly, the emphasis on hides as a trade commodity displaced women from their traditional role as agricultural producers and traders. Now men held the key role in trade as they negotiated hides.[77]

Tribes from the east who came onto the plains for the hide trade had to quickly adapt from a horticulture-based economy to a new, nomadic lifestyle. This required women to adapt to new subsistence strategies as well as social and economic changes. Among horticultural groups, the shift displaced them from the central role they held in their tribes due to their spiritual connection to corn. In a relatively short period of time, a generation or less in some cases, the acquisition of horses and the concurrent shift to hunting, processing, and trading buffalo hides wrought enormous changes to almost every aspect of northern plains tribal life. The effect was a culture that favored "men over women, young over old, and introduce[d] into plains societies class distinctions" that ran counter to the ethic of egalitarianism that had existed for centuries.[78]

Acquisition of the horse meant faster and more efficient hunting and, consequently, more hides for women to process. Some tribes, such as the Crow, increased expectations for women, looking with disapproval at the women who did not use new skins each year for their lodges.[79] The growing demand for women's labor to process hides led to an increase in polygyny. Sororal polygyny—the marriage of one man to sisters—had been the most common form of polygyny among northern plains tribes. However, as the need for women's labor to process hides increased, the practice of taking women workers captive increased.

Taking captives had long been a tradition in the Americas. The practice among Native peoples did not necessarily mean slavery in the Western sense; unlike African slavery during the colonial and early national periods of US history, Native captivity generally involved full integration into the tribe. Adaptation of the horse made raiding against neighbors and enemies much easier. Conflicts between rival bands became more frequent and violent, and while raids for horses became emblematic of the plains in the late 1700s, raids for captives became more frequent, too. Using horses, larger numbers of captives—generally women and small children—could be taken by raiding parties. Women often married into the tribe that captured them, had families, and learned the language and customs of the captor's tribe. Other captives performed services or duties of a tribal member who had either died or been taken in a raid. The fate of these "replacement" captives appears less secure. They could become integrated into the community at some level, rescued by their families, traded for goods or horses, or exchanged for people taken captive by other tribes.[80]

An example of the extensive network of taking and trading captives on the plains involves the story of Bird Woman, or Sacagawea. When Lewis and Clark arrived at the Mandan villages they learned firsthand that Indians typically took captives during engagements with other tribes. After her capture, Sacagawea, a Shoshone from the Wind River area in present-day Wyoming, had been traded east onto the plains until she ended up with the Hidatsas.[81] The story of Sacagawea is familiar, in part because she is an exception to the scant amount of information on Indian women, who, historian Patricia Albers notes, were "rarely visible as individuals or a category of people in the early journals of traders, missionaries, explorers, and government agents."[82]

But Sacagawea is also familiar because her life fits within the Euro-American genre of stories featuring Native women helping European explorers. The few historical examples available, such as Pocahontas, have "focused on the most notable Indian women," writes Devon Mihesuah, "because of their interaction with whites or success in the white world." The fact remains that the lives of ordinary northern plains women are not easy to narrate, or even discover. And as Mihesuah wryly notes, "while Sacagawea was helping Lewis and Clark, surely other Shoshone women were doing important things within their tribes."[83] While the lives of most Native women went unrecorded, in their obscurity they led complex and multileveled lives, centered on clan and family membership, dealing with the day-to-day challenges of family survival and the ever-present threats of warfare and dislocation through captivity.

The French continued to appear on the plains with their allies, periodically taking Lakota and Dakota Indians into captivity to work as slaves in the northern fur trade until the 1763 Treaty of Paris ended the French and Indian War (1754–1763), fought between France and Great Britain. In a separate agreement before the Treaty of Paris, the French handed over all land west of the Mississippi River to Spain, although Napoleonic pressures forced Spain to return the realm in 1800. Soon thereafter, in 1803, President Thomas Jefferson authorized the Louisiana Purchase and territory changed hands once again, this time to the young US government.

Although Thomas Jefferson is generally depicted as an enlightened and benevolent leader, he shared the ethnocentric views of his day. Despite his calls for equality, Jefferson scholar Anthony C. Wallace writes, "Jefferson saw 'the people' as a culturally homogeneous mass of equals. . . . [T]hose residents who could not participate fully in the civilized republic, either because of gender, racial inferiority, or cultural incompatibility were excluded or marginalized."[84] Beginning with the Lewis and Clark Expedition in 1804, the aggressive and expansionist United States began to diffuse its Anglo-centric attitudes about Indian people, public lands, and white Protestant morality into the northern plains and all of its inhabitants.[85]

In 1803, Native women had experienced relatively limited direct contact with Europeans, yet the effects of the newcomers had already altered their lives. While adapting to change had always been a part of women's experiences, after the Lewis and Clark Expedition interaction with Euro-Americans—and changes associated with them—increased dramatically. In particular, Euro-Americans sought to impose their concept of gender roles onto Native peoples. Interpreting the constant activity of the women at their many tasks through the lens of their experience, Euro-Americans assumed that only men who did not value or respect their women would allow them to perform such demanding work. They could not have been more mistaken. In a 1928 interview, Standing Bear discussed the respect and sense of equality Indian women earned from their contributions to their family's and tribe's welfare: "All the tasks of women—cooking, caring for children, tanning and sewing—were considered dignified and worthwhile. No work was looked upon as menial, consequently there were no menial workers."[86] The perception of women as mere drudges by the Euro-Americans missed completely the reality of the role women held since their earliest days in the region.

As origin stories and archaeological evidence show, women had always held respected and valued positions in their tribes. Revered as caregivers, their influence extended beyond their role as nurturers as they held central roles in their tribes for food production, trade, and rituals. Some women earned high status as healers or medicine women, others for their exceptional skills in beading or processing hides. And Native women earned respect for perpetuating the existence of their tribe. In the quiet dignity of day-to-day activities, they shared the lessons learned from their mothers—the skills, sacred stories, culture, and languages—helping a new generation learn to live on the North American plains.

# 2

# Glimpsing the Lives of Women on the Northern Great Plains, 1803–1862

## Sources and Perspectives

GRETCHEN A. ALBERS

Long ago the Mandan lived together under the ground near the ocean. Some hunters found a hole reaching up to the surface of the land we are now living on and climbed up to investigate. Before they reached the top they heard the bellowing of the buffalo herds. On reaching the top, they found buffalo herds everywhere. . . . When the people below heard that game was plentiful up above, they wished to come up at once, but the second chief of the people warned them that fat women heavy with child must not go up at that time.

The people started coming up to the top, but when about half of them were up, a large woman heavy with child started up. The people said she should not go up but should wait until her child was born. She insisted, but her weight broke the grapevine, and she fell down. This separated the people, half being below and half above.

Before coming out of the ground, Corn was a man. Everyone looked to him to give them success in raising their garden products. When the vine broke, he was still below, but his daughter, Waving Corn Stalk, succeeded in reaching the top. She looked back in the hole and cried when she learned that her father was separated from her. She cried, "What shall I do? I am up here all alone."

Her father replied, "You are old enough to understand all my ways of doing things. I give you the right to plant the corn anywhere you wish."[1]

A single sacred narrative about origins, in this case, about the origins of both ceremony and a people, can serve as a useful starting point for this brief survey of women's lives on the northern Great Plains in the years 1803–1862. The Mandan account could appear misleadingly straightforward at first glance, when removed from the complicated processes by which it was retold for a Euro-American audience and then set down in writing. This survey could appear to be mostly straightforward as well, but it would be similarly misleading to approach it as such. The above narrative was recorded by a Euro-American anthropologist named Alfred Bowers during one of the many interviews he conducted among the Mandans and Hidatsas of the Fort Berthold Indian Reservation, in west-central North Dakota, during the 1930s. The elderly Hidatsa woman who related it was known to Bowers as Mrs. White Duck. The conversations between Mrs. White Duck and Bowers would provide the anthropologist with much of his understanding of women's roles in Hidatsa society and in certain Mandan ceremonies. Their conversations would greatly expand the information on Native women that Bowers would eventually include in his two extensive volumes on Mandan and Hidatsa social and ceremonial life.[2]

A further search for the facts of Mrs. White Duck's life muddies the waters considerably. Her Hidatsa name was Rattles Her Medicine, variously translated as Rattles Medicine or Rattling Medicine. She was born and lived her life on the Fort Berthold Indian Reservation where, by the 1840s, the Mandans and Hidatsas who had survived the most recent onslaught of smallpox had joined together in the village of Like-a-Fishhook, on the Missouri River. In 1891, a census taker for the US government recorded Rattles Her Medicine to be thirty years of age, placing her year of birth in the early 1860s. This census taker also recorded that Rattles Her Medicine was married to a man named Frank Packineau, of Hidatsa and French-Canadian descent, and that the couple had two daughters by the names of Good Paint and Good Goods (or Good Lodge), and a son named Charles. Later in life, Rattles Her Medicine married for a second time, to a Mandan named White Duck. During this time she received her Christian name, Emma White Duck, from the Congregational missionaries. Years later, when Rattles Her Medicine met Alfred Bowers, her intimate relationship with a Mandan and the cultural sharing she experienced between Mandans and Hidatsas at Like-a-Fishhook allowed her to become an invaluable informant to Bowers. She provided him with information on both the traditional roles of women in her own tribe and the spiritual beliefs of the Mandans.[3]

Hence, a single story in one source on the lives of Native women introduces the complexities of a Hidatsa woman: a mother to children of Hidatsa-French heritage and a participant in a Christian faith, telling a sacred Mandan narrative in the Hidatsa language to a Euro-American anthropologist attempting to document Native "traditions" in the 1930s. The narrative itself, and what we can glimpse of Rattles Her Medicine's fascinating life, hint at a complex social, religious, and economic framework in which women were fully active and recognized participants. Suggested as well is the ease of cultural borrowing, adaptability, and change in a diverse society. With these types of sources, how does a twenty-first-century historian with no intimate ties to Rattles Her Medicine's culture attempt a straightforward narrative about women of her era? How would such a historian reach further back, to attempt depictions of the mothers of women such as Rattles Her Medicine, or for that matter, their grandmothers?

Before the 1860s, the number of women of European descent on the northern Great Plains remained quite small. An examination of women's lives between 1803 and 1862, then, logically focuses on Native women. Mandans, Hidatsas, and also the Arikaras, who joined them at Like-a-Fishhook in the early 1860s, still live on one reservation in west-central North Dakota. Although culturally distinct, they are referred to as the "Three Affiliated Tribes." All were originally agriculturalists who lived in permanent villages and made twice-yearly forays to hunt buffalo. Numerous villages strung up and down the Missouri River kept a vigorous and prospering trade with their neighbors who relied more heavily on the buffalo hunt than agriculture. Mandan, Hidatsa, and Arikara women had vital roles in this trade, as well as in agriculture, buffalo hunting, and the important ceremonies connected to these two activities.[4]

But even a partial discussion of northern Great Plains groups should also encompass at least a few of those tribes more oriented toward hunting buffalo than growing crops along the riverbanks. Important, too, are the Métis. Recognized today as a distinct political group in Canada, Métis peoples possess both white and Native heritage. In light of these many cultural groups, an attempt to describe the typical life of a northern Great Plains woman, to trace the average woman's childhood training, experiences in motherhood and marriage, and economic and spiritual pursuits, is far more than a mere challenge. There simply was no typical experience.

Rather than seek to describe the typical experience of a northern plains woman, this essay will instead examine the types of sources available for a study of women on the northern plains and the various perspectives of the people who created those sources. Glimpses of Native women's lives can be found in the writings of nineteenth-century missionaries—offering modern historians insights into ways of life that the missionaries themselves sought to eradicate. Fur traders who resided among the many groups in what are now the prairie provinces of Canada and the northern plains of the United States also recorded their perspectives of Native women. And finally, anthropologists and ethnographers who flocked to reservations in the early decades of the twentieth century recorded a great deal of information with the help of elderly Native informants such as Rattles Her Medicine. But all of these sources exhibit some form of bias.

This essay moves from an examination of the cultural groups at the heart of the northern plains, comparing missionary views of women with the later view of anthropologist Alfred Bowers, to an analysis of European fur trader documents, and concludes with a critique of a fictional work entitled *Waterlily*.[5] Critiquing the documents points us toward a broader understanding of what might constitute a source, and encourages readers to understand why it matters who has written about women of the northern plains during this time period.

Charles and Emma Hall, Congregational missionaries, arrived at the village of Like-a-Fishhook in 1876 by steamboat.[6] The first missionaries to visit the Mandans, Hidatsas, and Arikaras with the intention of settling among them permanently, the Halls had the dual aim of converting the Native peoples to Christianity and "civilizing" them by transforming their societies—including gender roles and division of labor—to match Euro-American standards. Hall wrote extensively about the Natives at Like-a-Fishhook. He intended to publicize and gain financial support for his mission, but his writings also provide important evidence that much of what could be termed traditional about Mandan and Hidatsa society had indeed survived the tumultuous times of the mid-nineteenth century. His writings were not without bias, however. Charles Hall ignored the fact that women played important spiritual roles in the ceremonial life of the Mandans and Hidatsas—roles that were inseparable from the vital economic functions they fulfilled within those societies. Instead, he saw Native women as leading degraded lives in which they bore the brunt of the physical labor and were treated as chattel in their marriages.

Charles and Emma Hall noted correctly that the gendered division of labor among the three tribes was very much in place. In his portrayals of Like-a-Fishhook, Charles Hall described the procession of women walking daily from the village to their fields, some leading their small children and others with babies on their backs. "A procession of women used to pass by the Mis-

sion, leaving the old village at break of day. . . . This long line of Indian wom-
en was on the march to the fields. There was a mile of garden—corn, beans,
squash, potatoes, sunflowers, on the bottom land. On this their living depended."[7] In this necessary work toward "getting a living," Hall wrote, "the Indian
woman was the one who had the hardest task."[8] Emma Hall would report in
her letters that the Native women of her new sewing group met with her twice
a week, quilting feverishly in order to be through by planting time. As she put
it, "our women are great farmers."[9] The Halls believed that Native men should
farm, as Euro-American men did, and that Native women belonged to a more
domestic sphere. Given their perceptions, neither missionary could see the
vitally important spiritual roles Mandan and Hidatsa women played in their
societies, roles that were inextricably bound to their position as the tribes'
"farmers." Anthropologists such as Alfred Bowers, arriving among the villagers by the 1930s, would take more of an interest in women's roles within the
contexts of their own societies. Anthropological sources are not without their
own problems, however.

The fieldwork of Bowers revealed that in Mandan and Hidatsa societies,
women's economic contributions enabled their male relatives to gain leadership. Women provided the finished buffalo robes and other goods that allowed their husbands and brothers to purchase the sacred bundles necessary
for their ascent in society. Men who aspired to high leadership positions needed the support of several wives and female clan members in order to gather
the necessary goods and to prepare the feasts for key ceremonial purchases.
Particularly among the Mandans, who passed down the sacred bundles
through the matrilineal line, women could also inherit and purchase rights to
these sacred bundles, allowing them to play important roles in the transfer
ceremonies to men who would officiate in the sacred rites.[10] Women served as
a conduit of sacred powers in other ceremonies as well. At special rites, young
men's wives at times had sexual intercourse or, alternatively, participated in a
symbolic exchange, with older men. Generically termed "walking with the
buffalo," such ceremonies were understood to transfer the elder men's powers
to the younger, ascending group.[11]

Women had their own societies. Among the Hidatsas, younger women
joined the Skunk and Enemy societies to perform celebratory dances when
men returned from war expeditions.[12] Rattles Her Medicine expressed to
Bowers that "the success or failure of a war party depended as much on what
the women at home did while the warriors were out as on what their male
relatives looking for their enemies did."[13] From an early age, Mandan and Hidatsa girls were taught that to fast and cry while their older brothers were on

an expedition would facilitate their safe return. Mandan women were eligible for war honors the same as men, if they had "struck" an enemy, and adult women also fasted for their own purposes. They could receive personal visions, just as men did.[14]

Charles Hall observed a spring ceremony that Native women performed, upon the breakup of ice on the Missouri River and prior to planting their fields. As Hall observed the women's prayers that planting would succeed, he noted that food had been brought outside in sacks, and poles with brightly colored cloth attached had been put up that reminded him of "somebody's washing hung out to dry."[15] Hall relates that a Hidatsa friend informed him as they passed the scene that "they prayed, too, as we did, and that they had music just as we did."[16] What Hall described in the 1880s was a woman-centered ceremony that had existed for many years prior to his arrival. Married women among the Mandans and Hidatsas would join the Goose society, which performed ceremonies considered vital to the success of their agriculture. They welcomed the water birds in the spring, asking for the protection of their fields, and sent them away in autumn with prayers of thanksgiving and ceremonial offerings. Women in the Goose society were often called on to perform ceremonies when drought or grasshoppers threatened the crops.[17] Women's participation in sacred rites grew in importance as they aged. Older women were eligible for the White Buffalo Cow society. This group's function was to call the buffalo in winter so that the men could hunt them in the wooded river bottoms rather than following herds out onto the open plains.[18] Through their ceremonies, which protected crops through spring, summer, and autumn and called the buffalo for the winter hunt, Native women were entrusted with responsibility for the entire tribe's welfare.

Both Mandan and Hidatsa society usually followed a matrilocal marriage system in which husbands joined their wives' families and female kin owned their lodges, fields, and implements in common. The two societies also practiced sororal polygyny, a marital arrangement in which a man is wed to two or more sisters. Therefore, a girl could expect to live her entire life surrounded by her sisters, mothers, and maternal grandmother. Young girls helped their mothers and grandmothers in the fields at an early age, learning to tan and decorate hides and perhaps to make pottery. They received an early induction into the reciprocal social system that delineated some knowledge as sacred through "paying" their mothers or grandmothers with a small present for every new skill learned.[19]

Marriage, an important marker in a young woman's life, received scant attention from Charles Hall. Hall either did not comprehend or chose to ignore the complex exchange of gifts and rituals that characterized both Mandan and Hidatsa marriages.[20] He dismissed these traditions through claiming that a Native man "could not marry a woman of his clan. Beyond that he was not restricted by anything but his ability to make a purchase."[21] Hall saved his most scathing critiques, however, for the Euro-American men—the fur traders and government employees—whom he found at his arrival to be living with Native women in accordance with Native customs, rather than in church-sanctioned unions. These "white wanderers," wrote Hall, had "wrought moral and physical ruin" among the Native peoples through exploiting their women.[22]

Although Charles Hall observed many spiritual activities and a gendered division of labor that could be termed "traditional," the fact that these marriages between Native women and white men existed suggests Native societies had vastly changed in the century before his arrival. Seeking to completely transform these societies to his standards, however, Charles Hall was not interested in examining the exact nature of these changes. Likewise, the anthropologists who recorded much about traditional ways of life in the 1930s were fascinated with what had been, and not with the significant adaptations Native peoples had made over the course of the nineteenth century. Turning back to the records of a third group of observers, the fur traders, helps put these changes into context.

Independent traders had resided in the villages of the three tribes since at least 1776, and the North West Company, a Canadian fur-trading operation based in Montreal, established a post among the Mandans and Hidatsas in 1794.[23] It would not be long before the Americans followed. After the purchase of Louisiana from France in 1803, an expedition led by Meriwether Lewis and William Clark set out not only to explore the nature of the new territory and its Native inhabitants, but also in large part to sway those Native groups away from Canadian and British entrepreneurs, such as the North West Company and its British-based rival, the Hudson Bay Company, and into trade with the United States. Lewis and Clark would winter with the Mandans in 1804–1805, hiring one of the independent traders long in residence in the area, Toussaint Charbonneau, as an interpreter and guide for the remainder of their voyage. Charbonneau's wife, Sacagawea, a Shoshone woman who had been captured by Hidatsas as a young girl, also accompanied the explorers on their trip to the Pacific Ocean and back.[24]

In contrast to anthropologists such as Alfred Bowers, Lewis and Clark recorded many instances of historical change—the presence of traders in the

Mandan village, for example, and also the devastating impact that disease had had on the tribes. When Lewis and Clark encountered the two Mandan villages in 1804, they visited the downstream remains of On-a-Slant—one of the nine flourishing villages abandoned only twenty years previously, and one, they would learn, that had been continuously inhabited for three hundred years before smallpox struck.[25]

While recognizing that the groups they encountered had undergone many changes in the last century, Lewis and Clark—as Charles Hall and Alfred Bowers would after them—observed and recorded Native practices and beliefs that had withstood even the devastation of epidemic disease and social dislocation. A few of these practices, particularly those pertaining to Native women's sexuality, conflicted with their Euro-American sense of propriety. As historian James P. Ronda writes, observing a Mandan buffalo-calling ceremony "simply baffled" William Clark, who "simply could not fathom how sexual relations between old men or white men and the wives of younger Indians could bring the animals closer and ensure good kills."[26] Rather than understand that among the Mandan, sexual intercourse functioned "like a pipeline that could transfer spiritual powers from one person to another," Clark was more inclined to associate this particular ritual with promiscuity.[27]

Within twenty years of Lewis and Clark's departure, US fur company interests were competing with each other in earnest on the Upper Missouri. Some of these Euro-American fur traders wrote down their observations about the role of women in Native societies and sometimes recorded their own discomfort or lack of understanding about these Native women, as well. One of these observers was Francis T. Chardon. Of French descent and from Philadelphia, Chardon was in the employ of the American Fur Company and stationed at Fort Clark among the Mandans and Arikaras when he wrote a journal between the years of 1834 and 1839.[28] A second observer, Henry A. Boller, who also hailed from Philadelphia, worked for a firm that was in opposition to the American Fur Company. His letters and records of the four years between 1858 and 1862 spent among the Hidatsas at Fort Atkinson formed the material for a book he published on his return home.[29]

Boller and Chardon revealed much about the vital role of Native women within the fur trade—in terms of both their work and their marriages to Euro-American men. Chardon was married to a number of Native women, giving him firsthand knowledge of women's roles in Native society. These sources suggest that Native women were active participants in the creation of fur trade society. Despite this evidence, early historians of the fur trade era in North Dakota largely echoed Charles Hall's biases, through assuming that Native women were degraded in marriages by Native and Euro-American men alike. In introducing Francis Chardon's journal, for example, a historian of the 1930s boldly asserted:

> In the days of the fur trade, Indian women were exploited just as surely as were the animals hunted and slain. . . . [T]hey were exploited, not alone by white men, but by men of their own families, by brothers, fathers, and husbands. If not promiscuous in their sexual relations before the advent of the trader, the less prominent of them inevitably were after.[30]

Clearly, a reassessment of sources left by these northern plains fur traders is called for.

Reassessing the role of Native women in the fur trade requires the focus of this essay to shift to the Canadian prairies. Here, Native groups such as the Plains Cree, the Assiniboines, and the Blackfoot Confederacy participated in the fur trade, as did the Mandans and Hidatsas. Modern historians more attuned to gender, notably Sylvia Van Kirk and Jennifer S. H. Brown, have provided a model for reading beyond the sources left by white male fur traders in order to glimpse the experiences of Native women. Although Van Kirk and Brown found the traders' portrayals to be colored by what was to them culturally alien, and therefore uncomfortable, about women in these societies, the picture that emerges is one of Native women who were active participants rather than passive victims.

Far from simply being exploited by traders, Native women actively encouraged trade. They welcomed the technology, such as kettles or woolen cloth, that made their lives easier.[31] And countering the idea that they were exploited by their own brothers, fathers, and husbands, Native women often sought to become traders' wives.[32] In Native societies, marriages did not necessarily entail unions for life. Native models, therefore, meshed with a fur trade society in which men might be transferred or return to their homes in eastern Canada or Great Britain at any time. A Native woman could expect, in these earlier years, to be welcomed back to her tribe along with her children following the dissolution of a fur trade marriage.[33]

As fur traders' wives, Native women performed work that became essential to the operations of the trade itself. Fur traders recorded again and again that it was Native women who made their moccasins, processed their meat, gathered supplementary food, and helped to make and also operate the birch bark canoes on which the North West Company, especially, depended for transportation. They served as interpreters, and most importantly, they dressed the furs on which the traders' livelihoods depended.[34]

Fur traders revealed in their letters and journals their discomfort with Native women's strength. As Van Kirk writes, "It did not accord with European notions of femininity for women to be strong."[35] Moreover, they tended to be uncomfortable with the autonomy, sexual and otherwise, that Native women possessed in their own societies and attempted to retain in their marriages to white traders. Similar to Lewis and Clark, fur traders often misunderstood the rituals and customs they observed among Native peoples, particularly polygyny, wife-lending, and the prevalence of premarital sex. They failed to understand that what from their perspective was promiscuous or adulterous did not seem that way to the Native peoples.[36]

Although assuming, in Eurocentric fashion, that Native women were degraded or overworked in their own societies and thus far better off being married to white men, fur traders nonetheless found it difficult to ignore the fact that Native women were accustomed to controlling their households and owning the products of their own labor.[37] Van Kirk suggests that some Native women perhaps did gain, materially, in marrying white traders and thereby securing access to the goods they desired. Moreover, some of the prairie tribes such as the Plains Cree, the Assiniboines, and the Blackfeet led a more mobile life than did the Mandans, Hidatsas, and Arikaras. For the women of these societies, taking up a sedentary life within the fur trade post could entail a lighter domestic workload, particularly in moving camp. Despite these advantages, Van Kirk points out that Native women "sacrificed considerable personal autonomy" in the process.[38] They also risked losing control of their children. In many Native societies, children were considered the property of the mother and the household was completely within her control. Marrying a white trader meant coming to terms with a husband who might send a child away to eastern Canada or Great Britain to be educated. Van Kirk describes a "perturbed discussion" in the fur traders' writings about Native women who were not as willing to submit to such patriarchal controls as the European men might have desired.[39] These were not simply the "submissive, attentive, and industrious" wives that some historians believed, or wanted to believe, that they saw.

What Van Kirk calls the "perturbed discussion" emerges on the other side of the border, in the writings of Henry Boller and Francis Chardon, who lived among the Mandans and the Hidatsas. Their accounts regarding the Native women with whom they came in contact require a careful eye to Euro-American bias. On the one hand, such traders acknowledged the vital economic and spiritual roles Native women played within the context of their own societies, as well as their essential contributions to the trade itself. Yet these Euro-American men could also betray discomfort with the evidence of female strength and autonomy that did not align with their notions of proper femininity.

Henry Boller was a young man of twenty-two when he arrived at Like-a-Fishhook by steamboat in 1858. His account, *Among the Indians: Four Years on the Upper Missouri, 1858–1862,* was written when he was again home.[40] One assumes that Boller shaped his account according to the expectations of an eastern United States audience that had an insatiable curiosity for descriptions of Native peoples. Boller fulfilled this expectation through careful depictions of daily life among the Hidatsas with whom he lived—and Native women's daily activities feature prominently in these portrayals. He carefully described women's daily work, betraying a certain amount of personal awe at their actions. Describing the Hidatsas' move to their winter quarters, Boller noted that he "could not help admiring the celerity and skill with which the [women] packed their plunder." In another instance, Boller observed Native women leaving the village to gather fuel, each harnessing their dogs to a travois and shouldering their axes. Upon their return, Boller noted in bewilderment that "each woman carries on her back . . . a bundle of wood of such size and weight that two would make a fair load for an Indian pony. Yet the women think nothing of it, and travel along, talking and laughing, as if it was play. Every day, year in and year out, this must be done."[41] Although impressed personally, at times it appears Boller wanted to shock his Euro-American readers through his depictions of Native women's chores.

Like the missionary Charles Hall, Boller could not help but notice what was the village women's most important economic role in their societies, that of farmer. He carefully described all aspects of the women's heavy labor in agriculture, beginning with breaking up their land in the spring, in which "every foot must be turned up and loosened with the hoe, a slow and toilsome operation."[42] He noted the processes of building fences made of willow branches, which the women had painstakingly gathered, of regularly hoeing their corn, and lastly of the harvest season, when the women's "long and patient labor is finally awarded with an abundant crop."[43] Even then, as Boller makes clear, the Hidatsa women's work was not done. Corn had to be hung on scaffolds to dry, holes had to be dug near the lodges so that a supply of food would rest undisturbed until spring, and they had to prepare for the Hidatsas' visit to their winter quarters for the buffalo hunt. Again, Boller probably wished to shock his Euro-American audience through depictions of heavy agricultural work that middle-class white women did not perform. But for the modern-day historian, what comes through most vividly in this account is the vital role Native women played in adding to the food supply. The "season of green corn," wrote Boller, was "one of festivity and gladness."[44]

Women's work was not limited to agricultural production, but rather extended into that arena commonly perceived to be solely Native men's sphere—the Hidatsas' twice-yearly buffalo hunt. It is significant that Boller, in providing his audiences with what was surely a requisite depiction of an exciting hunt, did not neglect to include the Native women's role in this operation. Van Kirk writes that Native women in Canada helped to build and operate the birch bark canoes upon which the traders relied; further south, Hidatsa women constructed and paddled the bull-boats that Native peoples along the Upper Missouri depended on for transportation. "These boats," wrote Boller, "which are necessary adjuncts to every [Hidatsa] lodge, are made of the fresh hide of a buffalo bull stretched over a framework of willow. In shape they resemble large wash-tubs, and will bear astonishing loads." The work of paddling the boats, continued Boller, always fell to the women, and since bull-boats were "ticklish craft to navigate," Boller concluded that it was "very laborious work" to do so.[45]

Women's work in paddling bull-boats becomes significant in Boller's depiction of the Hidatsas' buffalo hunt. The hunt itself was an awe-inspiring sight that Boller spent a great deal of time describing; he apparently felt that Native women's roles in helping prepare their hunters and meeting them after their return was worth noting, too. At the start, Boller writes, the men and women plunge into the Missouri, their bull-boats loaded with saddles and guns. Each woman "pushes the boat off and wades out with it until the water becomes sufficiently deep, when, steadying herself with her paddle she carefully takes her place. . . . [F]or a while, though the [woman] paddles with all her might, the boat makes no headway, but whirls around like a top."[46] In meeting the hunters afterward, each woman "help[ed] her hunter to saddle," inverted the bull-boat over her head and carried it back to the village, then returned to where the hunters were to pack up the meat.[47] The work of processing meat and tanning hides was entrusted to the women as well.

Significant, too, is Boller's inclusion of Native women's spiritual activities in his account, suggesting a general understanding that the women and their spiritual societies had a prominent place within village life. He described the young women who would celebrate the return of a war party, their cheeks painted with vermilion and yellow clay, and wearing their finest dresses. Boller wrote that this group "appeared rather tired," as they had been singing and dancing at every lodge within the village.[48] Boller witnessed the members of the Goose society dancing on the prairie behind the village. Their dance, according to Boller, was meant to

> remind the wild geese, now beginning their southward flight, that they have had plenty of good food all summer, and to entreat their return in the spring, when the rains come and the green grass begins to grow. . . . Each woman carries a bunch of long seed-grass, the favorite food of the wild goose, and at intervals all get up and dance in a circle with a peculiar shuffling step, singing and keeping time to the taps of the drum.[49]

As an outsider, Boller certainly could not have understood every aspect of the ceremony he witnessed. However, he was not seeking to radically transform the Native way of life and thus he did not include the same type of prejudicial commentary that Charles Hall would later espouse while observing the same ritual.

One of Boller's most intriguing depictions of women's spiritual activities involved the members of the most mature group, the White Buffalo Cow society. The sheer spiritual prowess of this society shines through Boller's account as the women succeeded in attracting buffalo after the men's efforts fell short. In Boller's account, men of the village, including an important leader, Four Bears, had attempted to "dream" so as to bring the buffaloes closer to the village for the winter hunt. None of their dreams had brought results. Boller writes that in this emergency,

> when all was doubt and uncertainty, the White Cow band, the *corps du reserve*, took the matter in hand, and as their medicine was never known to fail a better and more cheerful feeling soon pervaded the entire camp. . . . The great secret of the success of the White Cow band lay in the fact that when they undertook to bring the buffaloes the dancing was kept up vigorously night and day until buffaloes came.[50]

Soon enough, a huge buffalo bull entered the camp and charged about near the lodge where the women's society danced. All agreed "that the bull had been specially sent to show them that the efforts of the White Cow band were not in vain."[51] When a "fine band" of buffalo were spotted near the camp, Boller reported that "hearty congratulations on the wonderful strength and efficiency of the White Cow band were exchanged on every side."[52] Boller managed to convey not only the esteem that Hidatsa women garnered within their own society for their spiritual activities, but also some of his own awe at the unfamiliar traditions he was witnessing.

On the whole, Boller's account is remarkable for the level at which he sympathetically describes Native women's importance within their own societies, both economically and spiritually. Unlike many Euro-American observers, he could even take a balanced view of polygyny.[53] He admitted that in families with more than one wife, women could divide the labor between them, enabling them to "[get] along very comfortably."[54] He noted, too, that sororal polygyny was the most often practiced among the Hidatsa when he described one man whose wives were all sisters, and thus had "very little discord among them. His family lived well."[55]

Despite this rare understanding, at times Boller's writings could betray his own cultural biases against women who held positions of power, so unfamiliar in Euro-American society. He perceived such women as "viragos," by which he meant loud and domineering. His expectations of proper womanly behavior extended into his perceptions of Native women's appearances. Although he acknowledged the White Buffalo Cow society's importance, he wrote of one leading woman that her "charms . . . had long since faded. She had lost an eye and was quite lame, but her powers of speech remained unimpaired."[56] Despite these perceptions, Boller leaves no doubt that his very fort would not have functioned without Native women's work or their active participation in trade. "Trade went on very briskly. . . . [T]he [women] were dressing and bartering their robes as fast as possible," he wrote.[57] Trade completely depended on women's dressing of hides; in one surprising passage, Boller bemoaned the fact that because the women were busy repairing their lodges and doing their normal domestic work, they had not yet dressed any robes "except those which they traded to supply immediate wants." But, continued Boller, "upon the strength of what they would do when their robes were dressed the men lounged between the two forts. . . . Every Indian who had any robes at his disposal was therefore courted and treated with the greatest consideration."[58] Boller acknowledged that Native women were active participants in both producing hides for trade and in bartering them. He could, however, express discomfort with this active role at times. In describing a three-hour trading session with a group of Native women, Boller wrote that "many of the women were exceedingly angry when they found we would trade no more, and one old virago even went so far as to talk of cutting our goods to shreds in re-venge."[59] Much of the ambiguity in Boller's writings regarding Native women perhaps reflects his own ambiguous position at Fort Atkinson: as a Euro-American with his particular cultural attitudes about proper femininity and women's proper sphere, engaged in a business in which so much of his liveli-hood depended on women.

The contradictory ways in which Boller described Native women—as ac-tive agents within the fur trade and their own societies, worthy of admiration, or as "viragos" depended, in part, on the audience for whom he wrote. This is particularly evident in his letters, when he described other Native women tak-ing an active role in fur trade society by marrying white fur traders. The single Boller wished to reassure his parents that his "Christian education has been such . . . [that] I have so far maintained the high character that I had at home."[60] In other words, he wanted his family to know that he had not mar-ried a Native woman—although, as he wrote to his sister, he had had "offers of marriage from *two* of them, which you must allow is a different mode from that in vogue among the whites."[61] In describing a woman named Female Bear, whom Boller claimed wished to marry him, Boller revealed his own discomfort with such a reversal through writing that she was "rejected but is still prowling around, seeking whom she may devour."[62] In his personal let-ters, Boller expressed more negative sentiments about the Native women who married fur traders than was depicted in his book. He wrote to his sister that when Native women married fur traders, they became "very lazy and saucy, unless they are allowed to deck themselves in every species of finery that the trading store furnishes. When they get too outrageous, their husbands take a stout stick and give them a sound 'whaling' which exerts a most salutary influ-ence over them."[63] Boller's descriptions to his closest relatives, however, prob-ably reveal less about the actual prevalence of white men beating their wives than they do about Boller's own discomfort with women who attempted to exert influence over their fur trade husbands and gain advantages through their marital arrangements.[64]

While perhaps personally uncomfortable, Boller seems to have downright reveled in the shock that such cultural differences in womanhood might arouse in his mother and sister. Combining a stunning array of prejudices into one letter, he made sure to inform his mother that:

> these ladies are not remarkable for their purity, either of persons or
> morals. . . . [I]t is hot weather here now, and . . . the women, leaving off
> their fringed buckskin dresses, wear bed-ticking smocks, which, as they

daily hoe corn and pack firewood, it is considered unnecessary to wash. . . . As evening approaches bathing is the rule, and both sexes, young and old promiscuously take a plunge into the river.[65]

Despite playing into stereotypes, and perhaps taking pleasure in the thought of how his depictions would affect his mother and sister, in the end Boller betrays far more ambiguity than racism toward the Native women with whom he worked and lived. He admitted to his father, "If I wanted a wife, I would just as soon have an Indian woman as a white one, but I dislike taking trouble upon interest," revealing that Boller took financial obligations much more than color into account when refusing his supposed Native suitors.[66] And despite portraying Indian women as poor housekeepers for the bemusement (or satisfaction) of his mother, Boller nonetheless revealed his dependence on Native woman. In one touching passage, he begs his mother and sister to send "a complete woman's dress" so that he could give it to Susann, the Native wife of another trader. Susann "is like a sister to me; does all my washing and mending, or anything else I may ask her, and this is a great convenience to me, I assure you. . . . The keenest rivalry exists between the white men's [Native wives] at the two forts. . . . Such a dress as you could send her would place her far beyond competition!!"[67]

It is impossible to know the perceptions that a woman like Susann had of Henry Boller. Nor is it possible to know the exact motives or feelings that Female Bear had while she supposedly proposed marriage to Boller when, in his account, she carried logs of firewood to the village, past the fort gates, in order to "prove how valuable she was."[68] It is only possible to know the women from the glimpses Boller provides in his written records. Although riddled with cultural prejudices, his record reveals at least one truth: Native women were indispensable to the fur trade.

Francis T. Chardon, who lived at nearby Fort Clark among the Mandans and Arikaras, also revealed the indispensability of Native women to the trade. Writing in his journal during the years 1834–1839, he consistently noted that the women dressed the buffalo robes, scraped skins, cut up and dried the meat, and worked at their cornfields.[69] However, having an Arikara wife and three Dakota wives at separate times, Chardon had insights into the marriages between European men and Native women that the bachelor Boller perhaps lacked.[70] Contemporary readers of Chardon's descriptions of his own marriages, as well as those of his fellow traders, can easily find examples of the free will exercised by the Native women. This is quite a different interpretation from the historian who introduced his volume in the 1930s and asserted that Native women were exploited. Native women leave their marriages when they choose, and while Chardon notes the whippings that he gave his wives, he also notes a whipping that his Lakota wife gave to *him*.[71] Chardon's journal is distinct from Boller's account in one other important way—Chardon wrote through the 1837 smallpox epidemic, and thus left a firsthand account of that year's "ravages." While the disease likely affected him personally, with the death of his own infant son, he could not ignore the destruction all around him in the wider Mandan society.[72] His entry for August 31 reads: "A young Mandan that died 4 days ago, his wife having the disease also—Killed her two children, one a fine Boy of eight years, and the other six, to complete the affair she hung herself—."[73] By the next year, Chardon had resumed reporting on the fur trade and the vicissitudes of his and his colleagues' married lives. He does not comment on the lingering effects of this disaster for other unnamed Mandan women and their families who survived.

Whatever tantalizing glimpses we receive, it is impossible to fully understand the perspectives and motivations of Native women through reading the sources left by white Euro-American men. Ella Deloria took a fascinating approach to this problem in her novel *Waterlily*. In the book, Deloria put ethnographic research in an imaginative context to flesh out the experiences of Lakota women. This fictionalized account is set in the early nineteenth century—before the Lakotas (termed Teton or Sioux by Deloria), residing to the south of the Mandans, Hidatsas, and Arikaras, had experienced much direct contact with Euro-American traders such as Chardon or Boller. However, the characters in this fictional work did have indirect contact with Europeans in two significant ways: with horses and with germs. Deloria, a Yankton woman, worked with renowned anthropologists such as Franz Boas and Ruth Benedict from the 1920s until the 1940s. Writing at roughly the same time as Alfred Bowers, she had difficulty in obtaining the funds to complete her research. Without recognition, she was unable to publish more of her ethnographic materials.[74] *Waterlily* was published only in 1988.

Although Ella Deloria was not recognized in her lifetime, *Waterlily* includes much in the way of ethnographic information on Lakota and Dakota peoples, of which she was an expert—and it is unique in that it is told from the perspective of Lakota women.[75] The Tetons in present-day South Dakota relied far more on the buffalo hunt and a mobile way of life than sedentary agriculture. Appropriately, *Waterlily* begins with the camp circle on the move. A woman named Blue Bird drops behind the procession in order to give birth to a daughter, whom she calls Waterlily.[76] Through the perspective of Water-

lily, the novel proceeds to give a useful overview of what a Teton girl's upbringing and married life might have been like in the early portion of this
time period. In particular, the novel describes the tightly bound group of related households in Lakota culture, known as the *tiyospaye*, and the values a
young woman was inculcated with in this society.[77]

After Waterlily's mother separates from her husband, she remarries a man
named Rainbow, and the young Waterlily gains a brother by the name of Little
Chief and a grandmother called Gloku. Waterlily's new grandmother takes
charge throughout the novel in teaching the young boy and girl proper gender
roles, particularly one of the most fundamental kinship rules in Lakota culture, that "brothers and sisters must always place one another above all else."[78]
Waterlily receives her sharpest reprimand from her grandmother for acciden-
tally hurting her brother in play. Her brother is scolded as well, for crying.
Gloku sternly tells him, "[A] brother does not embarrass his girl relatives but
strives only to spare them and make them happy."[79] Whereas Little Chief is
taught to become a man and to fulfill his manly duty through providing for
his sisters, Waterlily is taught to sing her brother's praises. Her proudest moment as a young girl comes when Little Chief first counts coup, or earns great
honor through a brave confrontation with an enemy, and she has the right as
the warrior's sister to carry the scalp in his victory procession. As Little Chief
learns to perform his roles, Waterlily meanwhile preoccupies herself with caring for her new baby brother and following her grandmother, aunts, and particularly her mother everywhere.[80]

As Waterlily grows into adolescence, the lessons her mother is most anxious to impart revolve around proper courtship and marriage. Warning her
daughter to "never let a man take you anywhere alone," Waterlily's mother
expresses how vastly significant female purity before marriage was to this particular Native group, the Tetons. "Remember this," Blue Bird says, "your purity is without price; guard it well. Then your husband will be happy to think,
'I am of all men most fortunate, for I have married a virgin.'"[81] Waterlily learns
that lesson well, and when her time for marriage comes she weds in the most
respected form among the Tetons. She was "bought," and the man brought a
costly gift to her parents, rather than the families mutually exchanging gifts or
Waterlily simply eloping with him. Moreover, she honored her kinship obligations, as even though she did not know her suitor at all, she agreed to marry
him because his gift of horses would help her family.[82] When Waterlily goes to
reside at her new husband's camp circle, she comes into contact with plural
marriage, something that she had heard about but not personally seen. Her
father-in-law is married to two sisters and their cousin, and Waterlily found it

to be "a harmonious household. All the wives cheerfully shared the burdens of the family."[83]

Waterlily's work as a married woman is much like the work that Mandan and Hidatsa women did for the benefit of the fur trade: she dries meat after the hunt, then processes it, and finally packs it away. Other than lonesomeness among her husband's camp circle, she finds her marriage to be a satisfactory one. She knows, however, that if she were unhappy there would be "no economic need for her to endure in silence. She knew that her brothers and male cousins were ready to provide for her, and her own relatives to take her back into their midst. She did not have to hang on just to be supported by a husband."[84]

In the end, it is not divorce that separates Waterlily from her husband. The germs of an invading and unknown people hit her camp circle unexpectedly and hard. Waterlily's husband dies of smallpox, as do many of his family members. Waterlily does not die in this horrifying epidemic, however. She lives to bear a son, whom she calls Mitawa (My Own), and she eventually remarries. In this novel, Deloria manages to convey the dislocating tempo of historical change for Native peoples in the nineteenth century. She suggests, also, that some things had stayed the same for Native women in these tumultuous times. Waterlily focuses largely on family and on passing her people's values on to the next generation.

In a way, Waterlily is no more fictional than the Native women whom we glimpse only through the biased writings of missionaries, or fur traders, or Euro-American anthropologists. In the early nineteenth century, the real-life Lakota women who married, bore children, and lived out their lives without ever seeing a white man, although most likely suffering the effects of their diseases, did not leave written records. Nor did Rattles Her Medicine's mother, or grandmother, leave a written account—although they were probably among those women whom Boller said cut and dragged the timber for the trading post at Fort Berthold.[85]

With all the types of sources this essay has examined, it is important to keep the issue of bias in mind. Such biases limit the modern-day historian's ability to construct an unfiltered glimpse of Native women's actual lives. We cannot glimpse such women's perspectives and motivations. We can only imagine that they, like the fictional Waterlily, adapted to and invariably survived the onslaught of changes that characterized their diverse lifetimes.

**3**

# "Willing Challengers"

## Women's Experiences on the Northern Plains, 1862–1930

ANDREA G. RADKE-MOSS

Remembering her move to South Dakota in 1898 to marry a widowed homesteader, Grace Fairchild contemplated, "Looking back now on this crazy idea of moving into the dry plains part of South Dakota for the sake of free land, I think of the poem by Benet that goes like this:

> 'I took my wife out of a pretty house
> I took my wife out of a pretty place
> I stripped my wife of comfortable things
> I drove my wife to wander with the wind.'"

As she arrived closer to what would become her permanent home, Fairchild noted the sharp change in scenery from her native Wisconsin's "frame houses, churches and good farm land" to South Dakota's "sod shacks and log houses." To her it seemed to be a "desolate unknown." She marveled: "Funny though it never occurred to me to act like a balky horse and refuse to go any farther."[1]

Rachel Calof, a young Jewish mail-order bride, echoed similar sentiments in 1894, upon arriving at the North Dakota homestead of her fiancé's family.

> As we entered my heart turned to ice at what greeted my eyes. This was my first sight of what awaited me as a pioneer woman. . . . Shock and deprivation were no strangers in my young life, but seeing what faced us in this new and hostile environment I could hardly choke back my tears of grief.[2]

Both Fairchild's and Calof's initial impressions of the Dakotas in the 1890s suggest the submission and reluctance often negatively attributed to women homesteaders. This enduring stereotype is credited to Walter Prescott Webb, whose defining work, *The Great Plains*, described women as only marginal to the male plains experience. The plains were "strictly a man's country," only to be "dreaded" by women because the harshness of life there "precluded the little luxuries that women love and that are so necessary to them."[3] Certainly, rural and isolated homesteading marked a majority of women's plains experiences. However, in spite of initial timidity, neither Fairchild nor Calof were by any means unwilling or submissive participants in the settlement of the northern plains.

Like other predominantly white, middle-class women who settled eastern Montana, the Dakotas, and the Canadian provinces of Manitoba, Saskatchewan, and eastern Alberta between 1862 and 1930, northern plains women pursued personal and economic investment in the land to which they were bound. The daunting distances from town centers drove most women, not to despair, but to seek creative adaptations to their environment. For themselves and their children they sought domestic and cultural refinement, agricultural improvements through gardening and agricultural extension programs, primary and higher education, improved economic developments, and expanded political participation. The plains experience fostered in many women a pursuit of cultural and creative interests outside the home and farm, including literature, photography, school teaching, music, and political activism, especially in the temperance and woman suffrage movements.

Regardless of race, religion, ethnicity, socioeconomics, and marital status, women's experiences in the northern plains were largely connected by the central importance of agriculture in the plains economy. Women settlers came from many religions and ethnicities and included both single and married women. They comprised Anglo-American and British women who moved to the cattle-ranching areas of eastern Montana, Mormon women and their families who came to southern Alberta, significant Mennonite settlers from both the United States and Canada, Russian Jews who settled in North Dakota, African American "Exoduster" women, and other immigrants from Scandinavia and eastern and southern Europe.[4] In the United States, post-Civil War plains settlement also saw positive and negative encounters between these new immigrants and the northern plains Native women, primarily the Siouxan-speaking nomadic tribes—the Cheyenne, Sioux, and Crow Indians. In the Canadian plains provinces, native Cree, Blackfoot, and Métis populations had long interacted with European fur traders, creating more culturally and racially mixed populations. By 1900, both American Natives and Canadian First Nations women found themselves largely dependent on forms of agricultural production—either by force through reservation policy or by choice—just like their immigrant female neighbors. Indian women also turned to creative outlets of literature, music, poetry, and education to express their physical and spiritual connections to their environment.

Most challenging to Webb's theory of the "reluctant female settler" was that so many women drew from plains experience to depict enduring literary images of female life. Many Americans' and Canadians' first introduction to and popular conceptions of women's experiences on the plains have come from the writings of two significant plains authoresses, Laura Ingalls Wilder and Nellie McClung. Although different in genre and public renown, both writers drew from female homesteading experience to craft their semiautobiographical works, and both can be compared—at least in theme and inspiration—to two other important central plains authors, Willa Cather and Mari Sandoz.[5] That these four women took so much literary stimulation from late-nineteenth-century plains life, tragedy, and education—and that each chose to write semiautobiographically—suggests not an oppressive experience but one of deep physical and spiritual connectedness to their plains environment and culture.

For Canadians, Nellie (Mooney) McClung depicted homesteading experiences in Manitoba through the eyes of her fictional heroine, Pearlie Watson, a character based on McClung's own life. Born in 1873 in Ontario, Nellie Mooney came to southwest Manitoba in 1880 with her Scotch Irish immigrant parents, for the farming opportunities of the Canadian plains. Not turned off by the plains environment, instead Nellie "gloried in her new surroundings. She grew up a tomboy, ranging across the wide-open prairies she described so lovingly in her fiction."[6] And like Laura Ingalls, Mari Sandoz, and other plains daughters, McClung also briefly turned to teaching as an outlet for her educational energies. Three of McClung's four novels trace the lives of the Watson family on the plains of Manitoba: *Sowing Seeds in Danny* (1908), *The Second Chance* (1910), and *Purple Springs* (1921). The latter endures as her most famous work and as an important commentary on female activism in the Canadian plains.[7]

For Americans, famed children's author Laura Ingalls Wilder's memoir-inspired series Little House on the Prairie chronicled the lives of her parents and sisters as they homesteaded in various midwestern states. Five books of the Little House series take place near De Smet, South Dakota, where the Ingalls family lived from 1879 to 1894. De Smet is also where Laura married

Almanzo Wilder in 1885 and homesteaded herself as a young bride. The books—*By the Shores of Silver Lake* (1939), *The Long Winter* (1940), *Little Town on the Prairie* (1941), *These Happy Golden Years* (1943), and *The First Four Years* (1971, published posthumously)—have offered enduring images of typical life for women in the northern plains.[8] Indeed, the difficulties and joys experienced by Laura's family paralleled those of most northern plains families, and many would have recognized similarities in the descriptions of blizzards, grasshopper plagues, droughts, and illness. Further, the Little House books chronicled the poverty and the periodic moves inherent to the boom-and-bust cycles of the rural plains. In spite of these collective difficulties, rural women would have recognized Laura's celebration of the culture of music, religion, sociality, and education shared among neighbors. Both McClung and Wilder portrayed heroines who were independent, assured, connected to the plains, and driven by the desire for education. But most essential to the book themes of plains authors was the importance of domesticity, education, and agriculture.

First, the domestication of the plains was primarily driven by women's belief in an ideal described as "domestic ideology." The concept of domesticity that emerged in the 1830s had been thoroughly embraced by white, middle-class women in the antebellum era.[9] Barbara Welter's classic essay on domestic ideology as an analytical framework gained a distinctive western interpretation by Robert Griswold in the late 1980s, and more recently has been used to consider US imperial motives.[10] Arguing that "the development of domestic discourse in America is contemporaneous with the discourse of Manifest Destiny," Amy Kaplan used the lens of imperialism to reimagine the concept of domestic ideology, providing a new approach to northern plains frontier women's experiences, particularly in terms of relations with Native American women.[11] Despite refinements over time, two central components of domestic ideology remain: it justified middle-class women's restricted, home-focused activities with a meaningful role in society, and by acknowledging women's position as moral guardians and civilizers within the home it allowed them to expand their influence outside the confines of the home.

Whether in plains towns or in rural farm areas, domestic ideology was partly defined by the general acceptance that, as historian Robert Griswold states, "women's chief responsibilities were homemaking and child rearing, that females represented the moral foundation of the family and society, and that a commitment to family preceded and took precedence over a commitment to self." A major aspect of "domestic ideology" was housework itself, because "[d]omesticity for western Anglo women cannot be divorced from the productive labor they performed within the home."[12] So most women's diaries, journals, and letters contain descriptions of labor-intensive domestic chores, from cooking, washing, heating (usually with fuel collected from the prairie), sewing, quilting, mending, and child care, to hygienic duties that ranged from bathing children, washing clothes, and scrubbing surfaces, to sweeping and packing sod-house floors. Domestic ideology should not be limited to a perception of plains women as mindless drones slaving over stove and babies. Instead, the ideals of domestic ideology held a "powerful appeal to female settlers: they gave meaning to women's domestic work, made the blurring of sex roles culturally intelligible, helped confirm women's self-worth, offered a sense of stability in an inherently unstable world, and fostered bonds of friendship with other women."[13] At the same time, these widely held ideals became a useful justification for women to venture into the wider civil realm as they sought to domesticate the frontier environment through cultural refinement, education, and political reform.[14] Taken one step further, domesticity as a civilizing process brought northern plains women squarely into the very male business of conquering territories, subduing the land, and assimilating Native Americans.

Plains historians have expanded on the domestication process, showing how simple chores, domestic improvements, and the acquisition of material possessions were in themselves "personal symbol[s] of aspirations to middle-class refinement in spite of harsh conditions."[15] Middle-class domestication also meant upholstering inner spaces, using proper manners, and bringing cultural, musical, and material refinements into otherwise rough places.[16] As railroad shipping, Rural Free Delivery, and parcel post expanded into the plains, material possessions became more available to women through catalog ordering. By purchasing the cooking stoves, upholstery, clocks, china, silver, and house organs associated with middle-class refinement, the women of the northern plains could incorporate a very specific elegance into rural life that mimicked their eastern sisters. Domestication efforts, writes historian Chad Montrie, also included "subduing nature . . . by imposing domesticity on it, and over time this became their exclusive form of interaction with it."[17] To subdue nature, women might step outside of gender roles to kill a snake or a skunk. But mostly they planted flower beds, vegetable gardens, fruit orchards, and ornamental trees and shrubs. Later women further attempted to refine the natural environment through extension programs, which provided domestic science education and instruction in scientific agriculture, including new trials in hybrids, fertilizers, and climate adaptations.

Beyond the responsibilities of home and the private sphere, domestic ideology contained the seeds of reform by encouraging women to take their responsibilities for creating a civilized home into the civic sphere. The ideology drove plains women's actions to implement the foundations of Euro-American cultural, religious, and educational institutions. Not limited by some "abstraction called *civilization*," women transplanted the specific organizations and traditions that would "check male inspired disorder."[18] However, as Kaplan has argued, men and women together shared the work of imperializing the West, especially as they became "national allies against the alien."[19] So, while women's civilizing work in the plains took on a specifically domestic character, still the goals of men and women were the same. Thus, the concept of domestic ideology extended out of the private sphere into other areas that came under the influence of women's civilizing tendencies, such as "schools, churches, charity associations, [and] reforms."[20] Throughout the northern plains, women played an instrumental role in establishing schools, women's clubs, temperance and literary societies, and church groups like Catholic sisterhoods, Protestant charity organizations, and Mormon Relief Societies. These institutions brought the trappings of civilized culture to the plains that reinforced the goals of imperial expansion sought by plains men and women alike.[21] In fact, as Amy Kaplan has suggested, "part of the cultural work of domesticity might be to unite men and women in a national domain and to generate notions of the foreign against which the nation can be imagined as home."[22]

Primary in the implementation of this civilization were the attempts to establish institutions of both elementary and higher education. On the US side of the border, many states and territories refocused attention on universal free public education after the Civil War. Teaching was an appropriate pursuit, especially for single young women preparing for marriage, because, according to Suzanne Schrems, western schoolteachers represented those "who found teaching in the schoolhouses or mission fields in the West to be an acceptable alternative to the prescribed domestic sphere that society reserved for them."[23] Furthermore, through teaching, these young women gained numerous other benefits, such as supplementing their family income, saving money for land or marriage, and meeting others through socially and professionally approved interactions. Schoolteachers' benefits also allowed for women to "be able to make a contribution to society, to seek adventure, and to gain financial independence and self-realization."[24] So many young women taught school that Mary Hurlbut Cordier has estimated the numbers of teachers to be between twenty-five percent and thirty-five percent of all employed women in her study of Iowa, Nebraska, and Kansas in the 1880s, with other domestic, service, and agriculture opportunities making up the rest.[25] Similar percentages are likely for other plains states and provinces. Many daughters of northern plains families pursued teaching, even if only for one school year, as evidenced by the numbers of well-known plains women, including Ingalls, McClung, and Sandoz, who all taught for a while.

Education was often the first "improvement" attempted by women upon arrival at a new homestead in both the US and Canadian frontiers. Frequent moves and long distances made consistent primary education difficult in the rural plains; still most women sought some form of primary education for their children. In the United States, where the Land Ordinance of 1785 provided a mechanism for funding public education, the earliest schools were usually rural, first-through-eighth-grade inclusive.[26] Housed in simple structures like soddies or barns, the schools were staffed by a younger female with only a basic license for elementary instruction. On the South Dakota plains, Grace Fairchild started a school for the local children, using makeshift materials and hiring a seventeen-year-old teacher. She remembered, "Just having a school available made life look a lot better to me."[27] Difficulties included long distances, harsh weather conditions ranging from blizzards to dust storms, inadequate supplies, and low pay.

In the Canadian Prairie Provinces, as in the United States, establishing rural schools reinforced the idea that the future of the country lay with the advancing line of settlers, not with the Native Americans. In Canada, however, an important question centered on whether the education system would be based on a French system (private, Catholic, and voluntary) or an English system (nonsectarian, publicly supported, with compulsory attendance laws), developed in Ontario, largely from British and US models. The question answered itself with the large number of English-speaking migrants onto the Canadian Great Plains. As author Roger Manzer notes, the Anglo majority ensured it would "determine the shape of the new society," including which language and type of educational framework would take hold.[28] As in the United States, the first schools established in new towns tended to be small, grade-inclusive, and with young women serving as teachers.

No matter on which side of the border they lived, teachers had to contend with low pay, difficult conditions, and close scrutiny by parents and school board members as to their appropriate behavior. Despite the hardships, young women often chose to sacrifice higher-paying domestic work as laundresses or cooks, because teaching "offered more respectability." Teaching "also enabled educated women, who were usually barred from professional opportunities, to use their skills."[29] Thus the frontier "school marm" has endured both as an important mythical image and as a historical reality for many plains women.

During the 1870s and 1880s, in the northern plains on both sides of the US-Canadian border, the increasing numbers of female teachers became the subject of criticism, the teachers characterized as "anti-intellectual," claiming that the "classroom [was] a workshop for motherhood for the average female." Others have questioned this stereotype, instead portraying women as "dedicated" and "highly professional."[30] States and counties improved their attempts to professionalize teachers by setting up defined school districts, raising the licensing standards for rural teachers, and establishing normal schools for training purposes. With increasing emphasis on higher education, states, territories, and provinces also opened universities and land-grant colleges as coeducational institutions, offering higher learning to both males and females in numerous subjects. Most women students primarily took domestic science courses to become "scientific housewives," a further contribution to the spreading of domestic ideology in the plains.[31]

Besides the domestic ideology of homesteading wives, women's involvement in agriculture came in two other significant ways. Many farm and ranch wives departed from exclusively domestic duties by supporting agricultural production through actual farm labor. While women may have insisted on maintaining their connection to the domestic ideology, the reality of their rural experience led them to take on more diverse roles. Women's farmwork lay in a middle ground between the female-only domestic sphere and the male-only sphere in the fields. This part-home, part-farm extension of women's work involved gardening, orchard cultivation, and the raising of small livestock and poultry, such as pigs and chickens, usually to supplement the food provisions but at times for adding to the overall farm income. Beyond that, some women sought more active contributions to the male-dominated farmwork by venturing into less-traditional activities, such as "foddering livestock, [and] even planting or harvesting."[32] Taking on these new chores "could also be [seen as] a means of self-protection and attaining status," of taking control over the challenges they faced in their new environment, rather than exhibiting "mere passive endurance."[33]

Finally, single women—widowed, never married, or divorced—came to the plains to claim their own homesteads and try their hands at farming or ranching as female heads of household, as allowed by the Homestead Act of 1862. What perhaps most challenges the reluctant female settler image of Webb's thesis are the sheer numbers of plains women who either ran their husbands' homesteads or homesteaded on their own as single women. H. Elaine Lindgren's study of female homesteaders in North Dakota has shown a diverse spectrum of widowed women, engaged women, and sisters, brothers, and female friends who homesteaded together or on neighboring claims. Although difficult to find exact numbers, Lindgren's research of nine counties from the 1880s to the early 1900s has placed the percentages of female claimants between as low as four to six percent in the early years to as high as twenty percent in McKenzie County after 1900. In total, Lindgren argued, "[m]y data would indicate that in the area that is now North Dakota, thousands of women took land."[34] Regarding the work on these claims, women either rented to others, hired men to do the heavier farmwork, or performed their own labor, which ranged from plowing, threshing, and building fences to picking rocks and slaughtering livestock.

Comparable to the 1862 Homestead Act, Canada's 1872 Dominion Lands Act allowed eligibility only for widowed, divorced, or separated wives who had minor children; thus a majority of women homesteaders actually acquired land through purchase and not through the Lands Act. Still women's involvement in wheat farming has been well documented by Mary Kinnear, who has demonstrated that Canadian women at times shared in farmwork like clearing land, plowing, and home construction, but they were mostly tied to the traditional domestic work, especially as cooking demands increased with threshing crews. Women also supplemented farm income through cottage industries like needlework, or the selling of surplus produce, poultry, or livestock.[35]

Women's involvement in the farm economy could sometimes free them up for other creative and professional activities, such as art, photography, music, and literature. Famed Montana photographer Evelyn Cameron came to the Montana plains with her British rancher husband and developed her photographic talents while supplementing the Camerons' income with a photography business. Her photos have endured as some of the most revealing depictions of agricultural life for Montana women. Photographer Julia Tuell accompanied her schoolteacher husband to reservations in South Dakota and Montana, where she photo-documented the lives of Cheyenne and Brulé Sioux Indians. Artist and plains homesteader Ada B. Caldwell taught art at South Dakota State University from 1899 to 1937 and also worked in extension programs, teaching art projects to rural women. Montana farm wife Lillian Weston Hazen supplemented the family wheat income by publishing poetry and short fiction.[36] Cameron, Tuell, Caldwell, and Hazen represent how plains women found important connections between plains life and artistic expression. Women also devoted more time to the reform work of agricultural alliances, temperance activities, and political activism, especially woman suffrage.

Woman suffrage provided an important way for northern plains women to promote their own moralistic reform efforts, while also linking women to the expansionist aims that accompanied the goals of domestic ideology. The battle for woman suffrage in the northern plains states proceeded with difficulty. After the proposed Sixteenth Amendment for federal woman suffrage failed in 1870, national suffrage leaders took their fight to the individual states.[37] This process moved cautiously but steadily in plains states—with "close" victories in neighboring states of Wyoming, Colorado, Kansas—especially where middle-class women's clubs, including educational, agrarian, democratic, and temperance groups, provided grassroots support for the cause.[38] Among these groups, the nationally powerful Women's Christian Temperance Union (WCTU) provided important support after 1890, when the union's top leadership declared public support for woman suffrage. Between 1870 and 1919, numerous referendums for the female ballot were battled in plains states and territories. Following the creation of the Dakota Territory in 1861, the first woman suffrage bill came before the territorial legislature in 1872. It lost by only one vote. Later, in 1885, a Republican governor of the Dakota Territory vetoed a woman suffrage measure, arguing that if Dakota granted woman suffrage, "it might ruin the territory's chances at statehood."[39]

Woman suffrage gained its first victories in the arena of school suffrage, as the feminization of education demanded the service of women on school boards and in county and state superintendents' offices. Indeed, many plains states first granted school suffrage for women in the 1870s and 1880s, as school administration was accepted as the proper extension of domestic ideology. For instance, Dakota women received school suffrage upon the admission of North and South Dakota as states in 1889. This gave North Dakota another important first: Laura Eisenhuth was elected state superintendent of education in 1892, becoming the first American woman to hold state office.[40]

In spite of these victories, woman suffrage bills became closely tied to competitions over prohibition laws, especially in states with "wet" immigrant populations, who feared that legalized woman suffrage would lead directly to anti-alcohol laws. Indeed, the fear of temperance led to the defeat of the woman's vote in many states.[41] This tension certainly played out in the 1914 Montana election, which gained a victory for woman suffrage in spite of the liquor proponents, who were "particularly and vindictively active" against suffrage efforts; the same tension brought defeat in North and South Dakota, where the large number of German-Russian settlers who had moved into this region organized against the amendment.[42]

Following the statehood of North and South Dakota in 1889, the struggle for woman suffrage in these states was intermittent and often frustrating. The most volatile fight for woman suffrage in South Dakota came just one year after statehood, with a referendum Eleanor Flexner has called the "fiasco of 1890."[43] The referendum campaign was "one of the most rigorous that suffrage workers ever endured." Both Susan B. Anthony and Elizabeth Cady Stanton had toured the state—Anthony suffering blistering prairie heat during the summer, and Stanton enduring the cold of the autumn campaign, but just barely; she contracted typhoid and almost died.[44] The South Dakota referendum demonstrated two continuing struggles for western woman suffrage. Agrarian organizations often balked at supporting the franchise for fear of alienating immigrant farmers. In the 1890 battle, Anthony had counted on the support from these groups. Instead, the Knights of Labor and the Farmers Alliance launched a "third party, which refused to encumber itself with the controversial issue of votes for women," writes Flexner.[45] The second loss revealed by the 1890s Dakota fight was the continued "unhappy marriage" between the suffrage and temperance movements. Anthony had used the support of the Women's Christian Temperance Union in the state, which, by all accounts, had led to the defeat of the referendum. This failure later prompted Anthony to reject the WCTU's help in an 1896 California referendum.

Carrie Chapman Catt helped with the 1890 South Dakota campaign; she remembered the 1896 to 1910 period in woman suffrage as difficult and stale: "Only six state referenda were held," with one of those six another failed attempt in South Dakota. The experiences in South Dakota almost turned Mrs. Catt cold; during later "grueling and costly campaigns" in 1914 that included the Dakotas, she "branded the lot as 'tediously similar.'" According to Flexner, "Suffragists in growing numbers asked, what on earth was the use of one more unsuccessful campaign in South Dakota?"[46] Also instrumental during these tough years, Mary Shields "Mamie" Pyle served as the president of South Dakota's Equal Suffrage Movement from 1911 until state suffrage was finally achieved in 1918.

A failed 1913 Women's Suffrage Act in North Dakota revealed the recurring danger of close alliance with prohibitionists. Besides calling for abolition of the liquor trade, the WCTU also demanded reforms on child labor and obscene literature. These platforms further alienated North Dakota male voters, especially German immigrants and the railroads; not until 1917 would North Dakota finally win its battle for full suffrage, with the help of the Non-Partisan League, which put woman suffrage on its platform.[47] While women won the right to local and presidential suffrage only, two years later North

Dakota ratified the national amendment, and in 1923, voters elected two women to the state legislature.[48]

As the last northern plains state to pass suffrage, South Dakota finally accepted a suffrage bill in 1918. The victory came when suffrage activists united their cause with a bill to give all foreign immigrants citizenship. A failed 1916 attempt had again revealed the power of immigrant voters who feared prohibition laws. South Dakota women sought to gain the immigrant vote by giving their support to a bill that combined "woman suffrage and the qualification of citizenship for all voters."[49] This citizenship bill appealed to immigrant voters who finally turned from their fears of prohibition. One year later, South Dakota voters took advantage of a unique primary law that called party leaders together in November 1919 to prepare for the March primaries. The state also held conventions for the Republicans, Democrats, and Non-Partisan League. Carrie Chapman Catt and Nettie Rogers Shuler, in *Woman Suffrage and Politics*, write,

> The suffragists recognized this [as] a psychological moment when almost the whole Legislature would be on hand in Pierre, and readily obtained the consent of the Governor to call a special session if it could be done with no expense to the State. The suffragists then interviewed legislators and entreated them to go to Pierre at their own expense.[50]

A majority accepted this, and a call went out for December 3. National American Women Suffrage Association president Catt—herself a native Iowan and plains woman—was on the ground for the South Dakota reform and remembered the extreme hardship in the victory.

> For thirty-six hours telegraph and telephone lines hummed as the effort was made to reach legislators in the remotest parts of the State. The snow was heavy, the roads almost impassable, but the men came from all directions. One legislator used up three automobiles getting to the train from his home, many miles from the railroad; while another rushed from Minneapolis to Huron, called his wife to send his grip and just caught the train for Pierre. South Dakota had a unique ratification. It was the only State to hold a midnight special session and ratify between supper and breakfast.[51]

The suffrage battle for Canadian plains women was even more hard-fought. Manitoba would gain fame as the first province to pass woman suffrage in 1916, but not before a long, difficult fight there and in the other plains provinces, Saskatchewan and Alberta. The Canadian suffrage movement gained its earliest strong momentum in the 1880s among Icelandic women immigrants, who brought their ideals of political equality from their first country. Like the US suffragists, Canadian reformers also received extensive support from the WCTU, as well as agrarian and labor groups. Dr. Amelia Yeomans, the first female doctor in Winnipeg and an active WCTU member, staged a mock parliament in favor of suffrage in 1893.[52]

In 1912, a group of Winnipeg middle-class women formed the Political Equality League (PEL), the main provincial woman suffrage organization, which succeeded in moving the suffrage platform across the province through the leadership and speeches of a few dynamic women, especially the prominent reformer and author Nellie McClung. The PEL gained the support of the WCTU and others. Influenced by maternal feminism and the Social Gospel movement, McClung argued for Canadian women to reform the problems of alcoholism, poverty among women and children, and other ills.[53] McClung's literary works, especially In Times Like These (1915) and Purple Springs (1921), made a strong case for the reform of divorce, marital property, and child custody laws.[54] Battling the conservative government of Sir Rodmond Roblin in the election of 1914, McClung and her colleagues performed the famous pro-suffrage political skit, "The Women's Parliament," which mocked Roblin's conservative arguments against suffrage. Although equal suffrage failed in 1914, Roblin's government fell in scandal in 1915, opening the way for a new liberal government to pass the first provincial woman suffrage law in Canada in 1916.[55]

The parliaments of Alberta and Saskatchewan soon followed Manitoba in 1916, granting women "full provincial suffrage."[56] As in other plains states and provinces, the Alberta and Saskatchewan woman suffrage campaign received significant support from agrarian organizations like the Saskatchewan Women Grain Growers, the United Farm Women of Alberta, and the Non-Partisan League, which had extended its political influence into the Canadian plains from North Dakota in 1915.[57] Nellie McClung herself assisted with the Alberta suffrage cause, after moving there with her husband. She later served in the Alberta Legislative Assembly as a Liberal. In 1929, McClung and four others successfully argued before parliament for the right to have women declared "persons" under Canadian law. The "Famous Five" have been immortalized in Canadian women's history, with the legacy of a "Persons' Day" celebrating the victory.[58]

These political victories for white women did not mirror similar positive changes for Native women inhabitants of the plains, who "typically found themselves on the receiving end of manifest destiny," as historian Adrienne Caughfield notes.[59] Increased Euro-American movement into the northern plains in the years following the Civil War led increasingly into interaction with Native tribes of the northern plains. Usually this contact led to violence, as represented by the wars of Lakota resistance in the 1870s and the Métis rebellions in Canada of 1869 and 1885. Casualty numbers often included mostly women and children noncombatants, especially where US and Canadian military units would engage tribes within their villages or settlements. For instance, the 1876 Rosebud and Little Bighorn battles in eastern Montana both included uncounted numbers of noncombatant females. Further, the massacre at Wounded Knee on December 29, 1890, killed 146 Lakota, with sixty-two of those unarmed women and children. Many others died from exposure in the days after.[60]

The dovetailing of imperial expansion and domestic ideology are clearly seen in the gendered responsibilities of men and women as they shouldered their "duty to construct civilization in the wilderness, each with a distinct set of responsibilities"—men engaged in the political and military front, women the home front.[61] As a product of the white middle class, domestic ideology carried its racial overtones onto the frontier.[62] In the United States, the wives of military officers in the Plains Indian wars have provided the first detailed descriptions of northern plains women immediately following the Civil War. Elizabeth "Libby" Custer's writings following her husband's 1876 death at the Little Bighorn have provided a useful narrative to understanding how military wives viewed their sister Natives on the plains. Custer's descriptions were written with a mixture of curiosity, admiration, scorn, and sympathy. Using words like "repulsive," "repugnant," "cunning," and "crafty," Custer elicited a similar fear and caution felt by white women when encountering Natives. Following the 1868 Battle of the Washita, a few captured Cheyenne women met Mrs. Custer with curiosity of their own, touching and examining her. "I forced a smile of feigned pleasure at all the attentions bestowed upon me, and so hid my tremors and my revulsion," wrote Custer, "but inwardly I wished with all my heart that the younger and prettier women had been detailed as a reception committee."[63] After the Custers' move to Dakota Territory in 1875, Libby's interactions with Sioux Indians again elicited responses of sympathy for the Native women's oppression, especially in contrasting their plight with her own perceptions of the more elevated status of white women. She often commented on the lowly and pitiable state of "squaws" as contrasted with the "laziness" of their husbands for whom they worked unceasingly.[64] These ethnocentric portrayals of Native women's lives would echo in other white women's reactions found in firsthand reports.

As the Indian resistance came to an unsuccessful end and plains tribes moved to reservations, encounters between white and Native women mostly centered on the assimilation efforts of education and missionary work. It is interesting to consider how the white women reversed the concepts of "foreign" and "native" as they worked to assimilate Native women. Amy Kaplan puts this into the context of US expansionist aims when she writes, "To make Euro-Americans feel at home in terrain in which they are initially the foreigners, domesticity inverts this relationship to create a home by rendering prior inhabitants alien and undomesticated and by implicitly nativizing newcomers."[65] Domestic ideology combined with imperialism expanded women's role in the nation's expansion efforts while at the same time, "contracting women's sphere to police domestic boundaries against the threat of foreigners from both within and without" the United States, and helping justify their assimilation of Native women.[66]

The activities of white schoolteachers and missionaries on the Dakota reservations have been much examined by historians, with a common conclusion by white female missionaries that they acted as instruments of positive social, educational, and economic change for women on reservations. For example, beginning in 1875, Mary C. Collins spent time in Dakota Territory at the Oahe Mission and the Standing Rock Agency. Like other reservation teachers, Collins learned Lakota language and culture, then taught Christian values, self-reliance, and the importance of education, all while advocating for Indian rights.[67] Even more famous is Elaine Goodale, an unmarried, bilingual educator and Dakota superintendent from 1885 to 1891. Following the Wounded Knee Massacre (she heard the shots from eighteen miles away at the Pine Ridge Agency), she met Lakota doctor Charles Eastman at a makeshift hospital. A short time later they married. Goodale stopped teaching to raise their six children, but she continued writing poetry and short stories, and later wrote her memoir, *Sister to the Sioux*, published posthumously.[68] Often seen in the context of US assimilation policy, these and other women teachers still tried to act with sincere motives to improve the conditions of their Native sisters, according to their Euro-American standards.

In an examination of the "Gentle Evangelists," or Episcopal women teachers between 1867 and 1900, Ruth Ann Alexander has argued that

[a]lthough imbued with assimilationist ideas of their times and with Christian missionary zeal, the women usually liked the people they

served, advocated gradual persuasion in encouraging them to become Christian and "civilized," and tried to alleviate their suffering in adapting to reservation life.[69]

In contrast to this image, historian Margaret Jacobs has examined white female educators as instruments of cultural imperialism on the reservation, especially in their efforts to remove Native children to boarding schools. Women like Estelle Reel regarded the removal of Indian children as a "materialistic duty to rescue indigenous children from what [they] considered a savage background and to raise them instead in a 'civilized' environment."[70] Jacobs admits the difficulties in this interpretation: "An emphasis on white women as agents of colonial control in the American West may also be jarring in a field that has been so focused on westering white women's triumphs and tribulations."[71] And yet, women were the primary actors in this change, for Jacobs has shown that by 1900, eighty-two percent of teachers in Indian schools were women. White women's presence on northern plains reservations, as interpreters, missionaries, government employees, and especially educators, allowed them to use their domestic influence for encouraging Indian mothers to send their children to boarding schools.

The negative effects of familial separation are reinforced by Zitkala-S^a (Gertrude Simmons Bonnin), a Yankton Sioux reformer who remembered boarding school life. After the standard haircut meted out to Native children, she recalled: "And now my long hair was shingled like a coward's! In my anguish I moaned for my mother, but no one came to comfort me. Not a soul reasoned quietly with me, as my own mother used to do; for now I was only one of many little animals driven by a herder."[72] Zitkala-S^a's experiences with white education eventually brought her achievements as an author, poet, lecturer, musician, and composer, but "her success was dearly purchased. Caught in a tug-of-war between two civilizations, [she] sacrificed her relationship with her mother, yet was never fully accepted into white society."[73] Zitkala-S^a remained a harsh critic of US assimilationist policies throughout her adult life. Her reform efforts included advocating citizenship for Native Americans, "exposing corruption in the BIA, [and] insisting on the dignity of Indian religions."[74]

Other Native women benefited from US institutional education, but they also found themselves caught between acceptance within the larger American culture and the desires to stay reservation-bound in order to help their tribes. Most characteristic of educated plains women who returned to reservations were the LaFlesche sisters of the Omaha Tribe in Nebraska. After receiving education at the Presbyterian Mission Boarding Day School on the Omaha Reservation, the daughters of Joseph "Iron Eye" LaFlesche attended the Elizabeth Institute for Young Ladies in New Jersey and finally the Hampton Institute in Virginia. The oldest daughter, Susette "Bright Eyes" LaFlesche Tibbles, became an interpreter, activist, author, artist, and educator. Sister Marguerite LaFlesche Diddock became a field matron for the Office of Indian Affairs from 1896 to 1900, emphasizing the same cultural assimilation for Native women that had been thrust upon her as a young girl.[75] And in what would have been considered a surprising success even among white women of the time, youngest sister Susan LaFlesche Picotte became a physician after graduating from the Woman's Medical College of Pennsylvania in 1889. She then returned to the Omaha Reservation to practice medicine among her people, while also promoting education, land, and health reforms. Picotte also believed in assimilation as a necessary part of the progress and survival of the Omaha Indians.[76] Native women like the LaFlesche sisters who acted as agents of assimilation for their own people became part of the process of domestic imperialism, "which entails conquering and taming the wild, the natural, and the alien." Or as Amy Kaplan has argued, "[d]omestication in this sense is related to the imperial project of civilizing, and the conditions of domesticity often become markers that distinguish civilization from savagery."[77]

As part of the process of self-assimilation, some Native women left the reservations to gain higher education, and many sought training in the new professional fields of anthropology and ethnology. The work of a growing number of cultural anthropologists in the early twentieth century encouraged the recording and transcribing of many Native oral histories. Preeminent among these for northern plains women was the publication of the oral narrative of a Crow medicine woman. Pretty-Shield was interviewed by Frank B. Linderman through sign language and an interpreter. The resulting book was published in 1932 as *Red Mother*.[78] Pretty-Shield's biography—the first real biography of a Plains Indian woman—has been called the "feminine equivalent of *Black Elk Speaks*."[79] She includes much description of pre-reservation life before the demise of the buffalo and the removal of her people to the Crow Agency in southeastern Montana. Her depictions of Crow life are vivid and honest, with stories of games and dolls for children, as well as of the responsibilities for women and girls, which included setting up the lodges, dressing skins, cooking, and picking roots and berries.

Although not described much by Pretty-Shield and others of her generation who fondly remembered life before the coming of the whites, reservation life became the most important and traumatic period of transformation and adaptation for Native women. For although land politics such as the Dawes Act in the United States and the Canadian Indian Law enabled white women to acquire land on the northern plains, their gain came at the expense of Native women who had traditionally owned the land and the crops they produced. For example, during the early reservation period for Sioux women of Devil's Lake, North Dakota, Patricia Albers writes, "[w]omen were effectively excluded from agriculture, despite the fact that in the pre-reservation days cultivation was primarily the work of women. Men were awarded the equipment, stock, and seed. Nor did women have any say over how land was to be used, or how products were to be distributed."[80] Many Native women faced enormous difficulties adjusting to reservation life, including adaptations to new modes of subsistence for agricultural-based, seminomadic, and nomadic tribes alike, as well as changing expectations for gender roles, education, and child-rearing.[81]

In spite of a historical emphasis on Native women's loss of autonomy on the reservation, some historians have instead emphasized the adaptability and persistence of Native women. Sarah Carter has argued that "it was the more traditional work of women in diversifying the economic base of the community that saw the people through those lean years."[82] Further north in the Canadian plains, women of the Cree, Ojibwe, Blackfoot, and Métis populations had been significantly affected by contact with French and British fur traders since the 1600s. This interaction has been well documented by historians studying the marital custom called *a la façon du pays*, or "in the fashion of the country," and is described in fuller detail in the preceding chapter by Gretchen Albers.[83] Descendants of these intermarriages formed a large population of Métis, or those with mixed blood. Today, Alberta, Manitoba, and Saskatchewan are home to the largest numbers of Métis, with others living in Ontario and British Columbia and a few in the border states of Minnesota and North Dakota.[84]

Historians have tried to document the experiences of Native and Métis wives and daughters in Canada, in spite of limitations of class, ethnic prejudice, and literacy. Research has shown how mixed-blood children of Native and Métis women were able to alternate between and thrive in both cultures, in education, status, and marriage. The increasing persecutions and land deprivations against Native and Métis women between 1860 and 1930, however, often left them marginalized and in poverty, especially as First Nations moved to reserves. Tensions between Euro-Canadians and Métis came to a head in two significant "rebellions" led by Louis Riel: the Red River Rebellion in present Manitoba (1869–1870) and the North-West Rebellion in Saskatchewan (1885). The failure of these rebellions led to further erosion of Métis status, and by the end of the century, many families found themselves enduring cycles of poverty, domestic violence, and alcoholism.[85] In spite of this marginalization during the reserve era, many Métis women found methods of empowerment and adaptation by maintaining their Métis or French heritage of culinary arts, language and songs, religious faith, Native arts, games, and seasonal work in trading, hunting, fishing, and tanning hides for the fur economy.[86]

Educational policies in the Canadian plains followed similar patterns as those in the neighboring US plains. While a majority of Métis women learned at the feet of priests and nuns in their French-Catholic schools, other First Nations women gained their education from the evangelizing efforts of Protestant missionaries or their wives, or single female teachers, in the late nineteenth century. Historian C. L. Higham has documented these efforts among Canadian First Nations, while also comparing them to the educational assimilation of United States reservation and boarding schools. Both countries' policies were driven by similar racist views and the subsequent evolution of Indian portrayals from "noble savage" to "wretched savage" to "redeemable savage." Thus, in spite of different frontier histories between the United States and Canada, First Nations also experienced the imposing of racist stereotypes to justify imperial expansion and assimilation policies.[87]

Similar to the experiences of US Plains Indian women, Canadian First Nations and Métis women felt both positive and negative changes in their status due to reservation policies. The continued perseverance of these Native populations is mostly attributable to the persistence and cultural integrity of women. While white northern plains women felt drawn to their new environment and challenged by it at the same time, Native women felt deep historical and spiritual attachment to their land, subsequently tested, as reservation life required them to adapt to new ways of living and producing. For white, middle-class women, domestic ideology dovetailed with prevailing ideas of imperialism, giving women a role in their country's mission as they moved out onto the frontier. They sought persistence in their new environments as they created recognized and comfortable institutions of church, schools, clubs, and political activism. Native women sought persistence in their "new" environments of reservation living through the recognized customs of traditional Native ways but also through adaptation to white institutions like Christian churches, white schools, and creative outlets of reform and artistic expression. As historians seek new ways to examine the history of the northern Great

Plains, they are unavoidably drawn to the interactions between Native and Euro women—both the conflicts between cultures and the ties that brought their lives together. Indeed, the story of the northern plains is the story of women, both Native and Euro-American, who shared a common attention to their families, education, production, survival, and reform.

# 4

# Place, Gender, Ethnicity, and the Role of the Nation in the Lives of Northern Plains Women

SARAH R. PAYNE

The landscape of the plains changes slowly, almost imperceptibly, moving north from the Dakotas and crossing into the prairie states of Canada. Over the past few decades historians on both sides of the US-Canadian border have begun reconstructing women's historic roles on the northern plains, tearing down stereotypes and assumptions of what gender meant in this region, and showing that women played important roles in each country's economic, social, and political systems. Although crossing the border has been relatively easy, even in the twentieth century, the fact of the border remains. In their recent work, Betsy Jameson and Sheila McManus argue the role of the nation and its impact on western women is a largely unexamined area of study. Capitalizing on their call to link and compare experiences of women on both sides of the border, this essay examines stories of three diverse groups of women— African Americans, World War II war brides, and Indian activists—who moved onto the northern plains. Women within each of these groups shared distinct commonalities prior to making this region their new home. Depending on which side of the border they lived, however, their experiences illustrate how national laws, heritage, and cultural attitudes affected women across the spectrum of race, class, and ethnicity.

The autobiographical writings of Era Bell Thompson and Cheryl Foggo offer a starting point to explore how the role of nation can both link and provide avenues for comparison among black women on the northern plains.[1] In the post-Reconstruction era in the United States, many African American families moved out of the South to escape the entrenched racism and escalating violence. Some families, like Thompson's, took advantage of the opportunity to homestead land offered by the US government, settling onto the plains states of Oklahoma, Kansas, Nebraska, and the Dakotas. Other families, like Foggo's, moved farther north, enticed by offers of land in the Canadian prairies of Alberta and Saskatchewan. Thompson's and Foggo's families shared the horrors of Jim Crow laws and increasing violence against blacks, but the role of the nation in which their families settled would shape each of these women's lives in distinctive ways.

For Thompson, regional constructions of race often acted more forcefully to shape her life's experiences than did notions of gender. Thompson's autobiography, *American Daughter*, published in 1946, begins with her birth and early childhood in Des Moines, Iowa. Her father's career as a chef allowed the family to live a comfortable middle-class life. In 1914, when Thompson was nine, her father's increasing concern over racism and lack of opportunity for his sons compelled him to move the family north. Thompson's uncle, James Garrison, had already established a homestead in Driscoll, North Dakota, and encouraged the family to join him.

The next year, Thompson and her family moved to a farm of their own, west of Driscoll. In *American Daughter*, Thompson recalls learning the farm chores and falling in love with the land. She remembered driving their team of horses to the grain elevator, writing, "I loved the long, solitary ride through the golden autumn sunshine, during the brief North Dakota fall when the days stood still and the warm silence was unbearable in its pregnant beauty."[2] The fact that they were one of the few black families in the area as well as her father's success in raising a new crop—rye—gave her a freedom from prejudice she had not enjoyed before.

In 1918 Thompson's mother died from a stroke. As the only daughter, Thompson assumed the household responsibilities for her father and brothers until she moved to Bismark to begin high school in 1920. *American Daughter* progresses as Thompson details her experiences attending the Bismarck high school; working in St. Paul, Minnesota; studying at the University of North Dakota (funded by small family contributions, a track scholarship, and her work as a live-in babysitter); moving to Iowa where she attended Morningside College and earned her degree in journalism; and moving again, this time to Chicago, where she hoped to connect for the first time with a larger black community. Although much of *American Daughter* deals with Thompson's childhood in North Dakota during the 1910s and 1920s, the autobiography and its reception by literary critics shed light onto the gendered and racialized world of a black plains woman in the mid-twentieth century.

The way in which contemporary reviewers talked about Thompson and her book reveals much about the ways in which gender, environment, and race worked in the United States during the 1940s. A certain degree of what these reviewers and Thompson wrote was performative and did social work for its time, thus creating a space between text and reality.[3] In reviews, *American Daughter* was often posed counter to Richard Wright's *Black Boy*. Wright's 1945 autobiography of his experiences in the South was often described as "dark," "bitter," and void of hope. Reviews of Thompson's autobiography, in contrast, consistently noted the work's positive, optimistic, and patriotic tone. Reviewers hailed Thompson's work as "a moving recital, it is not racial but American," and lauded that she "never descends into bitterness."[4] Literary scholar Joanne Braxton argues that *American Daughter* is not, as is *Black Boy*, a work of protest; and, further, that Thompson is one of the first black female writers to depart from the form of black autobiography established by Wright and to establish a new tradition of black female autobiography.[5] It is significant, then, that reviewers of the time compared these two works much like apples and oranges.

The effect of these reviews went beyond mere comparison; gender and race are interrelated and, as reflected through the reviews, can work to define each other. The social context of this period is vital to understanding these relationships. In the United States, the emergence of the civil rights movement and the cold war acted to transform perceptions of race and gender. This transformation is illustrated in the reviews of *Black Boy*. While "brilliant and powerful," to one reviewer, it still repelled him "with its savage intensity."[6] Such commentary and the admittedly angry tone taken by Wright began to define a black masculinity of the 1940s and 1950s steeped in rage and reacting against black men's historically "marginalized and emasculated" social position imposed by "self-made middle-class white men," and reacting to a nascent civil rights movement.[7] Race, in this case, was a condition of an emerging masculinity—race worked to define gender. Thompson, on the other hand, wrote with "unaffected simplicity," criticized for being "too glad a Negro girl." One reviewer plainly linked race with gender: "Perhaps the problem of being a woman prevents her giving wholehearted attention to the problem of being a Negro."[8]

Scholar Margo Culley notes that *American Daughter* is an exception to most black women's autobiographies in that their titles usually reflect the author's identification with race more strongly than with gender. Thompson's title, *American Daughter*, hints not at her identity as a black person but as a woman and an American. In Thompson's work, then, gender seems to override the importance of race, but it does not define it. The way in which critics received Thompson's work reveals the degree to which American perceptions of femininity superseded conceptions of blackness.

*American Daughter* and its reviews also illustrate the importance of place in the construction of race. Thompson experienced both restrictions and power as a black woman on the northern plains in ways that were place specific to the region. Ralph Ellison, author of *Invisible Man* (1952), linked race and place unambiguously in his review of Thompson's work: "Because she [Thompson] knew an environment in which she was often the lone Negro child, her experience has been exceptional. She was free of the repressing effects of segregation; she knew whites intimately, both at home and at school, and she was able to see them in a more human perspective than is possible for the majority of Negroes."[9]

The observation of Thompson's unique experience with race on the northern plains was not a special insight on the part of reviewers; Thompson was well aware of the relationship, and she linked race and place metaphorically and overtly throughout *American Daughter*. The effect of the plains environment on Thompson is immediately recognizable in the text, appearing as soon as she arrives in North Dakota by train: "Suddenly there was snow. Miles and miles of dull, white snow, stretching out to meet the heavy, gray sky; deep banks of snow drifted against wooden snow fences along the railroad right-of-way. And with the snow went our dreams of Indians, for somehow they did not fit into this strange white world."[10] Literary critic Michael K. Johnson comments on Thompson's metaphorical use of the landscapes she encounters: "[Her] realistic winter landscape descriptions also allegorically represent the social situation of herself and her family." These descriptions represent as well "a sense of 'exile' in a predominately white western settlement."[11] Thompson's "exile" from a black community was not simply a metaphor. The total population of blacks living in North Dakota in 1910, four years before Thompson arrived, was 617, or slightly more than one-tenth of one percent of the total state population.[12]

Although historian Glenda Riley has shown that "Black women's writings point to great similarity between Black and white women's daily lives in the West," for Thompson, the discrimination she encountered while in North Dakota steered her toward life-altering decisions. For example, her social isolation in North Dakota led Thompson to go to Chicago in 1928 to find "her people."[13]

Despite the instances of racism that Thompson encountered on the northern plains, she still believed that the plains environment was less discriminatory than the East or South. She reflected in 1968 that she was "very lucky to have grown up in North Dakota where families were busy fighting climate and soil for a livelihood and there was little awareness of race."[14] At each instance of discrimination from her childhood recounted in the book, there is often a friendly white ally to temper the situation. For example, when Thompson's Bismarck High School track team traveled to Valley City, North Dakota, a diner waitress took the orders of all the white girls and did not ask for Thompson's. She writes, "Miss Wallace called her back. 'I believe you forgot her order.'"[15] On Thompson's first day of school in Bismarck, a young girl stayed on the other side of the street and refused to join Thompson and her Irish friend Jessie, who exclaimed, "That dirty snob! . . . Who in the hell does she think she is?"[16] And when Thompson and the track team attempted to go to a movie in Fargo, and Era Bell was refused entrance except in the balcony, the team later told her, "[Y]ou could of sit [sic] between us, they said you could of sit in the middle. . . . Don't you worry . . . it was a no-good show anyway."[17] Racism was at work in each of these instances, but through Thompson's telling, this racism was somewhat softened through the actions of her friends, allowing Thompson to argue that the northern plains was a less racially hostile place than other parts of the country.[18]

Hope for racial tolerance and opportunity also drew Cheryl Foggo's family north, from Oklahoma to the Canadian prairies. In her autobiography, *Pourin' Down Rain*, she writes, "At precisely the same time the Black Oklahomans were being brutalized by southern law, the Canadian government was taking out full-page ads in southern newspapers, offering 160 acres of land in its unsettled western provinces to anyone who could produce the filing fee of ten dollars."[19] Foggo's great-grandfather, Rufus Smith, responded to an advertisement in 1910, one of hundreds of black American farmers, mostly from Oklahoma, who left the South for the prairies of Saskatchewan that year.[20]

The Canadian government, expecting these advertisements to be answered by white settlers, found itself in the difficult position of trying to calm irate citizens concerned with the "dark invasion," and needing to continue advertising for farmers. The government found a simple and effective solution to end black migration—hiring "a few Black men to travel throughout the American Southwest, to warn Black churches and organization about the horrors of life in Canada."[21] The campaign worked, and black migration into the area ceased by 1912. Between 1908 and 1912, only about two thousand black families had settled in Alberta and Saskatchewan, and these numbers would remain small. Assessing their situation, the black community recognized that Canada was not the "racial nirvana" they had expected, but even so, their new homeland provided freedoms not possible in the United States: the right to vote, unsegregated education for children, "a relatively peaceful existence alongside their White neighbors, whose attitudes ranged from sullen tolerance to unfettered acceptance," and safety from lynchings and cross burnings.[22] It was hard, but as Foggo writes, "what they had left behind in the South was so dehumanizing that hardship in Canada was simply incorporated into the legend. God never promised it would be easy—He only promised the Promised Land."[23]

Foggo grew up a generation after Thompson, not in a rural farm town but in the small city of Calgary. The families lived close to one another, "the closest thing to a black community one would find in Calgary in 1961."[24] And as with Thompson's experience, the small number of black families in Calgary encouraged a sense of kinship while encouraging interaction with nonblacks. The children of a biracial family who lived down the street considered themselves black and enjoyed a feeling of belonging. "We played together," Foggo writes, "without isolating ourselves from the other children in the neighborhood and without any discussion of it, we sensed a link that transcended our environs."[25] And like Thompson, she took pleasure in walking through the open fields, or along the tracks by the river in the summer heat, where the sharp smell of creosote mingled with the soft scent of flowers and dust. "Until I was sixteen and we moved from the Bowness," she writes, "the journey along the tracks to the river, across the bridges and up into the hills was real life."[26]

Like Thompson, Foggo understood the difficulty of social isolation and the need for her community of relatives—most of them black, but not all—to stay in contact. In Canada, no laws prevented interracial marriages. Indeed, the black community was so small her family rather expected that both men and women would marry outside their racial group. Gatherings held at her grandmother's house brought the extended family together, allowing them to reinforce their racial identity and "affirm their Blackness," through food, stories, and moral support. "I learned a great deal, at an early age from those gatherings," Foggo writes. "I learned how to tell a story, the importance of our family, and our history and I began to learn the way Black people, at least the kind of Black people we are, use language." Her mother and aunts peppered their speech with "y'alls" and "uhhm uhhm uhhms" and other bits of rural black speech never used outside of these family gatherings. Talking "Black" allowed them to "*feel* Black," and tempered their feelings of isolation from larger black populations in the United States.[27]

It was overhearing her mother's phone conversation with the principal of her elementary school when Foggo was first introduced to the racism and Jim Crow mentality that her relatives endured in the United States. Her cousins, who had moved to Calgary, had punched a white boy for calling them names. Foggo's mother would not agree to talk to the children's parents about their behavior. "They come from a place where they can't fight," Foggo's mother explained to the principal. "Where they come from, a Black person doesn't have a chance against racists, and if Mr. Hayes has decided his children are going to fight name-calling with their fists, that's up to him."[28]

Individual examples of racism aside, Foggo wrote, "Some residual innocence, or naïveté from my childhood, allowed me to achieve adulthood with my belief in Canada as a non-racist society intact." African American families who moved to Canada from Oklahoma had not escaped from racism; discrimination existed everywhere. But in Canada it had not become as entrenched nor as institutionalized as it had in the United States. After a painful breakup with her first boyfriend, a white boy, and the difficulty of finding blacks to date, she confided to her cousins and sister, "'Sometimes I wish I lived in the States, . . . At least I wouldn't have to walk around in a sea of White faces there.'" The girls did not know their mothers were eavesdropping. "We heard them giggle from the kitchen," she wrote, "so outrageous did it strike them that a child of theirs would fantasize about living anywhere than Canada."[29] While the forces of race in the northern plains region impacted the lives of both Foggo and Thompson, the country in which they lived played a large role in shaping their lives. By stepping over the border in the early 1900s, Foggo's family entered a country whose legal system and cultural attitudes protected blacks from the worst of racial abuses and offered immediate opportunities for education, civic participation, and social freedoms decades ahead of the United States.

The northern Great Plains have always been spaces of ethnic diversity, from families of African descent like Foggo's and Thompson's, to Native peoples, Europeans, Russians, and Ukrainians, to religious minorities such as Mennonites and Mormons. These peoples both acculturated and maintained cultural traditions and languages, and even before the Canadian and US governments finally fixed the border at the 49th parallel, peoples continued to steadily flow into the region and to build lives and communities for themselves. In the United States the Depression, then the Dust Bowl, slowed the rate of newcomers into the northern plains beginning in the late 1920s; in Canada, the stream slowed to a trickle with the onset of World War II. For the first time, more people began to move out of the region than into it as women and men joined the military or sought jobs in wartime industries in urban centers.[30] The immigration tide turned as a new group, the war bride, made its way onto the plains.

The women who immigrated to the United States and Canada as brides (or to a lesser extent, fiancées) of soldiers constitute a very different type of immigrant. In the nineteenth century young, single men had ventured to the

United States and Canada, some with the intention of permanently relocating; others traveled back and fourth to their homeland in order to make enough money to return home permanently. Families and even large segments of communities had immigrated together, settling in ethnic enclaves. The war brides, however, immigrated by virtue of their marriages that had occurred during the Second World War, integrating as individuals into diverse areas of the United States and Canada, and leaving behind female networks and ethnic solidarity.[31]

Although a generalization, of course, for the most part the brides shared many similar characteristics. They averaged twenty-four years in age, came from working- or lower-middle-class families, met the compulsory requirement for schooling, worked outside the home to support their country's war effort, and had experienced the horrors of a war waged in their homeland.[32] Despite concerns of the women's family over dating foreign soldiers, they had dealt with the difficulty of having young men from their hometowns go away to fight the war and have them replaced with a flood of Allied soldiers. One British war bride recalled, "A few of us said we would wait for our lads to come home, but the wait was just too long, so one by one we started dating the GIs."[33] Although the overwhelming number of war brides came from Great Britain, they arrived on the northern Great Plains from all over Europe: England, Scotland, Ireland, Wales, the Netherlands, France, Germany, Belgium, and Italy. Each of the women had unique experiences on the plains based on their cultural backgrounds, their husbands' families, and their life experiences. But for many, it was the difference in the physical environment of their new plains homes that struck them hardest.

In Canada, soldiers fighting in Europe married and brought home more than forty-eight thousand young women as their new wives.[34] Soldiers met their loves at dances, in hospitals, and while stationed in small towns.[35] Although war brides settled throughout the country, many of them made their lives in the plains of Saskatchewan and Alberta. In fact, Saskatchewan had one of the highest populations of war bride settlers.[36] At war's end, the number of brides who had come home with their husbands greatly surpassed wartime estimates. In 1943, the high commissioner to London, Vincent Massey, estimated that sixteen thousand English and Scottish wives would come home with their Canadian husbands; the actual number was triple Massey's estimate.[37] The arrival of war brides, and their children (estimated to be some twenty-two thousand), has been called the "single largest wave of immigration since the Great Depression."[38]

Getting to their new homes proved to be an adventure. The process first involved acquiring approval to immigrate from the Canadian government through a complicated tangle of bureaucratic paperwork. Women boarded one of more than sixty ships and, under the supervision of the Canadian Department of National Defense, crossed the Atlantic.[39] For those who avoided seasickness, this part of the journey was relatively pleasant. Accustomed to wartime food rations, the sailing brides on many of the ships were treated with the luxury of fresh food. Numerous war-bride accounts note memorable delectables: "White bread, butter, fruit—utter bliss."[40] On the voyage, women made friends with whom they often kept in touch once they arrived in Canada, despite living across the country from each other. Expectation and imagination of what they would encounter in Canada helped to pass the time. Landing at Pier 21 in Halifax, Nova Scotia, the brides then embarked on the next part of their journeys by train to their final destinations.[41]

Once the journey into the Canadian plains commenced, the foreign physical environment left an indelible mark on these women's memories. Joan Reichardt recalled of her journey to her new home in Saskatoon, Saskatchewan:

> The landscape we passed through on that long journey was so different and wild compared to the little patchwork fields of England. . . . I remember being shocked by the intense heat and the wind (which I was to come to loath during my years on the prairies) when we got off briefly at some little whistle-stop in Manitoba and also astonished at the flat and featureless landscape we were passing through.[42]

The introduction to the plains landscape was shocking for Barbara Walsh, too. As she traveled across Canada to her destination of Regina, her "spirits fell lower and lower, seeing the flat prairies go on and on."[43] War bride Joyce Anderson, when asked her reaction to the prairie landscape, replied with a similar reaction to Walsh's. "You could see for miles and miles," she described, "but see what?"[44] The wind, the snow, the vastness of the open prairies was starkly different from home, and war brides found out that their new environments also meant new lifestyles.

Adjusting to rural life was a difficult change not only for women who came from large urban centers in Europe but also for women who came from smaller cities or had lived on farms and in small villages. In the 1940s, many rural Canadians lived in homes without electricity or indoor plumbing.[45] Nancy Pittet grew up in the industrial city of Paisley, Scotland, and found herself on a small Manitoba farm with no running water and coal-oil lamps.

When her mother-in-law brought in snow on washing day, she asked her husband why. "He said, 'Mum likes soft water to wash clothes.' Very intelligent, wasn't I," she scolded herself.[46] Learning the routines of farm life on the prairies came quickly out of necessity. Baking bread, churning butter, butchering and processing meat, and canning fruits and vegetables were just some of the work war brides conducted to survive on small farms. Marguerite Feist remembered of these and other activities on her farm in the Alberta prairie, "It was hard work, as we had neither electricity nor running water, only a well. . . . It was a rather isolated life, but we were happy."[47]

The tough adjustments were anticipated by some. War correspondent Paul Manning, writing in 1941, predicted social repercussions would upset both continents at war's end. He commented on what he saw as the difference between expectations and realities: "Many a girl believes that she is married to the son of some Canadian wheat king . . . [and will live] happily forever after on a 1000-acre ranch." "Some will find," he foretold, that those dreams do not materialize and "instead will come the routine of settling down to the rugged life of a small Canadian town."[48]

Even in the cities of the prairie, war brides still found the adjustment difficult. Connie Rust, a young woman from a London suburb, recollected: "When I came to Edmonton, I thought it was a dreadful place because it was so dull. I had lived just a half hour from London, and had done things, like going up to the London Palladium and hearing Kat Smith sing 'God Bless America.' And then I came to Edmonton and there was nothing."[49] For war brides, it was often hard to explain to family back home just what their new environment and lifestyles were like. Connie Rust attempted to describe Canada to her family: "We wrote long letters to my family telling them everything about Canada. They thought we were crazy, as we used to drive a hundred miles to go fishing on a Sunday and a hundred miles back. That's half way up to Scotland; they couldn't visualize the distance here at all."[50] The sheer size of the prairies required the adaptation of new modes of work, travel, and leisure, like Rust's hundred-mile fishing excursion.

Even though the landscape was radically different from their homeland, and for many war brides the lifestyle in the plains just as foreign, women found pleasant surprises and benefits to their new prairie lives. Hilda Bradshaw's first reaction to the Canadian plains was delight as she de-boarded her train in the city of Saskatoon. She was "tickled to see a city so clean after grimy London."[51] Living close to community and family, particularly for war brides living in rural communities, could be quite rewarding. Eileen Ironside lived on a small farm in Blackfalds, Alberta. Like all small farmers, she and her family worked hard but also took time for socializing. The Ironsides went square dancing *every* night; she found it "relaxing, even though we had to be up early the next morning for chores."[52] Although leaving European homelands was often heart-wrenching the Canadian plains became home. Nancy Pittet summed up her feelings about home and country: "It's [Canada] been wonderfully good. . . . I'll always have that longing for the country I came from. That will never go away. Yet I'm very proud and happy to be Canadian."[53]

In the United States, however, attitudes toward war brides were less welcoming than in Canada, especially during the first years of overseas deployment. From 1942 to 1946, US media representations of these marriages in newspapers, women's magazines, and armed service publications depicted them as undesirable and the women's motives as suspect. Barbara Freidman writes that in armed service publications, "women were first framed as predators who exploited American servicemen for their money and citizenship."[54] Likewise, newspapers charged the women with finding the "cheapest, surest and easiest way to enter the US." Suspicion over the women's intentions was expressed by Richard Russell, Georgia congressional representative and chairman of the US immigration committee. In 1946 he told reporters that he "did not see the appeal of foreign brides and in fact, 'deplored such foreign entanglements.' He proposed legislation that would allow British fiancées to enter the US . . . [only] to determine whether or not their intended grooms had 'changed their minds.'"[55]

Rules governing the ability of servicemen to marry foreign women changed as the number of marriages increased. Shortly after World War I, the requirement of obtaining a commanding officer's permission to marry had been dropped; in 1942, the escalating number of marriages, combined with concern over women's motivations, led to a reinstatement of strict rules. A soldier once again needed permission to marry. Moreover, a three-month waiting period was implemented. "The hope," Freidman writes, "was that subjecting the betrothed couple to an interminable waiting period, during which they had to endure embarrassing medical exams, interviews, and character investigations, might cause some couples to grow disillusioned and abandon their marriage plans."[56] Although the soldiers and their intended brides endured a bureaucratic labyrinth, more than one million women made their way to the United States, although the exact number who made the northern plains their home is unclear. During the spring of 1944, media coverage of the war brides shifted, casting them in a less threatening light (although considerable criticism continued). They were no longer considered "predators," but rather, "pioneers."[57] For the women who made the long and uncomfortable journey from Europe to Montana, this moniker seemed very appropriate.

Doreen Richard remembered her move from Birmingham, England, to a ranch twelve miles outside of Loma, Montana. She arrived in December, and driving to the farm she thought,

> it all looked alike. It was barren . . . and we'd go along and we would turn the corner, it was the same. No change. Absolutely none. That was the way it seemed to me. It went on and on for such a long time. I said to my husband, "Don't we ever come to a town?" "Oh, yes. We will be coming into Loma very soon." So I waited and I said to him "When will we be coming into Loma?" "Oh, we did." (laughs) That was it. I hadn't even noticed it.[58]

She grew to appreciate the land, although never quite adjusted to the immense quiet of plains ranch life.

Richard and her husband lived "in a little house over the road from his folks." It had "a nice stove and it was quite a nice kitchen," but with no running water, electricity, or phone, "it was so very different" from what she knew in England.[59] Cooking for a field crew was a new experience, too. She had never cooked a full meal while in England; her mother "couldn't have risked the rations to have let me cook."[60] She made good use, as she said, of her *Good Housekeeping Cookbook*. Although the Montana family she married into treated her kindly, Richard said, "I don't think I ever felt part of the family. . . . I was very fortunate, because as I say, they were very nice people," but "I don't think that they ever came to accepting me."[61]

Elvia Stockton, a war bride from France who moved to Grass Range, Montana, also was shocked by the wide openness of the plains. She arrived in May of 1946, her departure delayed by the US government until after the birth of the couple's first child. Although she recalled "a few stupid remarks, you know. Sexist remarks which, thank God I pretended I didn't understand . . . Jokes about French women," she felt welcomed into her new family and community.[62]

The couple lived on his mother's ranch, in an "old shack" on the property. Adjusting to rigors of ranch work with her husband did not daunt Stockton. "I like physical work, you know. We worked side-by-side. We didn't have a cent to our name. We didn't have any livestock. . . . [T]here was no fence. The renter had never taken care of that, so the first few years we spent fencing," she recalled. Although she had moved from Lyon, an urban area in France, life during the war had not been easy: "I was not a spoiled brat. I was very strong."[63] For Stockton, language proved her biggest difficulty, since she spoke very little English. But with the help of her family, and other French war brides she met in Billings, she adjusted. "Here," she said, "I have my little corner of France. . . . I really love Montana. And the people. I like the simple things in life."[64]

For the war brides making their homes in Canada and the United States, the differences in national attitudes and laws affected foreign women as they sought to construct new lives on the northern plains. When considering the experiences of Native women living on those same northern plains from the 1930s to the present, the shared history of unjust laws and discriminatory attitudes helped link Native women across national lines. For the Native women, of course, there is no single representative experience. Numerous Native cultures live in the region, and each deals with what it means to be a woman, or man, differently. In addition to cultural differences between Native groups, indigenous cultures also negotiate the gender norms imposed from outside their respective cultures by non-Natives. And while the role of the nation-state expressed the dominant culture's attitude toward Native people through laws and treaties, in the 1960s Native groups on both sides of the border became involved in the efforts to gain civil rights.

The lives of Mary Brave Bird, a Lakota born in South Dakota, and Anna Mae Pictou-Aquash, a Mi'kmaq born in Canada, became linked during the struggle to win recognition for the governmental abuses suffered by Native peoples. These women have reached iconic stature for their role in the Red Power movement, but their lives have only been minimally explored by scholars.[65] Beyond recounting the experiences of Native women, their stories can say something about how gender operates and intersects with ethnicity and place, transcending national boundaries to create spaces where power is accessed by or denied to Indian women.

Mary Brave Bird (known as Mary Crow Dog for part of her life) and her friend and fellow activist Anna Mae Pictou-Aquash contended with at least three frequently conflicting ideas of what it meant to be an Indian woman during the 1960s and beyond. First, Brave Bird and Pictou-Aquash were forced to deal with non-Natives' generalizations about Indian women, which were often steeped in racism and sexism. Second, both women negotiated the meaning of gender as they at once worked within and challenged the traditional or expected gender roles of multiple tribes. Finally, these two women lived in the context of renewed national feminist activism, but this predominately white, middle-class feminism that opposed patriarchy and anything perceived as oppressive or submissive, at times conflicted with tribal gender norms.

Brave Bird's autobiography, *Lakota Woman*, published under her married name Mary Crow Dog, tells of the hardships of her childhood on the reservation.[66] The book also relates the history of the 1973 siege at Wounded Knee—

a seventy-one-day protest made by Pine Ridge reservation members and the American Indian Movement (AIM) against the corruption and acquittal of tribal chairman Richard "Dick" Wilson, which led to Bureau of Indian Affairs (BIA) and Federal Bureau of Investigation (FBI) agents and Wilson's cronies surrounding the group and exchanging fire—and the death of Anna Mae Pictou-Aquash in late 1975 or early 1976. Brave Bird's second book, *Ohitika Woman*, tells the story of her life from 1977 to the autobiography's publication in 1993.[67] Brave Bird's works, especially *Lakota Woman*, have been received by Native audiences, scholars, and lay readers with mixed emotion. Her accounts are controversial, even among some Lakota women who believe her accounts "left out some things," as Brave Bird herself put it, emphasizing the negative aspects of Lakota female life at the time and omitting more positive ones.[68] The main sources of information on Brave Bird's life come from her own autobiographies and writings and should, like any other memoir, be read critically.[69] Consequently, while the books are valuable for the parts of her life they describe, it is perhaps more important for the purposes of this article what Brave Bird's works say about being Indian and about Lakota womanhood or manhood.

Perhaps the most traumatic of the gender systems encountered by Brave Bird were those of non-Indians on the northern plains. Born in 1953 on the Rosebud Reservation as a member of the Brulé band, Brave Bird focuses on the dark and tragic events in her early life in *Lakota Woman*. These dim moments reflect incidents when Brave Bird encountered regionally constructed notions of Native American women. More specifically, her experiences illustrate views of Indians held by non-Indians, and attitudes concerning acceptable treatment of Native women. Brave Bird's short but vivid account of being raped at age fourteen or fifteen provides only one example, yet reveals the vulnerability of Indian women living on the northern plains. Brave Bird writes, "The [rape] victims are mostly full-blood girls, too shy and afraid to complain. A few years back, a favorite sport of white [South Dakota] state troopers and cops was to arrest young Indian girls on drunk-and-disorderly [charges], even if the girls were sober, take them to the drunk tanks . . . and rape them."[70] Here, gender, ethnicity, and place combined to make being an Indian woman on or near the reservation physically dangerous.

At the same time that Brave Bird confronted non-Native plains notions of Indian womanhood, she confronted tribal gender norms. Both Brave Bird's and Pictou-Aquash's experiences illustrate how Indian women could simultaneously embrace and challenge the gender systems of their tribes and of the non-Native world. While women are respected and perform social, economic, and political functions in Indian cultures, as Patricia C. Albers has noted, colonialism changes the status of women, but its affects are varied, "and often contradictory, even within a single population."[71] This status change is especially evident in the figure of Anna Mae Pictou-Aquash.

In the foreword to *Ohitika Woman*, Richard Erdoes retells the most traumatic moment of the relationship between Pictou-Aquash and Brave Bird:

> But then there was the dark day that Mary and I were sitting in my studio, chatting. The phone rang. I handed her the receiver: "Mary, it's for you." I watched her listen, stiffening, her face distorted in grief. Somebody from the reservation was reporting that her best friend, Anna Mae Pictou-Aquash, had been found brutally murdered in the snow, her eyes picked out by crows or magpies, her hands cut off and missing.[72]

Anna Mae Pictou-Aquash's story stretches far beyond the boundaries of the northern plains, yet in many ways, her experiences there are the ones that have brought her into the public eye. Pictou-Aquash's involvement in the 1973 siege of Wounded Knee, her relationship with AIM leader Dennis Banks, the suspicions of some that she was an FBI informant, her interrogation by the FBI after the June 1975 murder of two agents, and her tragic and mysterious death have made Pictou-Aquash a controversial figure.

Like Era Bell Thompson and Cheryl Foggo's families who migrated north, or the war brides who came to this region from Europe, Anna Mae Pictou-Aquash arrived on the northern Great Plains from elsewhere. She moved through the plains, participating in the political environment of Indian activism, which itself stretched beyond the Great Plains. The Indian civil rights movement transcended national borders, and one of the most well-known events in the movement, the occupation of Wounded Knee, took place in the northern plains. Pictou-Aquash participated in the occupation, and through the mysterious circumstances of her death she became tragically linked to the northern plains forever. In her own words, she tells us why she went:

> All the injustices that have been going on, on the reservation here in South Dakota is something that has been bad for a long period of time. The FBI most certainly are racists. They don't have the ability to be able to comprehend that another people has another belief. I think that they want to destroy a nation.[73]

Pictou-Aquash belonged to the Mi'kmaq tribe from Nova Scotia. She grew up in poverty on the Shubenacadie reserve (similar to a US reservation). After her stepfather's death in 1956, she attended school off the reserve. Frustrated by continued racial slurs at school, and abandoned by her mother in 1961, Pictou-Aquash headed to the United States in search of a better life. She moved to Boston with her friend and later husband, Jake Maloney, also of the Mi'kmaq tribe. The couple had two daughters, but grew apart, and Pictou-Aquash left the marriage. The children lived with their father while she followed her own interests in helping other Native peoples. She had worked for the Boston Indian Council, and the Teaching and Research in Bicultural Education School project in Maine, then found her calling in 1970 when she participated with Russell Means and other members of the American Indian Movement (AIM)—a militant pan-Indian organization modeled after the Black Panthers—in painting Plymouth Rock red in recognition of the 370th anniversary of the first Thanksgiving.[74] Shortly thereafter, she met and became romantically involved with Nogeeshik Aquash, a Chippewa from Ontario. When the couple learned of the occupation of Wounded Knee in 1973, they headed together toward Pine Ridge.[75]

Around the same time that Pictou-Aquash became involved in AIM, so too did Brave Bird, who was a teenager then. Brave Bird met Leonard Crow Dog, a spiritual leader of the organization in 1971, and the two married several years later. At the age of sixteen, Mary participated in the 1972 Trail of Broken Treaties led by members of AIM.[76]

Brave Bird and Pictou-Aquash participated in the Indian civil rights movement; in the process, they challenged the gender roles of their tribes while also working within those constructs. During the siege of Wounded Knee, Brave Bird cooked, brought coffee to bunkers, sewed, and even gave birth to her son, Pedro. Pictou-Aquash performed domestic work during the siege, but she also took on more aggressive roles, including patrolling and digging bunkers.

Although several scholars have written histories of Pictou-Aquash's life and murder on Pine Ridge, historian Devon A. Mihesuah is the first to deeply interrogate the complex meanings of Pictou-Aquash's life and death as it relates to gender, race, and colonialism.[77] Mihesuah notes that when Anna Mae took on more masculine roles, male AIM leadership "did not seem impressed." Her personality and aggressive participation in AIM, according to Mihesuah, "intimidated some men" and caused her to lose support from "those who were most insecure."[78] While some male AIM members may have reacted negatively to Pictou-Aquash's challenge to what those males perceived as her proper gender role, women's overall contributions through a variety of activities was recognized by some male participants.[79] For example, in his autobiography *Ojibwa Warrior*, the prominent AIM leader Dennis Banks credits the work done by women at the siege as a major factor in the length of time they were able to hold out against the FBI, BIA, and Wilson's forces.[80]

The roles Indian women played during Wounded Knee sometimes put them in opposition to the feminist movement of the era. Brave Bird and Pictou-Aquash lived in the context of renewed national feminist activism, but this form of feminism, largely opposed to patriarchy and female submissiveness, could not always recognize the role played by ethnicity or culture in establishing power based on gender. At the siege, Brave Bird remembered, "a white nurse berated us for doing the slave work while the men got all the glory. We were betraying the cause of womankind, was the way she put it. We told her that her kind of women's lib was a white, middle-class thing, and that at this critical stage we had other priorities."[81] White feminists failed to understand that Native women, and men, regarded their tasks as essential to the cause of Indian civil rights and to tribal survival.[82]

This interaction between Native and non-Native activists illustrates how ethnicity can trump gender as a signifier of identity. For Brave Bird and Pictou-Aquash, at times being oppressed as Native Americans was more relevant to their lives than was a struggle for women's liberation.[83] Even within tribes and other ethnic groups, degrees of belonging complicate interactions. For example, early in the text of *Lakota Woman*, Brave Bird deals with her ethnic identity, painting for the reader the shades of "Indian-ness" encountered by full and mixed-blood Native Americans. Her father, a "part Indian, but mostly white," man was absent from Mary's life.[84] Brave Bird revisits the issue of her blood identity later in the book when she writes:

> To be an Indian I had to go to the full-bloods. My mother and grandmother were Indians, but I am a half-breed and I could not accept this. The half-breeds, the *iyeskas*, I thought, never really cared for anybody but themselves, having learned that "wholesome selfishness" alone brought the blessings of civilization. The full-bloods have a heart. They are humble.[85]

Brave Bird's account of full- and mixed-bloods reveals much about ethnicity and its definitions even among Indian peoples. Still today, Native tribes in the United States and Canada hotly contest the definition of being Indian, as well as the qualifiers to be used in determining whether or not one is Indian— blood quantum, participation in the culture, or other means.[86] Like Brave Bird's, Pictou-Aquash's ethnic identity was complicated and her interactions with other Indians sometimes tense. She was perceived by some Lakota women as an outsider, and even "snubbed" because of her Canadian origins.[87]

Balancing her gender and ethnicity, Brave Bird wrote, "There is an old Lakota song that begins: 'To be a man it is difficult, they say.' Well, to be a Native American woman is even harder. I do the dishes and I am again changing diapers. But I'm still fighting. . . . [I] try to make my kids understand what it means to be Indian . . . Try to help other women to cope with life."[88] Imposed and accepted ideas of appropriate gender and ethnic roles shaped the experiences of Brave Bird and Pictou-Aquash on the northern plains. The scarcity of scholarly work that addresses Anna Mae Pictou-Aquash and Mary Brave Bird reveals how far we have yet to go to understand these complicated relationships of how gender, ethnicity, and place connect the struggle for civil rights across a political border.

The life experiences of women living on the northern plains were shaped to different degrees and in different ways by the environment in which they lived, by the fact that they were women, by their class, race, and ethnicity. Since the northern plains, as a specific geographical region, extends into two countries, there is a need to see how the role of the nation impacts women's experiences across this invisible political divide. In the case of Era Bell Thompson and Cheryl Foggo, their writings both link and contrast their experiences on the northern plains. War brides who immigrated into Canada and the United States shared a commonality of experience as they adjusted to changes in living accommodations, modes of work, travel, leisure, and adaptation to the physical landscape of the northern plains. Yet the ease of gaining entry into the country of their new husbands, and the reception they received upon arrival, depended on whether the brides intended to settle in the United States or Canada. For Brave Bird, her ethnic identity and gender where sometimes at odds with each other, and at other times worked together in her struggles for a better life as a Native American and as a woman. Anna Mae Pictou-Aquash encountered similar tensions between ethnicity, place, and gender. Ultimately, each of these forces may have played a role in her tragic death. As scholars work to unravel the meaning of gender and place for women of all races and classes, the relationships between these forces will continue to form multiple and varied experiences for women living on both sides of the border that stretches across the northern plains.

Part II
# |The Central Plains|

Mari Sandoz, ca. 1938. Photo courtesy of the Mari Sandoz Heritage Society

# Mari Sandoz, a Vignette

SHANNON D. SMITH

In 1906, eleven-year-old Mari Sandoz secretly entered and won a short story contest conducted by an Omaha newspaper. Sandoz, living with her parents and four younger siblings in a rustic one-room homestead in northwest Nebraska, had learned to read, write, and speak English barely two years earlier when she started country school. When she excitedly showed her name and story in the *Omaha Daily News* to her father, Jules, he became infuriated. Claiming writers and artists were "the maggots of society," Jules beat Mari and locked her in the cellar. Six years later she stole away with the family's horse and rode eighteen miles to Rushville to take the eighth-grade exam so she could teach in rural schools. The other candidates would have been surprised to know that the shy, seventy-five-pound waif wearing a handmade dress was seventeen; she looked barely thirteen. Though Sandoz was nervous, intimidated, and desperately afraid of what her father would do, her grit, drive, and determination ultimately won out over fear of his wrath. This became the first of many brave and unconventional acts that characterized her fiercely independent life and literary career—a career that was clearly shaped by her childhood on the central plains.

Born on May 11, 1896, to Swiss immigrants who barely knew each other, Mari Sandoz grew up in the Sandhills of northwest Nebraska—one of America's last regions to be homesteaded—where Jules Sandoz had built a community in the rugged hills along the Niobrara River. Although coarse and frequently vulgar, Jules, who had been reared in a middle-class family in Switzerland, was multilingual, erudite, charismatic, and a tireless booster for the region. He was also a brutal, self-absorbed man who disdained women. When Mari's mother, Mary, found herself stranded at the tiny, just-opened Hay Springs train station, Jules was the only person around who could speak her German Swiss native tongue. Reluctantly, she accepted the filthy, unkempt man's offer to stay at his homestead. Within a few days, despite the squalor of his cabin and its meager surroundings, she had married him and turned over the small savings she brought to start a new life.

As the eldest child, Mari became the family workhorse—cooking, cleaning, and taking care of her younger siblings. She bore much of the wrath of Jules's explosive temper, but she also shared in many of Jules's notorious exploits. His primitive, rough-hewn homestead became a gathering place for his homesteading neighbors. Small groups of Lakota Sioux, who found a friend in Jules, would also camp next to his place on the Niobrara on their way to and from the Pine Ridge Reservation. Her upbringing in this multicultural immigrant-settler environment enabled young Mari to learn about the Sioux with no preconceived superiority. She found the Sioux to be no more unusual than the colorful palette of "immigrant Poles, Czechs, Irish, Dutch, French, Germans, Danes, Swiss, a few Serbs, a Bulgar, a Mohammedan, a Negro and . . . Texas cowboys" who visited her family's homestead.[1] Most of these neighbors' and guests' words, including those of the Sioux, were foreign to Sandoz, who spoke the Swiss German of her mother. Precociously inquisitive, Sandoz became adept at communicating with sign language and learned a great deal from her Sioux friends. As an adult she drew on these childhood experiences to develop a keen awareness of the Plains Indian worldview.

Shortly after she snuck away to take the rural teachers' exam, Sandoz began teaching in a one-room school; shortly thereafter she married. Five years later, in 1919, she ended the unhappy marriage and moved to Lincoln, where she began her epic literary journey. In 1929, the struggling, near-starving writer paid tribute to her recently deceased father by changing from her married name back to Mari Sandoz. The unconventional spelling of her first name reflected her father's European pronunciation, "Mah-ree," and reveals the conflict between her independent spirit and her connection to her father—who from his deathbed gave her permission to write his life story. In 1935, after more than fifteen rejections, *Old Jules*, Mari's candid biography of her colorful, eccentric father, won the Atlantic prize and changed her life forever.

With writing interests firmly grounded in the struggles and challenges she experienced as a child, Sandoz went on to publish some of America's most recognized books on Great Plains history, including *Cheyenne Autumn; Crazy Horse, the Strange Man of the Oglalas; The Cattlemen; The Buffalo Hunters;* and *The Beaver Men*. Because she knew firsthand the challenges and the promises of America's last "free" land, and she understood deeply the emotions, the spiritual nature, and the worldview of the Lakota people whom she knew as a young child, Mari Sandoz's work is among the most enduring records of the plains settlement years, and she has become known as the world's foremost chronicler of the men and women of the Great Plains.

# Introduction to the Central Plains

ROGER DAVIS

In his introduction to the *Encyclopedia of the Great Plains*, editor David Wishart asserts that "any region is both a real place and an intellectual concept."[1] In this section the central plains provides the place, while the intellectual concept is provided by a combination of the historiographical tradition regarding women in the West and the contemporary analysis of the scholarship of our four authors.

The central plains region is nearly 160,000 square miles of western Nebraska sandhills and a vast prairie grasslands that comprise the area of the states of Nebraska, Kansas, and eastern Colorado. The territory is bracketed by the Missouri River on the east and the foothills of the front range of the Rocky Mountains to the west. From north to south, a series of rivers drain into the Missouri. The Niobrara, Loup, Platte, and Republican waterways mark the Nebraska terrain. Kansas shares the Republican River, with the Smoking Hill, Kansas, and Arkansas Rivers weaving through the rest of the territory. The climate exhibits more sunshine than overcast days, and generally the humidity is low. This benign pattern is occasionally upset with the arrival of strong winds and violent thunderstorms that include tornados. Rainfall, while not as much as that to the East, is well distributed and, in conjunction with the river systems, allows the central plains to be a productive agricultural and grazing region supporting the production of prairie grasses, beans, and corn, and populations of buffalo, cattle and horses.

Nearly two dozen indigenous nations, including such tribes as the Arapaho, Omaha, Pawnee, Kiowa, Kansa, Ponca, Sauk, Osage, and Winnebago, hunted buffalo, planted corn and beans, and grazed horses across the central plains. Over the three decades from 1840 to 1870 more than three hundred thousand travelers headed west across the central plains on the Oregon, Mormon, and Overland Trails, thus beginning the process of challenging the Na-

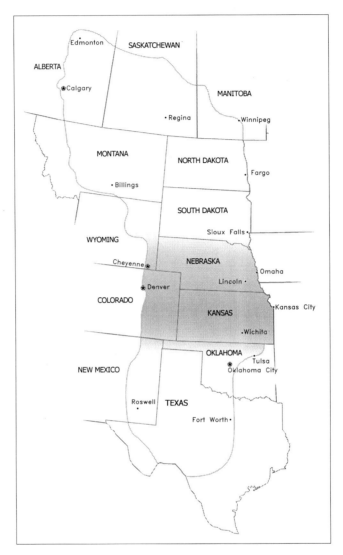

Map highlighting central plains region.
Copyright (c) 2011 by Carl Laegreid

tive communities. With the establishment of the western railways and the Homestead Act, nonindigenous populations arrived to farm the plains, plant urban communities along the water and rail routs, and set aside the Native populations in the name of progress.[2]

The historiography of women in the West is one of essential images and analytical context. In their seminal article, "The 'Gentle Tamers' Revisited:

New Approaches to the History of Women in the American West," Joan Jensen and Darlis Miller asserted three propositions about women and the region.[3] First, the authors proposed that it is within the concept of the frontier as "process" that images of women are created. Second, they argued that although historians had expanded on the array of images of women, moving beyond the "gentle tamer," to include the "sunbonneted helpmate, hell-raisers, and bad women," such images remained narrow and problematic. And third, the authors suggested a new multicultural framework of analysis to challenge traditional images and construct more realistic expressions of process and gender in the region. They called for a greater understanding of Hispanic and Asian women in the West, of the dynamics of immigration that brought them to the region, and for greater attention to cross-cultural relationships and socioeconomic factors essential for a fresh analysis of women in the West.

In separate works, Deborah Fink and Elliott West echo the call for scholarship with new and distinct perspectives. In her essay, "Putting Women into the Plains Picture," Fink notes that "gender has to do with both maleness and femaleness and with the constructions arising out of the relations between maleness and femaleness. While often such questions emerge in esoteric points that seem far removed from the reality of most people's lives, they are embedded in basic social and economic structures."[4] For West, one of the most significant of these basic structures is the family, arguing that it is within this milieu that much new can be learned about women's roles in the West.[5] The family as a social construct embodies five essential dynamics: a reproductive force, a productive unit, a conveyor of traditions and social form, a relationship of power, and a social bond. Of this construct of male and female, West concludes that "[n]o force in western history has been more neglected and none has been more important and revealing—as a weapon of conquest, as a vessel of culture, as a machine of change, and finally as a loom for new human weaves."[6]

This context of region as a maturing of intellectual and multicultural construction frames the contributions in this chapter on women's experiences on the central plains. Rebecca Bales's essay, "Mothers, Cultivators, and Traders: Central Plains Indigenous Women to 1803," emphasizes the economic and cultural role of indigenous women both within the context of the tribe prior to extensive interaction with European peoples, and then as a dynamic of the multicultural process. The sedentary agricultural life of the central plains was a factor unique to this region, and indigenous women defined the essential characteristic of this dynamic. This is a point illustrated in a comment by Deborah Fink, who observed, "Asked to draw a picture of a farmer, a Native

American would have drawn a woman."[7] Beyond indigenous women as agriculturalists, Bales focuses on the indigenous women of the central plains as "cultural mediators" who often defined, accepted, or rejected the material and cultural norms accompanying the growing contact with nonindigenous and other indigenous groups.

Dee Garceau analyzes another community of plains women in terms of mediating cultural traditions and social norms. Her essay, "Mormon Women at Winter Quarters," indicates that these women renegotiated traditional patriarchal authority within the terms of the theological and political structures of the community of church and family. Drawing on the resource of diaries, letters, and other reflective accounts, Garceau-Hagen finds that the familial arena provided ample social space for the construction of an alternative and critical Mormon perspective anchored in the gendered experiences of Mormon sisters, wives, and mothers. In addition to polygamy, essential issues such as fictive kin, "sealing" by proxy, and practices of "adoption" were given an independent analysis by the women of the Mormon camp and formed the basis for ongoing negotiation about gender relationships within the Mormon family. The Winter Quarters, as part of the trek west, was a place of process for Mormon women.

Another form of negotiation is featured in "'Poor old thing, I hope she is 'comph' at last': Crossing Gender Boundaries and Identities on the Great Plains, 1850–1900," by Peter Boag. Here the negotiation is one more internal for the women and men involved, as they challenge the most basic norms of gender by switching roles. Boag analyzes the cases of Mountain Charley, Tom King, and Joe Monahan, women who claimed a masculine role, successfully living in the West as men. Rejecting the traditional theory of "progress narrative," which emphasizes romance, revenge, economic security, and opportunity as the driving forces behind such gender choice, Boag argues for the significance of individual choice of gender identity. Offering the case of Old Nash, a Hispanic male who relinquished male privileges to live the life of a midwife and laundress, Boag brings into the process of the West the dynamic of multicultural transgender experiences.

The final offering embodies Elliot West's theme of family in the context of this social construct as "a machine of change" and "a loom for new human weaves."[8] In "Riding the Winds of Change: Education and Activism on the Central Plains, 1930 to the present," Renee Laegreid combines autobiographical accounts with contemporary oral history to demonstrate how rural white women, Native American women, and Asian and Hispanic female immigrants emerge as cultural mediators taking an active role in shaping the future for themselves, their families, and their communities. Dramatic changes in the process of place required all of these women to craft survival strategies of activism and engagement in definitions of gender roles. Laegreid demonstrates that from the Dust Bowl decade to the farm crisis of the 1980s, family farming on the plains has meant a rise in women's agricultural organizations and new voices from the once "gentle tamers" of the West. For Native American women, offsetting assimilation pressures has meant the creation of organizations to maintain tribal rights and pass traditional ways on to the next generation. New immigrants of the Fourth Wave, from Vietnam, Thailand, and Mexico, face traditional challenges of the melting pot, but the dynamics of modern transportation and communication networks function to enhance ethnic ties, thus redefining immigrant assimilation. The last half century of change on the plains has required these women to expand their political, social, and familial roles, laboring to reweave definitions of home and community.

Reflecting on the role of gender on the Great Plains, Deborah Fink comments that "[f]ew questions of gender in the Great Plains have been put to rest. They are being revisited in ongoing investigations, and debates are wide-ranging."[9] This is clearly the case. Just as apparent is the fact that these debates are richer and more meaningful as a result of the contributions offered by the scholars of this section.

5

# Mothers, Cultivators, and Traders

## Central Plains Indigenous Women to 1803

REBECCA BALES

Along the many rivers flowing through and intersecting the central plains of North America, indigenous peoples constructed villages and cultivated fields of corn, beans, and squash for generations. According to the origin stories of the many indigenous nations living on the central plains, the Creator not only placed them in the area but also instructed the people on how to live and how to sustain their societies. The importance of agriculture, corn in particular, emerges in the many stories passed down from generation to generation. As important is the maintenance of the earth, for it is the earth that sustains agriculture, game, water, and, in turn, the people. Consequently, the people refer to the earth as "mother." The reverence for female in these stories reflects and often dictates the status of women within their own societies.

The central plains region is distinguished from the northern and southern plains by the many streams and rivers that intersect in the region and the prairie grasses that grow there. According to archaeologist Patricia J. O'Brien,

> The Central Plains of the Great Plains of North America are traditionally bounded by the Rocky Mountains to the west, the Missouri River to the east, the Niobrara River to the north and the Arkansas River drainage to the south. The area is marked today by the modern states of Kansas and Nebraska and the flat eastern plains of Colorado and the southeastern fringes of Wyoming.[1]

Indigenous nations of the central plains include the Pawnee, Ponca, Omaha, Oto, Ioway, Sauk and Fox, Osage, Kansa, Kiowa, Cheyenne, and Arapaho. Because of the terrain, the introduction of corn and beans around 950 CE allowed those nations to develop a sedentary lifestyle based on agriculture with hunting (especially of buffalo) blended together.[2] Political and economic systems also developed along gender lines whereby both men and women carried out distinct roles. This distinction emerged in several ways, especially in relation to subsistence and familial expectations. Central plains women are set apart from their sisters to the north (namely the Lakota) and south (namely the Comanche and Lipan Apache) because of their central role in agricultural pursuits.[3] They defy the image attributed to all Plains Indians as nomadic hunters who followed the buffalo.[4] Historian Benson Tong addressed the roles of the Omaha women in his biography of Omaha Susan LaFlesche. He wrote, "The tallgrass prairies, river valleys, and mixed-grass plains served as the boundaries of their world. Within this world, the Omahas created a subsistence economy based on agriculture and hunting—an economy that offered security and sustenance."[5] Within this economy women established themselves as vital participants in their societies especially as mothers and laborers, a classification that included farmers, mediators, and traders. All of these elements of central plains cultures exist within the cultural and origin stories of each nation.

Some scholars have recognized the importance of stories and how these dictated women's status and roles. Authors Daniel Maltz and JoAllyn Archambault addressed the ways women maintained power within societies that seem to give them a higher status than men. The plains region falls into this category. They claimed:

> In a variety of Native American societies including the Plains, the Northern Athapaskan, the Inuit, the Creek, and much of the Eastern Woodlands, the case for male power over women is fairly strong. The question then becomes, what is it about these societies that allows women to place limitations on male power over them? Some answers to this question include cultural values on individual autonomy, alternative roles such as that of the "manly-hearted woman" open to at least some women, and mythological charters for women's status. In societies of this type, men control most power, but women have a variety of options for limiting it or gaining access to some of it.[6]

Women served an important function in their social, political, and economic organization and the origins of their societies. According to author

Paula Gunn Allen, indigenous women's place in society is imbued with and embodies the spiritual for indigenous people. In her groundbreaking work, *The Sacred Hoop,* she stated:

> There is spirit that pervades everything, that is capable of powerful song and radiant movement, and that moves in and out of the mind. The colors of this spirit are multitudinous, a glowing, pulsing rainbow. Old Spider Woman is one name for this quintessential spirit, and Serpent Woman is another. Corn Woman is one aspect of her, and Earth Woman is another, and what they together have made is called Creation, Earth, creatures, plants, and light. . . . At the center of all is Woman.[7]

This assessment of the centrality of female influence on the spiritual, found among many central plains tribes, is reflected in the oral stories passed down from generation to generation through the origin accounts of Native America. One of the most prominent elements in origin accounts is that of earth as mother.

Misinterpretations of indigenous women's roles and status in their societies emerged when Europeans, namely men, encountered the indigenous peoples of North America. The standards by which these men judged and wrote about the people they met rested on the beliefs and customs they brought from afar. Because Europeans kept records in written form, we have their assessments of their encounters with different cultures. The counterbalance to the biases Europeans wrote down can be found in oral tradition, especially the experiences and stories people passed down to their children and grandchildren. Especially important are the origin stories that set down expectations of the people.

The indigenous societies of the central plains imbued expectations of gender norms, as reflected in origin stories, early in life. The concept of Mother Earth is one example that strongly indicates the strength of woman. Ethnologist George Dorsey recorded a Wichita story in which she "gives birth to everything, is mother of everything, who keeps everything, even her bosom for the people to walk upon."[8] Furthermore, this Wichita story, as told to Dorsey, put women at the center of the moon's cycle, an element closely associated with women throughout Native North America:

> The Moon is the special guardian of the women, for she is a woman and possesses all the powers which women desire. She it was who taught the

first woman on earth and gave her power. She instructs the women as to the time of the monthly sickness, informs them when they are pregnant, and when the child is to be born.

. . . Furthermore, she regulates the increase not only of human beings, but of all animals, birds, and plants.[9]

The life-giving and -sustaining position of women permeates the entire social structure of indigenous societies. These attributes of women are often reflected in the power of water. According to Dorsey's Wichita informants, Woman-Having-Powers-in-the-Water (Otskahakakaitshoidisa) "is chief of all water potencies and things living in the water. She not only furnishes drink, but cleanses and heals the people by action of water."[10]

Pawnee origins also confirm the importance of women. George Dorsey extended his work to the Pawnees by collecting and recording several of their stories. According to the Pawnees, the first being created by the Creator Tirawa was a woman:

At the sound of his voice a woman appeared on earth. Tirawa spoke to the gods in the heavens and asked them what he should do to make the woman happy and that she might give increase. . . . Tirawa made a man and sent him to the woman; then he said: "Now I speak to both of you. I give you the earth. You shall call the earth 'mother.'

". . . In time you, woman, shall be known as 'mother,' and the man shall be known as 'father.' I give you the sun to give you light. The moon will also give you light. The earth I give you, and you are to call her 'mother,' for she gives birth to all things. . . . Never forget to call the earth 'mother,' for you are to live upon her. You must love her, for you must walk upon her."[11]

Reverence for earth as mother reflected the importance of women in Pawnee society. It extended to their role in forming and maintaining the lodge. She brought her power as an agriculturalist into the home; the fruits of the harvest sustained the family. "When they had completed the lodge," Dorsey continues, "the woman was the first to enter it. She had with her some corn that she had raised from seeds, and this she offered to the four gods, the southeast, southwest, northeast and northwest."[12] A clear parallel emerges in the origin accounts of earth and woman as sustainers and givers of life. Thus a logical

conclusion for most indigenous societies focuses on women as agriculturalists.

Ceremonial cycles revolve around planting and harvesting all crops. With
few exceptions in Native America, women planted and tended the fields, taking care that the harvest was plentiful. On the central plains, indigenous societies that depended on the harvest mirrored the general patterns of corn-
growing societies, with women at the center of the cycles of life. Oral stories
often include the origins of corn, one of the most sacred foods in Native
America, and its importance in the cycles of life. Originating in Mexico, corn
eventually made its way north, spreading throughout the continent and becoming a major staple in most indigenous societies.[13] Women's relationship
with corn reflected their importance in their societies.

Women sustained the people through their life-giving abilities as clearly
outlined in oral tradition. These accounts demonstrate the centrality of wom-
en and their significance to their communities in their capacity as agriculturalists, especially in relation to corn. In one account of the Wichita creation
story that George Dorsey recorded, women received corn so that the people
would survive. The following portion of the account focuses on women's role
in sustaining the people:

> He [Man-Never-Known-On-Earth (Kinnekasus)] also made a woman
> for the man; and her name was Bright-Shining-Woman (Kashatski-
> hakatidise). After the man and the woman were made they dreamed
> that things were made for them, and when they woke they had the
> things of which they had dreamed. Thus they received everything they
> needed. The woman was given an ear of corn, whose use she did not
> know, but this was revealed to her in her heart; that it was to be her
> food; that it was Mother-Corn; that it was to be the food of the people
> who should exist in the future, to be used generation after generation;
> that from Mother-Corn the people should be nursed.[14]

Women's economic role throughout the plains centered on the harvest from
start to finish. Central plains women followed these rules as did all other corn-
based cultures. The stories also mirror the cycles of life as well as the customs
and rituals distinguished by gender norms.

Anthropologist Robert Lowie's analysis of Plains Indians also addressed
the role that women played in agriculture on the plains. He stated,

Maize, beans, squashes or pumpkins, and sunflowers were the principal crops, the first overshadowing the others in importance [a reflection of the origin stories and the role of corn in them]. As usual in North America, except where agriculture was absolutely predominant, women did most or all of the cultivating. They had to struggle with the same difficulties that confronted subsequent White settlers—drought and grasshoppers. They lacked plows, draft animals, and fertilizer, and did not know about rotating crops. . . . Pawnee women cultivating at such a distance [5–8 miles from the village] were exposed to the attacks of hostile raiders; hence, they sometimes had bodyguards of armed warriors. Enemies of a different sort were the birds threatening the maturing plants; women erected stages from which they and their children frightened away intruders. According to an expert estimate the Kansa and Osage probably cultivated one-third of an acre for each person in the tribe.[15]

Women's roles were clear in all cultivation; corn, their staple crop, in turn, became a valuable trade commodity on the plains, thereby traveling to New Mexico and the northern plains.

Since time immemorial, indigenous peoples of the central plains maintained social, cultural, political, and economic norms that have influenced much of North America. Socially, women held a revered place in society because of childbearing and rearing, but each nation had certain rules and restrictions to be followed. Scholars, anthropologists in particular, recorded these social regulations that dictated gender norms (many of which can be found in creation stories). For example, the Cheyenne who lived on the most western portion of the central plains followed strict gender guidelines that K. N. Llewellyn and E. Adamson Hoebel addressed in relation to Cheyenne laws and jurisprudence. Men and boys could not violate Cheyenne women and girls who were known "for their chastity." Any violation could be turned over to the family of the girl, and the violator and his family recompensed the girl's family.[16] Indigenous societies of the plains frowned on the abuse of women because of their influence on successive generations. The reverence for women that is found in origin stories played itself out through customs that included courting, marriage, and gender expectations in these areas. Indeed, the marriage bond became the means by which families, clans, and nations solidified relations.

Courting and marriage customs throughout the plains included gift-giving and familial consultation.[17] A woman could choose whether or not to accept a suitor. If she and her partner chose to marry, then both families would negotiate the terms for completing the union. Scholar James H. Howard focused on the reciprocal gift exchanges, quoting Ponca Tribal Historian Pierre Le Claire, "When a boy wanted to marry a girl, he could do it in one of two ways. The first way he gave lots of presents to her family, such as horses and buffalo robes. . . . The second way was by arrangement."[18] Each society valued a woman's productivity, hence the reciprocal exchange of gifts that made up for the loss of her productive abilities in her natal family. Marriage formed the economic and political links within and to other nations. Through marriage, a woman passed on cultural norms to her children; these norms could change due to circumstance and interaction with other peoples.

During different time periods, migration and interaction with other Native nations brought cultural change.[19] However, drastic changes to their societies came with the incursion of Europeans and Euro-Americans into their territories with little or no regard for indigenous customs. Women were central to this change as it was their persistence and roles as cultural mediators that often defined interactions with outsiders while maintaining cultural norms.[20] The centrality of plains indigenous peoples made them extremely important in linking different regions and peoples with each other. Furthermore, as contact with new people increased, this central position exemplified how indigenous women of the central plains, indeed most indigenous women, maintained their roles in their own societies prior to and with European contact.

Territories shifted with movement of different nations. Movement onto and within the plains by different peoples can be traced through archaeological evidence.[21] Author Mark Warhus claimed that "[t]he Native American societies that [Juan de] Oñate encountered [in the late 1500s] had begun to migrate on to the Great Plains in the eleventh and twelfth centuries. Linked together by trade and traditions, they relied upon a combination of hunting, trade, and agriculture for their subsistence."[22] Another nation, the Otoes, were connected to the Missourias and made their way onto the central plains in the eighteenth century, affecting the tribal relations in the area. Similarly, the Wichita moved west when the Osage sought to gain control over the central plains. According to historian Elizabeth John,

> The best documented of Caddoan movements southward, and indeed the longest historic record, is that of the Wichitan peoples. Spanish and French sources attest continuing occupancy in the Arkansas Valley from 1541 until the mid-eighteenth century, when relentless Osage attacks

drove them southward to the middle reaches of Red and Brazos rivers. There they would dwell for a century until hostile Texans forced them back north across the Red River to the Washita Valley, which the Wichita tribe calls home today.[23]

Tribal relations set the boundaries of economic, territorial, and political interactions. In the case of movement, conflict often forced movement. According to Mark Warhus, "tribal animosities that shaped these societies were well established before the encounter with Europeans."[24]

Women's experiences depended on the stability of their own nations regardless of movement but were mightily influenced by it. The Otoes were able to set roots down on the central plains, adopting some agricultural practices there, but also continued to largely rely on game, especially the buffalo. According to Berlin Chapman, "The Otoes and Missourias cultivated small tracts of land, but probably secured more than half their food by hunting."[25] The Wichitas, on the other hand, had permanent villages. Warhus described them as "an agricultural people, taking advantage of the land to grow corn, beans, and squash. They lived in permanent circular grass houses formed around poles stuck into the ground."[26] Within the villages a distinct division of labor existed. Lowie noted women's and men's roles:

> The division of labor between the sexes followed a general primitive pattern in so far as the husband hunted while the wife supplied the vegetable fare. This meant that among the semisedentary tribes she did the cultivating and among the nomads dug up wild roots and collected berries. In all cases she prepared the meals, brought fuel and water, put up and took down the tipi, dressed skins, and made all the clothing.[27]

This division of labor created a system in which both men and women contributed to the security of the village, but the distribution of resources tended to fall to the women.

The success of indigenous nations procuring and preparing food and preparing goods or items for trade depended largely on the women and their skills. After the hunt, for example, the fruits of the men's labor was transferred to women, who dressed and cured the hides, prepared meat for meals and trade, and developed other parts of the game for agriculture (hoes), sewing (awls), and hides (housing). Wishart explained these roles:

Women in all the Indian societies of Nebraska owned the lodge, the tipi, and most of its contents, a right of ownership that American women did not have until the middle of the nineteenth century. The women also owned the fields, seeds, and implements of production. They often determined where to camp on the bison hunts and where, specifically, to pitch tipis in relation to other members of the clan. The senior wife was the main decision maker in the lodge and controlled the distribution of food. A woman had the right to refuse to marry a man selected by her parents, and she also had the right to divorce.[28]

Game acquisition and preparation played itself out in trade among Native nations and, later, between nations and Europeans. Items to trade depended on women's work; the better the work, the better the reputation a woman would gain. Better quality goods resulted in more trade, which directly reflected on both the woman who made them and her family and, if she was married, her husband.[29] A highly productive unmarried woman often attracted many suitors, who would gain both economic and social status, perhaps even political status, through the marriage. This economic situation clearly demonstrates the important role of women's labor in the market and at home. As important economic and domestic participants, women often accepted or rejected the materials and different cultural norms that entered their territories. Historian Paul Carlson explained the complexity and range of the trade system that developed on the plains. He wrote, "For centuries before the arrival of Europeans, people on the Great Plains had exchanged goods with peoples living on the region's borders. Fairly well-developed trade routes crossed the plains along water courses and through riverine horticultural villages."[30] These trade routes allowed goods and ideas to move throughout the plains and became the means by which European goods made their way into plains cultures.[31]

Clearly, women of the central plains played a significant role in trade with other Native nations; this continued when Europeans traveled onto the plains. The Spanish were the first Europeans to enter the central plains region. Francisco de Coronado's expedition reached present-day northeastern Kansas in 1540 and set the precedent for how the central plains Natives would interact with foreigners. Different nations welcomed or repelled the newcomers based on many factors, including how the newcomers acted, with whom the newcomers had positive relations, and what advantages the newcomers could gain through interactions. Women played a key role in the formation of these relationships, especially in terms of the perceptions that the newcomers developed; the first perception to emerge was, of course, based on physical attributes. For example, Herbert Eugene Bolton reported Coronado's description of indigenous women in *Coronado: Knight of Pueblos and Plains*. According to Bolton, "Coronado wrote: 'The people are large. I had some Indians measured and found they were ten spans tall. The women are comely, with faces more like Moorish than Indian women.'"[32] This positive description of the women of Kansas is more illustrative of the biases that the Spanish brought; that the indigenous women of Kansas looked "Moorish" and not "Indian" demonstrated, first, that not all Indians looked alike and, second, that the Spanish preconception of beauty often influenced their perception and most likely treatment of indigenous peoples, including women. The physical attributes that the Spanish described and recorded influenced the resources to be had on the central plains by way of the relationships the Spanish men entered into with "comely" women. In turn, these relationships gave Spanish men entrance into the Native nations they encountered. This emerged strongly with the French once they followed the fur trade onto the plains. Women's economic advantage began to outweigh the positive or negative perceptions of physical and cultural qualities.

As the French made their way onto the plains in search of beaver and other fur-bearing animals (the trade in buffalo hides would begin with the French, but it was not until the late 1800s that this trade would dominate the plains market), they engaged indigenous women in many of their pursuits.[33] Of particular interest to French fur traders was the economic position women played in cleaning and dressing furs that they began on the northern plains and further north. "In the early days of the fur trade," argues historian Nancy Shoemaker, "native women were crucial players in the development of the fur trade. Women processed hides, manufactured and sold pemmican (buffalo and berry jerky), and through alliances with French and British traders became the bilingual, bicultural intermediaries between Indians and Europeans."[34] Built into the burgeoning economic systems spreading on the plains was a cheap and available labor force—but not without a price to those who sought that labor. European men had to create alliances, not only with Native women but with their families and communities as well to sustain their economic activities. Wishart described the impact that the fur trade had on central plains women:

> The women erected and dismantled the tipis, built and repaired the
> lodges, produced the staple crops, collected wild plants, hauled fuel and

water, dug and transported salt, processed skins and furs, bore and raised children, and in general looked after the household.... In fact, this heavy workload increased in the early nineteenth century, as the fur trade raised the demand for dressed skins.[35]

Although the fur trade reached the central plains in its later stages, it still had an impact on women and political relations, especially between the southern plains nations and the central plains nations. For example, the Wichita became extremely important mediators as the Spanish and French vied for the upper hand in the trade.[36]

Economic, social, and political changes occurred with the incursion of Europeans and the fur trade. However, the focus of fur trapping changed as buffalo hides became a commodity. Although the buffalo hide trade was just beginning in the late 1700s, it would eventually create a severe crisis for all plains nations as well as the environment of the plains. The environmental impact would be felt much later, but it would begin with the Spanish and the French seeking and exploiting resources.

Europeans continued to trade throughout the plains and started to have a negative impact on the central plains nations throughout the eighteenth century. The Pawnees, for example, suffered from displacement and sought to protect their interests by shifting and merging their villages together. They were successful at keeping the Otoes out of their territory; this success, however, did not apply to Europeans. Indeed, European contact forced Natives to choose with whom they would ally. Wishart explained the causes for this, writing, "By the late eighteenth century, eastern Nebraska had become a dangerous place to live, as the westward penetration of Europeans and Americans into the interior compressed Indian space all the way from the Appalachians to the Great Plains."[37] This shifting land base dramatically changed the way that the central plains people lived. With less land women could not produce as much food as they had previously. In addition, a new commodity the Spanish introduced further compacted the plains and placed more emphasis on men's contribution to the diet. Indeed, the horse forever altered gender roles and trade.

The introduction of the horse had a great impact on the women of the central plains, changing the dynamics of food production and warfare ever after. Villages became more vulnerable as hostile nations could cover more ground in less time, and as movement became critical for the bison hunt, the stability of villages suffered even more with raiding becoming more prominent. In addition, horses made the buffalo hunt virtually effortless as men hunted at longer distances and more easily brought the buffalo back to their camps and villages. This dramatically and adversely affected women's roles as food producers. As Wishart states,

> By 1800 bison meat was displacing corn as the Indians' main source of food. Horses had enlarged the scale of hunting and transportation, and bison meat was generally plentiful and preferred. Corn and other vegetables became a delicacy to be eaten fresh at harvest time, or else stored for future use as an accompaniment to meat, as a buffer against famine, or as a trade item.[38]

Very quickly, agriculture became secondary to buffalo, and women, while they did take part in communal hunts, found their role as agriculturalists subsumed by men's roles in the hunt.

Europeans also brought disease, shifting the power relations throughout the plains. By 1803 smallpox had hit the central plains, creating a population decrease. As Wishart relates, "High mortality rates hindered the Indians' ability to carry out subsistence activities, and diseases of undernutrition and malnutrition killed many more, especially children."[39] Disease became the biggest threat to reproduction and family stability as it swept through villages. Also affected was the traditional medicinal practices that both men and women performed. Scholars have recognized women's ability to utilize herbs. For example, in his analysis of the Wichita, Dorsey noted, "She is also a great medicine chest, keeping upon her body various roots, etc., used in healing."[40] Yet, women's herbal knowledge could not defeat the diseases that they had never experienced before.

Inclusion of the role of indigenous women in the historical literature is scarce and often overshadowed by cultural and gender biases. However, some vital information can be gleaned from different accounts on the importance of indigenous women on the central plains. For example, chronicles and written histories of the Spanish invasion of North America extending into the central plains offer some insight into women's roles. Coronado's expedition perhaps reached as far as the Niobrara River, a geographical delineation between the northern plains nations and the central plains nations. His party's accounts of the women are few but do include some valuable descriptions for understanding the history of the central plains.

Furthermore, in the late 1500s Juan de Oñate led his expedition into Quivira, the term the Spanish assigned to the central plains.[41] Having lived in New Mexico, Oñate and his men compared the variations of the environment and the inhabitants of the central plains. Historian Marc Simmons stated,

> The handsome and prosperous Quivirans dwelled in large towns of round houses thatched with bundles of prairie grass. Oñate's followers marveled at the surrounding fields, fertile and heavy now with crops of corn, beans, and calabashes ready to harvest. The contrast with agriculture they knew in New Mexico was startling, for there farm size was strictly limited by the amount of land fit for irrigation. In this country, on the other hand, plentiful rains through the growing season watered cropland naturally.[42]

Although these particular Spanish chroniclers did not focus solely on women in their accounts, there is no doubt that the importance of women was present. The fields to which this description refers formed not only the basis of the subsistence of the Quivirans but also the roles of those who planted, cared for, and harvested the crops—women.

Two situations resulted from European contact and incursions. If a nation was friendly with Europeans then they reaped the benefits of that relationship. If a nation was not friendly with Europeans then, in their own best interests, Europeans would manipulate the fissures that grew between nations. This directly affected women (and the rest of society) by adversely challenging their central role as mothers and agriculturalists. Dependence on European goods and weapons shifted the balance on the plains, thus making villages and fields more vulnerable to raids and attacks. Equally important were the perspectives and judgments that Europeans pressed on women, from their physical appearance to their experiences and roles in their societies. Indeed, European men tended to describe these women as drudges and slaves to their men, while they perceived men as lazy. It is clear that this was certainly not the case. Wishart succinctly stated the biases that emerged from European accounts:

> The prevailing image of the role and status of Indian women was distorted by two major preconceptions. First, early travelers (at least the educated ones who wrote down their ideas) were blinded by their own cultural assumption that women were to be cloistered and protected. . . . [T]he understanding was that women were the weaker sex, both mentally and physically. The second, connected preconception was the

equating of hard physical work with low status, and nobody worked harder than Indian women. Belief in Indian women's low status was also confirmed by the men's domination of the political and religious spheres.[43]

The stories that have passed down from generation to generation directly counter the misperceptions that Europeans formed and perpetuated.

By 1803 a new entity came into play without the knowledge, let alone consent of the people of the plains. Thomas Jefferson bought most of the plains from France through the Louisiana Purchase. This massive land transfer and its consequent exploration brought pressure to bear on the plains nations, changing not only the cultural customs of these people but their gender roles and relations as well. Expectations of women in indigenous societies changed as the United States looked west for settlement. Central plains women felt this impact in many ways, especially as a new country challenged the cultural norms of indigenous societies and rearranged Native American demographics to fit westward expansion.[44] With this transference many of the plains nations had to negotiate their rights and renegotiate their customs as a new government brought pressure to bear on assimilation. According to Wishart, "Lewis and Clark wanted a council [with the Natives of present-day Nebraska]: eastern Nebraska was to be the testing ground for Jefferson's Indian policy and for their own diplomatic skills."[45]

Indigenous women of the central plains clearly played a critical role in their societies and between nations. As mothers, cultivators, and traders, they shaped and perpetuated their people and cultures. Current literature continues to emerge, shedding light on these roles throughout Native North America and restructuring beliefs about indigenous communities. New interpretations continue to surface as the voices of Native women find their place in the historic record, as well as through oral tradition and what can be gleaned from historic documents. Their stories fill in the gaps that have existed throughout history and set right the historical record. Their impact on history is remarkable and noteworthy because they shaped the plains as much as Native men and Europeans, and, more important, they restructure beliefs about gender throughout history. According to Klein and Ackerman, "Silence surrounds the lives of Native North American women."[46] Finding indigenous women's voices to fill the silence is certainly a challenge. The voices of central plains indigenous women before 1803 are difficult to re-create, but they can be found and illuminated through careful study and multifaceted and comprehensive questioning.

# "Poor old thing, I hope she is 'comph' at last"

## Crossing Gender Boundaries and Identities
## on the Great Plains, 1850–1900

PETER BOAG

"Strange country this," Edwin Thompson Denig incredulously exclaimed in the 1850s, referring to the Great Plains, "where males assume the dress and perform the duties of females, while women turn men and mate with their own sex!"[1] Today we inhabit a world where little along the lines of gender and sexual iconoclasm shocks us as it did Denig in the mid-nineteenth century. And yet we are likely taken aback by Denig's assessment of the place, and for the time he made it, for the very reason that gender and sexual nonconformity seem more matters of the modern, urban, and global age than they do for the bygone era of the frontier American West. But when we pause to consider that Denig's proclamation really concerned the Indian peoples of the Great Plains, calmer heads likely prevail; for some time now American society (or at least that portion of which the readers of this essay are likely a part) has known and accepted that large numbers of Native American tribes, and particularly those who inhabited the central and northern Great Plains at the time of European contact, recognized more than two (that is, feminine and masculine) genders. Not only did they recognize them, but they named them and associated them with specific and sometimes vital roles in their cultures.

Awareness of Native American gender and sexual tradition partially stems from the explosion of anthropological literature on the subject that began in the last quarter of the twentieth century.[2] And yet, there also exists a cross-gender tradition in the nineteenth-century history of non-Indian people of the Great Plains and, more generally, the American West. Less acknowledged and therefore less studied than that of the Native peoples, the crossing of gender and sexual boundaries in Great Plains Euro-American history is no less significant for understanding this region's history. Oddly, its relevance partially derives from the fact that it has been largely ignored. In other words, just as instructive as the story of crossing gender and sexual boundaries in Great Plains and western Euro-American history, are the reasons why scholars have neglected it. These include an inability to make sense of transgenderism within a historically binary gendered system, homophobia, and even race. For instance, Anglo-Americans have a strong historical tradition of associating sexual and gender impropriety with foreigners and nonwhites, which makes it inconvenient to recognize these among themselves and unproblematic to accept them among, for example, Native Americans.[3] Also, not until the early twentieth century did the Western world begin to recognize what only in the latter half of that same century would come to be understood as transgenderism and transsexuality. This constrains the ability of scholars in the modern day to conceptualize what appears to be the existence of these phenomena prior to 1900.[4] Some scholars have also uncritically assumed that crossdressers in Euro-American history are homosexuals and, therefore, according to certain prejudices, marginal and unworthy of investigation. By the same token, others who have attempted to legitimate cross-dressers in Euro-American history claim that readers need to get past the assumption of homosexuality among them in order to transform them into a credible subjects of study.[5]

This essay excavates from historical documents a "transgender" history of non-Native peoples of the Great Plains for the latter half of the nineteenth century.[6] It explains that Anglos, Mexicans, and African Americans who crossed gender boundaries on the Great Plains at this time and took on identities and personas opposite of what the dominant culture of the time associated with their biological sexes were not particularly unusual. Due to certain changing notions about sexuality and gender, however, they became, in time, somewhat problematic for inhabitants and writers of the Great Plains and larger West to countenance. As a result, a certain revision of the past took place. An assessment of transgenderism on the Great Plains for the latter part of the nineteenth century also demonstrates that reigning scholarly paradigms for explaining cross-dressers in the history of certain other parts of the Western world are not always appropriately applicable to people who crossed gender boundaries in this region; among other things these paradigms collapse the complexities of crossing gender and sexual boundaries into simple statements about economic rationale, disregarding the fact that identity can also motivate these activities. Finally, an examination of historical documents that depict the lives of several Great Plains cross-dressers tells us much about how and why Euro-Americans constructed womanhood in the way they did during the latter half of the nineteenth century in and for this particular region of the American West.

The discovery of gold in the West provides an appropriate place to commence with a consideration of transgendered people in the non-Native American history of the Great Plains. During the 1850s the quantity of all sorts of people on the plains increased sharply. Utilizing the well-established Oregon and Santa Fe Trails, they crisscrossed the central and southern plains in ever-growing numbers as they sought fortune in the Rockies and on the Pacific coast. These argonauts and adventurers included any number of individuals who dressed in the attire of the opposite sex. Take for example Mountain Charley, whose enigmatic and ubiquitous nature derived from the fact that there likely existed several different women dressed as men who claimed this moniker. An eastern news correspondent reported from Cherry Creek, Colorado, in 1859 that the Mountain Charley he met there had by that time driven cattle across the plains to California on three separate occasions.[7] In 1861 another, perhaps the same, Mountain Charley published her autobiography in Iowa under the name E. J. Guerin. In it Guerin included portions of an 1855 journal she kept while making the journey to the Pacific after departing her St. Louis home. Masquerading as a male, she traveled with a contingent that included "sixty men, fifty oxen, ten cows, fifteen saddle horses and mules." The party set out from Fort Kearney on the Platte River on May 31, traversed the usual route through today's Nebraska, ascended the continental divide in early July, and reached the Sacramento Valley in late October. This Mountain Charley returned to the states via Panama in 1857 and immediately headed across the plains again, this time driving a cattle herd all the way to the Pacific. A year later, back at her St. Louis home, Mountain Charley joined up with the American Fur Company as a trapper and followed the North and South Platte Rivers into the Rockies. When gold fever broke out in the Pike's Peak region, Charley then traveled the Santa Fe Trail into the southern Rockies.[8] Other women as men who prospected in the western gold rushes related similar accounts concerning journeys they had made over the plains. In 1859, western traveler Albert Richardson discovered in the Colorado diggings, for example, an individual who contended that by then, "she had twice crossed the plains to California with droves of cattle."[9]

The number of such women who headed across the plains to the Rocky Mountain gold rushes after 1858 is no easier to surmise than those who had headed to California between 1849 and the mid-1850s. Perhaps more such individuals appeared in the Rockies, or at least there exists good evidence for any number of them being there. The Colorado prospector who reported to Richardson in 1859 about her previous travels to California was only one of "several women dressed in masculine apparel" whom he encountered in the Rockies, "each telling some romantic story of her past."[10]

So plentiful and presumably problematic had such individuals become in the Rocky Mountain diggings, even in the otherwise chaotic and cosmopolitan atmosphere of the mining district, that Richardson also learned while in Colorado that when a newspaper there advertised in need of a "lad" to perform menial chores, it gave notice that "No young woman in disguise need apply."[11] In this case, the word *disguise* holds particular significance. No doubt prospecting and traveling overland trails proved less constraining in male garb, but a good number of those thus attired, as this advertisement suggests, endeavored to actually pass themselves off as men or lads. Consider the Cherry Creek Mountain Charley. The eastern correspondent who reported of him in 1859 described that when he initially encountered this character, he found him unsuccessfully attempting to light a cigar in the midst of a stiff breeze. "His movements" and inexperience raised the reporter's suspicions, for they "were not those of one who had been accustomed to male habiliments." Nonetheless, "only one other person in the diggins [*sic*] knew her sex, and she was smoking when I saw her *only to disarm suspicion*" [emphasis mine].[12]

This eastern correspondent, like Richardson, could detect among the male prospectors in Colorado actual women, suggesting that their camouflage sometimes failed them. The ability to see through clothing, however, was not a talent shared by everyone. For example, and also in 1859, *New York Tribune* editor Horace Greeley traveled westward with the Pike's Peak Express. While on the plains somewhere along the Kansas-Colorado border he encountered a "young clerk" at one of the Express's roadhouses and visited with him over supper. Greeley's dinner companion related a rather cheerless story about his recent experiences in the West. Instead of riches, the clerk had unearthed only misfortune. It all began with a rocky start during his journey out—he had frozen his feet while crossing the plains in winter. From there his adventure continued downhill, finally concluding with the decision to return to parents, home, and school in Indiana. The morning after this less than scintillating dinner conversation, Greeley and his companion departed in opposite directions. Only then did Greeley learn, and from his Pike's Peak Express conductor who apparently benefited from "more practical or more suspicious eyes," "that said clerk was a woman!"[13]

Other women who dressed as men came to or crossed the plains for reasons different from prospecting or driving cattle. Many of their stories, communicated in various secondhand chronicles of a slightly later day, are, not surprisingly, somewhat more apocryphal in nature than the primary documents from the gold rushes. To account for the existence of women who passed as men on the plains, writers of these narratives resorted to the motivating force of romance, failed or otherwise, interlaced with exciting tales of lawlessness and banditry. Take for example the legend of yet another "Mountain Charley," otherwise known only as Charlotte. Editor George West penned and serialized this tale over several issues of the Golden, Colorado, *Transcript* in early 1885. According to West's saga, after she married a "dandified looking young man" at age nineteen in Des Moines, Iowa, Charlotte gave birth to a "little dead baby" and then was deserted by her husband, who turned out to be not only a gambler but shady as well. "They told me," the disheartened Charlotte confessed, that "he had gone away with another woman, one with whom he had been associating for almost the whole time of our married life." Charlotte's love for her husband soon transformed into hatred and, not surprisingly, spread to the "low-down wench for whom he had left me." She committed herself to exacting revenge on the two and discovered that because they had departed for the "new El Dorado" of the Colorado diggings that she would need to pass as a man to pursue them "on the warpath." Now in the guise of Mountain Charley, Charlotte tracked her nemeses across Nebraska as she learned of their movements and crooked shenanigans along the Platte. She finally hunted them down at the base of the Rockies where she exacted her revenge. Shortly thereafter, Charley absconded for New Mexico, returned briefly to Denver, and then headed back to Iowa where, after serving a stint in the Union Army along the middle border, she reportedly resumed the dress of a woman, remarried, gave birth to more children, and passed "her declining years in a sphere suited to her sex, loved and respected by all who know her."[14]

Gilbert Allen of Alexandria, Indiana, recounted in 1906 for a western magazine another story of romance gone wrong on the plains and which involved outlawry and cross-dressing. The protagonist in this tale was a woman named Bess whose lover (or husband, it is not clear which) became involved in a life of crime and fled to the West to escape punishment, needless to say, deserting Bess in the process. But believing him innocent and desiring a reunion, Bess "played the part of a man," called herself Brown, and headed West in pursuit of her beloved. To support herself, but also apparently to broaden her prospects of encountering her paramour, Bess joined the Pony Express as a rider on the western reaches of the plains. "He rode the best horses," an informant who first encountered Brown on the overland trails described to Allen, "was trim as a dandy, [wore] corduroy pants, negligee shirt and slouch hat. He was small, graceful and handsome enough for a girl." One day, while making a regular run for the Express, a swarm of road agents descended on Brown. In an ensuing gun battle, Brown shot one masked man who, in a tragic twist of events, proved to be none other than her lost love. Unmasked, in his dying breath he admitted his guilt for the original crime that had resulted in the couple's sorrowful separation. "He thought to rob me," Brown exclaimed in anguish, "and my hand took his life. Ah! How my mad infatuation, my romance, ended." As the story goes, Brown soon gave "up his place as rider" and departed for the East by way of stage.[15]

Yet another frontier figure, Tom King, who escaped from a Kansas jail sometime during the winter of 1893–1894, was exposed by the Denver journal *Field and Farm* as a woman. She reportedly began a life of crime at age fourteen when "she eloped with a lover of doubtful reputation, and was afterwards proved to be a notorious horse thief who had been wanted for years by the federal authorities in Indian territory." Subsequently, Tom and her husband terrorized the South Canadian River country of Oklahoma and the Texas Panhandle. Even after her husband fell in a gun battle to US marshals, Tom continued a life of banditry along the border separating Kansas and Indian Territory, alternately slipping in and out of men's and women's clothing in order to fool and elude law enforcement officials.[16]

Outlawry on the Great Plains as well as romance gone wrong also factored into early twentieth-century explanations for Joe Monahan. For some forty years Joe lived and worked as a man near Silver City, Idaho. When preparing Joe's body for burial after his death around New Year's 1904, locals discovered that he was actually a she. Incredulous, they began offering imaginative stories to account for this enigmatic individual. One purported that Joe had in reality been none other than the notorious Kate Bender, a young woman who had mysteriously disappeared from Kansas in 1873 after authorities there discovered that her roadhouse-operating parents regularly robbed and murdered overland travelers, burying their bodies about the Bender property. That Joe had originally appeared in Idaho at about the time Bender had vanished from Kansas as well as the fact that Bender's whereabouts had never been discovered, lent a certain air of authority to the tale.[17]

Accompanying the emergence of the Monahan-Bender legend was another involving a failed love affair. In 1904 an *American-Journal-Examiner* dispatch from Boise claimed that "Jo" had actually been the daughter of a wealthy Buffalo family. Without her parents' approval, she eloped with a "well-known society man of dissolute habits" and followed him to New York City. After Jo gave birth out of wedlock, her lover deserted her. Finding life difficult as a single mother, Jo decided to leave her child with her sister in Buffalo, but being "disgraced" and "dispelled" from that town, she chose "to begin life anew in the West, that was then offering homes for the outcasts of all lands." But to do so, she felt that she needed to become a man.

Western Americans in various places and from various walks of life by the latter years of the nineteenth century and early years of the twentieth century knew well the tales of some women who had passed themselves off as men during the frontier era. This memory is lost to us today, but as the above stories illustrate, for some time westerners continued to tell, embellish, and refine their recollections according to their changing times and circumstances. As the frontier-era passed and the West became incorporated into the modernizing and urbanizing nation, fanciful notions about the region's past came to color the evolving chronicles of cross-dressing women. For example, the romantic idea of the frontier West as a larger-than-life man's world helps to explain the recurring theme in later cross-dressing chronicles that once the woman's true sex was revealed in the West through some astonishing event, she deserted the region for the East, but now as a woman. Alternatively, if she could not leave the West due to death, for example, the tale of her true womanhood was recovered only by turning to the East. These themes appear in Charlotte's, Bess's, and Joe Monahan's stories.[18]

At the same time that the growing romanticism about the West colored the evolving tales of the region's cross-dressing women, other factors, notably national and international alterations in understandings of gender and sexuality, also undoubtedly influenced this revising process. In the Western world in the late nineteenth century, incipient notions of both modern homosexuality and heterosexuality began to take shape at various levels from the popular to the scientific. This occurrence in part resulted from the increasing awareness that there existed in modern urban society some men who were sexually attracted to other men and some women who were sexually attracted to women. Rather than homosexuality per se, the formative notion of this was "sexual inversion." By definition, the male invert was really a female trapped in a man's body and the female invert, likewise, was a male trapped in a woman's body. Along with sexual mix-up came other tell-tale signs of inversion: the male invert, because he was really a woman in a male body, would behave and desire to dress in ways associated with the female gender while the female invert would behave and desire to dress in ways associated with men. By the end of the nineteenth century, then, one would find the term *mannish woman* commonly used to refer to those individuals who fit the latter scenario. Such notions did not really exist in the 1850s and 1860s, when the western gold rushes drew to them any number of women dressed in men's clothing, and so observers of the time generally did not assume such women to be anything other than women in men's clothing.[19]

This does not necessarily mean that these individuals met open acceptance. For example, in relating his encounter with several such individuals in the Colorado diggings in 1859, Albert Richardson also remarked of them, "all were of the wretched class against which society shuts its iron doors, bidding them hasten un-cared-for to destruction."[20] Rather than with sexuality per se, this contemptuous appraisal had more to do with transgressions of the boundaries that at this time starkly separated the male from the female sphere. In time, however, women who crossed the gender boundaries that had been established in the Victorian period became increasingly demeaned as the threat they posed to both male and female spheres seemed greater as both spheres crumbled under the weight of historical change. Inextricably linked to this increasingly threatening gender transgression was the emerging and negative notion of homosexuality.

By the latter years of the nineteenth century, broader society increasingly assumed sexual inversion for women who donned male attire. A negative assessment accompanied this supposition: medical experts explained sexual inversion as a degeneracy resulting from some horrible malfunction in the hereditary process or as a perversion contracted through dissolute living. It is no coincidence then that tales of cross-dressing women of the Great Plains either written or embellished during this period firmly asserted the "heterosexuality" of the subjects involved. Therefore, in 1885 George West's Mountain Charley chose male clothing only because of the desire to track across the plains her husband who had wronged her, but whom she had previously loved with "all my heart of hearts" and with whom she had had a baby. In 1906 Gilbert Allen's Bess became a man, called herself Brown, and rode for the Pony Express across the plains in hopes of one day reuniting with her lost male lover and fulfilling "my mad infatuation, my romance." In 1894 *The Field and Farm*'s Tom King took to men's dress in order more easily to follow "her desperado lover in many of his exploits" across the southern plains. And, another western writer maintained that Joe Monahan adorned herself in the garb of the opposite sex in order to cross the continent after her "lover" abandoned her with a child. To assuage other fears of possible mannishness or perversion, it was also necessary for writers to reveal the continued femininity or normalcy of these cross-dressers when they took to life as men. Thus, Gilbert Allen's Bess, even though she had become Brown, "was small, graceful and handsome enough for a girl." And George West explained of his Mountain Charley that "[i]n appearance she was merely an overgrown, pretty boy, but for a woman she was rather above the average size, fresh looking, and without the slightest indication of dissipation."[21]

When turn-of-the-century chroniclers of Great Plains cross-dressers called attention to the fact that women who became men did so for reasons related to opposite-sex romance, attraction, and love, they purposely popularized these people's heterosexuality, femininity, and normalcy. In doing so they consciously sanitized their region's cross-dressing history, which had become, from the modern perspective, rather messy. For truly, documents about women who dressed as men during this and the slightly earlier frontier era clearly indicate that a woman's gender could actually change into that of a male if she tarried too long in the incorrect clothing. E. J. Guerin revealed such a possible and dangerous transformation in her 1861 autobiography. Before heading out across the plains in 1855, Guerin had already lived as a man, working on various Mississippi steamboats and even the Illinois Central Railroad. Through all this she prided herself on her ability "to banish almost wholly, the woman from my countenance. I buried my sex in my heart and roughened the surface so that the grave would not be discovered—as men on the plains *cache* some treasure, and build a fire over the spot so that the charred embers may hide the secret." But even more, Guerin soon grew accustomed to masculine behaviors. "I began to rather like the freedom of my new character," she averred. "I could go where I chose, do many things which while innocent in themselves, were debarred by propriety from association with the female sex." So successful the transformation that during a brief period when she changed back into "my natural garments" and tried to resume her "feminine character" in St. Louis, she unwittingly discovered that "I could not wholly eradicate many of the tastes which I had acquired during my life as one of the stronger sex. Accordingly, at intervals, I would put on my masculine habiliments, and in this shape wander around St. Louis."[22]

Such evidence as this from the frontier past bordered dangerously close to notions of sexual inversion emerging at the turn of the twentieth century. During the tumultuous period of industrialization and urbanization that enveloped America at this time, the romantic myth of the Old West crystallized in popular culture as an antidote to modernization and its incumbent evils. As an effective elixir it had to expel from the region what could potentially be viewed as sexual and gender perversions, that is, the unsettling sexual and gender maladies increasingly associated with the modern age. Eliminating from the history of the Great Plains and West a reality that had only later become troubling, retrospectively imposed on the past a constructed woman-hood for cross-dressers that previously had not existed.

As noted near the beginning of this essay, one strain in the serious scholar-ship of later times has also attempted to clear from the cross-dressing past explanations for it that include gender and sexual identity. The reigning para-digm in this scholarship, known as the progress narrative, holds that the woman changed her clothing in order to obtain benefits not open to her be-cause of her sex, most notably gainful employment and in particular because she had a family to support.[23] Certainly, ample evidence supports the progress narrative. For example, E. J. Guerin supposedly took to male clothing and behavior precisely because a scoundrel known only as Jamieson murdered her husband on a Mississippi riverboat and left her a penniless single mother. "It was to dress myself in male attire," Guerin explained, "and seek a living in this disguise among the avenues which are so closed to my sex." "I had learned no trade," she continued, "and besides this, I knew how great are the prejudices to be overcome by any young woman who seeks to earn an honest livelihood by her own exertions." In another instance, newly freed slave Cathy Williams be-came William Cathay and joined the Buffalo Soldiers in 1866. Over the next few years she marched some thousand miles back and forth across the central and southern plains and was stationed awhile in New Mexico. As Williams explained to a St. Louis newspaper in 1876, "a cousin and a particular friend, members of the regiment . . . were partly the cause of my joining the army. Another reason was I wanted to make my own living and not be dependent on relations or friends."[24] That so many women appeared in male clothing while engaged in driving cattle across the plains or prospecting for gold offers ad-ditional and quite compelling evidence that supports the progress narrative.

Nonetheless, it seems plausible that some of these women who dressed as men on the plains and in the West in the latter part of the nineteenth century likely did so because they desired to satisfy feelings of gender and sexual dif-ference. The best way to demonstrate this is through the unusual case of Old Nash, a man who became a woman and worked as a laundress for Custer's Seventh Cavalry in Dakota Territory in the 1870s. Old Nash's story has come down to us through several popular firsthand sources. Elizabeth Bacon Custer's *"Boots and Saddles"* (1885) is the best known. The other major docu-ments are Katherine Gibson Fougera's *With Custer's Cavalry* (1940) and Gwendolin Damon Wagner's *Old Neutriment* (1934). Fougera constructed her book from the memoirs of her mother, Katherine Gibson, the widow of a captain in the Seventh Cavalry. It is written in the first person, as though by Gibson rather than Fougera. Wagner's *Old Neutriment* preserves the reminiscences of John Burkman, who served as Custer's orderly for nine years. Because these sources conflict on many particulars we may never get a completely accurate picture of Old Nash. They concur, however, on a number of major biographical points. Old Nash was Mexican. She joined the Seventh Cavalry to work as a laundress in about 1869, although Custer claims that she had first become aware of Old Nash while stationed in Kentucky, which was in 1871. In addition to laundering, Nash often performed midwifery for the women of the Seventh. She married at least three men in the company. It was only when she died in Dakota Territory in 1878 and her friends prepared her body for burial, as Custer explained, that "[t]he mystery which the old creature had guarded for so many years, through a life always public and conspicuous, was revealed: 'Old Nash'" was a man.[25]

The story of Old Nash subverts the rationale of the progress narrative. In this case, a cross-dresser gave up male privilege to become a woman. On the other hand, it may be that a man chose to become a woman at this place and time because certain benefits did await him. Some evidence in Old Nash's case supports this contention. According to Elizabeth Custer, Nash had become "weary of the laborious life of a man," and instead found that of the laundress easier.[26] Perhaps, but the lot of the laundress was far from undemanding. In addition to traveling over rough western trails, enduring remarkable want, and risking life and limb smack dab in the midst of the Indian wars, the actual work of the laundress required incredible strength and stamina. She had to wrestle bulky thirty-five-pound oak tubs, sometimes carry water over great distances, perhaps manufacture her own soap from caustic substances, scrub over a washboard, stir heavily soaked woolens and linens, chop and haul firewood, wield hot and heavy irons, mend clothing, and then take several days of the week to see the entire process (soaking, scrubbing, ringing, rinsing, bluing, starching, and drying) from beginning to end.[27] The laundresses of Fort Abraham Lincoln, Dakota Territory, which is where Old Nash's story unfolded, did all this while perched on a barren wind-swept plain—blistering hot in summer and arctic-like in winter! This was hardly an alternative for one "weary of the laborious life of a man," as Elizabeth Custer put it.

But economics might have played a role in Old Nash's choice to become a woman, for women as women could find the frontier a lucrative place and, within the context of the western army anyway, they could potentially earn more than men (this of course leaves open the question, why give up the prosperity they might enjoy as women in the West in order to become men, particularly in the army, as did Buffalo Soldier Cathy Williams?). In the third quarter of the nineteenth century the salary for enlisted men ranged from

$13 a month for the lowly private to as much as $34 for certain noncommissioned officers. On the other hand, a laundress might earn at a rate of from $1 to $5 a month per soldier and officer for whom she toiled. Each laundress washed for nineteen men.[28] Old Nash likely exceeded the uppermost limits that a laundress collected because officers' wives, generally from a higher class and having been dependent on servants back East to tend more menial chores, constantly reconnoitered for scarce workers such as Old Nash at western posts. "[W]hen the women of the garrison discovered her artistry in laundering delicate materials," Katherine Gibson's memoirs claim of Old Nash, "the enlisted men's washing knew her no more. Not only had she all she could do for the officers' families at [Fort] Lincoln, but some indiscreet woman had whispered the secret to the officers' wives of the infantry post as well, which brought her an avalanche of work." Even the Custers took advantage of Old Nash's competence. "She was our laundress," Elizabeth once noted, "and when she brought the linen home, it was fluted and frilled so daintily that I considered her a treasure."[29]

In the case of Nash, officers' wives and other women at Fort Lincoln also demanded her midwifery skills, which apparently kept her hopping. John Burkman later recalled that Old Nash "was a good nurse too, allus in demand to chase the rabbit when some woman was expectin' a baby." "[F]ew births occurred without her expert help," another observer explained. "She was a careful midwife, no less an embryo trained nurse, and she handled those babies not only with efficiency but with marked tenderness as well." While Fort Lincoln, like other army posts, employed a surgeon, midcentury physicians, particularly in the West, either had little formal training in their profession or, even if they did, generally lacked developed obstetrical skills. One historian discovered, for example, that as late as 1878 most physicians listed in the Wichita, Kansas, business directory did not even have medical degrees. And Fort Lincoln's "young surgeon" of the 1870s, according to Elizabeth Custer, "was wholly inexperienced in" delivering babies. In any case, the poor reputation of western doctors led many, whether pregnant women or no, to call them only at last resort.[30]

Rather, at army posts women tended other women in their time of need, just as they had done for centuries. Typically, laundresses rather than officers' wives performed this role, partly because they had ample experience giving birth themselves. Many post laundresses, though single, had children, in part because some also added to their coffers by working as prostitutes. Historian Anne M. Butler discovered for Fort Russell, Wyoming, in 1870 that of the nineteen single laundresses living there, seventeen had children. Obviously

Old Nash had not given birth herself (although as part of her ruse she claimed to have had two children who died in Mexico), but as Custer related, not surprisingly in light of Butler's findings, she did have "constant practice among the camp women."[31] Practiced she was. Old Nash claimed to have learned midwifery from her mother. This is plausible as the *partera*, or midwife, tradition of northern Mexico often generationally passed from female to female within the same family. But seeing that Old Nash was biologically a male, he may have simply learned from observation as a boy, for Mexican children were not always excluded from the event. In any case, pregnant women generally preferred midwives over doctors as the former were also expected to perform other duties that the latter would not, for example housecleaning, cooking, and even minding the other children, should they exist. Thus, when the officer wife friend of Elizabeth Custer, known only as Annie, hired Old Nash to attend her during the latter stages of her pregnancy, the laundress cared for her charge over the course of several days, only returning to her cabin in the evening to cook for her husband. During her time with Custer's friend, Old Nash proved to be "as skilful a physician as she was a nurse," and also seems to have bathed and dressed the newborn, until Custer herself developed the skills that permitted her to take over. In all, serving as midwife for Annie proved additionally profitable for Old Nash, for when she ended her duties, she departed "a richer woman by much gratitude and a great deal of money."[32]

Like the enlisted men for this period, laundresses with the army tended to be from the poorer and immigrant classes, especially the Irish. But laundresses in the West, and particularly with the army, also included Indians, African Americans, and Mexicans, like Old Nash.[33] Army wages might be seen as attractive to such women; so too the fact that as officially recognized members of the army the government also supplied them, however dismal these might be, with daily rations, quarters, bedding, fuel, transportation, and medical attention.[34] Moreover, they might earn money in a variety of ways beyond their official duties and as midwives. For example, because the fare of the enlisted men proved routine and limited, laundresses could also gain income, especially on payday, by cooking, baking, and selling their culinary creations to hungry, deprived, and momentarily flushed soldiers. Old Nash appropriately availed herself of this opportunity, often baking pies for Fort Lincoln's men. Her tamales were also the rage: even people as far away as Bismarck, one source averred, conceded them to be the best.[35]

Old Nash's skills as a seamstress likely provided her yet another source of income. Inhabitants of Fort Lincoln noted her sewing expertise—for example, in how she deftly refashioned the uniform of her last husband, Sergeant John Noonan, to display to full "advantage his well-proportioned figure." The demand and therefore potential earning capability of one adept at stitching and fitting in the western army of the 1860s and 1870s should not be undervalued. Up until the mid-1870s, most uniforms were bulky leftovers from the Civil War that enlisted men had to pay to be tailored. Old Nash did not reserve her sewing talents for army uniforms. She also salted away "stores of silk and woollen stuffs" and even laid her hands on "pink tarletan," all of which she fashioned into "gauzy, low-necked gowns" and veils that she wore to soldiers' balls.[36]

Reportedly, Old Nash found the life of a laundress, seamstress, midwife, and even chef for the Seventh Cavalry lucrative. According to Elizabeth Custer, Old Nash married three times during her time in the Seventh. Her popularity with the men in part can be attributed to her cooking skills, which one source used to account for her first marriage to a sergeant with a weakness for Mexican tamales, on which he grew fat and lazy. But also her popularity came from her remarkable enterprise and keen ability to make and save her earnings. At the time of Old Nash's passing, a Bismarck newspaper claimed that she was worth $10,000. One of her husbands had once reportedly boasted, "with the money that his wife was making, he intended, when his enlistment expired, to purchase a ranch and join the army of pioneers." Regrettably for Old Nash, her financial success also brought heartache, for apparently her first two husbands, once they obtained possession of her hard-earned money, in one case "several hundred dollars," deserted her.[37]

It is difficult to reconcile these fantastic accounts of Old Nash's cupidity and style in 1870s Dakota Territory with general assessments of the laundress's lot. "Laundresses lived in hovels without a single amenity," historian Anne M. Butler once described. "Their provisions minimal, their treatment grotesque, it seemed incomprehensible that anyone would willingly pursue the life of a military laundress."[38] But Old Nash soldiered on. She had a remarkable talent, for example, in transforming her otherwise dismal frontier quarters into delightful accommodations, quarters that were otherwise wretched. They might range from gunnysack-covered barrel staves to dugouts to tents. The laundresses at Fort Lincoln, however, benefited from the somewhat better appointed cabin, which Nash completely made over. "[W]e found the little place shining," Elizabeth Custer related. "The bed was hung with pink cambric . . . bits of carpet were on the floor, and the dresser, improvised out of a packing-box, shone with polished tins." Old Nash also applied her skills to occasionally transforming the otherwise drab Fort Lincoln dining hall into a festive pavilion for soldiers' dances, "darting up and down ladders, stringing bright-colored cheesecloth draperies here and there."[39]

Even with the financial and other benefits that life as an army laundress might conceivably bring, would a man likely choose such work and live as a woman? That Old Nash was a seemingly unique character helps answer this question. Moreover, westering men resolutely hated doing laundry, for example. When on their own, they sometimes waited three months to attend to this despised task. In other cases, particularly in gold rush areas, they might simply discard grubby garb and replace it with freshly purchased store-bought ready-mades. More than simply dreading the chore of washing, as Joan Wang aptly phrased it, men "have typically avoided doing laundry for reasons beyond its difficulty or triviality. The man who washed beside a washtub or picked up an iron took the risk of unsexing himself." This accounts for the occupation remaining women's work and then becoming racialized with the forced entry of Chinese men into the trade on the western frontier.[40]

So why then might a man become a laundress on the Great Plains during the third quarter of the nineteenth century? It may be, as Elizabeth Custer claimed, that Old Nash tired "of the laborious life of a man." Though this seems unlikely considering what he risked to lose and the fact that laundresses lives were equally, if not more laborious. Another story, this one re-created by Katherine Gibson Fougera from her mother's memoirs, claimed that Old Nash had actually been a political fugitive who fled north from Mexico. He disappeared from south of the border just when a certain Sergeant Nash happened to be stationed in the Southwest. As the story goes, one day "a swarthy man disguised as a woman approached" Sergeant Nash and bribed him into marriage. For the Mexican, the union would provide protection under the American flag. For the sergeant, in addition to the bribe, certain advantages awaited him: "Married soldiers enjoyed more freedom. . . . They were given individual quarters and did not have to eat in the barracks; moreover, their wives were permitted to work as domestics . . . thereby swelling the family exchequer." And, of course, this sergeant adored Mexican cooking.[41]

Because they differ so, it is impossible for both Custer's and Fougera's accounts to be wholly accurate. Likely neither is. In the former case, Old Nash had explained her history to Custer when Custer believed Nash to be a woman. Old Nash merely related some of her biographical details, including that she had at one time dressed "as a man in order to support herself by driving the ox-teams over the plains to New Mexico."[42] Only after the coming of the railroad threw her out of this line of work did she change back into her *original* woman's clothing. This, of course, does not speak to why Old Nash initially changed into a woman. Moreover, as we have seen, the life of an army laundress hardly provided a vacation from wearisome toil. Fougera's story, told in 1940, bears a striking resemblance to later chronicles about women who dressed as men for reasons related to outlawry and (in this case the appearance of) romance. Not surprisingly, considering what has been learned, Fougera's story also pretty much excludes the possibility of sexual impropriety.

The progress narrative does not make sense as an explanation for Old Nash. Moreover, what should be made of her remarkable dexterity at sewing and fitting officer uniforms and even gauzy ballroom gowns of silk and tarletan; cooking Mexican tamales that gained a reputation far and wide; laundering and fluting to such perfection that officers' wives vied with each other over her services; and transforming dismal domiciles into cheery quarters and frontier dining halls into festive dance pavilions? Such honed talents, typically at the time associated with the feminine gender, suggest that Old Nash did not just one day decide to take on the garb of and pass as a man. She likely perfected these skills over many, many years. Probably as a child she began to live life as a member of the opposite sex. Extant sources do not reveal much about Old Nash's early life. If she had in fact lived as the opposite sex, we can only speculate as to how this might have happened. Perhaps her parents encouraged her. Being Mexican she might also have been closer to certain Native American traditions that countenanced the changing of genders for those who had such proclivities. Although it is unclear where she came from in Mexico, likely it was the northern portion of the country and possibly that area taken by the United States in 1848. Suggestively on this account, Custer did claim that Old Nash had worked the Santa Fe Trail. The borderlands were a particularly risky area in the mid-nineteenth century as Native American raiders, particularly Comanche, Apache, and Navajo, often abducted Mexicans, especially children, sometimes adopting them into their tribes, other times trading them to other Indians, or even selling them back to Mexico. Occasionally such captives lived for year as Indians and only later in life made their way back into Mexican settlements. It may have been through such a process that Old Nash became the opposite gender, for both Apache and Navajo did have a male-to-female transgender tradition, although they valued such individuals differently.[43]

There is also the pesky problem of Old Nash's marriages; they numbered three within about a decade of her time with the Seventh Cavalry. That they each included sexual relations we may never know, though certainly her last marriage to Corporal John Noonan did. In an interview with Noonan after Old Nash's death, a reporter from a Bismarck, Dakota Territory, newspaper asked the bereaved husband, "You were a husband . . . a husband with all that the name implies[?]" "I was," Noonan replied, but added that, "so help me God . . . the later revelations mystify me. I can't understand it. She told me once that she was about to make me happy by presenting me with a child."[44]

Certainly by the latter nineteenth century sexual relations between members of the male sex were not unusual in the American West (in fact, they commonly occurred among working-class men); neither were they unknown in the army. Moreover, a modern male homosexual subculture had emerged by this time in Mexico, including in the cities of its northern borderlands. This subculture included distinct gender roles and identities for its male participants who performed in different sexual capacities. The penetrated were otherwise considered effeminate. They behaved in various ways associated with the feminine gender and might also at times dress in women's clothing. Of course, it might be that Old Nash had originated in such a milieu, but just how far back into the history of nineteenth-century Mexico this subculture extended is difficult to know. Evidence suggests it only emerged in the Porfirian era. By the very early part of this period Old Nash had already reached adulthood (her birth date remains unknown); she died, apparently of appendicitis, in 1878.[45]

The best evidence would suggest that Old Nash took on the dress, behaviors, and persona of a woman for reasons of sexual and gender identity rather than for reasons consonant with the progress narrative. This compelling example casts strong doubt, then, on the progress narrative as a universal explanation for various women who dressed as men and crisscrossed the Great Plains in the latter part of the nineteenth century. It also provides an intellectual opening in which gender and sexual identity might be considered as motivational causes for women to cross-dress as men. It may be that the relatively permissive social dynamics of the plains and the West in this era attracted to it not just women who desired to take advantage of the economic possibilities that awaited them there by passing as a member of the opposite sex, but also women who felt that the region, at least for a time, allowed them greater freedom to express their feelings of gender and possibly sexual difference.

Of course, this was only for a time. Elizabeth Custer recalled of Old Nash that when she had attentively nursed her friend Annie in her hour of need, the laundress often gently approached her charge's bed to inquire, "'Are you comph?'—meaning comfortable." Sometime later, when Annie read the Bismarck newspaper dispatch that described Old Nash's death at Fort Lincoln in 1878, "her only comment," Custer disclosed, "was a reference to the Mexican's oft-repeated question to her, 'Poor old thing, I hope she is 'comph' at last.'"[46] Custer related this story in 1885 precisely at the moment when those increasingly not "comph" with the Great Plains cross-dressing history began to rewrite it, disguising for subsequent generations evidence for a gender and sexual past for this region considerably more complex than what has been remembered. While these revised histories of passion and banditry as explanations for cross-dressing on the plains continue to provide us with romantic escape from the complexity and disappointments of modern living, in the end they cloak the real experiences of a variety of men and women who sought refuge on and from the likewise harsh realities of the late-nineteenth-century North American plains.

# 7

# Mormon Women at Winter Quarters

DEE GARCEAU

Mary Parker Richards described a conversation she had with Mormon elder John Taylor in the spring of 1846 at Winter Quarters, as follows:

> I had to call at Bro Taylors and get some letter Papper. . . . [H]e told me he had promised all the Elders in Eng [England] that he would go and see their wives when he got back to the Camp. . . . [S]aid he I feel some afraid of going to see the Sisters for the truble is they all fall in love with me. I expect it is somewhat dangerous said I . . . but I should be happy to have you bring Sister T with you when you come to see me. [A]nd if I should happen to fall in love with you I will try to keep it to my self.[1]

Mary Richards's dry wit and ready riposte are not ordinarily what come to mind when characterizing mid-nineteenth-century Mormon women. Mormons refer to their forebears in the epic migration West as "saints" and are likely to characterize the women as devout, self-sacrificing, or enduring. But the diaries of women at Winter Quarters tell another story, one that complicates the narrative of Mormon migration. They suggest that in a transient community of exiles where women outnumbered men, Mormon women expanded the boundaries of female self-expression and contested the reach of patriarchal authority over their daily lives.

Consider the circumstances of women's lives at Winter Quarters from 1846 to 1848. Mormon society in the 1840s was governed by a dense web of social controls that ordered daily behavior. Within its hierarchies, only men held positions of formal political and religious authority. Obedience to church elders was expected of all converts, men and women alike. At Winter Quarters, the need to impose order intensified, for this was a gathering of refugees who had fled from Nauvoo, Illinois, under threat of mob violence from non-Mormons. Displaced and dispossessed, Mormon exiles were pushed to their limits by poverty, profound loss, and an uncertain future. Winter Quarters became a way station on the Missouri River where they built lodging, grew crops, and prepared for their journey to a mysterious Zion, farther west.[2]

Mormons occupy a paradoxical position in western history, as both a persecuted minority and as colonizers who invaded Native American lands, dispersed missionaries to expand their influence, and enforced hierarchies of race that subordinated people of color.[3] To establish Winter Quarters, they negotiated an agreement with the Omahas to camp on the west bank of the Missouri River near present-day Omaha, Nebraska, "for two years or more" on some six hundred to eight hundred acres, "drained on the north and south by two creeks and bounded on the north and west with high bluffs." Here, the plains fell away in low swells carpeted with buffalo grass, grama grass, and bluestem grasses. Mormons could graze their livestock, draw water from the creeks, and travel by river if necessary. They promised to leave their buildings intact for Omaha use when they left, and assured the Omahas they would not use up the available timber.[4] For Mormons, the grasslands at Winter Quarters promised rest and respite from persecution. But this plains encampment quickly became more than a place to regroup. Far from the scrutiny of Gentile communities, Winter Quarters became a blank slate on which Mormons wrote their evolving notions of a religious utopia. Much has been written about the evolution of Mormon theocracy and contests over power at Winter Quarters. But few have noted that this was a gendered process.

Winter Quarters was not a democratic community, though Mormon men sometimes voted to endorse their leaders' decisions. Rather, it was a theocracy in which church patriarchs wielded executive power. Church leaders such as Brigham Young, Heber Kimball, Orson Hyde, and Wilford Woodruff delivered edicts, expected obedience, and threatened "disfellowship," or expulsion from the church, for those who failed to keep covenants. The church fathers' control reached well into everyday life. Apostles, the elite cadre of church leaders, instructed wives whose husbands were away on missions not to complain about missing them. Apostles lectured men to quit swearing and to stop their petty squabbling. Apostles chided women for wanting nicer households than their sod shanties. Apostles declared that men must tithe ten percent of their labor to the church or they would not be allowed to go West. Apostles reviewed requests to hold dances and approved those that served a religious purpose. Under these tight controls, women and men pursued their daily routines at Winter Quarters.[5]

Not only did church fathers promote obedience to authority, but they were very specific regarding women. Mormon theology preached the subjugation of wives to their husband's will. As Apostle Heber Kimball put it, "I am subject to my God, my wife is in subjection to me and will reverence me in my place."[6] Kimball articulated a hierarchical order with God at the top, under whose authority were men, who in turn, ruled over women. According to Kimball, women were created to serve men; man was "covenanted to keep the law of God," and woman "to obey her husband."[7]

> The man was created, and God gave him dominions over the whole earth. But he saw that he never could multiply, and replenish the earth, without a woman. And he made one and gave her to him. He did not make the man for the woman; but the woman for the man, and *it is just as unlawful for you to rise up and rebel against your husband, as it would be for man to rebel against God.*[8] [emphasis mine]

These teachings applied to all women; female deference to male authority was also expected from daughters toward their fathers and from sisters toward their adult brothers.

Against the background of patriarchal hierarchy, the experience of persecution and exile from Nauvoo in 1845 distilled the Mormon population into a community of believers. Under duress, those who harbored doubts left the church, and those who stayed affirmed their commitment to its doctrines. The converts who emigrated to Winter Quarters during the late 1840s were, for the most part, devoted followers.[9] Under these circumstances, one might expect women at Winter Quarters to faithfully apply the Mormon doctrine of submission to male authority in their daily lives. Instead, women at Winter Quarters left the impress of their humanity on a seemingly rigid social order. That is, they appropriated priesthood authority beyond official sanction, challenged patriarchal assumptions about women in their speech and writing, and expanded the scope of fictive kin ties to suit their purposes. Indeed, women's contestation of patriarchal power at Winter Quarters deserves a closer look.

Much has been written about Winter Quarters; in recent years historians have combed through firsthand narratives to piece together the nature of emigrant life there. We know, for example, that Mormons in flight from Nauvoo scattered across Iowa Territory in numerous temporary encampments, from Sugar Creek to Garden Grove to Mount Pisgah to Winter Quarters. By December of 1846, Winter Quarters boasted a population of 3,483, living in a hastily laid-out city of forty-one narrow blocks. Nearly eight hundred dwellings crowded these blocks, ranging in quality from one apostle's elegant "Octagon House" to one-room log cabins, sod dugouts, shanties, tents, and wagons. Illness plagued the exiles; scurvy, malaria, and pneumonia claimed more than five hundred lives in a two-year period. The prairie town was further decimated when the US Army recruited Mormon men to serve in the Mexican War. By the end of 1848, Winter Quarters housed only 747 men and 2,736 women and children. Women outnumbered men by more than 2:1.[10]

In a study of Winter Quarters, 1841 to 1852, Richard Bennett identifies it as the place where Brigham Young consolidated his leadership in the wake of Joseph Smith's assassination. There, Young and other apostles centralized church administration as they organized and coordinated the exiles' migration West. In an essay on Mormon migration to Utah, Stanley Kimball argues that the overland experience, including hardships at Winter Quarters, intensified social cohesion among the emigrants. In an investigation of women's work among Mormon emigrants in the mid-nineteenth century, Maureen Ursenbach Beecher finds that women engaged in home production of clothing and foodstuffs, within a local economy of exchange in which they traded household goods, tools, labor, and services on a daily basis. As in preindustrial rural communities, women's "visiting" sustained families. Frequent calls to each other's homes kept women connected through social networks that blended barter, health care, and emotional support.[11] Finally, numerous Mormon memoirs present their ancestors' trek west as an epic journey of faith and fortitude. These are celebratory accounts, which emphasize the theme of triumph over adversity for those who reached the Salt Lake valley.[12]

Few, however, have examined the historic significance of Winter Quarters for women. A handful of scholars mention Winter Quarters as a place of improvisation, where women expanded the boundaries of self-expression within a culture known for its strict behavioral orthodoxy. Maureen Beecher and Richard Bennett, for example, both observe that Mormon women at Winter Quarters exercised powers of the priesthood such as blessing others, prophesying, speaking in tongues, and healing the sick by laying on of hands. Although Joseph Smith, founder of the Mormon church, had approved the use of "gifts of the spirit" for men and women alike, Mormon theology formally identified men as the proper conduits for God's authority and power. Many Mormons at Winter Quarters disapproved of women's exercise of priesthood authority, saying it was "all of the devil," and "out of bounds."[13] In short, women's exercise of priesthood power at Winter Quarters calls for further investigation.

Another element of women's increasing self-assertion at Winter Quarters is evident in women's writing. In an analysis of Mormon midwife Patty Sessions's diary, Elizabeth Willis argues that Sessions's journal became a site of literary improvisation, where a devout Mormon wife registered her struggle with plural marriage and experimented with irony and black humor. Willis attributes Sessions's experimental literary voice to the makeshift nature of life on the road, which included Sessions's sojourn at Winter Quarters. Notably, Willis finds that Sessions's experimental voice was gradually silenced "within the masterfully organized state of Deseret."[14] Willis overlooks the fact that Sessions recorded actual conversations she had had, which also reflect Sessions's "voice" in daily speech. Willis's insights and Sessions's diary call for further study of Winter Quarters as a watershed in Mormon women's self-expression, spoken as well as written.

In addition, scholars who trace the evolution of Mormon social structure point to innovations in family organization that surfaced at Winter Quarters. They identify Winter Quarters as the place where polygamy became an open practice. In a demographic study of Mormon marriages, 1841–1846, George Smith suggests that the practice of plural marriage in Nauvoo provided the model for polygamy at Winter Quarters, where practitioners brought it into the open.[15] Most startling in Smith's essay is the data showing that some Mormon women had more than one husband under the doctrine of plural marriage.[16] Indeed, marital ties took a variety of forms among mid-nineteenth-century Mormons.

According to the doctrine of celestial marriage, there were two kinds of marriage: marriage "for time" and marriage "for eternity." A man and woman who married "for time" solemnized their union legally as well as spiritually, and they committed to a loving partnership for the duration of their lifetimes. A couple who married "for eternity" were not always legally united. Instead, they underwent a religious ceremony that "sealed" them together for the afterlife. Mid-nineteenth-century Mormon cosmology posited an exalted afterlife called the celestial kingdom, where righteous men could eventually become gods. One step toward attaining godlike status in the afterlife was for a man to take plural wives during his own lifetime, in imitation of biblical patriarchs. As historian George Smith explained it, "a woman's salvation depended on entering into a polygamous relationship with a man of high status in the church, because such men were thought to have made the greatest progress toward godhead on earth."[17] Thus, some women who already had married one husband "for time," married a second husband, a church leader, "for eternity." For example, Zina Huntington married Henry Jacobs for time, and several years later she was sealed to Joseph Smith for eternity. Likewise, Mary Elizabeth Rollins married Adam Lightner for time and later was also sealed to Joseph Smith for eternity.[18]

Though polygamous Mormon men often lived with several wives in one household, polyandrous Mormon women did not live with multiple husbands. After her celestial marriage to Joseph Smith, for example, Mary Lightner Smith continued to live with Adam Lightner. The Lightners had eight children together. Still, the practice of plural marriage sometimes left gray areas regarding with whom a wife lived. Nancy Marinda Johnson first married Orson Hyde, but when he left on a mission, she was sealed to Joseph Smith. At that point, she moved out of Hyde's home to a household chosen by Smith, which he presumably visited. Once husband Hyde returned, Nancy Marinda Hyde Smith returned to living with Orson Hyde.[19]

Thus marriage for eternity did not always entail the sustained intimacy of living together, sharing sexual relations, providing for a household, or raising children. Eliza Roxcy Snow, for example, was sealed to Joseph Smith for eternity in 1842, then to Brigham Young for eternity in 1846. Snow had no children with Joseph Smith, and she carried on a distant, perfunctory relationship with Brigham Young. In Snow's case, celestial marriage held the promise of an exalted afterlife but brought little partnership on earth.[20] A common pattern for church leaders such as Joseph Smith, Brigham Young, and Heber Kimball was to be sealed to as many as forty women, but to share quarters with only three or four of those wives. Additional wives boarded with other families.[21] For these women, celestial marriage to a church leader raised their status, social and spiritual, but lacked the comforts of daily intimacy.

On the other hand, some celestial marriages did combine the promise of the afterlife with daily partnership in the present. Households presided over by one husband with three or four wives were the ones that raised the eyebrows of non-Mormons and brought scandal and persecution to the Mormons. Winter Quarters offered relief from the judgment of non-Mormons. In this plains encampment of none but believers, households headed by one husband with several wives became an accepted fact of life.[22] Women at Winter Quarters would comment to each other, to their husbands, and in their journals how they disliked sharing a husband with other wives "for time," though none questioned the bond "for eternity."

If plural marriage was the most notorious of family structures among mid-nineteenth-century Mormons, it was not their only variation on family ties. The emigrants at Winter Quarters organized themselves into a bewildering array of quasi-familial associations. Whether to facilitate migration or to ease the pains of dislocation, Mormons created four kinds of fictive kin. First, unrelated men and women routinely referred to each other as Brother and Sister, as we saw in Mary Parker Richards's diary when she wrote about "Brother Taylor," and "Sister T." Occasionally, an elder woman like midwife Patty Sessions might also be called "Mother Sessions" by the women she ministered to. Similarly, elder men who held positions of respect in the community might sometimes be called "Father" by unrelated acquaintances. Not unique to Mormon society, these familial terms probably reinforced a sense of belonging and, in daily discourse, alluded to the group's shared religious purpose. Perhaps this helped to build community among converts from disparate regions or socioeconomic backgrounds. In any case, the journals of Mormon emigrants read like the chronicles of one giant family, with "Brother," "Sister," "Mother," and "Father" as terms of daily address.[23]

A second form of fictive kin had practical application. To organize their migration west, Brigham Young divided the emigrants into companies of tens, fifties, and hundreds. The smallest units, the tens, were ordered to function cooperatively like a family, whether or not they were blood relatives. Sharing wagons and "mess," each company of ten would rely on its members to cook, stand guard, drive oxen, and the like. Family-style loyalty to one's company was intended to prevent potential shirkers from incurring resentment and breeding discord.[24]

A third quasi-familial category occurred with the practice of stand-ins for religious ceremonies. Sometimes a Mormon patriarch pledged to wed a plural wife for eternity, but the disruptions of exile and migration prevented him from attending the actual "sealing" ceremony. In these cases, if a woman pressed to go forward with the celestial union, then another man, sanctioned by church leaders, could stand in for the missing groom. The stand-in went through the ceremony with the bride so that the union was solemnized. Patty Sessions, for example, married Joseph Smith for eternity in 1846 without benefit of a temple ceremony. In 1867, Sessions requested that the ceremony be redone in a temple, though by then Joseph Smith was long dead. Joseph F. Smith, the groom's nephew, stood in for the deceased at the 1867 ceremony. Mormons referred to the practice of substituting a living person for a deceased one, for ritual purposes, as "by proxy." Thus Patty Sessions was sealed "by proxy" to Joseph Smith in the 1867 temple ceremony. After 1894, the practice of plural marriage for eternity to revered church authorities was discontinued. In its place, Mormon leaders called for children to be sealed to their parents for eternity, going back through the generations as far as one's ancestry could be traced, uniting extended families in the afterlife. For the ritual of sealing ancestors in a temple ceremony, living relatives could stand in for the dead, making the ceremony complete by proxy. In this practice, stand-ins became fictive kin only for the duration of the ceremony.[25]

Fourth, and most intriguing, the Mormon "law of adoption" created fictive kin who provided converts with another route into celestial heaven. As historian Gordon Irving noted, Mormon doctrine held that apostles like Brigham Young or Heber Kimball "were somehow directly related, by blood," to the royal lineage of the ancient patriarchal order, and thus destined for exaltation in the afterlife. Through "adoption" by such a patriarch, ordinary men, men not related by blood to the biblical patriarchs, could still make their way to celestial heaven. The practice of adoption resonated with Mormon men, perhaps bolstering their security in a chaotic world by affiliation with a powerful father figure. In the wake of traumatic exile from Nauvoo, many men sought adoption as "sons" by one of the Quorum of Twelve, the recognized patriarchs of the Mormon church. Orson Hyde, one of the Twelve, "invited as many of the unattached as he could to become adopted sons in his family."[26] Brigham Young, Wilford Woodruff, and Heber Kimball each adopted about forty "sons." Over time, the law of adoption was abandoned, but at Winter Quarters, the practice flourished among men.[27] Little is known, however, about how women negotiated the law of adoption for their own benefit at Winter Quarters.

Historians' work to date thus invites further questions about women's experience at Winter Quarters. There is more to be revealed about Mormon women's appropriation of spiritual authority, self-assertion through the spoken and written word, and negotiation of family ties, both marital and with fictive kin.

Patty Sessions was fifty-one years old in 1846 when she and her husband reached Winter Quarters. She had left behind three adult children in Illinois, two others had died, and she missed them all. Added to the stresses of separation from her children were the strains of a plural marriage. Her husband, David Sessions, had taken a second wife, Rosilla. Patty and Rosilla shared a household at Winter Quarters, but the two women shared little else. They disliked each other, though Patty tried to work cooperatively with her sister-wife. Rosilla, a headstrong young woman in her twenties, would have none of it. Patty sought solace in prayer meetings with other women and in her work as a midwife.[28] She also kept a daily journal. "The Sessions diary," writes Elizabeth Willis, "is self-expression beyond the utilitarian"; it reflected Sessions's need to define the significance of her experience "independent of values pre-scribed by any totalizing system."[29] That is, Sessions validated her authentic voice within the diary, recording her spoken resistance to an unhappy plural marriage, and marking the spiritual authority she claimed as a midwife.

Rosilla Sessions was every plural wife's nightmare: she was openly hostile and disrespectful toward Patty Sessions; she spread rumors that Patty mis-treated her; she refused to do her share of household work; and she tried to turn David Sessions against Patty.[30] Mormon church fathers counseled for-bearance on the part of first wives toward younger sister-wives. The patriar-chal assumption was that first wives could accept and adjust to the presence of sister-wives in their households.[31] Throughout the fall of 1846, Patty Ses-sions tried repeatedly to make peace with Rosilla and to get her to do her share of the household work, but the young woman responded with insults. "I went and tried to talk with her but she was very abusive toward me," Sessions wrote.[32] Perhaps Rosilla disliked plural marriage as much as Patty did. Ses-sions then enlisted her husband's help, which was difficult because David Ses-sions had sided with Rosilla and often distanced himself from Patty. Sessions recorded in detail her own, her husband's, and her sister-wife's behavior as the drama unfolded:

> Mr. Sessions and I had a talk with Rosilla she was very willful and obsti-nate. . . . I told her it was a big cud for me to swallow to let her come in after she had abused me so shamefuly. . . . [H]e [her husband, David Sessions] knew he had done wrong and abused me bad and he was sorry. . . . I said if she come in I should be boss over the work and she must be carefull how she twisted and flung at me.[33]

Notably, Patty Sessions was unapologetic regarding her own direct objections to mistreatment; she was no model of forbearance. Indeed she was rapidly losing patience, and on November 2, 1846, she described the following con-frontation with Rosilla: "[S]he talked very saucy to me and when I could bear it no longer I told her to hold her toungue and if she gave me the lie again I would throug the tongs at her."[34] Here, too, she recorded her spoken words without apology or dissembling, and she rejected the martyrdom implied by church fathers' counsel on wifely behavior. Patty Sessions was fed up trying to keep house and provide for a sister-wife who would not shoulder her portion of the work, and she told her husband so. "He went and talked with her last night then wanted me to find provision for her to live some where else. I said I could do it but it was hard as old as I was to have to maintain her without work." When Patty Sessions refused to arrange lodging for Rosilla elsewhere, her husband got "mad and turned his back said . . . she [Rosilla] must have a living if she would not work."[35] But Patty held firm in refusing her husband's request that she find living quarters for the lazy and rude sister-wife. David Sessions realized he would have to find lodging for Rosilla if he wanted her to stay at Winter Quarters, so he arranged with "a woman close by" to house and board Rosilla in exchange for her help with housekeeping. Rosilla turned down this offer and instead tried to persuade David Sessions to run away to Maine with her and leave Patty at Winter Quarters. A terse entry on December 3, 1846, reveals the outcome of this conflict: "Rosilla started for Nauvoo."[36] David Sessions had been unable to find housing that pleased Rosilla, and she left the marriage, never to return.

In the end, Patty Sessions prevailed in her refusal to sacrifice dignity, household harmony, or work routines to the demands of a difficult sister-wife. Then, too, Rosilla effectively rejected a plural marriage that worked poorly for her as well. With hindsight, one can see that the two sister-wives had more in common than they realized. Both abhorred plural marriage and made this union fail. Like Rosilla, a substantial number of women expressed their resistance to plural marriage by leaving the relationship. Historian Lawrence Foster observes that among seventy-two Mormon church leaders who had a total of 391 wives, there were fifty-four divorces, twenty-six separations, and one annulment. He adds that it was primarily the wives who initiated divorce in these cases.[37] Patty Sessions expressed no regrets that her sister-wife, Rosilla, felt compelled to leave the marriage. Significantly, Sessions's diary contains no backpedaling from her final opposition to Rosilla and no ritual expressions of self-sacrifice to the cause of plural marriage. Instead, she reinforced with the written word what she had given voice to with the spoken word—her resistance to oppressive treatment at the hands of a sister-wife or a polygamous husband. Mormon women at Winter Quarters may have been devout believers who accepted the spiritual promise of plural marriage in eternity, but Patty and Rosilla Sessions were loath to accept its injustices in real time.

Patty Sessions's diary at Winter Quarters suggests that Mormon women renegotiated patriarchal order as they lived it. Indeed, Sessions was not the only one to validate spoken resistance with the written word. Like Sessions, Mary Parker Richards kept a diary of her sojourn at Winter Quarters, where she logged her opinions and feelings as well as daily activity. And like Sessions, Richards found her own objections to certain patriarchal assumptions newsworthy and duly recorded them.

Mary Haskin Parker, a youthful convert from England, migrated to the

Mormon "Zion" at Nauvoo in 1843. There she met, fell in love with, and married Samuel Richards. When mob violence drove the Mormons out of Nauvoo, Mary Parker Richards fled with her parents-in-law, Phineas and Wealthy Richards. Meanwhile, husband Samuel went overseas on a mission. Mary Richards's flight brought her to Winter Quarters in 1846, where she lodged with her parents-in-law but frequently stayed overnight with her sister-in-law Jane Richards as well. Mary's life at Winter Quarters, 1846–1848, was busy with social rounds. Visits, dances, rides, meetings, and more visits filled her days.[38]

Mary Richards was open and passionate about her love for Samuel. During his two-year absence she wrote him long, detailed letters peppered with declarations of affection. From a letter written May 26, 1846, with the heading, "Evening on the Praira": "Dear Samuel, I dreamed I was with you this morn. it is indeed pleasant to dream of you. but is not so to awake & find it a mistake." From a letter dated June 3, 1846: "Tis a beautyfull evening. wish you was here to take a walk with me." And from a letter written June 6, 1846: "I am very glad to hear that you are going to send me your likeness though would much rather see the Boy that wears the curl." Across the bottom of the page she wrote, "Thank you Samuel for the kiss you sent me and here is kisses for you" [dotted line drawn around the word *kisses*].[39]

Mary Richards's affectionate reveries were shattered when she received a letter from Samuel requesting that Mary arrange for him to marry a second wife. Specifically, Samuel asked Mary to speak with Ellen Wilding on his behalf and convince her to marry him when he returned from his mission.[40] Mary Richards wanted to please her husband by doing as he asked, but she recoiled from the prospect of sharing Samuel with another wife. Expressions of anger mixed with her love in a long, newsy reply to Samuel, penned July 15, 1846. Richards began by describing a party she had attended, and she listed every man with whom she had danced—Brother Littlefield, Robert Burton, William Cory, W. Hyde, W. Kimball, and even the august leader, Brigham Young. She followed this list of her admirers with a jab: "I expect by this time you will think I am pretty rude." Then she hastened to reassure him of her love: "[T]he recreations in which others enjoy themselfs afford but little comfort to me while he whom I love above all others is abcent from me."[41] Then she broached the issue of plural marriage:

> As regardes the request you asked of me concerning Ellen you know my
> dear. I have ever tried to do all that you desired me to. yea the love [the
> word *love* is crossed out] affection that dwells in this bosem to wards

you compels me to do it although it deprives me of the hopes of happiness for ever. I was in hopes that after your retorn you would have been contented to have lived with me alone for a little season. . . . if you had seen what I have seen. you would not wonder why I thus wrote for there is no such thing as happiness known here where a man has more than one [wife].[42]

Mary Richards expressed her commitment to her husband and to their marriage through her willingness to do as he asked. At the same time, her anger surfaced in the "rude" counting of her beaux to her absent husband and in crossing out the word *love* and replacing it with the more tepid *affection*. If in one line she acceded to his request, in another she wrote him the truth as she saw it: "[T]here is no such thing as happiness known here where a man has more than one." Like Patty and Rosilla Sessions, Mary Richards did not accept plural marriage with equanimity. Instead she pointed out the emotional costs in no uncertain terms. Like Sessions, Richards challenged the patriarchal complacency of Mormon husbands who assumed their first wives would willingly facilitate the addition of extra wives.

Sessions and Richards were not unique. Even plural wives connected to the most powerful church leaders at Winter Quarters criticized the practice. Richards's diary entry for February 10, 1847, mentioned "a very pleasant visit with Ellen [Helen Mar Whitney]":

> [S]he repeated some verses to me that her mother, Sister Kimball had composed the next morn after her little son Solomon was born. *the first verse is all* I *remember. it is as follows* "The Lord has blessed us with another Son / Which is the seventh I have Born / May he be the father of many lives. / *But not the Husband of many Wives.*" [emphasis hers][43]

The "Sister Kimball" whom Richards mentioned was Vilate Kimball, revered as a "Mother of Israel," sealed to Joseph Smith and married to church leader Heber Kimball. It is striking that she penned these lines, for she was known publicly as a model of Mormon female piety. Evidently this verse made the rounds among the female faithful, and no doubt provided relief, comfort, or laughter to those who struggled as plural wives.

Vilate Kimball may have limited her critique of polygamy to the company of women, but Mary Richards was not so circumspect. In a letter to husband

Samuel dated February 2, 1847, Richards commented on the breakup of her father's plural marriage: "[T]he knot that was tied between dady & sister Morse has slipt. so we find the key that locks will unlock."[44] Richards thus made the point to her husband that plural unions for eternity are vulnerable to dissolution in this life. In doing so, she implied that either her marriage to Samuel or perhaps his union with a second wife might not last. Again Mary Parker Richards challenged her husband's complacency regarding the difficulties of plural marriage for women. In short, Mary Richards's diary demonstrates her antipathy to polygamous marriage, and her letters indicate that she spoke her truths directly to her husband.

Plural marriage was not the only doctrine to raise the ire of Mormon women. Mary Richards engaged in verbal sparring with male elders, and she recorded these conversations in detail. Her diary entry for March 2, 1847, describes one such argument, worth quoting at length:

> I had a confab with father [her father-in-law, Phineas Richards] who undertook to make me beleve that Adam never transgressed . . . and that the Woman alone was under transgression. but the man was not. I then asked him why it was that man was Cursed if he had not transgressed . . . why it was. that he was to Eat of it in sorrow all the days of his life and get his bread by the sweat of his face. he [Mary's father-in-law] then read me a line from the Prophesy of Enock were it says. the Man was not deceived but the woman being deceived was in the transgression. this says I, does not prove to me the Man was not under transgression. if you should tell me I must not eat a sertin thing and I should go and *eat* that thing would I not have transgressed your commands & C & C.
>
> said he I did not tell you that man was not under transgression
> I most certainly understood you so, said I . . . I knew I was not mistaken.
> . . . our debate lasted More than an hour. Eve was sewing.[45]

Mary Richards deemed this verbal contest with her father-in-law over religious doctrine newsworthy, and she recorded it in full. Even more significant, Richards challenged the patriarchal tenet that Eve, or woman, was responsible for man's fall from grace. Instead, she saw human fallibility shared equally by women and men. Moreover, Richards's confidence in her own judgment about these matters surfaced with her concluding joke, "Eve was sewing," meaning she, Mary, had been sewing during this exchange.

As well as challenging patriarchal assumptions about women, Mary Richards noticed when other women stood up to male authority. When her sister-in-law Jane Snyder Richards defied insult from her father-in-law, Richards wrote, "[F]ather spoke some things that hort Jane's feelings. But she spoke noble in her own defence and made father draw in his horns."[46] Perhaps Richards recorded this family spat because a woman resisted verbal domination by an overbearing male relative and successfully stood her ground. Evidence like this suggests that at Winter Quarters, women like Jane and Mary Richards contested patriarchal authority when it offended their self-respect.

If some Mormon wives challenged men to rethink their assumptions about women, others asserted greater spiritual authority than that formally sanctioned by the church. Patty Sessions believed that women could act as conduits for God's wisdom and power, through speaking in tongues, prophesying, and laying on hands to heal the sick. Conventionally, such powers were attributed to the male priesthood, but at Winter Quarters, women claimed such powers and exercised them freely.

Patty Sessions routinely recorded her work as a healer of both physical and spiritual ills. "Went and laid hands on the widow Holman's step daughter," she wrote in March 1847; "she was healed."[47] In addition, Sessions also wrote about the women's prayer meetings she attended, where those present experienced "gifts of the spirit." Her diary entry for May 1, 1847, described a visit to Sister Leonard's: "[N]one but females there we had a good metting I presided. . . . they spoke in toungues I interpreted some prophesied it was a feast."[48] Sessions's phrases, "I presided," "I interpreted," and "some prophesied," indicate that some women felt empowered to hear, translate, and transmit words and energy from the divine. Sessions often gave these women's meetings more space in her diary than the Sunday meeting presided over by church fathers. On Sunday, February 14, 1847, for example, Sessions wrote, "[W]ent to meeting then in the evening collected Zina Jacobs, Eliza Snow, Sister Marcum at Sister Buels. . . . we prayed sung in toungues spoke in toungues and had a good time."[49] Though historians have acknowledged women's appropriation of spiritual authority at Winter Quarters, Sessions's enthusiasm for women's prayer meetings suggests that this phenomenon merits a closer look.

Patty Sessions described one meeting of women that approached ecstatic spiritual experience:

June 1, 1847

> We had a feast in the afternoon at sister Miller's . . . then we blessed
> and got blessed . . . layed my hands upon her [Sister Kimball's] head . . .
> and the power of God came upon me I spoke great and marvelous
> things to her she was filed to the overflowing She arose and blessed the
> Lord and called down a blessing on us and all that pertained to her,
> sister Hess fell on her knees and claimed a blessing at my hands I then
> blessed her sister Chase claimed a blessing of sister Kimbal she blessed
> her with me, she spoke great things to her the power of God was poured
> out upon us.[50]

The frequency and fervor of women's prayer meetings intensified just before
they left Winter Quarters to head for a "Zion" unknown to them. From
May 27 to June 4, 1847, the final week before their departure, Patty Sessions
and the women in her prayer circle met five times. Each time they gave full
expression to their spiritual voices, speaking in tongues, prophesying, and exchanging blessings. Though their women's prayer meetings would continue
on the road west, they would be far less frequent.[51]

It was during this time of intensified preparation for the trek westward
that Patty Sessions's female peers linked her spiritual authority to her role as
midwife. On May 29, 1847, Sessions "went to a meeting to Eliza Beamans with
many of the sisters." There,

> sisters Young and Whitney laid their hands upon my head and predict-
> ed . . . that I should live to stand in a temple yet to be built . . . *and there
> I should bless many and many should be brought unto me saying your
> hands were the first that handled me, bless me, and after I had blessed
> them their mothers would rise up and bless me.* [emphasis mine][52]

Sisters Young and Whitney's vision held that Patty Sessions's abundant spiritual powers grew out of her work as a midwife—it was the mothers she had
helped in childbirth, and the babies she had safely delivered, whom they predicted would confirm Sessions's spiritual authority by asking for, receiving,
and giving blessings. This is significant, for it represents a uniquely female vision of spiritual authority not formally sanctioned by church fathers.

Just as Patty Sessions's female prayer group took the role of visionaries, so
too did individual women at Winter Quarters claim the spiritual authority to

"see" beyond daily material existence. When Lucy Meserve Smith arrived at Winter Quarters in 1846 with a new baby, disease pocked the makeshift town. During the winter and spring, emigrants lost their sources of vitamin C, and scurvy wore them down. Meserve Smith wrote, "I took the scurvy not having any vegetables to eat. I got so low I must wean my babe and he must be fed on cornbread, when he was only five months old." When the baby's health failed, Meserve Smith wrote, "[M]y only child died I felt so overcome in my feelings I was afraid I would lose my mind."[53] Several months later, Lucy Meserve Smith experienced a vision in which three angels appeared by her bed and sang a hymn. "Then my little son appeared to me," she wrote,

> I tried to hug and kiss him but I felt no substance. . . . I said to him, "Why did you leave mother dear?" He answered . . . "Because I had a greater work to do somewhere else." I said, "God bless you dear," and he disappeared and left me as wide awake as I am at this moment.[54]

Whether one believes in such visitations or not, this event is telling in that Lucy Meserve Smith trusted her own capacity for spiritual vision. Her conversation with her deceased son helped her to come to terms with his death; it was "a great consolation to me," she wrote. Like Sessions, Meserve Smith marked her connection to the divine by recording the visionary incident in her diary. And like Sessions's female prayer group, she validated her intense religious experience outside the orbit of male priesthood authority.

Women's improvisations at Winter Quarters also included seeking privileges associated with "adoption" by a church patriarch. Recall that the law of adoption was practiced by men at Winter Quarters who wanted to become "sons" of church fathers. Not only did adoption by a church leader promise access to celestial heaven, but it also brought rewards on earth. Historian Gordon Irving observed that "adoption gave one special status."[55] That is, attachment to Brigham Young's, Heber Kimball's, or another apostle's family meant greater social prestige and better housing at Winter Quarters. According to Richard Bennett, "Winter Quarters was apportioned along family lines, with Young's division occupying most of the center of town, Heber Kimball's company in the more southerly neighborhoods, Wilford Woodruff and his forty families occupying one block . . . and Cutler's clan along the riverbanks."[56] The Young, Kimball, Woodruff, and Cutler families, which included fictive kin by the law of adoption, had the better cabins. Those left outside the apostles' extended families camped on the peripheries, in tents, wagons, and shanties, or dug into the bluffs. These dwellings offered poorer shelter than the roofed cabins with paned windows enjoyed by some of the apostles and their kin. Not surprisingly, men at Winter Quarters "scrambled to gain acceptance into one or another of the greater families."[57]

Although it was men who typically sought the advantages of adoption, some women at Winter Quarters also pursued adoption, or something resembling it. Eliza Roxcy Snow yearned for a place in Heber Kimball's fictive family. She did not need adoption by Kimball to enter celestial heaven, since she already numbered among Brigham Young's plural wives. Her spiritual marriage to Young brought few temporal benefits, however, except for the intangible of status as a "Mother of Israel." In daily life, Snow neither lived with Young nor partook of his wealth. Instead, she was forced to live with the Markhams, a married couple whose family discord wore on Snow's nerves.[58] Meanwhile, her closest friends included Sarah Kimball, and she "dreamed of being in elder K's mess."[59] Fortunately for Snow, as Kimball organized his company for the journey west, the Markham household—including Snow— was included among his "fifty."[60] Now that she claimed membership in Kimball's company, Snow took matters into her own hands, and boldly asked for adopted status within his fictive family:

> Elder Kimball was passing my "study" today when after the usual compliments, I told him as I was number'd among his children, I wished to know if he would acknowledge me as one. He said he would.[61]

Once Kimball affirmed Snow's place in his family, she pressed for more:

> I told him that I should claim a *father's blessing*. He said he would give me one. I asked when? To which he replied "*now*" I told him I was ready; he said to me then, "*A father's blessing shall rest upon you from this time forth*." [emphasis hers][62]

"From this time I call him *father*," she wrote with satisfaction [emphasis hers].[63]

Having established fictive kin ties to the Heber Kimball clan, Eliza Snow began to reap the benefits. Two months later, she wrote, "[M]ov'd into a house

built of logs. . . . we find ourselves very comfortably & commodiously situat-
ed."[64] Snow continued to enjoy the social and material benefits that came with
membership in the Kimball family. In February 1847 she described a party at
which one hundred assembled guests, including extended and fictive family
members, "supp'd at a table that would have done honor to a better cultivated
country."[65]

Eliza Snow may be the most well known woman who lived at Winter
Quarters because she wrote poetry celebrating the Mormon mission and its
leaders.[66] Given her position as a celestial bride of Brigham Young, her literary
renown, and her creative imagination, it is not surprising that Snow extended
her privilege by claiming the relationship of "daughter" to Apostle Kimball.
More surprising is that lesser-known women who moved on the peripheries
of Mormon society also drew on the concept of fictive kinship with powerful
members of the church to improve their own position. Elizabeth Gilbert, a
destitute young widow stranded in Nauvoo, wrote to Brigham Young requesting help with travel to Winter Quarters. In her letter, she asked Young to care
about her as he would a sister or a daughter:

> My body is almost worn out a struggling to get a shelter for my head. . . .
> if you think it wisdom for me to come out this fall how shall I gather
> [i.e., travel to Winter Quarters]? Council me as though I was your child
> or Sister and Whatever you say that I will do.[67]

There is no record of Young's reply, but it is worth noting that Gilbert appealed to Brigham Young's sense of obligation toward fictive kin and placed
herself in that category.

Finally, while Elizabeth Gilbert's plea reflected her economic emergency,
some women used Mormon society's expanded sense of family in more playful ways. Recall that men and women could stand in for deceased or absent
persons in order to carry out sacred adoption, baptism, or marriage ceremonies "by proxy."[68] At Winter Quarters, Mary Richards and her sister-in-law
Jane Richards invented lighthearted secular ceremonies "by proxy." Mary
Richards drew the attentions of a young bachelor, "Brother Littlefield," during
her sojourn at the encampment. On April 16, 1847, she attended a party given
for Littlefield shortly before his departure on a mission. "I danced . . . with
Bro Littlefield," she wrote, "twice, once as he said for himself. and once he
danced by proxy for Samuel [Mary Richards's absent husband]."[69] Littlefield

liked Mary Richards and took every opportunity before he left to spend time with her. Two days after the dance, he asked her out for an evening walk. Together they strolled to Jane Richards's cabin, where they

> spent the evening very plesently. He then walked home with me. while going he asked me if I did not wish it was Samuel I was walking with instead of himself I told him I would if it was not that it was a vain wish. but as it was . . . I was very well satisfied with my company & C & C.[70]

Then, one week after leaving for his mission, Brother Littlefield returned to Winter Quarters. In a cryptic aside, Richards wrote that he returned "for some purpose or other best known to himself." "He desired me to meet him that evening," she continued, "at Sister Janes as he wished to spend the eve with us both."[71] During the evening, both Mary and Jane Richards asked Littlefield to convey messages to their absent husbands once he joined them in England. This "he said he would remember to do."

> He then arose to take his leave when Jane proposed that we each send a kiss by him to our Husbands which he seemed pleased to convey. and asked permission to take one for himself. which we permited him to do.[72]

Mary Richards, Brother Littlefield, and Jane Snyder Richards's playful interactions show how three young adults used the concept of stand-ins for sacred ceremonies in a lighter vein, creating their own social ceremonies of harmless flirtation. Their exchanges of spousal affection "by proxy" spoke to the Richards wives' wish to see their absent husbands and to bachelor Littlefield's desire for female attentions. Mary Richards and her friends' lighthearted version of the sacred stand-in, to meet their social needs, reveals more subtly the improvisational nature of life at Winter Quarters.

At a makeshift community amid bluffs overlooking the Missouri River, the possibilities for reordering society could be as open as the prairie that stretched westward or as constricted as the tightly platted streets and rigorous rules of devotion. A temporary encampment in which women outnumbered men, Winter Quarters became a cultural space in which women tested their voices and flexed their authority. Although women eventually lost the freedoms that emerged in this way station on the plains, their improvisations remain testament to gendered contests over power in the history of Mormon culture. Indeed, the evidence from Winter Quarters, 1846–1848, suggests that Mormon women renegotiated patriarchal authority in their daily lives. Women like Mary Richards, Patty Sessions, Rosilla Sessions, and "Sister Morse" challenged the complacency of husbands who expected women to facilitate plural marriage with equanimity. Equally important, women like Richards and Sessions validated their authentic voices, recording by written word their spoken resistance to patriarchal assumptions about women, whether it was that a first wife should "find provision" for a surly sister-wife or that woman was solely responsible for man's fall from grace. In these ways, Mormon women showed their husbands, fathers, and brothers the limits of male authority over their thinking and behavior. They forced a social system ordered by hierarchical gender norms to bend to their humanity. In addition, Mormon women at Winter Quarters appropriated powers of the priesthood and linked these spiritual powers to the female experiences of motherhood and midwifery. Finally, some women also experimented with the concept of fictive kin, demanding the privileges of quasi-adoption from church fathers or turning the concept of sacred stand-ins to secular purposes. For women taught to cultivate deference to patriarchal leadership, these improvisations represent bold initiatives. Taken together, they indicate Mormon women's resistance to subordination and complicate our understanding of gender relations among the founding generation.

# 8

# Riding the Winds of Change

## Education and Activism on the Central Plains, 1930 to the Present

RENEE M. LAEGREID

Southwind dust flying considerable. . . . Thelma & all the family where here for dinner. Thelma and Verna went to Syracuse started at 1–30 got home at 3–45. . . . Mo Baked Bread & Churned, was home all alone in after noon Very blue & clowdy day for Mo her heart was busted. We got a Letter, also Card from Ervin to day. . . . wind was singing a sad tune.[1]

Mary Knackstedt Dyck, Kansas, November 10, 1936

When the decade of the 1930s opened on the central plains, it held an uneasy alliance with its frontier past. Many of the same patterns of rural life, Native American-white relations, and immigration persisted, but changes were in the wind. Rural farm women, like Mary Knackstedt Dyck, endured the environmental and economic conditions of the 1930s and suffered the heartache of children leaving the devastated region in search of work. The increasing rural out-migration and concern over land use, however, would encourage a later generation of women to take a more activist role to protect their families, communities, and the land. Native American women entered the 1930s still under the yoke of federal assimilation policies, but shortly thereafter John Collier's administration would begin the slow, halting move toward legitimizing Native Americans' rights and acceptance of their traditional ways. Immigrant migration had played a key role in settling this region in the nineteenth century, and immigration would surge again. In the later part of the twentieth century, Hispanic and Asian women, part of the Fourth Wave of newcomers to the central plains, would find themselves in the middle of a new controversy over an old question—would people so "different" fit into or destroy the established Anglo society in the West?

The theme of continuity and change underlie the experience of these three, relatively discrete groups of women on the central plains. There is remarkably little overlap among rural white, Native American, and Forth Wave women, and yet in each case, ethnicity, gender, and environment played a significant role in shaping their experiences. More important, as the century progressed, women in these groups became increasingly aware that education and activism would allow them to take a stronger role not only in determining their individual conditions but also in helping to shape the future for their families and communities.

For rural farm women in the 1930s, attitudes toward gendered labor and farming the arid land had not changed significantly since the frontier era.[2] The paternal structure of the farm family remained strongly intact, reinforced by federal and state institutions that promoted scientific farming for larger, commercial markets while supporting traditional gender division of labor.[3] Serious contemplation of how to profitably farm in the arid central plains would only come about because of the Dust Bowl.

The practice of farming the central plains with techniques developed for wetter, less arid regions had been going on since the Homestead Act passed in 1862. Land speculators, or boosters, put a positive spin on Stephen Long's description of the region as the Great American Desert, declaring it the new Garden of the West.[4] Despite the modern reader's inclination to consider this fortuitous reinterpretation completely self-serving and unprincipled, Ferdinand Hayden's belief that rainfall increased "in all our western regions under settlement" rested on the best scientific evidence of his day.[5] Families who moved onto the central plains brought with them attitudes toward farming and the land shaped by culture and tradition, including concepts of humanity's relationship to the land based on the biblical injunction, "fill the earth, and subdue it."[6] The atypical rainfalls that coincided with the passage of the Homestead Act encouraged the belief that farming on the plains could succeed using the same techniques that had been practiced so successfully in the wetter, wooded regions in the East.

Women who moved onto the plains brought cultural traditions as well, a way of viewing their natural surrounding through a gendered perspective. Julie Roy Jeffries examined frontier women's diaries to show how gender played a role in the way "Americans evaluated visual characteristics of the Great Plains."[7] Jeffries described pioneer women's concept of the plains environment, based on class, location, and women's responsibilities—child rearing, family safety, security, and sustenance. These responsibilities centered on the domestic sphere of the home and radiated outward to include the family garden, the chicken coop, and the dairy barn. The men took care of the land farther out—the fields and ranges—and most women would not challenge their husband's decisions of crops to plant, or how to work the land, even when traditional practices that had worked so well east of the plains seemed untenable in the face of heat and lack of moisture on their new farms.

When Dust Bowl conditions began in 1929, historian Pamela Riney-Kehrberg observes, "the residents of the Plains, in a broad swath from western North Dakota south through west Texas, suffered the indignity of the worst sustained environmental and economic disaster ever to affect the United States."[8] Ma Joad, John Steinbeck's character in *The Grapes of Wrath*, became a symbol of the tenant farm wives, the newer folk on the land, who up and left, leaving the impression that all roads became one-way streets out of the region.[9] But by and large, people stayed. Except in the hardest hit areas, rural folks who owned their farms, like Mary Dyke's family, chose to tough it out, hoping conditions would improve rather than risk losing their investment in the land. While some members of the younger generation, like Dyke's children, did move around in search of work, many others could not afford to abandon their support networks. The perception of a mass rural to urban migration within the region is unfounded as well. As the director of the 1940 census writes, "the earlier rapid movement toward urbanization came to a halt," although he accurately predicted a return to rural out-migration once conditions improved.[10]

For the rural families who stayed, women played a vital role in helping their families survive by employing a variety of strategies. First, they contributed by increasing subsistence food production, a tough job even in years with normal rainfall.[11] Second, they reduced household expenditures, doing whatever they could to cut costs—making clothing from flour sack cloth or giving up luxuries like coffee and tea. *Nebraska Farmer* magazine printed essays on how some farm women managed to cut corners in the family budget. One woman wrote in to suggest that if other wives followed her rigorous example—grinding their own grains; raising and canning pinto beans, string beans, tomatoes, cherries, and apples; and butchering and canning beef and pork, curing hams and rendering the lard—they could cut their grocery bill as she did, from $700.00 in 1929 to $249.00 in 1932. In an era when rural women had more time on their hands than money, engaging in labor-intensive chores saved scarce dollars for the family.

Women also found ways to generate income by selling goods produced within their gendered sphere. Women sold ducklings and chicks, canned goods, salads, cottage cheese, and cakes. Some women raised canaries while others made craft items, such as hooked rugs, to sell in town for cash. Via Bourret, in Stickney, South Dakota, became anxious over the increasingly low prices for commodities and decided to write a letter, "woman-to-woman" to Eleanor Roosevelt. "Everything which we have to buy has gone up," she explained, "and the things we have to sell are going down in price: eggs, cream, chickens. This is the woman's share of the farm and small town money."[12] Her letter demonstrates a popular form of women's activism during the Depression, explaining their dire condition to politicians who obviously did not understand the severity of their problems, then proposing solutions. Through letters such as Bourret's, women asked for a voice in policy making in areas that directly affected their lives.

Despite falling prices, the commodities produced within the women's sphere still added valuable income to the family coffers. Caroline Henderson, who lived on the Kansas-Oklahoma border, wrote of the Sunday market in her town during the worst year of the drought, 1936:

> Cars kept driving up and people coming in with pails or crates or cases of eggs. Cream was delivered in containers of all sorts and sizes, including one heavy aluminum cooker! . . . In many cases the payments were pitifully small, but every such sale represents hard work and economy and the struggle to keep going.[13]

As the drought and depression wore on, women began to look for jobs off the farm—teaching, housekeeping, sales clerk positions—to bring in needed cash.[14] For the most part, however, their activities fell within the concentric rings of women's traditional responsibilities that Jeffries had identified: home, garden, and farmyard. As Henderson noted in her letters, it fell to the men to decide to continue planting wheat, hoping for a rain that did not come, or if it did, fell in such torrents as to be useless.[15]

The dire economic conditions on the plains led to a government investigation into Dust Bowl conditions. Published in 1936, the report indicated that settlers' misunderstanding of farming in an arid region, compounded by misguided federal farm policies that encouraged large, commercially oriented farms, had created a "disquieting picture."[16] Rather than recommend the removal of marginal land from production, the report advocated irrigation and provided a detailed plan of action to transform the plains "from a risky adventure and a recurrent liability into a stable basis of economic and social profit."[17] Not surprisingly, the US Census showed a significant jump in the amount of irrigated acreage from 1930 to 1940, and sustained increases thereafter.[18] The success of deep well irrigation, a relatively new technology in the 1930s, led one USDA official to claim in the early 1970s, "We have achieved a climate-free agriculture on the Plains."[19] The specter of drought had ceased to be an issue—mankind had finally subdued the plains.

While some claimed victory over nature, the 1970s saw a rise in women's organizations that challenged the methods of progressive agriculture. During World War II, while women took on many responsibilities on farms and ranches as men went off to war, they did not orchestrate a challenge to the prevailing gendered labor system. Similarly, during the 1940 through the 1960s, women participated in agricultural organizations, but as an auxiliary to men's organizations.[20] The rise of the feminist movement in the late 1960s, however, encouraged rural women to argue for a voice based on their association with domestic concerns—health and well-being of their family, a desire to stay on the land, and concern for the vitality of rural communities. The "invisible farmers," as historian Carolyn Sachs writes, began to gently challenge the structural girders that had supported "patriarchal farm families through extension programs, government loans, and marketing policies" by educating themselves on land usage, alternative crops, and farming practices for the benefit of their family, their communities, and the land itself.[21]

Activism began, and continues, as a gentle challenge to male authority and privilege.[22] Rather than adopting the more individualistic and often strident strategies of urban feminists, rural women have worked within their area of concern, focusing on communal needs specific to their communities. For example, women found a venue to address their concerns with pesticide use and the increasing power of agribusiness by working at the grassroots level in the Sustainable Agriculture movement. Beginning in the 1970s, the movement's interrelated goals of environmental health, economic profitability, and social and economic equity have the ultimate objective of providing the necessary agricultural produce for the present without damaging the needs of future generations.[23] Although both men and women are involved in the movement, as one member explained, "most of the pesticide education work and environmental awareness on the local level is done by women. I've noticed that conferences tend to be attended by a lot of six-foot tall white men, but . . . the kind of work that has kept the organization stable has been done by women."[24] Women have been able to effect change—sustainable agricultural policy is now common policy—without challenging either their traditional gender roles or their position in a patriarchal society.[25]

The farm crisis of the 1980s, which affected medium-sized farm families hardest, reinvigorated women's activism in an area where women felt most vulnerable—farm management. Jane Green and Deb Rood developed the University of Nebraska's Women in Agriculture program in 1985. Their mission, "To educate women involved in agriculture on relevant business management skills," has been met by providing educational resources to help women to survive in a male-dominated business.[26] This has become increasingly important as the number of women with primary responsibility for farm management, either as widows, daughters, or women who chose to become farmers, continues to rise.[27]

In the 1990s, Denise O'Brian, founder of Women, Food, and Agriculture Network (WFAN), wrote, "There is a new type of Agriculture on the horizon. That new agriculture involves women as they have been involved before, only they are taking leadership roles."[28] Concern over farm issues, and the need to rethink fundamental aspects of farming in an arid region, compelled Annette Dubas to run for the Nebraska state legislature. "A farmer is an eternal optimist," Dubas reflected; "they go out and plant the same thing every year, and hope for the best."[29] Women are slowly but surely adding their voices to help farmers think differently, "because of how these decisions are affecting their families. Women will look at different ideas if they think it will create a safer, more secure environment for their families."[30] Although the basis of Dubas's concerns seems gender-related, they transcend women's traditional sphere. "I think we will have to look at different crops and ways of farming," she argues, "especially in the more arid areas of our state because water is going to become more and more of an issue as time goes on. What are more sustainable ways to farm? Do we need to get bigger or will scaling the size of our operations down be more efficient and profitable?"[31]

Ruth Chantry, outreach coordinator for the Nebraska Sustainable Agricultural Society, remarks that farming has been and continues to be considered a man's business; there has been resistance to including women in decision making.[32] But patriarchal attitudes are "shifting and loosening," Sachs notes, moving away from the patriarchal idea of farm wife, with its implications of straightened gendered responsibilities, toward "equal partners in labor, ownership, and decision making."[33] Chantry writes that she and her husband have "a different way of looking at things, which is often, but of course, not always, gender based. . . . I think men think more linearly and women think more circuitously. The benefit of this for a farm couple that works together and solves problems together is that you can have the best of both worlds, if/when it works out that way."[34] Chantry reflects a widespread view among farm women and scholars that reject women as being inherently more nurturing and connected to the land, arguing that this view corners women into a biologically determined nurturing role, which perpetuates the traditional, male-oriented power structure.[35]

Unlike their nineteenth-century predecessors, rural women are finding ways to have their concerns heard. To be sure, many farm women continue to earn income to help keep their families stay on their farms, following gendered concepts of labor and responsibilities that emerged in the 1930s— working off the farm to supplement the family income.[36] However, the once "gentle tamers" of the West are organizing to educate themselves and become activists in order to stay on their land, to maintain their rural communities and way of life that at once reflects and transcends their traditional gendered sphere.

When the decade of the 1930s opened, rural women entered an era that witnessed shifting dynamics between change and continuity, mostly unaware that in remote areas of the central plains, Native American women also faced a future of profound change. Winona Caramony, a member of the Omaha tribe, was born on the reservation in the northeast corner of Nebraska in 1924, the year the Indian Citizenship Act passed, declaring Native Americans citizens of the United States. During her life both on and off the reservation, Caramony's experiences illuminate many of the political, social, and cultural changes that affected Native American women throughout the central plains during the twentieth century.

Although the momentum for change had begun in the late 1920s, as the Indian Citizenship Act indicates, significant transformation toward Native American policy began with John Collier's appointment as director of the Bureau of Indian Affairs (BIA) in 1934. His dedication to preserving Native American culture began in the 1920s, when he worked with the Pueblo Indians in Taos, New Mexico. But his concern with indigenous cultures also reflected a growing concern among Americans over the destructiveness of modern civilization and the belief that Native Americans possessed the "natural, sylvan characteristics" that "must be preserved for human rejuvenation."[37] While director at the BIA, Collier initiated a break from the federally sponsored assimilation policies determined to bring Native Americans in line with their Anglo counterparts in the "civilized" United States.

During the nineteenth-century and into the early twentieth, while reservation agents worked relentlessly to transform Native American men into farmers modeled in the Anglo image (patriarchal, individualistic, and self-supporting), Native America women found themselves subjected to efforts to mold them into gender roles aligned with Anglo concepts of middle-class domesticity. The field matron program, for example, operating from 1895 to 1927, included "cooking classes, religious services, and child care seminars all [of which] offered tribal women much more than practical help in adapting to sedentary reservation life."[38] The Anglo and assimilated Native American women who worked as field matrons had a very clear agenda: "To help Native American women adopt Victorian Anglo-American standards of womanhood."[39] The efforts of assimilation proponents significantly affected the tradition of egalitarian gender roles among Native Americans that had supported the political, economic, and social structure of tribal life.

The shift in federal policy that began under Collier's administration offered cautious hope for Native Americans struggling to maintain Indian traditions and values. The Indian Reorganization Act (IRA), or Indian New Deal, eased pressure on Native American families by ending allotment and restoring some tribal land. The IRA also allowed tribes to create their own constitutional governments, protected tribal resources, and encouraged the preservation of traditional customs. Many of the central plains tribes passed referenda to accept the IRA, a major milestone in allowing Native Americans to vote whether to accept or reject federal Indian policy. Although Collier could not get all the programs he promised to Native Americans passed, his administration made a significant break from more than seventy years of forced assimilation in the region.[40]

The political changes initiated by Collier did not significantly improve the economic condition of Native Americans on central plains reservations, and the drought and depression that affected the region during the 1930s increased the hardships. Decades of governmental efforts to destroy traditional subsistence networks, culture, and traditions had also affected gender roles among Native families. While both men and women struggled to adapt to the imposed changes, women faced increased responsibility to provide for their families. In Caramony's family, for example, her mother worked to support their family. "They were hard times, when I think back now," Caramony recalls. "[I]t seems like my mother had to provide for us."[41] Her father found employment with the Works Project Act, "but he also drank a lot." Her mother, Mary Lieb, assumed responsibility for their family. "She was a good provider," Caramony reflected. "[S]he was a very strong woman."[42] To support her eight children, Caramony's mother walked three miles to the main highway to catch the Greyhound bus for her job at the Winnebago Hospital. She also worked at the reservation school and made craft items to sell to the white teachers at the school.[43]

Mary Lieb made and sold traditional handcrafted items that would have been banned under earlier administrations. The creation of the Indian Arts and Crafts Board in 1935 encouraged Native Americans to engage in craft work "to rebuild the economies of Indian communities and to encourage the perpetuation of Indian customs and values."[44] But craft work was a double-edged sword. Regarding a similar revival effort directed toward southern plains Hispanics, Sarah Deutsch argues that "private and government arts proponents defined and limited the development of that culture."[45] The emphasis on creating traditional-styled crafts—"hard work, a long time ago," Caramony admonished—meant a low wage-to-hour income. Although craft work did bring in needed income, especially to women on reservations, it was not enough to support a family. Focusing on craft work, too, meant developing skills that had limited use or economic value, which did not hold much promise for either integration into Anglo society or significant economic improvement on the reservations.[46]

Despite, or perhaps because of, the difficult times, Caramony's mother stressed the importance of education for her children. As a young woman she had attended Carlisle Indian Institute in Pennsylvania. Winona Caramony's experiences with education followed a familiar pattern for Native American children of her era: attending elementary school on the reservation, then for those who could, attending a regional BIA high school. Caramony's experience at the BIA school in Flandreau, South Dakota, opened her eyes to potential opportunities off the reservation. Once she had moved off the reservation, she recalled, "I just left because it was so much better outside. . . . I could work for the summer and then come back to school [the Flandreau Indian School], so that's what I did."[47] After graduation she attended Haskell Indian Institute in Kansas, which had recently implemented a two-year post-high school vocational program. At Haskell, as had been the policy with Indian schools in general, gender determined the course options for students; Caramony entered the commercial, or secretarial, program.

In 1945, after completing a year at Haskell, Caramony married a member of the Omaha tribe and spent almost twenty-five years with her husband, an electrician in the Navy Air Force, rearing four children and traveling. Her experiences highlight two important and interwoven themes for Native Americans during this era: continuation of the martial tradition among Native Americans and out-migration from the reservations. As young men left to follow their tribe's warrior tradition by joining the armed forces, women organized dances to honor the servicemen and auxiliaries to assist the WWII veterans—the war "thus reinforcing the martial role of women in Plains Indian societies."[48] Many Native Americans also left the reservation to work in wartime industries, thereby helping to establish urban pan-Indian communities.

When John Collier resigned as director of the Bureau of Indian Affairs in 1945, his ideal of cultural pluralism effectively came to an end. Members of Congress who had opposed the Indian New Deal moved to reinstitute assimilation policies by developing two mutually supportive programs—termination and relocation. Termination, they argued, would wean Native Americans from federal appropriations and dissolve the tribal affiliation with the US government as well as the reservation, while relocation would move reservation Indians into urban areas, thereby speeding the assimilation process.[49] In 1953 Congress passed the Termination Act, initiating ten years of intense efforts to terminate tribes. Native American leaders took their grievances to both the Kennedy and Johnson administrations, which led to a reassessment of the policy; Nixon ended it. By then, however, the Northern Ponca tribe in Nebraska had been terminated and more than two hundred thousand Native Americans nationwide had left their tribal homelands, forced to relocate, mainly in urban areas.[50]

Ironically, termination did not have the assimilation effect legislators and reformers had hoped. Coercing Native Americans off their reservations led to the development of urban enclaves and inspired "a renewed interest in tribal values [that] was the exact opposite of what the relocation program was supposed to achieve."[51] These enclaves became a center for the emergence of Native American civil rights groups.[52] One of the first Native American women activists on the central plains, Helen Peterson, a member of the Omaha tribe, joined the National Congress of American Indians (NCAI) and served as executive director from 1953 to 1961. In her essay, "American Indian Political Participation," Peterson argues against the post-WWII Congress's attacks on Indian rights and property, a philosophy "harking back to the days of the General Allotment Act."[53] She argued for the importance of Native Americans' participation in political organizations, "the Indian's best hope of having some part in determining their own future and in continuing to exist as Indian tribes."[54]

Native American women played key roles as activists as the groups became more radical. In 1968 Mary Jane Wilson cofounded the American Indian Movement (AIM), along with Dennis Banks and Clyde Bellecourt. Unlike other civil rights groups, Native American women focused "less on integration with dominant society, and more on maintaining cultural integrity."[55] They centered their efforts in areas that would benefit tribes as a whole, such as enforcement of treaty rights, gaining back land, and empowering their tribes, rather than on individual rights. And Native American women used the traditional concept of egalitarian society to counter arguments by Native men against their taking part in political activism. Calling on their traditional rights, they insisted on their right to participate in activist activities, arguing that "acting sexist was a sign of being assimilated . . . a way of exhibiting ignorance of Indian traditions," thereby reinstating themselves into the center of political activism.[56]

A few activist groups emerged in the 1970s specifically devoted to women and children's issues. The organization Women of All Red Nations (WARN) focused on the sterilization abuse of Native American women discovered when AIM occupied the BIA office in Washington, D.C. There they found documentation confirming what Native Americans had long suspected—sterilization procedures conducted on Native women with neither their knowledge nor their approval.[57] The WARN activists engaged in energy and environmental issues as well. Their emphasis on tribal rather than individual rights, however, put them at odds with feminist organizations. Caramony reflects the wider view among Native American women that while some are interested in feminist issues, tribal concerns still take precedence and will most likely continue to do so until larger issues are resolved.[58] As David Wishart notes, "by virtue of any important socioeconomic indicator (life expectancy, infant mortality, per capita income) Thurston County, home to the Omaha and Winnebago, is still by far the poorest place in Nebraska."[59] Caramony, however, is confident that before too long, women will be able to turn their attention to feminist issues.

Education for tribal members became Caramony's focus when, after her husband's retirement, she returned to the Omaha reservation in the 1980s. A self-proclaimed "advocate for education" she has taught for many years and served on school boards three different times.[60] She has witnessed an increased interest in obtaining a college education among Omaha women who are still quite often the main providers for their family. The number of women attending the Nebraska Indian Community College on the reservation has increased, as has the number of young women pursuing college degrees off-reservation. Her children have all earned college degrees, and she notes with pride three of her nieces are physicians. "The Omaha women I know are aggressive," she said, "they're educated. All the ones I know who are nurses, they are teachers. In fact we . . . just hired two Indian Omaha teachers down there." In tribal politics, too, women are reasserting their right to have a role in shaping tribal issues by taking leadership roles on the tribal council. Caramony continued, "Before I used to hear them say women are not supposed to run for council, they're not supposed to. And women don't belong in the council. I used to hear that a lot, too. But it's different now days, things are changing. I guess that's because women are beginning to be more aggressive and they're more vocal and educated, and know what to do."[61]

As they have in the past, women, and especially grandmothers, continue to play a strong role in teaching traditional ways to the younger generations. Caramony's concern that "the younger ones are kinda losing it a little bit" encouraged her to work with other women to teach culture, crafts, social dance, and games to children on the reservation. Native language is being taught to children on the Omaha reservation, beginning in the preschool Head Start program, a stunning reversal from Indian boarding school days when federally funded programs punished children for speaking their native language.

Back in the nineteenth century, one of the main goals for assimilation proponents had been to open up Indian-held land for Euro-American settlers to farm. The accepted position of the time was that Indians would either abandon their nomadic ways and become acculturated into American society or vanish. Native Americans did not vanish. However, Winona Caramony acknowledges that the remote location of reservations leads to an out-of-sight, out-of-mind attitude, noting: "I think even nearby towns don't know that we even exist here." And yet for her, the ability to move between her Native and Anglo worlds is crucial. "I think I've accomplished a lot because I know what it is to live in the white man's world," Caramony reflects, "and I also know my Indian ways. Diversity. I like that word—*diversity*. Because in my work, at times I can go to a meeting and probably be the only Indian woman there. Then I come back, and take part in my Indian events." Contemplating the idea of moving back and forth between Indian and non-Indian worlds, Caramony continued, "I think we have to live with the outside world, too, not just right here. And that's the way we've got to [educate] our children."[62]

The experience of isolation, alienation, and cautious interaction with the Anglo-American society familiar to Native American women can be found in another group of women as well—twentieth-century immigrants on the central plains. The town of Hastings, Nebraska, provides an example of the diversity of immigrants coming into the region and the ways in which education and activism factor into their lives.

Standing on the corner of First and Hastings Streets in Hastings, Nebraska, is both a step back into the town's history and a vision of its future. The boom of railroad cars being yarded fills the air, along with the dust and the heat and the smell of creosote. For Hastings, as with most plains towns, the railroad was its reason for being, the lifeline connecting an isolated town to outside markets. From this spot one also finds a glimpse of the town's future: a Vietnamese grocery store, just one of the several Vietnamese-owned businesses in town. Across the street at La Aztec Grocery, Ana Garcia, a Mexican immigrant, helps a customer send a fax, gives information to another on how to send money to relatives in Mexico, then pauses to put freshly baked rolls into a worker's lunch bag. Just down the street are two cafés owned and operated by Mexican immigrants; a Mexican leather goods store is just out of sight. Around the corner a grocery store and a dry goods store, both owned by Cuban refugees, are thriving businesses, as is a sewing shop owned by Guntamanee (Ead) Mattley, from Thailand. As this ethnic economic enclave suggests, Hispanics and Asians represent two of the fastest-growing ethnic groups on the central plains.[63]

In many ways, the experiences of Asian and Hispanic women moving here echo their New Immigrant counterparts who arrived almost a century earlier. Distinguished by the fact that the newcomers migrated predominantly from eastern and southern Europe in the nineteenth century, thousands of New Immigrant women left their homeland to either follow a husband or join other family members in America. The women faced precarious dependency exacerbated by discrimination, language barriers, and a responsibility to maintain cultural continuity with Old World traditions. The patriarchal family structure encouraged women to construct enclosed ethnic networks in which male members of the family, or children, provided the link to the dominant society.

While nineteenth-century New Immigrants were just that—immigrants who ventured to the United States primarily for economic reasons—newcomers to the central plains in the post-1930s era represent a broader range of motivations for movement: political refugees, immigrants, seasonal laborers, and illegal immigrants. People in each of these categories face specific challenges as they try to create a permanent home, a temporary settlement, or furtive life on the margins of society. Recent newcomers to the central plains, like Kate Nguyen from Vietnam, Ead from Thailand, and Ana Garcia from Mexico, represent the diversity of Fourth Wave women's experiences.

Kim Nguyen was twelve years old when she moved from Saigon, South Vietnam, to Hastings, Nebraska, with her mother, grandmother, great-grandmother, younger sister, and an uncle "just tacked on" to the otherwise all-female immigrant group.[64] Kate's grandmother had married an American soldier during the Vietnam War. Because their child, Kate's mother, was considered an "American Baby," the family faced overt prejudice from their community. The US government began to help political refugees and children of US soldiers move out of Vietnam in the late 1980s, and in 1994 Catholic Social Services helped Kate's family by sponsoring their move to Hastings.[65]

Nguyen recalls that when the family first arrived, "there were not a lot of Vietnamese [in Hastings], and the culture here had a hard time accepting the family and accepting me for a while." Entering the public school system helped Kate integrate into Anglo society far quicker than would have been possible for a nineteenth-century immigrant girl, but her rapid acculturation created concerns among the older women of the family. In Vietnam, young girls did not participate in sports, or have slumber parties, or "hang out" with friends after school, and Kate's mother wrestled with the tug of maintaining traditional ways and the lure of the new before giving her daughter permission to participate in American activities. Nguyen credits her mother for being more open-minded than many other Vietnamese immigrants and allowing her to engage in activities considered entirely inappropriate for girls in the old country.[66]

As the eldest daughter, Kate felt the greatest responsibility to become a bridge to their new community. She learned English quickly: "It took me two years to get the English down," she said, serving as translator for the older women in the family. Children serving as translators for nineteenth-century immigrant women was a common phenomenon, one that allowed women to continue ethnic traditions separate from the larger, dominant society. A significant difference with current plains newcomers is that despite language barriers, women do not stay within the protective surrounding of their home. Despite the unusual female composition of their family, Kate's mother, grandmother, and great-grandmother are typical in that they all found employment immediately. Meat-packing plants in the area employ a large number of Vietnamese because, as Kate noted, they don't require their workers to "speak a lot of English."[67]

Working outside the home creates a paradox for non-English-speaking women. Although they are working outside the confines of the home, the women experience a greater sense of isolation than earlier immigrants. Their work is physically demanding and at the end of the shift, "they go home, and they pretty much get worn out." Unlike previous immigration waves, this leaves little time for women to perpetuate traditions and develop a strong sense of community among their ethnic group. Kate recalls, "A couple of years ago Mom tried to do something like that for all the women, you know, kind of a woman group kind of a deal. But it didn't work because a lot of people are busy."[68]

Vign Ngo came to Hastings in 1994 as a political refugee and served as director for Vietnamese settlement with Catholic Social Services until the program ended in 2001. Aside from their finding jobs in meat-packing plants or manufacturing, Ngo notes the willingness of Vietnamese to start small businesses. He owns one of two Vietnamese grocery stores in town, and his daughter owns Rosy Nail Salon, one of the four Vietnamese-owned nail salons in Hastings. "Vietnamese women don't get their nails done," Ngo remarks, "because they are too busy and too careful with their money. But in any town of 20,000 people there will be a nail shop run by a Vietnamese."[69] Ngo also notes the lack of a cohesive Vietnamese community in Hastings. By contrast, bigger cities on the central plains, such as Lincoln, Nebraska, have a larger Vietnamese population, which encouraged the development of a vibrant ethnic community.[70] Hastings not only lacks numbers but also a cultural center, such as a church that provides services in Vietnamese, that would provide a focus and a venue for women to socialize.[71]

One striking difference between nineteenth-century immigrants and current arrivals is that with faster and cheaper transportation, many Fourth Wave people have the ability to visit their homeland, renew language skills, see relatives, and keep current with cultural changes. Both Ngo and Nguyen note that a combination of factors, such as an improved political situation in South Vietnam, maintaining strong ties to family in Vietnam, and relative wealth gained in the United States, encourage many Vietnamese to return to their homeland when they retire. Kate's parents are considering the move back. It is unlikely Kate will return with them. She graduated from college in 2004 with a degree in business management and is building her career in the banking industry. In Vietnam, women "have very limited rights, and it's pretty much woman is there to cook, clean, and stay home and take care of family. There is not much of a career for woman over there," notes Kate. "The thing that I really see with the woman is, here, my God, I mean . . . compared to Vietnam, we're pretty much in heaven."[72]

The opportunity to break from traditional gendered restrictions and pursue opportunity are the reasons Ead Mattley stayed in her new hometown—even though her reason for coming to Hastings was based on cultural obligations of the eldest daughter to care for family members. Back in Bangkok, Thailand, Ead had resigned herself to her fate: remaining single so that she could take care of family and helping her father in his tailoring shop. Her plans changed in 1980 when one of her sisters, married and living in California, asked her parents to send Ead to help care for her young children. Ead recalls, "In the first beginning, in three months, I want to go back home. I couldn't speak English. . . . I talk to my Mom, and I said, 'I'm going to go home.' And she said, 'Everybody come, it very difficult, why you just stay for a while.' I say, 'I couldn't speak any English, how I going to stay here!' And she said, 'I think you go to school.'"[73] Despite the difficulty of learning through the English as a Second Language program, Ead determined to master the new language.

Ead's other sister, Ranee, had moved to Hastings to attend Central Community College. The seemingly odd connection between the small plains town and Bangkok began when a Hastings agribusiness manufacturer conducted business with one of Ead's cousins in Thailand. The Hastings booster encouraged Ead's cousin to send his family to Hastings, and over the years, a number of her cousins, as well as Ead's sister, had attended the community college there. While going to school, Ranee decided to open a small candy and gift business. She asked her mom to send Ead to help; honoring her family obligation, Ead arrived in 1993, planning to stay three years at the most, then return to Thailand.[74]

During her first week in Hastings, however, Ead met the man who would become her husband. She fulfilled her three-year obligation to her sister before marrying. Despite initial resistance, her parents gave her permission to marry on the condition she return every year for a visit. Shortly after she married, Ead opened her own tailoring business. She also enrolled in English-language courses again, because, as she said, "I couldn't speak with the customers!" For Ead, education was the key to becoming a part of her new community. The difficulty now is holding on to her traditional ways, which she does by cooking Thai food and speaking her native language when she can. "You know when I talk Thai?" she asks. "With the dog! . . . He's bilingual."

Traveling to Thailand and back helps Ead keep in contact with family, friends, and her culture, just as it does for many Vietnamese immigrants. The ability to maintain connections between new and old worlds is the reason Ana Garcia and her three children moved to Hastings from Ciudad Juarez five years ago. She speaks very little English, and what she knows she learned from her children. Translating for her mother, nine-year-old Cinthia explains, "When she has to speak to Americanos sometimes her children speak for her." Garcia separated from her husband in Mexico, but he refused to give her child support. "She came here," Cinthia continued, "because in Mexico there is not enough work for women over forty."[75]

Garcia did not settle on Hastings by accident; rather, she followed the family migration pattern. Her brother came to Hastings about fifteen years ago and owns La Aztec Grocery, where she works. Garcia's sisters and mother followed in a succession of moves over the past twelve years.[76] First-generation immigrant women in particular, like Ana, recognize the parallel ethnic communities that exist in Hastings and other central plains communities. For the most part Americanos and Hispanics function unaware of each other's existence, with only a small zone of interaction. "She goes to Spanish-speaking church services, all friends, family speak Spanish," explains Cinthia. Unlike the Vietnamese, who describe a sense of isolation, the Hispanic community is strong and socially active in Hastings, and Garcia feels comfortable here.[77]

Ana's move to Hastings can be seen in the context of what Sara Deutsch describes as a regional community.[78] Deutsch's study of Hispanics' migration patterns—from their villages in New Mexico and Mexico to mining and agricultural areas on the western edge of the central plains in Colorado and Wyoming—examines the motivations for their move, their reception by Anglos, and the shift from a predominantly migratory pattern to establishment of Hispanic enclaves in the United States. Dire economic circumstances compelled men, and later women, into a seasonal migration pattern north in order to maintain their villages. The emphasis on leaving their village to sustain it helps explain Hispanic disinterestedness in integrating into Anglo society—villagers intended to return home. While the 1921 and 1924 per centum limitation laws, or quota laws, severely restricted the influx of immigrants from other countries into the United States (and in doing so encouraged assimilation among those ethnic groups), protests by agricultural advocates gained exemptions for seasonal Hispanic laborers, such as the bracero movement.[79]

In a later essay, Linda W. Reese explains the reasons seasonal migration evolved into permanent Hispanic enclaves on the plains, and how this shift led to a diminution of status for Hispanic women within their homes and communities. Beginning in the 1940s, Hispanic women in agricultural areas on the central plains became involved in labor activism. While activism helped renew women's importance in their communities, it also brought about criticism from Anglo society.[80]

This is perhaps where similarities are most pronounced between nineteenth-century New Immigrants and contemporary Fourth Wave newcomers to the central plains: the culture they are entering maintains its predominantly Anglo-Saxon character and the perception that the newcomers represent a threat to established Anglo society. When twenty-three million people entered the United States between 1880 and 1920, a wave of fear spread across the country that the sheer number of new arrivals, with their different religions, traditions, institutions, and cultures, were a threat that would overwhelm the melting pot.[81] Much as Old Stock Americans—people who had been in the United States for more than one generation—feared these strange New Immigrants would destroy American culture and political institutions, it did not happen.

The melting pot concept worked, in large part because the immigration laws prevented newcomers from reinvigorating ethnic culture. In particular, immigrant women learned English and became involved in the larger community. The traditions that seemed so disturbing to Old Stock Americans, such as ethnic music, food, and even language, ultimately enriched the fabric of American culture and society without the need to reassess or redefine American core values. On the central plains, people whose grandparents or great-grandparents faced discrimination for their Old World habits became part of the mainstream who are now worried about the "alien" invaders.[82]

Writing on the threat new immigrant groups pose to the dominant culture, Brian Fry notes that most Anglo-Americans don't consider themselves part of "a" group—they are "the" group—Americans—who know who they are "by knowing who they are not."[83] They are not "those guys" who look, act, and speak different from how they do. The physical distinctions between Anglo-Americans and non-Anglos have the unfortunate affect of perpetuating racist attitudes toward newcomers far more profoundly than what nineteenth-century immigrants experienced. For example, Ester Rickert's grandparents moved to the United States from Mexico during the 1920s. By all measures her family has assimilated into US culture and achieved middle-class status: attaining college degrees, engaging in professional careers, and marrying outside of their ethnic group. She noted with dissatisfaction, however, the Anglo-American prejudicial habit of lumping all Hispanics together based on physical appearance, and usually assuming them to be "the worst kind"—illegal Mexican immigrants. Ead, too, mentions that people who do not know her treat her differently because she looks Asian. "I think they think you're not educated [because] you can't speak good English," she said. "I tell them I've been here longer than I'd been in my country. I know what's going on."[84]

The challenges faced by women on the central plains, like Ead, Esther, Anna, or Kate, who represent Fourth Wave newcomers, seem in many respects a variation on the difficulties faced by New Immigrants a century earlier: language barriers, discrimination, and the difficulties of adapting to a new culture. But for Fourth Wave women, and indeed when comparing Native American and rural women to their nineteenth-century counterparts, education and activism have played a key role in allowing central plains women to determine their futures and shape the future for their families and communities.

Part III

# The Southern Plains

Frieda Hambleton with Edith and Mae, Bradley, Oklahoma, 1927.
Courtesy Sandra Scofield

# Frieda, a Vignette

SANDRA SCOFIELD

Frieda Katherine Hambleton, grandmother of author Sandra Scofield, lived from 1906 to 1983. Born in Indian Territory, during her lifetime she labored as a tenant farmer, a railroad gang cook, and a union worker in a flour mill. In this brief reflection, Scofield captures a moment in her grandmother's life, deftly illustrating the impact of environmental and economic changes, migration, effects of the war, and the ways that those historical movements effected changes in poor families, and in what a woman could do independently, particularly on the southern plains.

## April 1937, Devol, Oklahoma

Frieda rose before first light and took her bag out to her brother Lou's car. He worked for the Santa Fe Railroad, and he had gotten her a job as a cook for a crew in Desert Valley. Coming back in through the porch, she drew water from the barrel for the kitchen. Then she made breakfast for the men: Lou and their stepfather, Daddy Hill, and their mother's brother, Uncle Albert. The men ate without talk, slurping their coffee.

Albert went to the barn. Lou and Daddy went to the wheat field. Frieda and her brothers had come to this farm as teenagers after their own father had died in a farming accident, and though Lou never took up the plow himself, he liked to watch a day break with a farmer. He'd been a help to Frieda and Ira, Frieda's husband, when they tenant farmed in Bradley, but there wasn't enough help to be had for dry dirt, wind, bad luck. So Lou got Ira a job with the state highway, and there, on a day as clear as blue glass, a dust devil picked Ira up, tarp and all, from the back of the truck, and threw him to the highway, headfirst.

Frieda tried to make it on her own. She took in boarders, worked in an office for four dollars a week, and sent little Mae, nine years old, out to babysit. It wasn't enough, so she went to her mother's farm, and here the children would stay, while she and Lou drove west within the hour.

She made more biscuits and bacon and watched her children creep into the kitchen with their wounded faces: Edith, age twelve and frail as a stalk of cracked glass. Eulah Mae, a year younger but stalwart. And Sonny, six, looking like a miniature Ira, with high cheekbones and bright eyes.

They sat with Frieda's mother at the table, all of them quiet, hardly able to swallow. Her German mother, Sophie, with her own hard history, finally snapped to. These children will thrive, she said. Milk and eggs, chores and school, church and waiting.

Waiting. At that, Sonny sprang up and ran outside, banging doors. Frieda saw her mother's mouth go grim. Edith gave a cry and threw herself facedown in Frieda's lap. Mae didn't budge. Sophie got up and cleared the table.

Shh, shh, Frieda said to Edith. I'll send for you as soon as I'm somewhere settled. You can't go into that inferno. I'll be living in a boxcar.

We'll all be together again.

She looked straight at Mae. You look after Sonny, and mind Mama all the ways you can.

There was nothing left but leaving. Children sobbing on the steps, the awful waving. Daddy stood to the side, his hands tucked into the bib of his overalls.

It would be Christmas 1940 before she would see her children, in Gallup. Then the war would save them: a factory job in Wichita Falls, across the river from her mother's farm. She packed flour twenty years, and tried to remember where it came from. She worked in nursing homes, and cared for her aged parents. The only earth she would till again was the patch for okra and tomatoes she raised every year back of her house on Grant.

# Introduction to the Southern Plains

SANDRA J. McBRIDE

"We once suggested that the first steps we needed to take in western women's history were to see the West through women's eyes and listen to women's words."[1] So recalled Elizabeth Jameson and Susan Armitage in their introduction to *Writing the Range: Race, Class, and Culture in the Women's West.* These may seem like baby steps from our perspective here in the twenty-first century, but as every formerly crawling child learns when she first totters on two feet, the view changes radically with even a small change in elevation. The world she now explores is far more beautiful, complex, and compelling than the one she previously enjoyed.

Such has been the experience of western women's historians over the past few decades of multicultural history. Their contributions have done much to bring to light the diversity and richness of women's experiences, and the view of the West has changed and deepened. This enlarged vision has not come without difficulty, though. Organizing principles of gender, race, class, sexuality, and culture have become more common, but also more contested. Women of color have received more focus, but as Antonia Castañeda argued in "Women of Color and the Rewriting of Western History: The Discourse, Politics, and Decolonization of History," using the lens of the middle-class white women without a recognition of how life may differ for women of color distorts history.[2]

The incredible diversity of women's experiences on the Great Plains complicates the seemingly simple act of "looking through women's eyes." Jameson and Armitage noted that historians must "imagine how a common historical space appeared from many different lines of sight."[3] They argue that "common lenses" can be found if we "look at the experiences of women of different racial ethnic groups through such lenses as work, intimate relationships, sexuality, reproduction, and access to power."[4] These lenses will help to provide

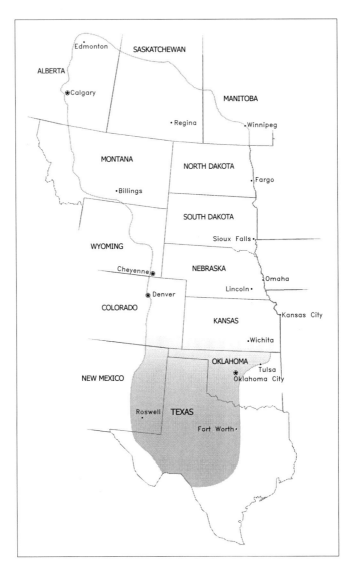

Map highlighting southern plains region.
Copyright (c) 2011 by Carl Laegreid

the multiple lines of sight necessary to create a multicultural history of the southern Great Plains.

The "common historical space" the essays in this section examine is the southern plains, a rough third of the Great Plains that includes parts of New Mexico, Texas, and Oklahoma. This space defies stereotypes, just as the women who lived and worked here did. Though it shares with the rest of the Great

Plains a gradual eastward slope, the southern plains region is not flat: it boasts tilted plains like the Llano Estacado in New Mexico, hills such as the Osage in Oklahoma, and rolling plains, including the Red River Rolling Plains of Oklahoma and Texas. The most dramatic feature of the weather, tornadoes, are most prominent in Oklahoma, but most of the time the sun shines, the wind blows, and the humidity stays in low ranges.[5] Some major metropolitan areas such as Oklahoma City and Austin draw water supplies from the Arkansas, Red, Brazos, and Colorado Rivers, as well as from aquifers like the Ogallala.[6] Areas of the region unsuited to raising crops provide excellent grazing land for cattle, sheep, and goats. Corn, soybeans, sorghum, winter wheat, and cotton often depend on irrigation to counter the low rainfall.[7]

The essays offered here provide lines of sight for four historical periods that inhabit this space. In the first, Caroline Castillo Crimm, in "Patricia de la Garza de León, Spanish/Texan Pioneer," creates a portrait of a woman whose life spanned the transition from Spanish Texas to Texas statehood. Like many pioneer women, Patricia moved to the frontier with her husband, Martín, to establish a ranch. However, she did not experience the isolation and loneliness often associated with homesteading women, because Patricia and Martín, as a Spanish family, moved with their extended family, servants, and workers to a mission town to await the construction of their ranch. Castillo Crimm makes clear the importance of "*compadrazgo*, the creation of an extended family, a powerful network of friends and family who could be depended on in time of need." Patricia de la Garza de León moved to the frontier to claim the promise of New Spain. Strong family networks helped her to survive the death of her husband, her family's competing loyalties to warring governments, and multiple moves to protect their lives and investments.

Donna L. Akers illuminates the intersections of indigenous, African, and Euro-American peoples in Indian Territory to provide the context necessary to understand why the murder of an African American woman was met with relief rather than retribution. "Killing Winged Celia: Gender, Race, and Culture in the Southern Plains" demonstrates how the Choctaw tried to preserve a society in which clan membership was traced through mothers, and women held different but complementary powers with men. For instance, Choctaw women were traditionally farmers, because their powers included the creation of life. Akers focuses on the influence of Euro-American forces, such as patriarchy and a market economy, and how those forces caused some Choctaw to sever the roots of their culture and familial relationships, both within the tribe and with their African American slaves, in order to assimilate.

According to Jean Stuntz, Comanche, Hispanic, and Anglo women brought with them specific forms of civilization when they settled on the southern plains. In "Civilizations of the Southern Plains, 1862–1930," we see Comanche women, largely nomadic, gained status through skill in activities such as cleaning buffalo hides. Hispanic women faced a difficult transition, from holding a central role in rural villages to working for wages in emerging urban areas. Their role within the family, combined with the discrimination they encountered outside of their barrios, led to the emergence of protofeminist activists as early as the 1910s. Stuntz also presents Anglo women who moved to the southern plains, illustrating how they helped to establish or work ranches and farms, bringing with them their vision of civilization in forms as wide-ranging as churches, colleges, saloons, literary societies, and civic clubs that beautified cities by planting flowers and trees in parks. They were drawn to land they could cultivate, and they carried their desire to cultivate civilization from dugout to frame house to Amarillo's first skyscraper.

Since 1930, extreme environmental conditions in the southern plains have challenged women committed to the land. As Linda W. Reese points out in "Risky Business: Southern Plains Women and the Tradition of Place," this environment, "ripe with possibility and fraught with danger influenced the women who settled the southern plains in the twentieth century and remain determined to stay on it." Reese focuses on those who withstood the Dust Bowl and those who continue to farm, in spite of cyclical drought and other challenges. Not only did these women have to contend with an extreme environment, but they also had to negotiate racial diversity, increasing mechanization, and the effects of government programs like the Rural Electrification Administration. Reese highlights several women, such as Fabiola Cabeza de Baca, a New Mexico Extension Service agent who "united women of every race," and "succeeded where others failed because she capitalized on traditional values and kinship networks while introducing new methods." Modern women farmers have continued to succeed by affirming traditional values, such as family-owned farms, while simultaneously introducing new methods, such as specialty crop farms.

As these essays demonstrate, seeing through women's eyes and listening to women's words are still the steps that western women's historians must take to create an increasingly inclusive history. They clearly demonstrate Castañeda's claim that "[w]omen of all races, classes, and cultures are active subjects, not passive objects or victims of the historical process."[8] Our vision of the southern Great Plains is now more beautiful, complex, and compelling as a result of these historian's contributions.

# 9

# Patricia de la Garza de León, Spanish/Texan Pioneer

CAROLINE CASTILLO CRIMM

The Great Plains drew women not only from the East Coast of the United States but also from the areas south of the Rio Grande. The years of living on the northern frontier of Mexico had made Hispanic women tough and resilient, able to adapt and accommodate to the challenging environment of the Great Plains. Northern New Spain is a land that once encompassed Texas and, therefore, shares the same arid landscape. The great northern migration, led by José de Escandón in the 1740s and 1750s to settle the river valleys of northeastern Mexico, brought people who had experienced living in the arid north. The women who moved into Texas after 1800, such as Patricia de la Garza de León, had already spent much of their lives learning to adjust to the environment and had developed lifestyles necessary to survive periods of drought and months of scorching heat as well as frigid northers that blew across the dry plains. They had also learned that the grasses of the Great Plains provided fodder for cattle, sheep, horses, and mules, the mainstay of their economy and source of their wealth, minimal though it might be. The difficulty of living on the dry plains was mitigated, especially for the women, by the methods of settlement chosen by the Spanish colonists. The Spanish families who came north, unlike their Anglo counterparts, would never set out alone to establish a small cabin on some barren grassland or some lonely creek bank. The Spanish came as large groups of settlers with livestock, ranch hands, and servants who carefully chose large ranches close to broad, deep rivers. Not far away were the mission friars sent to Christianize the local indigenous peoples, and soldiers to protect the small communities from any outward threats.[1]

The Spanish women who moved to the frontier successfully re-created their lifestyles by building families on the ranches with the same kind of cattle-based culture they had left behind. The spaces within which they lived were based on the Hispanic culture they had learned in northern Mexico and on the Catholic religion that dominated their lives. These two ruling principles would later set them at odds with the newly arrived Anglos who settled in Texas. The greatest influx of new settlers came with the transition of Mexico from Spanish Empire to independent republic. The new Mexican government hoped to settle its northern frontier much as the United States was settling the Great Plains. There the American government offered ten- and twenty-acre farmlands for sale at $1.25 to $10 an acre. In Texas, however, the temptation of nearly five thousand acres of land for mere pennies an acre was sufficient inducement for thousands to flock to this edge of the Great Plains after 1821.

The first Anglo settlers wisely adopted the methods and customs of their Hispanic neighbors, in particular the Catholic Irish who settled near the coast in Refugio and farther south in San Patricio. The Mexican settlers already living on established ranches along the San Antonio and Guadalupe Rivers taught their Anglo neighbors to survive on the dry grasslands by shifting from farming to cattle ranching. For the women, this new interaction with people outside their social structure remained friendly as long as the two groups had a common cause—surviving in the environment—and a common enemy— the indigenous people who objected to having their land taken. The interrelations became more difficult in 1836, when Mexican Texas came under the dominance of the Anglos, who resented the original Mexican settlers who still owned thousands of acres of land. The Anglo world that rapidly surrounded them could, and often did, threaten their security. The stories of land loss, when a husband or father was shot by Anglo marauders and the women were forced to sell out, made many of the old Mexican-Texan families resentful of the Anglos in whose hands the land had come to rest. But resentment did not dominate their lives. They were too busy making a living within their own community.

Patricia de la Garza de León, mother, rancher's wife, and community leader, shared with other Hispanic women the dangers of warfare, invasions, and changing governments in the years from 1780 to 1850. With her husband, Martín de León, Patricia helped establish two ranches in Texas, and together they founded the empresario settlement of Victoria. She also bore ten children and lived to see her children and grandchildren make the successful transition from Spanish Texas to Mexican Texas to the Republic of Texas and finally to statehood under the United States government. Three times, she established her space within the Great Plains, re-creating her Hispanic world. When her space was taken, she found ways to accommodate and accept the differences, while still retaining her Hispanic heritage.

Patricia de la Garza was a product of the northward expansion of the Spanish Empire during the 1740s. Spain's Enlightenment ruler, Carlos III, concerned about the French settlements in Louisiana, funded one of the first great land rushes in the New World and encouraged the settlement of northern New Spain, the area of modern Texas and the northeastern Mexican state of Tamaulipas. Patricia's father, José Angel de la Garza, and her mother, whose name is unknown, came north from central Mexico in December 1748, with more than twenty-five hundred other settlers to join the colony established by José de Escandón, the great colonizer, along the northeastern coast of Mexico, known as Nuevo Santander. The de la Garza family had originally planned to settle at the Villa de Vedoya on the Nueces River, which would have marked the northernmost settlement of Nuevo Santander. Escandón never founded the town of Vedoya and the de la Garzas moved with other settlers to the new port of Soto la Marina on the coast just north of Tampico. The three thousand to four thousand settlers in the northern colonies profited from the sale of hides, tallow, wool, cotton, and salt through Soto la Marina, until Mexico City merchants closed the port in 1776. Rather than leave the port city, the settlers, including the de la Garzas, turned inland to Saltillo and Monterrey to sell their goods.[2]

Patricia was born at Soto la Marina around 1775. During her early life on the de la Garza ranch, she was trained in all the womanly skills, including preparing food, healing illnesses and injuries, teaching religion, and educating the young. Although it is unclear whether Patricia ever learned to write, she placed a great deal of emphasis on education for all of her own ten children, both boys and girls, who were taught to read and write. She also learned to ride horses and developed ranching skills that would serve her well in later years.

By the time she was fifteen, Patricia was expected to choose a husband. Among the young men whom Patricia met was Martín de León, a young, ambitious muleteer, who spent much of his youth in the dangerous job of carrying goods by mule train across the northern expanses of New Spain. In 1790, perhaps at Patricia's instigation, Martín gave up his muleteering job and returned to his home town of Burgos, where he joined the local militia unit, known as the Fieles de Burgos, for a ten-year enlistment. With the Fieles de Burgos he helped to defend the Escandón settlements from raids by small Native tribes who lived in the mountains of northeastern Mexico and resented the encroachment of Spanish settlers on their lands.[3]

In 1795, twenty-year-old Patricia de la Garza married thirty-year-old Martín. Patricia could not expect great wealth from Martín, although he had just been promoted to captain of the regiment and could promise Patricia a grant of land when he finished his enlistment. In exchange, Patricia could offer a sizable dowry, property that she brought into the marriage to help the family get a good start in life. The money and goods remained legally hers, and when she did sign them over to her husband, she could reclaim them upon his death. Dowries for young women in the larger cities, including Monterrey in northern Mexico, consisted of clothes, linen, jewels, furniture, and silverware. On the frontier, however, dowries were more practical, consisting of money and animals that could be used to start a ranch.[4]

As her dowry, Patricia de la Garza received from her father twelve mares, four two-year-old colts, five tame horses, five unbroken colts, two proof jacks, sixteen breeding cows, one yoke of oxen, one donkey for plowing, one jenny (female donkey), and one cow. Of far greater importance was the 9,800 pesos in cash, which was the gift from her godfather, Don Angel Pérez of Soto la Marina. The largest amount listed for the brides of Monterrey, the principal city in the north of Mexico during this period, was 5,000 pesos. Her dowry of nearly 10,000 pesos placed Martín and Patricia among the wealthy upper classes.[5]

During the next five years, Patricia and Martín made their home in Burgos, where Martín served out his enlistment. By the time the first two children were born, Fernando in 1798 and María Candelaria in 1800, the young couple had decided to use Martín's captain's grant of land and Patricia's dowry to establish a ranch for their growing family in the river valleys of the area that would come to be known as the Great Plains. They planned to hire vaqueros and servants to come with them to settle and build their ranch. In addition to protection by their own vaqueros and servants, the two to three dozen settlers at the small ranch settlement could expect help from the presidio, or military fort, of La Bahía del Espíritu Santo, two days' ride to the northeast, or from San Antonio de Bexar, another town and fort, a two days' ride to the northwest.[6]

Martín and Patricia chose their land at the Paso de Santa Margarita on the Nueces River. It was an important low-water crossing on the road from Escandón's border towns along the Rio Grande to the presidio and mission at La Bahía. Unlike the Anglo women moving westward onto the Great Plains, Patricia would never have been left alone in a log cabin to wait while her husband went in search of food, better land, or barter. Spanish families always moved in large groups consisting of a central family, including relatives with servants, ranch hands, and farm help, and they remained at missions or towns while the strong and defensible ranches were built. While Patricia waited at La

Bahía, caring for four-year-old Fernando and two-year-old Maria Candelaria, and pregnant with José Silvestre, Martín took his ranch hands down to the river crossing in 1802 and began the construction of the ranch.[7]

Acquiring the land and building the ranch was a slow process. The Spanish crown, and its many bureaucrats, maintained careful control of the lands and it often took years for the paperwork to reach Mexico City and Seville, Spain, and be returned with the required permits. While Martín traveled back and forth from La Bahía to the Nueces River site, Patricia gave birth to José Silvestre in 1802. With the couple still waiting on their land title, another daughter, María Guadalupe, was born two years later, and their fifth child, Félix, was born in 1806, just before the completion of the ranch headquarters and the family's move to the ranch.[8]

The Rancho de Santa Margarita, Martín and Patricia's ranch, provided protection and a place for travelers to stay while crossing the Nueces River on their travels from the towns on the Rio Grande and La Bahía to San Antonio. The deed describes the ranch as arid and gives the legal description: "[B]ounded on the South by the said [Nueces] River; on the North by the village of the Apaches and from this point toward the West, they are bounded by the creek *Nombre de Dios* and toward the East they extend as far as the lands owned by the Mission del Rosario."[9]

Their ranch headquarters was built on high ground overlooking the Nueces River at the site of the modern town of San Patricio, Texas. The river was close enough to provide water for the ranch while avoiding the yearly spring floods. While Martín and the vaqueros worked the horse herds, trained mules, and rounded up cattle, Patricia, her daughters, and the house servants worked to make the house comfortable. Together the women produced food for the many ranch hands, wove cloth, washed the clothing, cleaned the house, and produced such salable commodities as candles and rose-scented soaps made from lye and lard. In addition, the girls and their brothers learned their catechism, were taught to read and write, and received baptism and communion when a priest happened by the ranch.

The couple made a modest living for almost ten years from the cattle, mules, and horses that roamed the flat, dry grasslands. The couple never did complete the paperwork necessary to receive a title to the ranch, but with the vast lands available in Texas, the government did not demand titles of its citizens.[10]

By 1805, Martín and Patricia welcomed an increasing stream of visitors at the Santa Margarita Ranch. French leader Napoleon Bonaparte had sold the Louisiana territory to the Americans, abrogating the agreement made with the Spanish king. Spanish settlers from Louisiana needed a refuge and the Spanish viceregal government wanted more settlers in the frontier province, as long as they were settled far from the border with Louisiana, where they might engage in contraband. Martín and Patricia hosted settlers going to found the new town of Santísima Trinidad de Salcedo on the Trinity River as well as those fleeing from American Louisiana who had decided to move back to New Spain to establish homes in Nuevo Santander, Monterrey, or Saltillo.

Patricia, concerned for her children's education, both religious and secular, hired a tutor who lived on the ranch and taught the children to read and write. She was said to have insisted that her children not carry guns, since she believed that only hooligans were armed. During 1806, the Nuevo Santander and Nuevo León militias had been called out once again to defend Texas from Thomas Jefferson's explorers, Lewis and Clark, although the two men never entered Texas and remained far to the north. Lieutenant Zebulon Montgomery Pike, on the other hand, of Pike's Peak fame, did come through Texas, although he was unimpressed by the small settlements.[11]

By 1810, Patricia, now the mother of seven children, Agapito having been born in 1808 and María de Jesús in 1810, had to find godparents from among the other ranch families at La Bahía. These *compadres* and *comadres*, the co-parents, promised to help the parents protect the infant throughout their lives and bring the child up in the Catholic faith. For Patricia, the concept of godparenthood had expanded to become *compadrazgo*, the creation of an extended family, a powerful network of friends and family who could be depended on in time of need. With each child born into the de León family and the addition of another set of godparents, the communal bond grew. Since the godparents were as close or closer than family, everyone in the small community was often related to one another either by blood or through the church.[12]

Mexico was in turmoil in 1810 and the repercussions were soon felt at the Santa Margarita Ranch. Patricia was concerned over the safety of her children as soldiers headed north to put down rebels stopped off at the ranch. The independence movement led by Father Miguel Hidalgo y Costilla had begun in Guanajuato in the center of Mexico in 1810, but by 1811, rebels staged a brief revolt in San Antonio. Although that revolt failed, mercenaries from New Orleans invaded Texas and captured La Bahía at the end of 1811.

Patricia grew increasingly concerned when the invasion forces began raiding the nearby ranches, including the Santa Margarita. Patricia insisted on moving the family, with all eight children—including Refugia, the newborn—back to her home at Soto la Marina. By the end of August 1814, the royalist General Arredondo had reestablished control and Patricia and the de León family returned to Texas. This time, Patricia insisted that the family establish a new ranch, closer to the safety of the military units at La Bahía. The second de León ranch was settled on the Aransas River in 1814.[13]

For the next three years, Patricia and Martín profited from the sale of horses, mules, cattle, hides, and tallow at San Antonio and perhaps as far away as Saltillo. They also needed to buy a trousseau in New Orleans for their eldest daughter, María Candelaria. At the marriageable age of fifteen, young women in Texas were introduced to the society of La Bahía and San Antonio. Patricia had found a suitable young man for her eldest daughter in José Miguel Aldrete, the son of the neighboring Aldrete family. The plans for the marriage had to be halted, however, when more rebels invaded Texas in 1817, threatening the de León family on the Aransas River ranch. Martín, Patricia, and the family could do little but barricade themselves on their ranch and wait for help from General Arredondo, who crushed the rebels in the fall of 1817. The ranch families around La Bahía were once again at peace, and the wedding between José Miguel Aldrete and María Candelaria de León took place the following year in the small chapel at the presidio of La Bahía.[14]

During 1821 Patricia gave birth to their last daughter, Francisca, destined from birth to care for her parents in their old age. The same year, Mexico declared its independence from Spain and the new government in Mexico City began plans for more colonization. The new government hoped to emulate the United States and bring in settlers to strengthen its northern frontier. The requirements included loyalty to Mexico and adherence to the Catholic religion; Moses Austin was among those who wished to colonize Texas. He claimed Spanish citizenship because of his residence in Spanish Louisiana for the previous ten years. Austin died before he could carry out his plans, and his son, Stephen F. Austin, took over his contract to bring settlers to Texas.[15]

With the advent of the new government and the imminent arrival of Austin's colonists, Martín and Patricia were concerned about acquiring land for their own children. In 1824 Martín de León hastened to San Antonio to request an empresario contract, which required that he establish settlers in his colony and provide for their welfare. Each settler was to be granted a league of 4,428 acres for a ranch, and a labor of 177 acres for a farm. As empresario, Martín was also to act as judge and militia leader and to handle all the paperwork necessary for surveying and granting title to the lands. As the head of the colony, he and Patricia received the honorific titles of Don and Doña, and their sons and sons-in-law would become the leaders of the colony. Martín received a contract to settle forty-one families on the banks of the Guadalupe River at a town that he called Nuestra Señora de Guadalupe Victoria, shortened to Victoria.[16]

Doña Patricia's children were reaching marriageable age, and, as leaders in the community, the de León sons and daughters were attractive marriage prospects. Within the first five years of the Victoria colony, Doña Patricia had married off six of her ten children, all of whom settled in either Victoria or the nearby settlement of La Bahía, by now renamed Goliad in honor of Father Miguel Hidalgo, the Mexican liberator. The remaining children, Refugia, age twelve, Agustina, ten, and Francisca, eight, remained with Don Martín and Doña Patricia in their new home in the town of Victoria.[17]

After the success of the first forty-one families, Martín expanded his settlement of Victoria by requesting and receiving a second contract for 150 settlers. Among the new immigrants were Placido Benavides and José María Jesús Carbajal, both well-educated and influential members of the colony's government. In 1832, Benavides, the colony's teacher and militia leader, married eighteen-year-old Agustina. The same year, Carbajal, who had been educated in the United States and had been hired as a land surveyor for Texas, married twenty-year-old Refugia. Benavides and Carbajal were both advocates of the new liberal ideas and influenced some of the family members to join them in their opposition to the Mexican government.[18]

During the summer of 1833 and 1834, cholera struck Texas with devastating effect. The disease was introduced by the Irish colonists arriving from New Orleans and spread with horrifying speed throughout the colonies. During 1834 Martín and Patricia remained in Victoria to care for the sick and dying. Sixty-eight-year-old Martín contracted the disease and died on July 18, 1834, leaving Patricia, her two daughters, and her granddaughter in the big Victoria townhouse.[19]

With Don Martín gone, Doña Patricia stepped into the role of matriarch of the colony. While her sons and sons-in-law took over the day-to-day running of the government, Doña Patricia, who made it her business to know everyone, saw to the health and cleanliness of the town. She made sure the sick were cared for and that church services took place as often as a priest was available. She continued the school for the children and insisted on law-abiding citizens in the town. As with most Hispanic matriarchs, her children obeyed her commands, and although she had no legal standing, her word was law for both her family and the citizens of Victoria.

The Anglo-American settlers in the colonies to the north had begun to coalesce in opposition to the new government established by Santa Anna in 1834. In late 1835, Santa Anna sent Martín Perfecto de Cos, his brother-in-law, north to arrest the rebels who opposed the new government. Among the rebels was Doña Patricia's son-in-law, Carbajal, who fled for his life to Victoria. There Doña Patricia's family and Carbajal's Anglo-American friends protected him from the troops who arrived in hot pursuit.[20]

Doña Patricia did not have the luxury of choosing sides as Texas slowly slipped into war during 1835 and 1836: half of her family sided with the rebellious Anglo-Americans, and half opposed involvement in the escalating conflict.[21] During December 1835, Doña Patricia's sons and sons-in-law were involved in the defeat of General Cos at San Antonio. Everyone felt sure that the war was over, but by January 1836 it became evident that Santa Anna would not rest until Texas was punished for its insurrection.

Doña Patricia could not have been pleased when she learned that her eldest son, Fernando, and José María Jesús Carbajal had driven a herd of horses to New Orleans to exchange for arms and ammunition. Returning with the supplies, Fernando and Carbajal were captured and imprisoned at Casa Mata in Matamoros. Perhaps at Doña Patricia's insistence, Placido Benavides helped his two brothers-in-law escape and the trio returned to the de León ranches in Victoria.[22]

Doña Patricia grew increasingly concerned for her family. While she would have preferred that her family stay out of the fray, her son Fernando had received a commission with the Texian army, and Placido Benavides rejoined the Texas militia, which effectively harassed General Urrea's forces on their way through Victoria.[23] As Santa Anna marched toward San Jacinto, General Urrea took control of Victoria and was informed that Fernando de León, as one of the town leaders and a supporter of the Texian independence movement, was hiding supplies destined for the Texian army. Much to Doña Patricia's dismay, General Urrea jailed Fernando and forced him to disclose the location of the supplies. When Fernando finally revealed the cache, he was still not released from his confinement and instead remained in the Victoria jail, where, it is believed, Doña Patricia cared for him until the arrival of the Anglo-American forces in May 1836.[24]

With the defeat of Santa Anna at San Jacinto in April 1836, General Urrea released Fernando and retreated toward Mexico. General Thomas Rusk, who had been appointed to take the place of the wounded Sam Houston as commander of the Texian forces, arrived in Victoria and, at the insistence of Anglo-American enemies, jailed Fernando again, this time as a traitor to the Texian cause. When Fernando was finally released, Doña Patricia moved the family out to the ranch for protection from the roaming bands of Anglo-American marauders, most of them newly arrived volunteers who had missed the fighting and saw the de León family as Mexicans who should be punished. Furious at the affront of having vagabonds stealing her property, Doña Patricia protested the treatment directly to Rusk, demanding his protection from the wild and uncontrollable Texian troops. There was little Rusk could do, as he had no food or supplies to give the troops.[25]

In June 1836 Rusk received word of another attack planned by Mexican forces and ordered the removal of the Mexican families. Just as Patricia and Martín had taken their family to safety to avoid raids by rebels during the first decades of the nineteenth century, Doña Patricia gathered the whole family to leave Texas. She was only able to save fifteen mule-loads of goods, mules rented from Phillip Dimmitt for which he later demanded payment from General Rusk. According to Fernando de León in a claim made in 1848, General Rusk:

> gave a special order for your petitioner [Fernando] and his family to embark on board of a government vessel, then at anchor in Matagorda Bay, bound for Galveston and New Orleans. . . . Previous to leaving, in compliance with the order of General Rusk, your petitioner and his family had been forcibly deprived of a large amount of property, consisting of clothing, furniture, plate and jewelry by men professing to be patriot volunteers . . . who won their chief laurels by taking the ear rings and jewelry from the persons of helpless females belonging to your petitioner's family. . . . Your petitioner was hurried off on foot (his corral being full of horses at the time, but it was said, they were all needed for the army) to the Government vessel and landed with his family in New Orleans.[26]

The family set sail from Matagorda for New Orleans on the barque *C.P. Williams* in June 1836 along with more than seventy other families. [27]

Upon arriving in New Orleans, Doña Patricia arranged to sell one of the two ranches that Don Martín had been granted as compensation for his empresario efforts, claiming the main ranch in its entirety as her dowry right. Hispanic women had the right to reclaim their dowry before any of the property of a marriage was divided among the heirs, and since all of her children had ranches of their own, Doña Patricia felt no compunction in taking all of the property. Pleasant Branch Cocke of New Orleans paid $10,000 for the twenty-two-thousand-acre main ranch, just the amount she had brought into the marriage almost forty years earlier.

The family did not remain in New Orleans, but moved to Opelousas, Louisiana, where they stayed with Placido's Benavides kin. Women, in particular upper-class women such as Doña Patricia, had limited opportunities to make a living. Smart businesswomen knew that they had to protect themselves by investing their funds wisely. Owning land and mortgages provided a steady income and Doña Patricia invested much of her money in mortgages in Louisiana, as well as holding a mortgage on the home in downtown Victoria. These mortgages provided her with a comfortable income until the end of her life and were later passed on to her two youngest daughters.[28]

Within two years, Doña Patricia packed up the family once again and moved back to Soto la Marina. Although conditions in Texas were still unsettled, Placido's brothers and the Linn family, early Irish settlers who had become friends of the de Leóns', returned to Texas, where they jointly maintained tax payments on the property belonging to all of the de León family members.[29]

When Texas finally became part of the United States in 1845, Doña Patricia decided to return to Victoria. With the beginning of statehood in Texas and the invasion of Mexico by US troops in 1846, numerous Mexicans now sought refuge from the fighting by returning to their Texas homes. Caravans of wagons, coaches, and riders brought visits from family in Tamaulipas to the Texas ranches. Doña Patricia welcomed her family back to Victoria, where she held marriages and baptisms for her grandchildren at St. Mary's Catholic Church, which had been built on the town tracts donated by the de León family.[30]

Another good reason to return to Texas was the family's hope of recovering their lands. Under the government of the Republic of Texas, the laws were written to allow the new Anglo settlers to take over the land of Tejanos who might have "forfeited the land in consequence of having abandoned the country and given aid and comfort to the enemy."[31] Much of the de León land was invaded and taken over by claim jumpers who falsely claimed that the de León family had sided with Santa Anna. Upon her return, Patricia de la Garza de León brought suit to regain her family's lands. The Spanish laws of community property had long given women the right to own land in their own right and to regain their dowries upon the death of their husbands. Women also had the right to represent themselves in court and to sue and be sued. Fortunately, these legal rights for women had been adopted by the State of Texas and Doña Patricia and her daughters made good use of these laws to regain their property.

The Treaty of Guadalupe Hidalgo, which ended the Mexican-American War, had given the original Mexican landowners the right to reclaim their lands. The Texas Supreme Court was forced to reverse many of the rulings made under the Texas Republic and restore land titles to the Tejanos since "once a legal grant had been made by a previous sovereign, whether Spain or Mexico, the property belonged to the grantee regardless of citizenship."[32] Notwithstanding the family's right to the de León lands, many of the Anglo-American claim jumpers refused to move. If Fernando and Doña Patricia and the other Tejanos wanted their lands back, they had to undergo the long and expensive process of reclaiming their titles through the courts. Doña Patricia, by this time seventy-one years old, did not hesitate to leap into the legal quagmire, and she encouraged her children to do likewise.[33]

She was concerned about protecting her investments. Sometime in 1845 or 1846, Robert Carlisle and Bridget Quinn had bought the de León family home on the Victoria town square. Doña Patricia, already well acquainted with the advantages of holding income-producing mortgages from her years in Louisiana, took a mortgage for $7,000 on the property. The couple had been paying $700 a year on the note until sometime in 1849. When they stopped paying, Doña Patricia took Carlisle and Quinn to court. In 1851, shortly after her death, a jury returned a verdict for Doña Patricia's estate, and her two youngest daughters continued to receive the income from this mortgage for a number of years.[34]

Because of the Spanish laws that gave them the right to own property, Hispanic women were often the source of funds for those who needed it within their communities, and they readily made loans to their kin, although they often held mortgages as protection. Doña Patricia had taken on the responsibility for her three orphan Benavides granddaughters when Placido and Agustina passed away in Louisiana. In 1847, she petitioned the court of Victoria County through W. H. Delano, her attorney:

> She has been placed in charge and care of [her granddaughters] [María] Pilar, [María] Libriata [sic], and Matiana [Benavides] for the last four years and six months. Support of said children has come from her own purse. During the whole period of her said charge she has received nothing from the estate except $100 and a small amount of clothing and necessaries. . . . She is pained to say that poverty renders her incapable of doing this any longer. She is informed that the Guardian [her son, Fernando de León] has no funds in his possession. She prays that the court make an order for sale of a portion of the real estate. She prays also that a house in the Town of Victoria known as the Round Top House, a part of the property of said estate may be appropriated for the use of the heirs.[35]

Ysidro, the girls' uncle, who had taken good care of the girls' inheritance, had died in 1845. During the following four years, Fernando, Doña Patricia's eldest son and the girls' uncle, was appointed guardian. Fernando, evidently, gave his mother nothing for the care of the girls. Although he may have claimed he had no money to give, the court records indicate that the Benavides estate was still providing $381.20 in rents and income every year. By the same token, Doña Patricia was not destitute either. She was receiving income from mortgages on property in Louisiana and $700 a year on a mortgage on the family home in downtown Victoria. Admittedly, she may have been tight for cash, since she had just loaned $6,000 to her son-in-law, José María Jesús Carbajal, for his revolution to establish the Republic of the Rio Grande in northern Mexico. As a result of her appeal, Fernando was relieved of his duties as guardian, and a relative from Soto la Marina, Cesario de la Garza, was appointed by the court to take over the care of the girls' estates. The three Benavides daughters, upon reaching their majority, took over the care of their own property and became accomplished businesswomen.[36]

By October 1850, Patricia de la Garza de León, then about seventy-five years of age, was dying. She had prepared her will with the help of Edward Linn, an old and faithful Irish Catholic family friend, and Cesario de la Garza, her new son-in-law, both of whom would serve as her executors. As part of her will, she began by listing the advances made to her children over the years, including the following:

> Fernando de León received $1,611 in cash and stock.
>
> Silvestre de León (deceased) received $777.
>
> Jesúsa Manchola received $955.
>
> Guadalupe de la Garza received $417.
>
> Félix de León received $910 received $519.
>
> Agapito de León (deceased) received $350.
>
> Candelaria Aldrete received $580.
>
> Refugia Carbajal received [illegible] money and stock.
>
> Francisca Dosal received $850.[37]

If it was true that she could not read or write, she did an admirable job of keeping track of her funds. With everyone informed of their debts to her, she then began the list of her bequests to each of them. To Fernando, her eldest, she left nothing, and took the additional and surprisingly vengeful step of bequeathing "to each of my children [except Fernando] equal portions of the $1,000 that Fernando borrowed from me to pay debts."[38] Whether this was in part to punish him for not having taken care of his three nieces five years earlier or for his possible conversion to the Protestant religion or for some unknown insult is unknown.

Fernando tried to make amends by marrying forty-year-old Luz Escalera de León, a dedicated Catholic, who would become the de León family matriarch during the next thirty years. In August 1850, the newlywed couple had also attempted to mollify Doña Patricia by adopting fifteen-year-old Francisco Santiago, the son of Fernando's brother Silvestre, who had been living in Soto la Marina with his brothers since the war for Texas independence. Neither act restored him to his mother's good graces.

Patricia evidently liked her two sons-in-law, however. She left "to José María Carbajal the $6,000 he owes me and to Miguel Aldrete the $1,000 he owes me." The rest of the property she divided among the widowed daughters and her grandsons. The remaining sons and daughters all held their own land and had substantial wealth.[39]

Doña Patricia was concerned about her two youngest daughters. Women were often favored in wills in both Latin America and the United States because of their financial vulnerability and the difficulties they faced in making a living through their own work and diligence. In the new Anglo world, American laws prevented women from owning property in their own names, and women were often required to call on a male relative to handle their business affairs. Women were also expected to stay at home and care for the children on the ranch or farm. Jobs in the towns for young women were limited to teaching or helping their husbands in mercantile establishments. Doña Patricia had lived as a widow for fifteen years, and although she had significant support from her mortgages and her extended family, she knew the struggles and hardships that women faced. Patricia's daughter, forty-year-old María de Jesús Manchola, widow of Rafael Manchola, had large quantities of land, but she had been forced to depend on her brothers to handle her business affairs for her in the new Anglo world.

In 1850, Francisca, Patricia's youngest daughter, at thirty-two, was at last given permission by Doña Patricia to marry and was freed of her traditional Mexican duty as the youngest daughter to care for her mother. With her mother's blessing, Francisca married Vicente Dosal, a tailor from Zacatecas, Mexico, of whom Patricia evidently approved. It was to these two daughters that Doña Patricia left the mortgages she owned in Louisiana after deducting the lawyers' fees. She left the title to two of her building lots in Victoria on which she held income-producing mortgages, one each, to María de Jesús Manchola and Francisca Dosal. Her cattle were to be portioned out, one-third to María de Jesús and one-third to Francisca, with the remainder of the cattle and one yoke of oxen going to her fifteen-year-old grandson, Francisco Santiago de León, who had just been adopted by Fernando and Luz Escalera. Francisco Santiago, as well as his two brothers, Francisco Grande and Martín, both with new wives and families of their own, received one each of the Louisiana mortgages.[40] The remainder of the family was doing well and Patricia did not feel she needed to divide her limited funds with them.

Doña Patricia, well aware of the political power of their old family friends, Edward Linn and Texas Senator John J. Linn, asked Edward to serve as her executor, jointly with her son-in-law, Cesario de la Garza. Linn was an Irish Catholic and she knew he would carry out her wishes in remembering her religious duties. Linn was to "pay to the Catholic Church all the dues that my parents owed" from the debts that were owed her by the State of Texas for her losses during the Texas Revolution. There was, by late 1850, some realistic hope that Texas would be able to repay the debts incurred in 1836, since the United States government had promised to pay $10 million to Texas as part of the Compromise of 1850, and as a powerful political figure, Senator Linn might have been able to regain Patricia's money from the state. Whether Doña Patricia's heirs ever received payment is unknown, but they had inherited a sufficient amount to continue to live comfortably throughout their lives. On her deathbed Doña Patricia had done what she could to protect her children. Their success within the Anglo-American economy was up to them.[41]

Until the 1880s, Patricia's descendants remained on the ranches and drew wealth from carting, hides, cattle, and land sales. The wealth in the hands of the matriarchs, such as Patricia de la Garza and, after her, Luz Escalera, provided a readily available source of cash from which members of the family and *compadrazgo* network could borrow. Numerous sisters, in-laws, cousins, and friends worked together as business partners, bought and sold from each other, and shared the communal wealth. Called together by the mothers to celebrate religious festivals, families gathered a dozen times a year or more to keep the Mexican traditions alive. Through the power of the women, they preserved their language, their food, their culture, their religion, and their pride. Once they left the ranches and moved to town, they insulated themselves in their barrios and the mothers, sisters, and godmothers continued to extend protection over their children and godchildren. With their male kin to call on in times of need, with the strength of the families and their religion, with the resourcefulness of their culture, the women of the de León family and the Tejanas of Victoria could live out their lives in comparative peace, passing on to the next generation new matriarchs, new godparents, and a community populated by descendants of Patricia de León.

# 10
# Killing Winged Celia
## Gender, Race, and Culture in the Southern Plains
### DONNA L. AKERS

In 1879, an old African American woman was chased through the woods by a man with a loaded gun. She ran through the underbrush, searching for a hiding spot, frustrated with her ancient body's lack of agility and stamina, and finally emerged into a small clearing, with her pursuer right behind her. She came out into the light, turned to look him in the eye, straightened her posture, and waited for death. It came swiftly, without delay; the blast of the old rifle echoed in the quiet woods.

She fell to the ground, mortally wounded, but still alive. As she waited in terror and pain, she saw the man moving toward her without the rifle. He stooped over and picked up a large rock, switching the wooden stake he held from his right hand to his left, and then he advanced. In one swift moment, the old woman died, pinned to the ground by a wooden stake driven through her heart. And there her body was left for the buzzards.[1]

"Winged Celia" was killed in Indian Territory in the early 1870s.[2] No one knew where she lived—she had no fixed abode, and only made sporadic visits in the little African-Choctaw settlement near the woods. She was killed by an African-Choctaw man who was rendering a service to his community—or so he believed. You see, Winged Celia was not a human being. She was a witch; and as such, she posed a frightening threat to humans.[3]

The killing of Winged Celia in this small, backwoods clearing in the old Choctaw Nation dramatically illustrates the diverse experiences of women living in the southern plains after the Civil War. The intersection of race, culture, and identity in Indian Territory developed from a unique confluence of disparate peoples—indigenous, African, and Euro-American. Winged Celia's murder highlights how, over time, cultural beliefs and norms are diffused and shaped to suit the needs of a society.

The story of Winged Celia took place in the years after the Civil War, when many small African American communities dotted the landscape of Indian Territory. At least twenty-five African American settlements were created in the post-Civil War years in Indian Territory, almost exclusively made up of former slaves of the Choctaw, Cherokee, Chickasaw, and Muscogee (or Creek) peoples.[4] These large Indian nations had been forced into permanent exile in Oklahoma from their southeastern homelands during the so-called Indian Removal of the 1830s and had brought slavery with them from the Old South.

In Indian Territory, a few families of mixed white-Indian ancestry owned large farms of hundreds of acres, on which they grew cotton for the US market. Dozens, and in some cases, hundreds, of African American slaves labored on these plantations, most of which lined the banks of the Red River. For example, Robert M. Jones, of mixed white-Choctaw heritage, owned five large Red River plantations, the largest of which was more than five thousand acres where more than five hundred African people in bondage labored. He transported his crops to market in New Orleans via five steamboats he owned that plied the Red River between Indian Territory and New Orleans.[5]

The great majority of slaves among the Native peoples of Indian Territory were owned by a small number of men who participated in the market economy, growing crops such as cotton to sell in New Orleans. Aside from these few men, the vast majority of indigenes in Indian Territory engaged in subsistence farming, and sometimes they had a slave or slave family living with them. The nature of slavery among the Indians has been the subject of a scholarly inquiry over the past few years. Scholars such as Tiya Miles and Theda Perdue argue that Indian slavery was more lenient and less onerous than that practiced by white slaveholders in the South.[6] It was apparently rare for slaves belonging to the Indians to be whipped or punished physically, and many former slaves reported that they shared equally with the Indian family in terms of produce and work and had the freedom to engage in outside work, from which they kept all or most of their earnings.[7]

Slavery had been practiced for centuries among the Southern Native peoples, but unlike the white, Southern form of chattel slavery, the indigenous system had been in a transitional state in the process of moving from captivity to adoption. Before 1700, slavery in the Southern nations was not hereditary and was not a part of the economic system. Captive women and children performed work as "slaves" until a clan or family adopted them. Adoption was a physical and spiritual experience, believed by the Choctaws to totally transform the outsider into a Choctaw person. After this process, the captive was no longer a slave and had all the rights, privileges, and responsibilities of natural-born Choctaws.[8]

Slavery as a system was not static, however. During the eighteenth century, as part of the French, English, and Spanish struggle for influence and allies, southeastern indigenous nations were played against one another. European governments encouraged strife and factionalism and turned the Chickasaws into slave hunters against the Choctaw people. Hundreds of Choctaws were sold into slavery in the Caribbean through British slave traders in Charleston, South Carolina. Slavery was again transformed during the nineteenth century—imported from American society in a new and virulent form of lifelong, hereditary bondage.

After the American Revolution, white men came into the Choctaw Nation as traders, refugees, criminals in flight, or adventurers, and they married Choctaw women. The first of such men we have on record were isolated individuals who were the progenitors of families of mixed heritage, many of whom became prominent in nineteenth-century politics. These men sometimes brought up their male children as participants in the American market economy, and a handful were successful in achieving economic prosperity that mimicked that of white Southern slave owners, adopting the outer markings of what they thought was "civilization." This included raising crops for the market, selling for profit, and exploiting slave labor in an oppressive colonial relationship between Choctaw families and Africans, similar to that of Southern plantation owners.

These white intruders imported the ideology of patriarchy along with other ideas from American culture. In traditional southeastern nations, matrilineal kinship was the norm, and women and men engaged in complementary, although distinct, spheres of power, labor, responsibility, and privilege. When white men married into the tribe, the resulting children were recognized as clan members of their mothers in the usual manner of matrilineal peoples. Their white fathers sometimes taught them English and, in some cases, introduced Euro-American thought, behavior patterns, religious beliefs, and other aspects of white ways of living into the lives of their Native family. Intermarried white men were agents of change within the indigenous nations, introducing patriarchal male dominance as "civilized."[9]

Choctaw gender roles differed greatly from those of the dominant white society. For example, in the Choctaw Nation, women traditionally were the farmers. They planted and tended the crops as a natural expression of the Native belief that women had special powers to create and nurture life. The farming that indigenous women performed was subsistence farming: growing enough to meet their needs, with an occasional small surplus that they would sometimes sell. According to white American norms, farming was performed by men, while women tended the home and children. Historian Theda Perdue relates that with the gradual expansion of men's dominance into the agricultural economy of the southeastern indigenes, gender roles "became blurred." Most of the prosperous men of mixed heritage either hired tenants to farm their land or had slaves perform the work. Many of them viewed farming as undesirable labor—perhaps due, in part, to the residual effects of Choctaw belief systems that labeled farming as feminine. Jeffersonian ideals of independent, yeoman farmers forming the basis of American society were never embraced among the Choctaws.

Patriarchy, the market economy, and Christianity expanded within the Choctaw Nation over the nineteenth century, leading to drastic alterations in indigenous societies that had practiced true equality between the sexes for millennia. These hegemonic relations of domination and subordination so typical of Western Christian societies deformed indigenous societies and led to a myriad of adverse and negative consequences, not only for women but for the entire society. The resulting declension of female autonomy, equality, independence, and power introduced pathologies common in white societies, for example, the impoverishment of women and children, the increase in domestic abuse, as well as the devaluing of womanhood and femininity.[10] Theda Perdue and Sarah Hill argue that although gender roles changed over time, "the story of Cherokee women . . . is not one of declining status and lost culture, but one of persistence and change, conservatism and adaptation, tragedy and survival."[11]

Although the number of intermarried white men was very small in 1800, by the time the infamous forced dispossessions began, some had gained influence and prominence among their adopted Native nation. Take, for example, Peter Pitchlynn, the son of a white trader and a woman of mixed white and Choctaw heritage. He was well educated and bilingual, and he served as the Choctaw Nation's representative to the United States government. He lived in Washington, D.C., for many years and attended many social occasions in the "best" circles. He also maintained a large farm and family in the Choctaw Nation and served as the principal chief of the nation during the Civil War. The Pitchlynns were related to all the prominent families of mixed white-Choctaw heritage, including the Folsoms, whom we will meet later in the story.

As in any group of people, there were varied attitudes toward white civilization, but as aggressive American colonization proceeded and its rhetoric of superiority took hold, many people of mixed heritage believed the indigenes should and could "progress" and become "civilized." Little did they realize that they could never become "civilized" enough that Euro-Americans would accept them as equals. Albert Memmi points out that once the difference between the colonizer and the colonized has been isolated, "the gap must be kept from being filled. The colonialist removes the factor from history, time, and therefore possible evolution. What is actually a sociological point becomes labeled as being biological."[12] In the early years of the nineteenth century, the American government and missionaries told indigenous peoples that they had to become educated and acculturated to eschew their "savage" ways; then they would be welcomed into mainstream American society. This rhetoric was believed by many of the Choctaws of mixed heritage, who internalized this propaganda and strove to meet white American measures of what constituted a "civilized" person. But just as Memmi describes, white Americans codified the distinctions between themselves and the Other as biologically determined. Thus, "Indians" and blacks could never be equal with whites, no matter how acculturated they became.

Many Choctaws of mixed heritage were shocked when they came face to face with white racial attitudes after adopting many of the accoutrements of white society. Rather than being welcomed into the brotherhood of the dominant society, they found themselves rejected not because they were "savages" in manners, lifestyles, attitudes, or beliefs, but solely based on their so-called race. Persons of mixed heritage, even those who appeared to be white, were resoundingly rejected from equality with white Americans along with their darker-complected kin. A vivid example of this took place when Peter Pitchlynn's sons were arrested for murder and tried in the federal court in Arkansas by an all-white jury in 1859. A couple of drunken white men got into a fight with the Pitchlynns at the home of the latter in the Choctaw Nation. The altercation resulted in the death of one of the white men, and the Pitchlynn sons were immediately arrested on a charge of first-degree murder. Despite the complete lack of testimony against the Pitchlynn sons from anyone other than the second white man involved in the fight, the Pitchlynns were convicted and sentenced to long jail terms. Peter Pitchlynn became extremely embittered when he found that the Arkansans were so patently and flagrantly racially prejudiced that his sons could not receive a fair trial and were instead tried and convicted of Indianness. This was indeed a bitter lesson to learn, after spending a lifetime embracing the supposed superiority of white ways.

Although a minority of Choctaws strove to acculturate, the majority continued to live in traditional ways, despite the decimation of the matrilineal clan system during the dispossessions of the 1830s. The Choctaw system of kinship that incorporated balance and equality between genders continued. Nothing in southeastern indigenous belief systems posited the inferiority of women; indeed, quite the opposite. Women were esteemed as the givers of life, the repository of female mystical powers with which they created life. Men likewise had masculine domains—warfare and hunting. In their own spheres, both men and women could call on special, gendered spiritual powers that were regarded with respect and awe by the opposite gender. The vast majority of indigenous southeastern men and women continued traditional views about women's roles, but from about 1830 on, one can locate the increasing intrusion of the American system of patriarchy.

A huge blow to gender equality and the matrilineal clan system of the Choctaw people occurred in the 1830s, as a result of their expulsion from their homelands. At that time the United States sent Colonel William Armstrong to the Choctaw Nation to list all Choctaws on a roll. This dispossession roll would be of great importance and long-lasting influence, ultimately having dire consequences for Choctaw society. It was to be used as the basis for claims for compensation for improved lands that the Choctaws were being forced to abandon, to distribute rations during the horrendous Trail of Tears, and afterward, for dispersing supplies the United States was obligated to provide under the terms of the Treaty of Dancing Rabbit Creek. In addition, to apply for permission to stay in Mississippi and become a citizen of that state, Choctaw families had to be listed on the eviction roll.

The imposition of white American gender norms, accomplished in part through these eviction rolls, and their repeated enforcement over the years resulted in long-term damage to Choctaw gender relations. Households among the matrilineal Choctaws were usually composed of an elder female, her daughters, and their families. Only in families formed by white men, or their children, were nuclear male-headed families the norm. Nevertheless, on the form Colonel Armstrong created for recording each household, the first and most important person listed was the "male, head of household." The patriarchal norms of white society were thus imposed on the matrilineal norms of Choctaw society. Choctaw families were extended families, or clans, people descended from a common female ancestor. Most Choctaws were matrilocal and lived in houses or compounds of dwelling places headed by a woman. Her husband, all her grown daughters and their husbands and children, and any unmarried sons either lived in the same house or in a house next door. Therefore, in the Choctaw Nation, the head of a household was the eldest female, not male. The house and everything in it belonged to the women of the family or clan, as did the children and the produce from the fields that were planted and tilled by the women. The imposition of this alien kinship organizational strategy divested women of their power over lands and crops by assigning their ownership to males. Upon the Choctaws' arrival in Indian Territory, the United States continued to recognize only men as heads of families, thus striking a major blow against the matrilineal kinship system that was integral to Choctaw society.

Patriarchal oppression went hand in hand with US colonialism, imposing a hierarchical imbalance of power between men and women that proved devastating to indigenous women and children over time. Of course, elevating men to positions of authority and economic, political, and social power took some time, but by the late nineteenth century, many more households partially assimilated Euro-American gender norms. The devastation of tribal societies in which women and men were valued equally, and whose strengths and natures were recognized as essential and commendable, represents a sad loss for all humanity.

Ten or fifteen years before Winged Celia was murdered, Nancy Fulsome [also spelled Fulsom] was a slave on one of the Folsom plantations. At that time slaves of the Choctaws lived their daily lives as coworkers and childhood playmates of the Choctaw people, and through this contact, they learned to speak Choctaw fluently and understand most, if not all, of the Choctaw beliefs and values.[13] Often because of their knowledge of English, Africans served as interpreters and advisors for the non-English-speaking Choctaws. The blacks who lived in such close relationships with the Choctaws influenced and were influenced by Native practices and beliefs. As time passed, many Choctaw values and cultural attributes seeped into the Africans' culture, internalized and adapted to suit their needs. Some African slaves within the Indian nations were so thoroughly integrated into the indigenous culture of their "owners" that they spoke only the indigenous language of the Native group—no English at all.[14]

Many cultural beliefs of tribal African peoples, especially those of western African origin, blended quite easily with Choctaw belief systems and practices. For example, historian Tiya Miles, in her excellent study, *Ties That Bind:*

*The Story of an Afro-Cherokee Family in Slavery and Freedom*, tells us African folktales featuring a trickster rabbit combined with southeastern Native tales about the same hero; African medicinal practices became enmeshed with Native knowledge about uses of indigenous plants; African women's basketry patterns were woven into Native women's crafts; and corn, the staple of the southeastern Indian diets, became a signature ingredient of what we now call soul food.[15] Cultural beliefs and behaviors are modified over many years of contact. Most often these changes result in an enhancement of existing practices, rather than an either-or choice between the traditional and new. Choctaw society and freedmen society incorporated elements that were attractive to each group, while other attributes were rebuffed.

After the Civil War freed the slaves of the Indian nations, many freedmen remained in Indian Territory in hopes of receiving land from the indigenous nations. The post-Civil War treaties that reestablished relations between the Indian nations and the United States included clauses in which the nations agreed to extend the rights of indigenous citizenship to the former slaves of each nation.[16] But the Choctaws did not want to share their lands and wealth with the African Americans, nor did they want them to become members of the Choctaw tribe. One reason for this was the fear that if the United States confiscated the Choctaw lands, as they had done in 1830, and forced the Choctaws to divide the land into individual holdings, there would be less land to divide if the African Americans swelled the total number of "Choctaws."[17]

A second, and more important, motivation for Choctaws to reject incorporating former slaves into their body politic was that the Choctaws who interfaced more frequently with the United States understood that white Americans firmly rejected African Americans as equals. They watched the institution of Jim Crow laws, the creation of white Southern systems of terror to keep blacks "in their place," and the array of legal, political, an economic tactics used to return Africans to slavery in all but name. Justified under the guise of biological intransigence, white Americans demonstrated with stark clarity that nonwhite citizens would not be extended the rights and protection of the US Constitution.[18] Because of the repeatedly demonstrated perfidy and treachery of the United States government in relation to indigenous treaties, the Choctaws feared that the Americans would once again confiscate their lands. In anticipation of this event, the Choctaws sought to distance themselves from blacks. They certainly did not want to join people of African descent as targets for the racial hatred of white Americans.

Along with white American ideals of patriarchy, Christianity, and capitalism, Choctaws of mixed heritage imported racial hatred of people of African descent. They created a racial hierarchy that placed themselves on par with cultured and educated whites, ranked white tenant farmers, lessors, and laborers as beneath them, and placed blacks, free-born or formerly enslaved, at the bottom. Choctaw laws adopted from 1830 to 1860 demonstrate the increasing oppression of African slaves and the imitation of slave laws used in the American South. For example, a law passed October 6, 1836, in the Choctaw Nation included provisions against teaching slaves to read or write or "sit at table" without the permission of the owner. A later law prohibited freed Choctaw slaves to continue residence in the Choctaw Nation; within thirty days of emancipation, the former slave had to leave. Philosopher Albert Memmi explains that "the oppressed man initially attempts to divorce himself from his own culture and tries to forge a new identity apart from his own experiences. . . . There is a tempting model very close at hand—the colonizer. The latter suffers none of his deficiencies, has all rights, enjoys every possession and benefits from every prestige." [19] Some of the Choctaws of mixed white-Choctaw heritage eagerly adopted white racism in a misplaced attempt to create a "not-colored" identity for themselves—and, they hoped, to one day become on par with the oppressor. These Choctaws lived in dread of a white conflation of Indians and blacks into one "colored" category.

The United States tried to force the Choctaws to accept responsibility for their former slaves in the treaty of 1866, which reinstated the former relationship between the United States and the Choctaw Nation. Surprisingly, however, the Choctaws and Chickasaws retained the right to decide whether or not to adopt their former slaves, as well as the right to request that the United States government expel them from the Nation to the western half of the Choctaws' lands, which the United States had confiscated. The Choctaws simply ignored the former slaves for almost forty years, until the United States forced the Choctaws to allot their communal land holdings in the early years of the twentieth century. At that point, the United States also forced the Choctaws to enroll the former slaves as members of the nation. But in the intervening years during which the freedmen were treated as noncitizens, they formed small communities, banding together in extended kinships that were similar to those of the Choctaws themselves. The Choctaws left them alone, treating them as simply another "foreign" group with at least tacit approval to remain there. Meanwhile, the Choctaws turned to what they saw as the far more important and pressing matter of staving off the continual barrage of proposals in the US Congress to create a new US territory out of the Choctaw Nation, which they knew would lead once again to their dispossession.[20]

The community in which Winged Celia was murdered was an isolated

African settlement in the midst of the Choctaw Nation. The people in the community had grown up with the Choctaws, spoke their language as well as English, and had adapted many of the traditional beliefs of the Choctaw culture. One resident of the community related,

> One arm Celia lived in our settlement. No one knew where she lived for she always made her appearances suddenly. She lived by stealing. All of our people were afraid of her and she would come into our houses and get anything she wanted.
>
> She had wings that folded out from her body and when we heard the chickens cackling in the yard, we knew that winged Celia was coming.
>
> She would be seen, perched on some one's housetop ready to come in and get what she wanted. Children and grown people would throw rocks and clubs at her but could never hit her.
>
> She was a conjurer and was responsible for all the bad things that happened in the community.
>
> She never left our community. When we would beg her to go away and leave us alone, she would laugh and make a noise like a chicken.
>
> She was a terror to our community for several years, but finally a white man told us that she could be killed with a silver ball.
>
> The white man sent to a foreign country and got a silver ball. One of the negroes put the ball in his gun and went hunting for winged Celia. He found her in a small cleared place and shot her with the silver ball. She fell and the man who shot her drove a wooden stake thru the middle of her body into the ground, pinning her body to the ground. And there they left her to rot and for the buzzards to pick.[21]

The storyteller, Nancy Homer Fulsom Cox, bore the maiden surname of one of the large, influential families of the Choctaws. The Choctaw Folsoms descended from Nathaniel Folsom, an Englishman who entered the Choctaw Nation when it was located in the old homelands in Mississippi, about 1778. In all likelihood, he deserted from the British Army and took his chances in the backwoods of southern Indian country. Folsom married into the Choctaw tribe, his wife the daughter of a chief and a member of a large clan that had power in the nation. As was common among whites of the time (but not among the Choctaws), Folsom sired at least fourteen children, and they each produced large families, spreading the Folsom name and kinship networks throughout the Choctaw Nation. The Folsoms were interrelated with many of the other white-Choctaw families, whose progenitors were, likewise, often Scotch Irish who came into the territory and married Indian women.[22] The Folsom descendants were generally better educated than other Choctaws, spoke English and Choctaw, and embraced Christianity and acculturation.[23] Nancy was a Folsom slave or descended from one, and she would have worked on one of the many plantations and farms owned by them. She would have been brought up in a milieu of Choctaw-African-Anglo beliefs, a unique culture that blended attributes of three distinct societies.

Winged Celia was an outsider to the African-Choctaw community in which she lived. Nancy Cox tells us that "all of our people were afraid of her" and relates the entire story as "we" versus "her." Choctaw society was based on kinship—everyone was a member of a clan, and this clan protected its members from harm from any other member of Choctaw society. Fictive kinship was created to bring outsiders into the fold of Choctaw relations. These kinships, even though fictive, were scrupulously honored by all parties. But Winged Celia had no champion, and the old clan system of the Choctaws had broken down. She remained an Other to the community, and from what we know, no attempts were made to bring her into the community web of relationships.

In the Choctaw world, strange and persistent anomalies that they could not otherwise explain might be attributed to witchcraft. They attributed very little to chance or accident. There was usually a reason for something going wrong. Most often, they suspected that someone had not followed the rules of ritual separation, causing an impurity or imbalance. The Choctaws were extremely concerned with maintaining purity and following strict guidelines because if they did not, the order of the universe could break down, threatening the well-being of the individual and the entire community. Anomalies and abominations were a very real threat, and the Choctaws wold be very anxious to restore their world to harmony and balance. Celia, as a "thing"—a chicken-woman—was such an anomaly.

Witches attacked people because they wanted to add the life of the victim to their own. The Choctaws respected elderly people and many of them had great power, but they also frightened some people and could be distrusted. In the case of Celia, her age and fearlessness, coupled with her bizarre behavior, would have been terrifying.

Witches could assume human shape but were not human and, thus, were outside the social order. As nonhumans, they threatened the well-being of individuals and the community; therefore, they had to be discovered and stopped. Suspicion, fear, and jealousy often operated in identifying a witch—she could be masquerading as one's neighbor, friend, or companion. Since nonhumans could not be members of the human community, they were outside the law, and there would be no retribution for their death. Indeed, many Choctaws believed that the death of the witch or wizard made the community safer, and so sanctioned the killing of such things.[24]

Traditional Choctaw beliefs in the existence of witches and wizards continued throughout the nineteenth century and well into the twentieth. An interesting episode in Choctaw lawmaking demonstrated the continuing power of these traditions within Choctaw culture, in the decade of the 1820s. At that time, Choctaw leaders—mostly Choctaws of mixed white and Native heritage—were striving to illustrate to the dominant white society that the Choctaw people were assimilating with beliefs and ways of living, progressing toward "civilization."

According to this ideology, the state of white society justified the confiscation of Choctaw lands and their expulsion to the far west. To demonstrate their progress and thereby stave off dispossession, Choctaw leaders passed a series of laws mimicking those of the dominant society, outlawing the behaviors that whites had labeled evidence of savagery. White missionaries had decried the execution of witches by the Choctaws, dismissing their beliefs as superstition and demanding the Choctaw government put an end to such acts. In response, the Choctaws passed a law in 1829 that limited the circumstances under which witches could be killed. The new law stated that a person accused of witchcraft could be executed only under the following circumstances:

> if any person or persons shall find at any place the entrails of a wizzard or witch, the said entrails going from or returning to the body, the said body shall be put to death at the place where it may be discovered, an[d] the said body shall be cut open, by a proper person and an examination be made to see whether it has in it any entrails, an[d] a report be made of said body.[25]

This in itself is a fascinating example of the attempt by the Choctaws to bring their society into conformity with that of white Americans, at the same time dealing in a peculiarly Choctaw social belief entirely unacceptable to educated, Christian whites of the time.

Winged Celia was identified as a witch with ease. She was distinctly different from the other members of the community. In tribal societies, deviation from the norm is undesirable, since peer pressure is key to maintaining order. Celia's sudden appearances, her lack of social integration, and her bizarre behavior marked her as an Other.[26] Celia was also evidently deformed so that her arms took on the appearance of wings. The African Choctaws would possibly have seen this deformity as part of a witch's power to transform herself into shapes of different creatures; witches had the ability to take on the form of human beings or animals and were able to change their shape at will. Furthermore, not only did Celia take on the appearance of a bird, it seems she could communicate with them as well: "[W]hen we heard the chickens cackling in the yard, we knew that winged Celia was coming."[27]

The people of this community lived in great fear of people who they thought might be witches. Tribal people the world over have common beliefs in witches, conjuring, and witchcraft. Inexplicable occurrences and abilities in their lives must be explained so that the group can make sense of the world. The Choctaws, like most other Native Americans, believed in an orderly world where everything had a place that was knowable and defined. Their language even grouped similar items together. For example fingers are in the same category as logs, pencils, and other cylindrical objects. The fire and sun belong in the same category. Things that do not fit into a distinct category—that is, things that have no relationship to other things—are considered abominations, and the Choctaws loathed and feared these aberrations. For example, when Anglos introduced hogs into Choctaw society many centuries ago, the animal did not fit into any of the Choctaw categories, because of their cloven hooves. Therefore, Choctaws absolutely refused pork as a food, seeing it as an abomination. Celia did not fit into either animal or human categories, making her an abomination. Celia threw off the world's balance in the African-Choctaw community and, therefore, was a threat to its health and well-being that had to be removed.[28] Cox related that "[c]hildren and grown people would throw rocks and clubs at her but could never hit her." In other words, the people tried to rid themselves of this witch, but their tactics were ineffective. Ultimately, they begged her to go away and leave them alone, but "she would laugh and make a noise like a chicken."

Although many Choctaw beliefs can be seen in the reactions of these villagers to Winged Celia, they were not simply Choctaws. Although they lived among the Choctaws, and some would have been born among them, they were also of African descent. In addition, many of the Choctaws who owned slaves had adopted various practices and beliefs from the dominant white society, and these too would have been reflected in the worldview of the people of this Choctaw-African community. The villagers were in contact with men from eastern Europe who came to work in the mines in the Choctaw Nation. As Nancy Cox told us, after trying for several years to rid their community of Celia, one of the men traveled to a neighboring town and met a man there who claimed to know how to kill her: with a silver ball. This man likely understood the terror of the people in confronting this nonhuman in human form, for tales of vampires and the infamous Count Dracula would have been known to many immigrants from eastern Europe. Although unfamiliar with Choctaw beliefs about witches, he apparently knew how to deal with the "undead." Like vampires, Winged Celia could be killed only by using special techniques—a wooden stake through the heart and a silver bullet.

The Cox account does not provide much information about the white man who gave the African-Choctaws the answer to their problem, but we can guess at a few details. In the 1870s and later, hundreds of Europeans immigrated to the Choctaw Nation to work the coal mines located in the region. Italians, Englishmen, Swedes, Germans, Belgians, and Eastern Europeans came in to work in the Choctaw mines. Mining camps were located around present-day Lehigh and Coalgate, Oklahoma, near Cox's settlement. Europeans had a long fascination with the vampires and the undead. As one historian has noted, E. T. A. Hoffman, Joseph Sheridan Le Fanu, Edgar Allen Poe, and Bram Stoker "spread stories of bloodsucking vampires and hideous ghosts, and recounted all forms of terrifying deeds on the part of the dead who would not rest in eternal belief."[29] In Victorian England, for example, tales of vampires and werewolves constituted a unique and popular genre. Not only were there tales to make one's hair stand on end, but procedures for killing vampires also entered the popular culture. The answer to the dilemma of a witch whom they could not catch and who refused to leave seemed simple, according to the European formula. This nonhuman creature could be killed by being shot with a silver ball and having a wooden stake driven through its heart.

Killing a witch was not a crime under the Choctaw traditional law because the creature existed outside the clans. In US law, Winged Celia's killing was murder, but in the backwoods of Indian Territory, the only recognized law was that of the community; and no one outside the community would have been informed of the killing. Celia, alone and outside the kinship network, was "different" and feared. Perceived to be the cause of all the "bad things that happened in the community", she was killed. In keeping with Choctaw law, the community acted to defend itself from this outside threat. Years later, Nancy Cox made no apologies, nor did she seem ashamed of the incident.

Perhaps her point in relating the story was to illustrate her community's success in dealing with the supernatural. A community, threatened by a witch, managed to extinguish that threat.

When Cox was interviewed for the WPA project in 1935, her interviewer referred to her as a "Choctaw Freedman." In the interviewer's introduction to the story, she stated that "[t]he story originated among the negroes and Indians who lived on Red River, in the Southern part of what is Oklahoma." In early Oklahoma, after the United States confiscated the last lands of the Choctaws and other indigenous peoples and dissolved the Indian Nations, skin color overrode all other considerations of a person's identity—"negroes and Indians" instead of "people." The white interviewer reflected the dominant society's quick identification of "negroes and Indians" as the Other. The Choctaw fear of being relegated to a category with African Americans was finally realized. But perhaps the white superiority implicitly claimed by the interviewer was somewhat compromised by her introduction of the story, wherein she stated, "It was believed to be true and the woman who told it says she saw the person or *whatever it was* many times" [emphasis mine].[30]

Celia's story dramatically illustrates the impossibility of generalizing women's experiences in the southern plains in this era. Her position as an outsider placed her in considerable jeopardy. Living in this African-Choctaw community subjected her to the worldview of people who were biologically of African descent but whose culture and belief system represented a unique mixture of indigenous Choctaw beliefs, their African heritage, a smattering of European superstitions, along with at least some influence from the dominant American culture. All this took place in a geographical space carved out of the Choctaw Nation during the late nineteenth century, where Choctaw government ruled in uneasy contention with the US government, which by treaty had solemnly agreed to Choctaw sovereignty. However, the same forces that had dispossessed the Choctaws from their ancient homelands in Mississippi in the 1830s, and thrust them into permanent exile in the west, were gathering and consolidating political power under the Dawes Act, with the goal of once again dispossessing the Choctaws. This time, however, the US government would not only take their communal lands but also unilaterally dissolve the Choctaw government, in essence accomplishing through the edict the oft-repeated American mantra that Native Americans were simply "vanishing." Within the context of American colonization, the story of Winged Celia illustrates the remarkable combination of ethnicity, language, and culture that formed and re-formed in response to changing conditions in Indian Territory. It began with the arrival of the dispossessed Choctaws in the 1830s and continued with the emancipation of African slaves after the Civil War. The eastern European miners came into contact with Celia through the economic forces that led the way for completion of American colonization of the indigenous peoples of Indian Territory.

Celia's story illustrates the endless combinations, adaptations, and selectivity of cultural beliefs and attributes that formed the background and context of the stories of real women living in Indian Territory in the nineteenth century. This complexity defies the simple cultural categories often suggested through racial or ethnic labels—Celia and her community were not simply "African" or "Indian," and certainly not "white." Their complex, dynamic cultural milieu included aspects from three distinct cultures or worldviews—a context that one suspects may be much more common than not. The story of Winged Celia presents us with an opportunity to understand how women negotiated issues of race, ethnicity, and gender in new and richer ways.

# Civilizations of the Southern Plains, 1862–1930

JEAN STUNTZ

Heat, drought, cold, and wind; the climatic extremes of the southern plains have played a crucial role in shaping the modes of subsistence, cultural traditions, and demographics in this region. Native Americans—focusing on Comanches for this essay—Hispanics, and Euro-Americans all lived on the southern plains from 1862 to 1930. Women in each of these ethnic groups developed strategies to cope with the environment as they bore and raised children and took care of their families by preparing food, creating clothing, and performing work within the gendered expectations of their specific society. But forces from outside the region have had an equally profound impact on women. Placing the arrival of these groups within the broader context of social, political, or economic influences encourages a deeper understanding of how the intersection of diverse civilizations shaped the lives of women in this region.

The Comanche people, arguable the strongest Native group on the southern plains at the opening of this era, illustrate what archaeologists term the "considerable interaction" of Native peoples in this region.[1] Their move onto the southern plains, as well as their place in the shifting power structure, fits within the ongoing dynamics of change evident in this region for generations. Prior to the Comanches' arrival, the Wichitas and Apaches had dominated the region, engaging in a predominantly pastoral economy. The tribes had learned to survive in this environment, locating their villages near rivers, where the women grew corn, beans, and squash in the fertile bottomlands, harvested wild fruits and nuts, and traveled with the tribe onto the high plains for semi-annual hunts.[2] Southern plains tribes developed extensive trade networks with peoples outside the region. Their trade included captives as well as goods, leading to the creation of multiethnic cultures long before the arrival of Europeans.

When Spanish explorers such as Vasquez de Coronado and Juan de Oñate entered the southern plains in the mid-sixteenth century, they did not stay long; disappointed that the tales of fabulous riches were nothing more than fabulous tales, they returned to the Spanish colonies further south. Yet while Europeans "largely ignored the Southern Plains until almost a century later," historian Loretta Fowler writes, their introduction of disease, metal, and the horse set into motion changes that "revolutionized the lives of the native peoples on the plains."[3] When the Spaniards turned their attention back to the southern plains in the late seventeenth century the impact of their earlier visit, especially the introduction of the horse, had helped set the stage for the Comanches to move into the area and rise to dominance.

The Comanches began as a branch of the Northern Shoshones around present-day southern Wyoming. Adapting remarkably well to the horse, which they acquired in the years after the Pueblo Revolt of 1680, they moved onto the southern plains in 1706; by the late 1730s, they had displaced the Apaches as the region's dominant tribe.[4] Pekka Hämäläinen writes that when the Comanches moved onto the southern plains, they created a nation "in a state of constant and at times uncontrolled change, a society that creatively reinvented itself while scrambling to absorb outside pressures."[5] Their adaptation to horses allowed greater mobility and better access to hunting, but these advantages did not come without cost. Maintaining the herds and processing the increased number of hides that mounted hunters could bring in created a need for a shift from their previously nomadic lifestyle to a mixed pastoral-nomadic economy and a corresponding increase in the demand for labor within the bands. These new responsibilities fell heavily on the women.

European accounts of Comanche women's lives stress what they considered to be excessive amounts of work, even compared to other Native women. In the late 1820s, Mexican official José María Sanches described Comanche women as "real slaves to the men, who occupy themselves with war and hunting only. The wives bring in the animals that are killed, they cut and cure the meat, tan the hides, make the clothes and arm the men, and care for the horses."[6] Sanches, with his European conception of gendered responsibilities, did not appreciate the status women earned through their contributions to their family's and, by extension, band or tribe's increasing wealth. Nor did he have insights into the gendered hierarchy within the private confines of the women's sphere or the importance of women's moral authority within the band.[7]

In the Comanches' patriarchal-dominated society, each small group, or band, was entirely autonomous, and individuals had much personal freedom within their band.[8] Women enjoyed a great deal of personal choice, especially on choosing husbands. When women married, they did not leave their birth family, as happened in European marriages. Instead, these women retained their ties with their fathers, brothers, and uncles, and so had a male support system that tended to prevent excessive domestic abuse. Not only did women have a say in who they married, but they had the authority to chastise an erring husband. If a husband displeased his wife she could choose to punish him by having an affair, thus causing the husband to lose honor within the tribe.[9]

Because of the bilateral nature of their kinship system, married women also retained their ties to their female kinfolk.[10] Aunts helped in the care of children, and in the case of the death of a mother, the children would be handed over to the mother's sisters, as the maternal aunts were considered their mothers, too. Within their domestic sphere, women's work patterns followed the rhythms of the seasons, as they moved tipis, processed food and hides, and reared children.[11]

As cherished members of their society, children were included in the daily activities of tribal life from the earliest age. Tucked into cradleboards, which allowed their mothers to keep their hands free for work, the children were at eye level with family members, able to socialize with the people who would play an important part in their young world.[12]

In polygamous families, or in families that included female captives, a hierarchy existed, with the first wife having a position of authority over other women in the household. The position of captives was fluid; Comanches did not consider slavery a permanent state, and for the most part, captives became full tribal members through adoption or marriage. The inclusive attitude meant that captive women could hope to find some amount of protection, if not compassion, among Comanche women. An Anglo-Texan woman, Sarah Ann Horn, had been "informally adopted by an old widow woman who worked her hard as a hide dresser but also protected her against sexual abuse." According to Horn, "greatly did she contribute, by her acts of kindness and soothing manners, to reconcile me to my fate."[13]

The status women gained for their labor not withstanding, José María Sanches's observation was right—women worked hard to support the Comanche economic system. The demands on women, in addition to the loss of band members through disease and warfare, drove the need to augment family labor sources. Their solution, a "creative reinvention" of traditional practices, combined a rise in polygamous marriages with an increase in captive taking, especially for women who could be adopted into the tribal kinship system as wife laborers.[14] Men who acquired many wives and/or female slaves could become very wealthy and powerful within their tribes. Women, though, carried "the burden of market production" in this growing, quasi-capitalist economy, scraping and curing the hides that were the backbone of this financial system. An Anglo woman named Rachel Plumber, taken captive in Texas, "remembered how robe tanning kept her 'employed all the time in day-light': 'Often I would have to take my buffalo skin with me, to finish it whilst I was minding the horses.'"[15] While women processed the hides, the hides belonged to the men, who, as Hämäläinen notes, garnered "the prestige that flows from the control and redistribution of the critical wealth-generating goods."[16]

To procure labor, raiding for captives among Native enemies, Spanish settlers, and Anglos increased dramatically, and raiding for Hispanic captives became a "veritable industry."[17] As noted earlier, captive taking had a long history in the region, with motives as diverse as possibilities for the captive's fate. A captive might be taken for revenge, to replace a family member who had died, or as "a blatant affront designed to signify the weakness of the enemy," and once captured, might be killed immediately, traded, or integrated into their captor's tribe.[18]

The story of a Comanche woman participating on a raid for Lipan Apache horses, then taken captive after a fight ensued, gives insight into the role of women in intertribal raiding and captive taking.

> A single Comanche girl was there, too, out on the raid with the Comanche. . . . She saw the Lipan men and called, "Here come the Lipan!" . . . The girl got on her horse; the chief mounted his horse, too. He told his men to go out and fight. They met the Lipan and had a real fight. Pretty soon the Comanche began to back off. When the woman saw her men weakening, she got off her horse and hit the horse in the face, sending it away. She did this instead of riding to safety because she wanted to do a great war deed. If she were on foot, her men would have to stay and protect her and show their bravery. Among the Comanche, the women had their minds on such things. The Apache were going to give her a chance to escape at first, but she wouldn't take it. Sometimes when Comanche women wanted to fight, they fought. . . . The Lipan fought so fiercely that even the Comanche man had to go on, leaving the woman behind. The [Lipan] man who took this woman did not marry her. He took care of her. After she had been there for three years, one young Comanche boy who was there (a boy who had been captured years before and had grown up with the Lipan) married her. So this man who had captured her had a relative-in-law when these two Comanches married.[19]

The girl, not adopted by her captor, occupied a role "somewhere between that of a servant and that of a family member."[20] Her ambiguous status ended, however, when she married. Once adopted through marriage, the woman—regardless of her ethnic heritage—was considered a pure Apache, fully integrated into the tribe's kinship system.[21]

When Europeans returned to the southern plains in the late seventeenth century, they initiated a fundamental shift in the captive-raiding practice. Raiding for captives to trade for goods or to cement alliances with the Europeans became a priority, and once tribes discovered the European desire for women, women captives became a valuable commodity.[22] Women also played a role in diplomatic strategies. Through ransom or redeeming, writes Juliana Barr, "female captives became the bargaining chips by which make captors negotiated truce and alliance."[23] Women would also take the initiative in mediating between their bands and the Spanish by their presence in diplomatic or trade parties. However, as the Comanche need for labor increased, the bands had more use for captives as laborers—Native, Hispanic, or Anglo—than the money they might bring in from rewards, sale, or ransom.[24]

Stories of Anglo women and children taken captive by tribes as they moved into the region held a horrifying fascination for settlers. One of the earliest and most famous of the Anglo captive stories occurred in 1836, when ten-year-old Cynthia Ann Parker, daughter of American settlers in Texas, was taken by Comanches during a raid on Fort Parker. Adopted into Comanche society, Parker became the wife of Chief Peta Nocona and mother of future chief Quanah Parker. She had at least two chances to return to white society but refused to do so. In 1860 she was re-kidnapped by Texas Rangers and forcibly returned to her Anglo family. Recounting oral history passed down from his tribe where Parker lived, William Chebahta recalled, "Cynthia Ann was taken back to Texas, where she pined away, always remembering her Comanche home."[25] Her contemporaries found it inexplicable that she continued to grieve for her Indian husband and children and never reacclimated to white ways.[26]

Since Parker spoke little English and did not give any interviews, her preference for Comanche culture and her experience with the tribe remained a source of mystery. Piecing together evidence from stories of other Anglo captives, the reasons they give for choosing to remain with a tribe proved diverse and complex. But the Comanche process of integrating captives into kinship units, and thus providing a feeling of belonging, proved a powerful factor in their willingness to stay, especially for those who had been taken captive as children and reared among the bands.

During the US Civil War, while the federal army and many Anglo men had turned their attention to distant battlefields, the Comanches enjoyed a resurgence of power. Their raids for captives, horses, and cattle increasingly terrorized settlers. In 1867 the federal government determined to end Comanche sovereignty; during the Medicine Lodge Conference, held that same year, government agents pressured Comanche leaders to sign a treaty that would confine them to a reservation in Indian Territory. Despite signing the treaty, Hämäläinen notes, tribal leaders did not consider it "an infringement on their traditional ways."[27] They continued their lifestyle of the plains, hunting, raiding for captives and, increasingly, for cattle as bison became scarce, and moving near the agency only in the winter so they could receive rations.[28] They also continued to fight the encroachment of Anglos onto what they considered their hunting grounds. In 1871 Colonel Ranald Slidell Mackenzie led five thousand US Army troops into the southern plains to force the Comanches to move onto the reservation. The final battle of his campaign took place in Palo Duro Canyon, where Mackenzie found the Comanches in their winter camp along the creek. Although only a few Indians died, Mackenzie ordered all the Comanche horses slaughtered and their supplies destroyed. To prevent total starvation, Chief Quanah Parker had little choice but to lead the remaining Comanches onto the Oklahoma reservation.[29]

Once confined to the reservation, Comanche women faced intense pressure to conform to Anglo notions of civilized behavior, particularly from missionary women. Women reeducating women to new societal expectations had occurred earlier between the two groups; Comanche women performed a transition ritual on Anglo women captives to incorporate them into the tribe. The "process of 'natal alienation' rendered the captives utterly powerless and dependent," allowing them to be "reborn as Comanches."[30] On the reservation, Anglo women missionaries reversed the roles and widened its scope. Working closely with Comanche women, missionaries believed, as special agent for Indian School Service Merial Dorchester did, that "[n]o uncivilized people are elevated till the mothers are reached."[31] Personal interaction between Comanche and Anglo women would facilitate the process of Christianizing the Native women and instructing them in Euro-American ways, allowing for a "trickle-down" civilizing effect throughout the family and, by extension, the entire tribe.

Like so many Native women in this situation, Comanche women found ways to continue practices that sustained their traditional values. Sanapia, born in 1895 on the Oklahoma reservation, continued her mother's role as an eagle doctor. Her grandmother had a strong influence, encouraging Sanapia to remember the traditional stories and ways. Sanapia recalled, "[S]he's the one who told me to take my mother's doctoring-way when I was getting older. . . .

[M]y grandmother said that soon in the future there wouldn't be hardly any Indian doctors left."[32] Using traditional cures, she helped her people deal with illnesses and, in particular, with Ghost Sickness, an affliction that emerged from the hardships and uncertainties of post-reservation life.

Sanapia's experiences illustrate how women reached out to help others during an era of extraordinary challenges. In more private ways, too, the women found avenues to continue traditions that held particular meaning. Comanche mothers continued to make cradleboards for their infants, but after 1871, they began embellishing cradleboards with elaborate beadwork using design motifs, passed down for generations, that linked child to family and family to band.[33] Nestled in its beautifully worked cradleboard, the child "signified honor, patience, respect, love," a connection to their past as well as hope for their future.[34]

Like Comanche women, interracial and intercultural relationships formed the basis of many Hispanic women's experiences. Since the early sixteenth century, the mingling of indigenous, European, and African people had been an intimate part of their reality, where so many women "saw daily reminders of its consequences in the faces of their children."[35] Hispanic settlers had begun the movement into their country's northern frontier after Mexico won its independence from Spain in 1821. These women were either part of *pastores* families, sheepherders who migrated from New Mexico and established isolated villages, or as Caroline Crimm described in Chapter 9 of this book, part of a small elite who came to the area with substantial financial means.[36]

The thin grasses on the southern plains demanded that rancheros and villages be widely spaced to allow adequate forage for the sheep; the need to irrigate garden plots continued the Native tradition of situating villages near rivers. Although sex and age factored into the designation of chores, men could attend to domestic duties—cooking, cleaning, and ironing—and women could work in the fields, herd sheep, or fix fences if needed. In these communal villages, though, "women had their own world in addition to the one they shared with men . . . realms of expertise that served the entire village, and a society and economy of their own."[37] Women helped one another as healers, and midwives, and they also could own property, manage their own livestock, and raise produce, such as chilis, for market.[38]

Increased contact with Anglo-Americans transformed the lives of women in the villages. Even before parts of Mexico had been brought into the United States, Hispanic and Anglo women's lives intersected. In 1846 and 1847, for example, newly married Susan Magoffin traveled the Santa Fe Trail with her husband. Her first encounter with Mexican women illustrates a middle-class

Anglo perspective on civilized—or what she considered uncivilized—behavior. One woman "shocked her by combing her hair in the presence of a man," and she found their revealing style of dress disconcerting.[39] "To her American eye," Virginia Scharff writes, "the Mexican women were creatures of some exotic species, not sisters, not even fully human on her own terms."[40] After the United States usurped Mexican territory, Spanish-Mexican women "clung to, and even embellished" cultural traditions—smoking, gambling, dancing in public—that distinguished them from other ethnic groups.[41]

The racism apparent in Susan Magoffin's journal factored in the marginalization of Hispanics after the US-Mexico war, as Anglo settlers began colonizing the territory. Despite promises by the US government, Hispanics had to contend with legal challenges to their land titles, and overwhelmingly, they lost those challenges. As William Robbins notes, the court cases led to a "massive transfer in land titles—with all the customary forms of chicanery and outright violence—from Mexican to Anglo ownership."[42] As a group, ninety percent of resident Hispanics lost their land.[43]

This loss had a profound impact on the lives of Hispanic women as they dealt with husbands and male family members forced to leave villages for work. Increasingly, women found themselves compelled to abandon a way of life centered on family and a land-based economy and to take wage-based jobs that involved interaction with Anglo society. Facing this difficult transition, "women relied on one another for mutual support." The combination of wage work and mutual assistance strategies "persisted well into the twentieth century across region and generation."[44] The shift to wage labor had several implications. First, while the move from rural to urban undermined women's position of authority in the family, their role as caretaker of the family continued. Second, racial discrimination limited job opportunities to the most physically demanding and the lowest-paying of all jobs. Working as laundresses, seamstresses, or domestic workers kept them at the bottom of a wage-based economy.[45] The combination of Hispanic women seeing themselves as the foundation of the family, the discrimination they faced in the workplace, and their segregation into ethnic enclaves (barrios) created a self-conscious awareness among Hispanic women. In their roles as wives and mothers, workers and civic-minded individuals, they collaborated to improve the quality of life at work, at home, and in their neighborhoods.[46]

Although the majority of scholarly work on Hispanic activism focuses on the post-1930s, in 1910, the stirrings of a protofeminist movement have become evident. The Tejana socialist labor leader and political activist Sara Estela Ramirez wrote the following poem to call Hispanic women to action:

Rise Up! To Woman
Rise Up! Rise up to life, to activity, to
The beauty of truly living, but rise up radiant
And powerful, beautiful with qualities, splendid
With virtues, strong with energies.[47]

The next year, in 1911, the El Primer Congreso Mexicanista met in Laredo, Texas. As part of the "first civil rights assembly among Spanish-speaking people in the United States," women delegates from South Texas and across the border in Mexico "addressed discrimination, land loss, and lynching."[48] Soledad Peña admonished both Tejanos and Mexicanos of "our duty . . . to educate woman; to instruct her and to . . . give her due respect."[49] The next Congreso would not take place until 1939, but as early as 1910, Hispanic women, and in particular wage-earning women, had begun to tackle labor and civil rights issues.

So far this essay has examined the experiences of Hispanic women who lived in an area that had changed from Mexican to US jurisdiction. But new immigrants from Mexico into the southern plains occurred during this era, as social and political events in Mexico spurred a massive migration to the North. A soaring birthrate—up fifty percent between 1875 and 1910—combined with ninety-six percent of Mexican families losing land under dictator Porfirio Diaz's modernization policies and the political uprisings lasting into the 1920s, compelled nearly one-fifth of the Mexican population to emigrate to the United States. Between 1910 and 1930, more than one million Mexicans crossed into the United States.[50]

While most women crossed the border into the United States with husbands or other family members, there is an increasing awareness of women who left Mexico alone. Vicki Ruiz tells the story of Pasquala Esparza, who secretly left "the family home with nine-year-old Jesusita at her side and one-month-old Raquel in her arms" to escape an abusive marriage.[51] Pasquala intended to go to California, to live with her married sister. When she arrived in Ciudad Juarez, she found she did not have enough money to obtain passports to El Paso. Renting a room in a boardinghouse and taking a job across town as a housekeeper, she worked for the next six months to earn the money for her small family to cross the border. During this time, the older daughter took responsibility for herself and the baby. Ruiz tells her story, writing,

Jesusita remembered that as part of her daily routine she would carry
Raquel a long distance to an affluent home where their mother worked.

After preparing the noon meal for her employer, Pasquala would anxiously wait by the kitchen door. When her children arrived, she quickly and quietly ushered them into the kitchen. While nursing Raquel, she fed Jesusita a burrito of leftovers. Then Jesusita would take her baby sister into her arms and trek back to the boardinghouse to await their mother's return in the evening.[52]

Even after earning the money for their passports, Pasquala had to convince the border guards that a single woman with children should be allowed to immigrate into the United States. Only after several tries, and ultimately skirting the law by applying for a different type of visa, did she succeed.

As part of a family chain migration, Pasquala could rely on her sister to help with the adjustment to a new life. But her move to California is illustrative of other Mexican immigrants who moved into southern plains communities. Resident Hispanics, those whose family had lived in the region before it became a part of the United States, found themselves outnumbered almost two-to-one by newcomers like Pasquala and her daughters. As their barrios developed into heterogeneous communities, conflicts between the two groups erupted. Mexican Americans faced not only economic competition from the newcomers but also "daily decisions about who they are—politically, socially, and culturally."[53]

Anglo-Americans also became concerned with the rising number of Mexican immigrants. This phenomenon, which occurred concurrently with an era of unprecedented immigration to the United States from southern and eastern Europe, created anxiety among Anglo-Americans, who felt their civilization under siege from the flood of foreigners. This perceived threat led to the creation of the Americanization Movement, designed to encourage rapid assimilation of foreigners into the States. President Roosevelt articulated the rationale behind the movement in 1915, when he stated, "The foreign-born population of this country must be an American population. . . . It must talk the language of its native-born citizens, it must possess American citizenship, and American ideals."[54] Since Anglos did not distinguish between Mexican Americans and recent Mexican immigrants, all Hispanics became the target of Americanization reformers.

Repeating the pattern seen with Anglo women working with Native Americans, Americanization reformers focused on Hispanic women as the most effective means to assimilate the group into Anglo society.[55] Convinced that Hispanic women had either been "thrust outside their true role (in the home)," or had been cast "as martyrs to domestic ignorance, their bad housekeeping

making them slovenly and impoverished," as Sarah Deutsch describes it, reformers created evening school classes for women to teach them cooking,
home nursing, sewing, and the importance of cleanliness.[56] And yet, as Frank
Van Nuys argues, the "intensity and persistence of discrimination worked
against Hispanics adopting Anglo-American values and cultural norms."[57]
While Anglo women saw their programs as a way to give Hispanic women a
role in the Americanization process, as both student and teacher, and an opportunity to become part of the American mainstream, Hispanic women remained skeptical. For many, they recognized that Americanization would not
move them "from margin to center in Anglo society, and would certainly not
return them to the center of Hispanic society."[58] In their barrios, in the fields,
and in the factories, Hispanic women found support among themselves. By
the early 1930s, they had begun to organize as activists to negotiate a place in
society on their own terms and consistent with their own values.[59]

The interaction of Hispanics and Native American women with Anglo wom-
en had been fairly minimal until 1870, when Euro-Americans began arriving
in increasing numbers. Some Anglo women moved onto the southern plains
as single women to work on reservations or in Hispanic villages; most came
with families to settle on farms in the newly developing towns; but all brought
with them the imperative to instill their vision of civilization on the southern
plains. "White women," writes Virginia Scharff, "played a crucial role in the
process of settlement. It was their job to transport, enact, and reproduce the
customs of American domesticity, the habits at the heart of American social
life." At every level of society, from mission work to philanthropic funding of
hospitals to caring for a geranium on a dugout windowsill, as "westering
women advanced [they] carried a little piece of empire along."[60]

   This region had come under US control after the US-Mexico war of 1848,
but settlement had been slowed by the onset of the Civil War, after which the
combination of devastated economy and abundance of feral cattle initiated
the era of cattle drives.[61] In the 1870s, the boom era of cattle ranching began;
the Comanches had been relegated to reservations, and men who either began
cattle drives or worked those drives saw land that was both unclaimed and
good for ranching.[62] The harsh, arid climate did not lend itself to the settlement of small family farms, like up in the central and northern plains. Here,
large tracts of land would best be suited for cattle, and this would require
significant financial investment. William Robbins puts the development of
large-scale cattle ranches in the context of an emerging capitalist market, noting, "This new age in the ranch-cattle business, no matter what its scale, was
tied firmly to eastern and overseas markets."[63] Large cattle ranches, financed

in good part by wealthy British capitalists, would further shape the economic, political, and cultural development of the southern plains region.

Cornelia Adair and Mary Ann ("Molly") Goodnight exemplify Texas ranch women who were connected with the emerging capitalist markets and who acted as harbingers of Anglo civilization onto the plains. Their experience shows, too, how class status played a role in determining how much influence an individual woman could exert to disseminate her ideals. In their own ways, Cornelia Adair and Molly Goodnight used their positions to bring Euro-American ideas of civilization and refinement to the West Texas plains.

It is hard to picture Cornelia Wadsworth as a western woman; she always dressed in the latest fashions, even when posing with the ranch cowboys. Born into a wealthy Philadelphia family she had grown up surrounded by luxury. In 1869 she met John Adair, a moneyed English-Irish aristocrat, at a ball in New York City; they married soon after. The couple moved to the Wadsworth family estate in New York, where John Adair helped manage her family's business affairs. In 1874 Cornelia convinced John they should take a buffalo-hunting excursion in Nebraska. This was a common holiday for very wealthy Americans and Europeans, and for Cornelia, an expert horsewoman, it provided an opportunity to experience the western frontier that had captivated her since childhood.[64]

The trip out west did not disappoint either of the Adairs. Before setting out to hunt the buffalo, Cornelia wrote in her diary, "The morning was most beautiful, and the clear delicious air put us all in the highest spirits; and then the intense, delightful excitement of starting out on such a novel expedition, not knowing what adventures we may have."[65] The beauty of the plains, and the potential for investment, encouraged the couple to return in 1877. On this trip they met Charles Goodnight, one of the founders of the Goodnight-Loving cattle trail and longtime rancher. Goodnight had been looking for a partner to invest in a new ranch; Adair was looking for an opportunity to invest in western enterprise and to leave what by then had become an uncomfortable business arrangement with his in-laws. Shortly after they met, John Adair and Charles Goodnight formed the JA ranch, located in the Palo Duro Canyon.[66]

The Adairs left the day-to-day management of the ranch to the Goodnights, dividing their time between the ranch and their other estates in England and Ireland. When they did spend time on the ranch, Cornelia had a "sporting impulse to learn the cattle business."[67] She and Molly Goodnight accompanied their husbands and the ranch cowboys on a twelve-day, four-hundred-mile cattle drive from Trinidad, Colorado, to Palo Duro Canyon. It was highly unusual for women to ride the cattle trails, but Cornelia rode side-saddle the entire way while Molly drove one of the four-mule wagons.[68] When

John Adair died in 1885, Cornelia became Goodnight's partner. She proved to be an astute businesswoman. Cornelia lived on the ranch for months at a time, closely overseeing its management and acquiring more land. In 1887 she bought out Goodnight's share of the JA; when she died in 1912, the ranch had expanded to half a million acres.[69]

Molly Goodnight's story also begins in the East. Born Mary Ann Dyer, she moved from Tennessee to Texas with her large family when she was fourteen. Although Molly did not enjoy the same level of wealth as Cornelia, she came from a prominent and influential Tennessee family. Soon after the move to Texas, both of her parents died and she took the responsibility of rearing her three younger brothers by herself, teaching in various central Texas schools to support them. She met Charles Goodnight in 1864, perhaps when one of her brothers worked for him as a drover, and they married in 1870.[70] While she never had any children of her own, Molly came to be known as the Mother of the Panhandle. Widely admired and respected, she embodied all the characteristics expected of a middle-class Victorian-era woman living on the Texas frontier, serving as nurturer, nurse, caretaker, and homemaker for the men who lived and worked at the JA ranch.[71]

Both Cornelia Adair and Molly Goodnight led, by example, the Euro-American idea of civilizing the plains through their philanthropic activities. Cornelia used her resources to improve the town near the JA ranch. She focused her financial contributions on social causes that promoted nineteenth-century women's vision of civilization, such as funding the Adair Hospital and generously supporting the YMCA and the Boy Scouts.[72] Molly Goodnight also fulfilled her role as civic leader, most notable as one of the founders of coeducational Goodnight College in 1898 in conjunction with the local Methodist church.

Aside from institution-building, Molly Goodnight's most famous project, preserving the buffalo (or bison) that once thrived on the southern plains, illustrates eastern reform ideas for encouraging "civilized" behavior applied to the western frontier. Her plan to save the bison fits within the newly popularized effort to protect animals. The first US chapter of the Society for the Prevention of Cruelty to Animals (SPCA) opened in New York City in 1866. Humanitarian efforts to educate the public and enforce anticruelty laws for domestic animals were couched in terms of advancing civilized behavior and encouraging "the national character and national instincts."[73] In Texas in the 1880s, most bison had been killed through overhunting and as part of the US government's strategy to force Native Americans onto reservations. According to Michael Thurgood Haynes, Molly Goodnight "pitied the orphaned calves that were left to die because their hides were not large enough for commercial use."[74] Taking the SPCA's idea of protecting domestic animals, she effectively applied it to a nondomestic endangered species by raising orphaned buffaloes. The Goodnight cowboys helped her project by bringing in calves they found while out riding the range. Through her efforts, the bison herd increased in number within the safety of Palo Duro Canyon.

Because of their wealth and position in the cattle business, Goodnight and Adair have become iconic figures in Texas history. But the historical record is replete with less-well-known women. Since it was not uncommon for literate, middle-class frontier women to keep journals, some of which have been published, one sees how they set about civilizing the plains. For the earliest settlers, just holding onto the ideals of a civilized life proved a difficult challenge. The wives and daughters of cowboys had vivid recollections of their early years on the southern plains. Nancy Jane Baird, who came to the Texas Panhandle in 1888, lived in a tent for the first two years. At that time there were only two other women in the county. She remembered that there were lots of skunks and gray foxes who wanted to share the tent with them. Dolly Thompson recalled that the trip from Parker County, Texas, to Canyon in 1889 took a month because they all got measles on the way. Her family traveled with two wagons and twenty-five to fifty head of cattle. She was eleven years old when they moved, and they lived in a half-dugout, which is a house with a frame section built onto a dugout. As a child she enjoyed taffy pulls, fish fries, masquerades, and picnics. For her, the transition to frontier life was not traumatic because her family had been farmers before they moved.[75]

Most people who did not live in town lived in dugouts—literally rooms dug out of a hillside—or sod houses. Emma Jane Ferguson Hough described her dugout:

> It was warm in winter and cool in summer. . . . We had two rooms in the dugout: one was a long room twenty feet square. This was our living room and sleeping quarters. The other room was smaller and served as both kitchen and dining room. The dugout had a plank roof and glass windows on top that opened on a pivot. The dirt walls inside of the house were lined with canvas and the ceiling was papered with some very hard-to-get wall paper.

They had an organ in their home and people came from miles around to sing on Sunday afternoons. In 1901 they moved to Hereford, Texas, and built a large house with seven rooms. In this they were unusual. Most families lived in isolated dugouts for decades.[76]

Nellie Perry first came to the southern plains in 1888 when she visited her brother, George. Perry was quite disconcerted on arriving at her brother's sod house after a long, tiring trip from Iowa. The little house (about twelve feet by fourteen feet) had strips of carpet over the door and window openings and a dirt floor. George was a bachelor and not much of a housekeeper. Nellie was appalled at the way everything was simply hung on a wall or on the rafters or in a heap under the bed. The furniture consisted of a bed, a stove, a makeshift table made of two planks, two chairs, and a small cupboard. When she went visiting that Sunday, however, she found that sod houses could be much fancier than her brother's. The Bates family, who lived in the next section, had divided their large sod home into two well-furnished rooms. The kitchen, in one part of the house, had a dirt floor, while the living/dining/sleeping area boasted a carpeted floor and bookcases set into the walls.[77]

One of the first towns to appear on the southern plains was Tascosa, in 1876. It began as a trading post and meeting place for *Comancheros* (Mexicans who traded with Indians, especially Comanches), *pastores, ciboleros* (Mexican buffalo hunters), and later, cowboys. In the 1880s Tascosa was known for its saloons, gambling, and prostitution.[78] As more women moved into the new southern plains towns, they very consciously began to clean up what they considered uncivilized and immoral frontier behaviors in order to re-create the society they cherished back home.[79] William B. Hutchinson, from Wichita, Kansas, noted the importance of women in the Tascosa's transformation from raw outpost to genteel community. "Women and children," he wrote, "give us an air of respectability and civilization."[80] Imbibed with the Progressive Reform spirit of their day, middle-class women worked tirelessly to abolish prostitution, promote temperance, and make their cities clean. They organized churches, schools, and clubs, and they brought about the transformation of the area from what they considered a wild frontier to one that met with their expectations for decent living.

Focusing on West Texas settlements as a representative example, one can see how middle- and upper-class women promoted their ideas of civilizing the plains through their support of religion, education, social clubs, music, and the arts. The earliest church services recorded in Potter County took place at the Frying Pan Ranch. The only woman on the ranch, Mrs. W. W. Wetsel, held Bible readings and hymn singing for the cowboys. Twice in 1888 an itinerant minister held services at the ranch. The brand-new town of Amarillo had only about 150 residents then, and most of them lived in tents, but the women were determined to build a church. The Methodist Church South was organized on November 25, 1888, and the first chapel, called Union Church because it was open to all denominations, was completed in the summer of 1889. Methodists, Baptists, Christian Church members, and Presbyterians were each allotted one week a month, but all were welcome to each service. As more people came to town, though, the denominations grew apart. In 1892 the Presbyterians built a church on Fillmore Street, in 1898 the Christian Church members built their own church on Taylor Street, in 1904 the Methodists built their first church for their exclusive use on Polk Street, and in 1907 the Baptists built their own church on Taylor Street. Episcopalians held services in the courthouse beginning in 1891 and built their first church in 1893.[81]

Just south of Potter County lies Randall County. Itinerant preachers also made their way to tiny Canyon City beginning in 1889. The first Sunday school was organized in 1890, with Miss Emma Turner serving as its first teacher. All denominations held services in the courthouse once it was built, and the county's only organ was also put into the courthouse so that everyone could use it. In Randall County, the Baptists were the first to build their own church, followed by the Methodists. The Methodist women formed the Women's Society of Christian Service in 1901, which raised money for the church and held Bible studies. The Baptist women formed the Women's Missionary Union in 1907. The Presbyterians, the last of the "union church" members to build their own structure, did so in 1902. The first Christian Church in Canyon was built in 1905, and the Christian Women's Organization began its fund-raising efforts. Many Germans lived in the area, and the first Lutheran Church was organized in 1908. Episcopalians held services in a large tent until 1917; St. Ann's Catholic Church was built in 1925.[82]

In Lubbock, the same pattern prevailed. All denominations shared the use of the courthouse for union services beginning in 1896. The Baptists built the first church with the help of people from other denominations and shared its use until the others could build their own. The Baptists and Methodists shared a union choir and union Sunday school through the 1910s. The women of all the churches organized a chapter of the Woman's Christian Temperance Union (WCTU) in 1909. Prohibition and religion were closely linked on the southern plains. Lubbock voted itself dry in 1910.[83]

Religion also linked itself with education. Several schools and academies began in connection with different faiths. Father Anastasius Peters founded the Mercy Academy in Martin County in 1881 as a theological center for Carmelites. In 1894 the Sisters of Mercy opened Mercy Academy. It quickly became a boarding school for young ladies, and many West Texas ranchers sent their daughters there as it gained a reputation as a finishing school. As noted earlier, Molly Goodnight helped found Goodnight College in 1898. Originally aligned with the Methodist Church, in 1905 the college transferred allegiance to the Baptist denomination; competition from other schools led to its closure in 1917. Hereford Christian College and Industrial School opened in 1902; in 1904 the Disciples of Christ took over financial responsibility. The Methodist Episcopal Church, South, opened Clarendon College in 1898 after the city eliminated all saloons from the town. (Donley County voted itself dry in 1902.) The first Clarendon College was replaced by a nonsectarian Clarendon Junior College in 1927.[84]

Other colleges were not associated with churches. The first Amarillo College began in 1897, and two of the four faculty members were women, Maud Tannehill and Mrs. James Bolton. It lasted until 1910, the year that West Texas State Normal College opened in Canyon. Although people in the area had wanted an institute of higher learning since 1900, it was not until 1923 that Texas Technological College opened in Lubbock. All of these institutions were coeducational.[85] The people who moved to the southern plains valued education, and they brought with them the belief that higher education could transform the frontier settlement into the type of towns they had left behind.

Women's social clubs also functioned as a means of self- and civic improvement. In Lubbock, women formed the Twentieth Century Club in 1909. It was a combination literary society and civic improvement organization. The members were influential in forming the Lubbock library, and they donated books to the school library. These women also aided in cleanup days for the city and promoted child welfare. By 1925 many other women's clubs had been formed in the city. The Civic League took over the city beautification projects with planting trees and flowers, the Junior Twentieth Century Club began several groups of Camp Fire Girls, the Lubbock Music Club brought entertainers to the city, while many other clubs contributed in similar ways.[86]

In Amarillo, the first women's club was formed on October 26, 1900, and was called Just Us Girls (JUG). It was educational in nature, and early on they decided that the city needed a library. The members collected and donated books for a small library that opened to the public in October of 1902. JUG continued to collect books and raise money for the library that in 1908 was turned over to the Amarillo Public Library Association (another women's group). Other clubs in Amarillo included the Social Dames Club, an art and literary league; the Civic League, which planted trees and flowers in parks and elsewhere; and the Federated Club, which began in 1913. One of the Federated Club's early campaigns was to wipe out, or at least reduce, the flies in the city. They offered prizes to the people who killed the most flies. The winner (if one could call him that), Earnest Webber, collected thirty-one quart jars full of dead flies.[87]

Amarillo also had social events of a more aesthetic nature. The Philharmonic Club, formed in 1905, raised money to bring musical performances to town. In 1922 Amarillo had its own band, and several of the area music teachers, many of them women, held recitals throughout the years. The Amarillo Symphony Orchestra began in 1924 through the efforts of the Philharmonic Club and the symphony's first director, Miss Grace Hamilton.[88]

Smaller towns also had their organizations and social life, replete with book clubs, city orchestras, suppers, ice-cream socials, plays, recitals, and lectures given by and for women. The small town of Hereford had its own women's club, the Monday Afternoon Club, that, like its big-city sisters, organized the town's first library. An even smaller town, Ochiltree, had its own Chautauqua and a community orchestra by 1915. Life on the southern plains in the first two decades of the twentieth century was amazingly crowded with social events that promoted a well-ordered, middle-class point of view.[89]

In many ways, Anglo women living on the southern plains, like their counterparts living in the big cities of the United States, felt the urge to make things better. And, like their eastern sisters, they ventured into the public arena under the guise of "municipal housekeeping" to change the southern plains into an area that conformed to their concept of civilized society. Comanche, Mexican, and Hispanic women had, of course, attempted the same when their groups held sway in the region. But from the 1870s to the 1930s, Anglo women, backed by the power of their convictions and the expansionist aims of the country, enforced their concept of civilized society onto the region, suppressing those of the Native American and Hispanic women.

By the 1930s, while the lives of Anglo women were not much different from those living in any other rural area in the United States, the lives of Indian and Hispanic women had been dramatically altered. Within half a century the area had changed from Comanche winter camps and scattered Hispanic villages to thriving towns, from isolation to urban centers. Taking a long view, numerous influences from outside the region had contributed to the movement of Comanche, Hispanic, and Anglo women onto the southern plains. From 1862 to 1930, however, the civilizing efforts of Anglo women became a ubiquitous force, shaping the lives of all women in diverse and profound ways.

# Risky Business

## Southern Plains Women and the Tradition of Place

LINDA W. REESE

The leading story of *The Oklahoman* newspaper focused on the severe drought enveloping the region. Above a photograph of parched ground, the headline on January 15 asked, "When will the rain come?" The Lugert-Altus Lake registered eighteen feet below normal, and four hundred thousand acres had been scorched by wildfires. "We've got a lot of fields where wheat seeds [planted the previous October] are still just laying there," a southwestern farmer reported, and another rancher grumbled, "A lot of people are just selling out." This article is not a report retrieved from the historical archives of the Dust Bowl days in the 1930s. This is an account of the drought of 2005–2006. It is a certain understanding that the southern plains of the United States, a vast area that includes portions of Oklahoma, Texas, and New Mexico, experiences extremes in environmental conditions. High winds, rapid temperature changes, storms, and drought alternate with periods of temperate beauty and abundant rainfall. This regional environment, ripe with possibility and fraught with danger, influenced the women who settled here in the twentieth century and remain determined to stay on it. Farm women who spend their lives on the land contend with the forces of nature and life and time. Their bond consists of a love and commitment to the land embedded in a foundation of hope that defies the odds of survival in the face of drought, dust, and agricultural market uncertainty. As Donald Worster has written, the southern plains is "next year" country. Given the dramatic population shift from rural to urban in the Trans-Mississippi West since 1930, this essay examines the forces that challenge and affirm women's resolve to continue a tradition of life on the land they cherish.[1]

Without doubt, national attention to the southern plains region reached its peak in the era of the Dust Bowl of the 1930s. Wide-scale devastation of the landscape produced heartbreaking suffering and poverty that led to the exodus of thousands of families out of the region. They traveled to far western states where they hoped to put down roots on the land again and to build a new future of plenty. The history of the so-called Okie migration has been told in numerous historical studies, films, and memorable novels such as John Steinbeck's *The Grapes of Wrath*. The story of the people who remained behind, however, especially that of women and their impact on family survival, is largely neglected. Drought and hard times were not new to these sturdy pioneers, and neither made a difference to their reverence for a sense of place or a refusal to accept defeat. Fabiola Cabeza de Baca, in her 1954 memoir of growing up on the Llano Estacado, the Staked Plains, near Las Vegas, New Mexico, wrote, "Life so cruel and at times so sweet is a continuous struggle for existence—yet one so uncertain of what is beyond fights and fights for survival."[2]

From a very early age, Cabeza de Baca learned the distinction between money and wealth. "People who live from the soil have abundant living and, compared with that of the wage earner, it can be classed as wealth," she wrote. She did not believe that her family had ever been poor because they lived on the land. Rain was far more important than cash. Rather than counting money, she counted the weeks and months between rains. The closing chapter of her book discusses the drought of 1918, when most homesteaders gave up farming in the area and the plowed land became sandhills covered with tumbleweeds. Wartime prices and rationing demanded cutbacks in hired help and in the essentials of life. Her father was forced to exchange the large ranch he had always lived on for a much smaller one. By the 1930s, the Cabeza de Baca family did not lack familiarity with Dust Bowl conditions.[3]

Historian Joan M. Jensen's prodigious research on rural women in the 1980s sketched the significance of Cabeza de Baca during the Great Depression. After receiving a degree in home economics in 1929, Fabiola joined the New Mexico Agriculture Extension Service where she worked as an agent for the next decade. In New Mexico the characteristic that united women of every race between 1900 and 1940 was poverty. As Jensen's research revealed, demographically, New Mexico women were largely illiterate in English, "rural, young, married, likely to have children, and to see many of them die in infancy." Jensen credits Cabeza de Baca with enabling farm families to increase their productivity, stabilize their families, and remain on their land during the state's harshest depression.[4]

Cabeza de Baca crossed boundaries of race and gender in establishing adult clubs that reached eighty percent of the farm families in her area. She organized volunteers to supervise children's clubs and encouraged gardening at home, canning foods, and selling produce and poultry. She helped them obtain new technology such as canning equipment, sewing machines, and water systems for their homes by creating collectives and by cultivating a bartering system of labor for cash. In addition, she promoted Native handicrafts to be sold at the Santa Fe Native Market and at roadside stalls to supplement family income. Those she did not reach personally, she influenced through her newspaper column, "Ciencia Domestica," in *El Nuevo Mexicano*. By the end of the decade, death and infant mortality rates had dropped, a majority of New Mexico women were literate in English, and in Cabeza de Baca's area more than 90 percent of the women had home gardens and sewing machines. While New Deal relief programs assisted families, Cabeza de Baca succeeded where others failed because she capitalized on traditional values and kinship networks while introducing new methods to obtain necessities and to reinvest savings in improving their homes and lives.[5]

Perhaps no Dust Bowl woman farmer has received more historical recognition than Oklahoma's Caroline Henderson. Her "Letters from the Dust Bowl," published originally between 1931 and 1937 in *Atlantic Monthly*, chronicled the environmental disaster that tested the resolve of homesteaders throughout the region. Henderson's portrait of life in the Oklahoma Panhandle illustrates the daily struggle to survive and remain on the land while others bowed under the weight of defeat. Henderson sent her 1935 letter, "Dust to Eat," previously rejected by *Atlantic Monthly*, to Secretary of Agriculture Henry A. Wallace in anticipation of an advertised trip he planned to make to Amarillo, Texas. "Now we are facing a fourth year of failure. There can be no wheat for us in 1935 in spite of all our careful and expensive work in preparing ground, sowing and resowing our allotted acreage. Native grass pastures are permanently damaged, in many cases hopelessly ruined, smothered under by drifted sand," she wrote. "Fences are buried under banks of thistles and hard packed earth," she continued, "or undermined by the eroding action of the wind and lying flat on the ground. Less traveled roads are impassable, covered deep under sand or the finer silt-like loam." Henderson gave credit to "[t]he enduring character of our people" during this time of extreme stress. Her letter became the classic description for historians of the effects of drought and dust storms on the region.[6]

Henderson finished her master's thesis in literature, entitled "The Love of the Soil as a Motivating Force in Literature Relating to the Early Development of the Middle West," for the University of Kansas during the worst dust storms of the 1930s. One chapter in the thesis defined the role women had played in the development of the land. As she analyzed seven prominent Midwestern writers who published works on pioneering, she revealed her own perspective about women and commitment in the midst of failure. Sometimes "the hard won things are the most precious," she wrote. A longer explanation of her feelings appeared in *Atlantic Monthly* in 1936. "Naturally you will wonder why we stay where conditions are so extremely disheartening. Why not pick up and leave as so many others have done?" she wrote to a friend.

> . . . I cannot act or feel or think as if the experiences of our twenty-seven years of life together had never been. And they are all bound up with the little corner to which we have given our continued and united efforts. To leave voluntarily—to break all these closely knit ties for the sake of a possibly greater comfort elsewhere—seems like defaulting on our task. We may have to leave. . . . But I think I can never go willingly or without pain that as yet seems unendurable.[7]

For Caroline Henderson a sense of defeat loomed close, but she refused to deny her love of the land and the power of her hope for a dream yet to be fulfilled.

As Alvin O. Turner, Henderson's biographer, maintains, her significance lies in more than just her descriptions of the conditions in the 1930s. Henderson began homesteading as a single woman in 1907, before her marriage to her husband, Will. The couple lived on that same land until near their deaths in 1966. The body of her writing provides a window on the changing nature of the southern plains in the twentieth century and the continuing challenges of drought, storms, isolation, and economic uncertainty to farm stability. They also supply a remarkable woman's perspective on rural life that endured through extreme adversity and found fulfillment, if not in wealth then in friendship, in ideas, in writing, and in a deep appreciation of beauty. Abundant rainfall in the region in the 1940s and high agricultural prices accompanying World War II briefly regenerated the farm and Henderson's hopes. Her letters in the 1950s and 1960s, however, reveal the brutal, honest evaluation of her failed dreams. In June 1952 Henderson wrote to her daughter Eleanor, "It is hard to write under such depressing conditions when we see our living disappearing before our eyes. . . . This is the fourth successive day of extreme heat—98–100 degrees—and uninterrupted blasting winds." By September her letter to Eleanor remarked, "It is sad to tell you that my gloomiest forebodings about the wheat coming were completely justified. I have looked over the 60 acres on this place pretty carefully. . . . [N]ow one can find only dry seed in dry ground and scarcely any moisture." Still, Caroline Henderson refused to give up on her land until her health made it impossible to continue to live there.[8]

Homesteading in the Oklahoma Panhandle carried with it at least the promise of eventual security and prosperity. Farther south, in the Texas cotton lands, this possibility came only to a fortunate few. Rebecca Sharpless's brilliant study, *Fertile Ground, Narrow Choices: Women on Texas Cotton Farms, 1900–1940*, documents the lives of farm women caught in the sharecropping farm structure held over from the nineteenth-century South. Unlike Henderson and Cabeza de Baca, this group of women belonged to families who did not own their own land and rarely realized the opportunity to accomplish that goal. These were exceptionally poor women: wives, mothers, daughters, and agricultural laborers whose lives were dictated by the rhythms of the cotton crop. Most often they lacked suitable housing, electricity, running water, access to medical care, and nutritious food. In their triple roles as housewife, mother, and field laborer, women discovered survival of the family depended on how well they coped with the endless nature of their work. When that era ended after 1940, Sharpless maintains that "[f]ew former farm people wax nostalgic about the old days. No one misses the near-starvation, the shacks, the rags that sometimes passed for clothing." She admits, however, that adjusting to city life proved difficult for some rural people. Etta Carroll always remained a farm woman at heart and remembered those days fondly. "We worked hard, but we were used to it," she said. "And I think that back in those days we were just as happy with our lives then as we are now. I'd just as soon live in the country. You could get up and do what you wanted to do. And when you're in town, you do what the other person wants you to do."[9]

In Hester Calvert, Sharpless identified one of the more successful women of the cotton region whose family saved enough money to purchase their own land and develop a dairy near Waco, Texas. A lifelong reader, Calvert had finished only a sixth grade education. At age twenty-six she married, and like most families of the region with little access to birth control they followed the socially and economically sanctioned practice of birthing a large family. In the space of eighteen years, she experienced ten pregnancies. The Calverts were luckier than most couples who generally lost one in five of their children. Hester miscarried at age forty-five, but only one child died shortly after birth, and the remaining eight reached adulthood. In addition to the eight children, the Calverts housed and cared for her husband's aged parents and Hester's mother. They moved often, as sharecroppers did, frequently living in cramped, unpainted shacks. Hester made do with most circumstances except that she refused to live in a house that did not at least have screens on the windows. At one point their sharecropper house burned, taking nearly all of their possessions. They lived in the basement of a vacant school aided by donations from their neighbors until they could make a crop and move again.[10]

Hester cultivated a large garden, but without any canning equipment until the late 1920s, these vegetables were eaten only in season. The staple diet, typical of Southern sharecropper families, consisted of pork, cornmeal, and molasses. Hester cooked on a wood-burning stove and washed clothes in the yard with a tub and scrub board. She made nearly all of the family's clothing, borrowing sewing machines until she was able to buy her own with butter, egg, and turkey savings. While Hester did not engage in cotton fieldwork, all of her children did by the time they were six or seven years old. The Calverts were able to save enough to buy their own mules and move up to tenant farmer status. By the 1930s, they had become landowners. According to Sharpless, "Hester's chores were identical to those done by her daughters thirty years later." Such a burdensome life could only have been managed through an intrinsic energy capable of absorbing both joys and sorrows and incorporating these with a determined work ethic that refused to surrender. Not only did women like Calvert influence the quality of their own families' lives, but they also enabled Texas to become the leading cotton-producing state in the union.[11]

Farm women in each of the areas discussed here recognized the injustices of racism in the United States. As isolated as Caroline Henderson seemed to be on her land in the Oklahoma Panhandle, she kept informed of the changes taking place in the state, and she expressed her opinions openly about the civil rights debate that engaged the nation in the 1950s and 1960s. After the Ada Lois Sipuel and George McLaurin court cases forced integration at the University of Oklahoma, Henderson wrote to a New York friend, happily informing him about the final removal of the classroom ropes that separated black and white students. In 1955 she expressed her resentment toward the determination of the Southern states to obstruct the *Brown v. Board of Education* decision. "Really it isn't the young people in the school that are making trouble," she wrote. "It is the older people still clinging to their doctrine of states rights and white supremacy. But I sincerely believe that except for that minority group the drift or tendency now is in favor of justice and equal rights for all our citizens." Concerning Native Americans, she contributed to charities that assisted New Mexico Navajo missions and considered the treatment of Indian peoples a travesty in US history.[12]

Historians Sarah Deutsch and Rebecca Sharpless more emphatically identified levels of racial oppression for Hispanic women in New Mexico and African American women in Texas. With the onset of the Great Depression, the seasonal movement of Hispanic people from agricultural villages to wage work and return across the American Southwest faced serious limitation. As demand for restriction of Mexican immigration escalated, the US House Committee on Immigration considered three quota bills as early as 1930. The government enlarged the US Border Patrol and increased penalties for illegal immigration. Approximately four hundred thousand Mexicans and their US-born children were repatriated to Mexico. In spite of the recruitment of workers from New Mexico by sugar, sheep, and railroad companies, the governor of Colorado declared martial law and blockaded the southern border of Colorado in 1936 with the National Guard. Depression-era economic conditions and government policy reduced the ability of Hispanic families to sustain themselves with wage work, and the prolonged drought crippled the agriculture on their small land holdings. Still, one Hispanic woman remembered, "People on the farm were better off than downtown—we had our gardens." By the middle of the 1930s, relief rolls in northern New Mexico villages swelled to 60 percent of the population.[13]

Anglo resentment toward Hispanics increased as conditions worsened. Unfortunately, Harry Hopkins, director of the Federal Emergency Relief Administration, exacerbated the situation. He dropped recipients who would most likely work the beet fields from relief rolls at the beginning of sugar beet season. This forced families into migrating for seasonal labor at low wages, taking their children out of school, and jeopardizing their relief status as village residents. Their only recourse was to leave the women and children at home and send the men out to earn wages too small for survival. According to Deutsch, "The federal government adopted as the official view the myth that only Chicano labor would or could perform beet and other underpaid work." In addition, many officials and social service workers believed that Hispanics were accustomed to an inexpensive diet and lower standard of living than Anglos. These views triggered a return to the promotion of traditional Anglo conceptions of appropriate roles for women onto Hispanic culture. The number of Hispanic women teachers, clerical workers, and health-care workers increased, and many, of course, engaged in domestic service. In the villages, mothers and daughters hired out to clean and do housework for wages below other domestic workers. In addition, some relief officials also discriminated against Hispanic women. New Mexico State Relief Administrator Margaret Reeves wrote to Washington offices, "I do not believe that there should be many more working women in New Mexico, nor many more projects for women than we have at present." Referring to a seventy percent Spanish-speaking population, Reeves said, "I feel that women projects are better adapted to Anglo-American communities and to industrial areas." Reeves also suggested that Hispanic women needed to be in the homes with their large numbers of children. In agricultural villages, however, agents of change like Fabiola Cabeza de Baca prevailed when they incorporated new technology, services, and women's programs into traditional values and patterns of behavior. New Deal personnel in New Mexico experienced the same racism, political power struggles, and sexism as in other areas of the country. Rather than bringing innovation, most New Deal programs preserved the economic structure. Cabeza de Baca represented the exception in the New Mexico Agriculture Extension Service.[14]

Texas cotton areas experienced rapid racial transition in the twentieth century, but nineteenth-century racial attitudes lingered on in the segregated society. Texas Indian peoples, mostly Tonkawas, Wichitas, and Comanches, had been forced into what became Oklahoma by the 1860s, but fear and racial slurs persisted in Texas. African Americans brought to the state as slaves before the Civil War were joined by increasing numbers of freed people. By 1920 some of the cotton-producing counties had a black population as high as twenty-two percent. Mexican immigrants also made their way to the cotton lands after 1910 in growing numbers. Racial inequality, the result of distrust and segregation, affected the lives of black, brown, and white women throughout the region. Hester Calvert, herself a struggling sharecrop mother of eight, believed that black women could be hired for washing and cleaning, but according to her daughter, "Mother wouldn't have had a meal that a black around us cooked. . . . She just wouldn't think they'd be clean or know how."[15]

Inasmuch as cotton producing was labor-intensive work, crews consisted of entire families, both the male and female members. While the quality of family life improved when women did not have to spend substantial amounts of time in the fields in addition to their household chores, as several studies have found, this aspiration rarely matched reality. For African Americans, female fieldwork was too reminiscent of slavery days. For white women, fieldwork contradicted social attitudes about race and class status. Many men and women, therefore, frequently denied or underreported the amount of time women worked in the fields, but a majority of women contributed to the cotton labor force. Women often took their young children to the fields with them and worked between seven and nine hours a day. The numbers of women and the time spent differed according to race. Sharpless's statistics indicate more than fifty percent of white women and Mexican women and more than ninety percent of black women engaged in fieldwork. The majority of white and Mexican women spent between three and six months on field labor, and the majority of black women were in the fields more than six months. Women primarily engaged in chopping and picking the cotton rather than plowing and cultivating. Generally, the higher the level of poverty of the family, the longer the women worked in the fields, with the exception of Mexican women whose fieldwork numbers approximated white women in spite of a significant difference of status.[16]

White women went to their homes at the end of the workday, but black and Mexican women usually came as part of a crew brought into the area to complete the harvest. They camped in tents, shacks, smokehouses, or pickups near a creek on the farm. They were told to leave as soon as the harvest was over. A single male relative or representative, known as a *patron* in Mexican culture, negotiated the work contract and supervised the crew. He arranged the hours worked, terms of payment, and working conditions. Women dragged fifty to seventy pounds of cotton in a full sack to the weigh station where the landowner's wife or teenage daughter recorded the accounts. Excellent workers sometimes picked approximately five hundred pounds a day. Many were illiterate, and Mexican women generally did not speak any English. They worked at the mercy of their employer's ethical and moral character. Landowners sometimes shorted the pickers in the number of pounds reported or required the pickers to buy supplies at inflated prices at a farm-owned store. Cotton wages during the 1930s dropped to as low as thirty-five cents per hundredweight. Black women often picked cotton part of the day, and then reported to landowner or tenant farmer houses as domestic workers. One black picker's son remembered his mother's work ethic: "She didn't mind wrapping us kid[s] up and go scrap the little cotton left on a burr, or walking for five mile to do house work for a cupple of doller [sic]."[17]

As the decade of the 1930s came to an end, the conditions of the Depression and the Dust Bowl lessened. Like so many other aspects of national life, World War II and the Cold War dramatically changed the nature of agriculture in the United States. Mechanization and improved crop sales affected not only landowners but also their families as a whole. Farm women had not always been enthusiastic about New Deal programs. The Agricultural Adjustment Administration (AAA) in particular drew significant female criticism. Many held the 1933 crop reduction contracts that favored large landowners responsible for their plight. Oklahoma homesteader, oil woman, and author Sue Sanders unified a large group of stranded migrants in Bakersfield, California, when she called the AAA the "Agricultural Ouster Administration."

She planned to go to Washington in 1939 to convince the government to allocate money to return the migrants to their homes. "They don't want anything given to them," she said of the migrants. "They just want to borrow a little and get a piece of land and they'll make it."[18]

Katherine Jellison's study of farm women and technology, however, identified a symbiotic relationship between the needs of US farm women and the Rural Electrification Administration (REA) established in 1935. Farm electrification meant a higher standard of living for families more in keeping with levels in urban areas as well as the acquisition of labor and time-saving devices for the home. Secretary of Agriculture Henry Wallace appealed directly to farm women to support the REA because "[w]omen make a more important contribution to farming than they do to any other single industry." The Roosevelt administration foresaw not only a means to retain population on the farms but also a way to boost US manufacturing in the sale of new appliances. Although most farm women did not enjoy the advantages of electrification in the 1930s, the 1940s and 1950s would see a dramatic increase in its extension in the southern plains. Texas farm woman Helen Catlett composed a woman's time line for the last sixty years of the twentieth century. "Rural electrification and farm-to-market roads probably changed the lifestyle the greatest in the 1940s and 1950s," she said. "In the 60s, the [birth control] pill and fewer children; in the 70s acceptance of women working because it was necessary rather than because she wanted to. Prediction for 80s: inflation and energy cost will influence lifestyle again." The modern farm woman received greater recognition of her centrality to the agricultural economy.[19]

Population studies done in Oklahoma in the 1940s indicated that rural farm families moved rapidly to replenish the state's population loss of the 1930s. In comparisons of urban and rural farm areas of the state, fertility ratios, determined by the number of children under five years of age for every one thousand women aged fifteen to forty-four, showed that the rural farm ratio was nearly twice the urban ratio. The highest rate of reproduction occurred in the livestock, subsistence, and cotton agricultural areas, and the lowest, in the wheat-growing Panhandle area. Unfortunately, wealth had an inverse relationship to fertility. Those areas with highest fertility were also areas of the lowest valued land. The presence of poverty in the state was additionally borne out by the rates of government assistance. Since the beginning of the federal Social Security program in the 1930s, Oklahoma had ranked first in the nation in old-age assistance rates. This embarrassment was only one of several issues related to land, water, and agriculture that caused outgoing governor Johnston Murray to exclaim in the *Saturday Evening Post* that "Oklahoma is in a Mess!" The highest numbers requiring assistance resided in those areas with the poorest land, practicing subsistence agriculture, and having the highest reproduction levels. Additional factors that influenced the need for assistance were, not surprisingly, families with seven or more occupants in the home, low levels of schooling, families also receiving aid to dependent children, race, and gender. Black and Indian citizens experienced higher assistance rates than their numbers in the population would have indicated. Men outnumbered women in the elder population at this time, and they applied for assistance in greater numbers than women. The author concluded with a warning that a sharp decline in farm prices, droughts, insect plagues, or floods would certainly raise demands for public assistance even higher.[20]

Indeed, the 1950s brought another drought to the southern plains. The rains of the 1940s and the high prices for wheat, cotton, and beef spurred by war mobilization convinced farmers to plow up three million acres of marginal land unfit for cultivation in Texas, New Mexico, and Oklahoma. Destruction of the vegetation holding the soil and overgrazing by cattle led to dirt drifting in the high winds of 1950, and dust storms became common again. By 1954 drought, unusually warm temperatures, and high winds had eroded the topsoil of 11.5 million acres of crop land and more than 5 million acres of rangeland. The years of 1955 and 1956 were the worst, leading to the contemporary description of the time, the "filthy fifties." Historian Douglas Hurt described blowing dust storms "reducing visibility to zero at times, drifting soil along fence rows, piling sand dunes twenty to thirty feet high in some fields, ruining crops, and scouring paint off license plates." But the utter tragedy of the 1930s was not repeated in the 1950s. Conservation techniques such as contour plowing, strip cropping, and grazing management as well as irrigation reservoirs and crop diversification kept farmers operating. In addition, federal assistance through low-interest loans from the Farmers' Home Administration, the Commodity Credit Corporation, and the US Department of Agriculture allowed farmers to hold onto their lands until the drought subsided.[21]

In the presence of another sustained farm crisis, what changes occurred in the reality of the lives of farm women and how did this reality diverge from the image promoted for farm women by the leading farm journal and national advertisers? Between 1945 and 1960 farm consolidation, improved technology, higher labor productivity, and decreased farm income dramatically lowered the presence of the farm sector in the American economy. With fewer farm families, fewer women lived on farms and raised their children there. In this period the proportion of farmers in the total population fell from 17.5 percent to 8.7 percent. The number of farms declined by 34 percent and family farm income in relation to nonfarmers dropped to 47.7 percent in 1956.[22]

These numbers illustrate the contradiction between the postwar US mentality of anticommunism, explicitly defined gender roles, and consumerism promoted by farm mass media and the life experiences of farm women. Distinctions among women based on ethnicity, race, scale of operation, and community virtually disappeared from meaningful discussion. Options possible in the immediate aftermath of World War II had no visibility by the mid-1950s. According to anthropologist Jane Adams, "the normative farm family was relatively prosperous, white, nuclear, male headed, and church going." Men concerned themselves with farm productivity, and women with homemaking and child rearing. Immediately after World War II, articles in the *Farm Journal* envisioned an American woman who would be an actor not only in her own home but also in her community and her world. Ruth Sayre, vice president of the Associated Women of the American Farm Bureau Federation, encouraged women to instill the virtues of "reasonableness, generosity, and tolerance," within her own home. But she declared, "We cannot build a wall about our own family. It is women's part to do in the community the kind of things they do for their own homes. Keep it clean, orderly, and healthy. See that it has education and is well governed; be the guardian of its ideals." *Farm Journal* editorials told readers, "[W]omen find a lot of satisfaction in being well informed, and in taking an intelligent part in any conversation. We feel better about ourselves if we're able citizens." Ohio Congresswoman Frances Payne Bolton appealed to farm women to become involved in politics, saying, "Because our woman's responsibility in the Eternal Economy is to give life and to protect it, we can no longer draw back."[23]

Homemaking and child rearing replaced public participation as the centrality of the farm woman's life, according to the *Farm Journal* in the 1950s. Advertisements and editorial policy reflected the decided promotion of free enterprise, and only infrequent articles appeared on rural poverty, migrant labor, and abbreviated land tenure. In a 1952 article, *Farm Journal* editor Gertrude Dieken compared the lives of nineteenth-century farm women with the conveniences of contemporary farm life. Dieken mentioned in the article carpets, electric stoves, refrigerators, washer-dryers, television sets, cars, and airplanes. Women experiencing the drought of the southern plains in 1956 could only dream about the consumer advantages the *Farm Journal* took for granted. Advertisers and the journal itself acknowledged farm women as productive workers on the land, but their position as partners during World War II and its aftermath faded to one of part-time hands in the 1950s. Adams noted a 1956 article that recognized the farm woman was in charge of the home, garden, and children, but "when Bud whistles, she'll drop her work to get a part for the cultivator, or drive the tractor during rush season." Women now served as support staff for their husbands in the business of running the farm. During this decade women were pursuing off-farm employment in increasing numbers, a trend that escalated over the next decades. By 1960 the number of farm women working off-farm jobs reached twenty-three percent. Yet the image remained one of privatized homemakers, enjoying the fruits of US modernity, rather than income earners and citizen activists, until the social movements of the 1960s.[24]

Throughout the decades religious faith has been an important part of the resilience of rural farm women. In good times and in bad, the farm woman has incorporated religious observance into her life and the lives of her children. Delois Alexander and her husband raised three children and five grandchildren on the 750-acre cotton farm her parents homesteaded in 1902. Thinking through the many challenges of farm life since she took over the farm in 1949, Alexander said, "You can get really close to the Lord in the middle of a cotton field." The environmental hazards of the southern plains led many of its inhabitants to place little reliance on science, technology, and human authority, and a great deal of faith and trust in divine intervention. Protestant fundamentalist religions emphasizing biblical literalism and individual morality predominate, especially Baptist, Methodist, Church of Christ, and Pentecostal Holiness churches. During the days of the Great Depression and the Dust Bowl, these beliefs provided solace, release, and answers to the incomprehensible acts of providence visited on the land and its people. In addition, churches served as refuges of continuity amidst great social upheaval. While overall state populations declined, church memberships and Sunday service attendance increased. Many believers saw the economic ruin as a sign of God's displeasure at humanity's sin. Revivals and church services abounded with calls to repent evil ways and return to a righteous life. Remembrances of the horrific black dust storms time and again refer to the belief that the end of time was near, and the second coming of Christ was imminent. Panhandle resident Delores Marie Wilmot remembered, "We thought the end of the world was surely coming, you know because, well, we went to church all of the time and they had these traveling evangelists, and they preached the old fire and everything else was going to fall on you anytime."[25]

Cotton-region women of all races found consolation, strength, and social leveling through prayer, Bible reading, and church attendance. Most families followed home religious practices in which the Bible was the ultimate authority. Bible reading, prayer, and song afforded a means of unifying a family and passing on family history and experience. Women who could not read often memorized long biblical passages and created stories or sermons used to instruct their children. Catholic families constructed home altars and recited the rosary together. Etta Carroll explained, "If we didn't have faith to pray and the Lord answer our prayers, what would this world be? Because he made this earth and he made everything on the earth. . . . You don't do anything by yourself. You have to have help." This kind of divine help strengthened them through poverty and family crisis. Churches functioned as relief agencies, centers for social life, forums of community morality and discipline, and places of worship. Formal church services were strictly segregated by race and gender. In white churches, only men could hold positions of authority. African American women exercised much greater authority in black churches as preachers and lay leaders. Within those boundaries, however, social classes attended and supported their church together. Landowners, tenants, and sharecroppers experienced community during worship service.[26]

Church membership also provided the basis for single-sex organizations such as Missionary Societies and Ladies' Aid Societies, which supported the work of the local church, sponsored community sings and youth social activities, and organized relief efforts for needy individuals and "love offerings" to distant communities. These religious groups took the place in rural areas that study clubs and social organizations occupied in urban areas. Members learned about other parts of America and the world, international events and different cultures, and socialized with each other, all in the name of good works. African American women's groups also provided consolation from racial harassment and violence. Alice Owens Caulfield attended prayer meetings for "a man with Christian belief to head the government," and the protection of members of her community from lynchings. She explained her faith:

> I understood that God was always close to you or to me. When I felt friendless, when I felt like I wasn't being treated right, I felt like there's a better day. . . . [W]hy be afraid when God is going to protect? . . . But as I'm in this world, . . . dealing with racism and taking it coolly and never saying too much. See there's no hate. We believe that we're all God's children; he's got 'em in many colors, in many lands, born to one blood.

Religious practices gave her strength for the present and hope for a greater afterlife.[27]

Popular country music between 1930 and 1950 reinforced a set of rural values that reflected these religious sensibilities. One of the most enduring and influential country music groups among the rural population was the Carter family—A.P., Sara, and Maybelle—whose recordings dominated radio in the South and West in the 1930s and 1940s. According to historian William W. Savage, Jr., "In their music, families were strong, mothers made sacrifices, sinners were saved and everyone was encouraged to keep a cheerful disposition." Their song "There'll Be No Distinction There" admitted that times were difficult, but heaven would bring relief from this world's problems, and poverty and prejudice would cease. In another recording, "Behind the Stone Wall," the Carters charted the dangers of leaving home and family for the larger world. A young man and his friend's misadventure in New York City landed them a long prison term. The message is clear as Savage maintains, "One ought not to leave home, and certainly one ought not to go to the city, for there one might fall into bad company with dire consequences." Maybelle Carter's daughter, June Carter Cash, together with her husband, Johnny Cash, continued this music tradition well into the 1990s.[28]

Farm trends begun in the 1950s have persisted to the present: population movement, especially among young people, away from the farms, declining levels of farm income, and the necessity of greater off-farm employment to sustain a hold on the land. For the southern plains, the periodic recurrence of drought is expected. None have been as devastating or as widespread as those of the 1930s and the 1950s, but each brought its own set of troubles. For periods of the 1960s, 1970s, 1980s, and 1990s, drought returned, parching the land and destroying crops. In 1996 President Bill Clinton ordered $70 million in federal aid mostly for drought-stricken Texas and Oklahoma. By August 1998, one hundred people had died in Texas in heat-related deaths, and more than five hundred people stood in line at the Department of Human Services in Oklahoma County for financial relief. The Oklahoma National Guard distributed hay to hard-hit cattle areas across the state. Still, farmers stayed on the land because of previous water development programs, conservation strategies, crop insurance, and disaster relief.[29]

The participation of farm women in agriculture continued to evolve as well, and new research better indicates the dimensions of the lives of women who stay on the land. Farm women contribute more now than ever to the successful operation of the farm and maintenance of land tenure. The decisions she makes about her work directly affect the viability of the farm. A 2003 study made by Penn State University Department of Agricultural Economics and Rural Sociology found that farm women holding off-farm jobs increased from thirty-seven percent in 1980 to fifty-two percent in 2001. The majority of these women worked full-time jobs in addition to their household tasks and farm labor. A major motivation for off-farm employment rested in the employee benefits of health insurance, life insurance, and pension plans. In addition, female wages add substantially to the total farm income, sometimes making the difference between success and failure. The study revealed that farm women with higher educational attainment were more likely to bear fewer children and to work off-farm, remaining in the workforce until middle age. This substantial increase in women's employment has been blamed, however, for rising rates of divorce among farm couples. Oklahoma, Texas, and New Mexico rank in the upper levels, at roughly sixteen percent each. Only the highly urbanized states register greater percentages. Lower fertility generally associated with education also affects the divorce rate in that the presence of children, especially young children, serves as a deterrent to divorce. Female off-farm employment, then, appears to have both positive and negative affects for farm families.[30]

Approximately half of the women in the Pennsylvania State University study engaged in fieldwork, and three-quarters tended farm animals, ran errands, took care of the bookkeeping, and managed gardens and animals for home consumption. A shift took place between 1980 and 2001 in women's work emphasis, however. The farm woman today is more likely to do fieldwork and less likely to work in tasks associated with home consumption or the supervision of hired labor or family workers. Lower fertility rates and Mexican immigration in the southern plains have increased the dependence on a Hispanic workforce. Male respondents perceived women's participation in these farm tasks lower than female respondents, but in terms of women's involvement in major farm decision making, males rated their involvement higher than women did. Farm women are fully aware of the extent of their chores, but are more likely to see their decision-making power as subordinate. This is generally true unless the farm has been transferred through her family. If the farm passes to the couple through the woman's family, even if both names are on the deed, she is more likely to work off-farm and be more directly involved in major farm decisions such as buying, selling, and renting land, major equipment purchases, and substantial changes to land use. If the farm is received through his family, the man is less likely to pursue off-farm labor and more inclined to assume all major decisions. Education, employment, fewer children, and transfer paths of land affect the levels of female empowerment.[31]

Another change in agriculture concerns the increase in the number of in-dependent female farmers—that is, women who are the sole operator or indi-vidual owner of a commercial farm. Since 1978 the number of women farmers in the United States has risen from 5.2 percent of all farmers to 7.5 percent. In addition, women in the United States currently own forty percent of all private agricultural land. Oklahoma and Texas rank in the leading five states with women as principal farm operators, and New Mexico and Texas are listed in the top five states in acreage operated by women. These women are active not only in all aspects of their farms but also in the major farm organizations of their states. Previous comparison studies documenting differences between independent male operators and female operators failed to distinguish be-tween farmers on the basis of size of farm and type of farm operation. In 1998 Kimberly A. Zeuli and Robert P. King conducted a thirteen-state survey that included Oklahoma and Texas, correcting for these omissions. The average age of female farmers is only slightly higher than males (50.7 years versus 49.9 years). A much higher percentage of women have education beyond high school than men (57.8 percent compared to 45.7 percent), and more than twice as many women have graduate or professional degrees. Zeuli and King found that a much larger proportion of women manage specialty crop farms than men, as predicted, but their study refutes the accepted understanding on size of acreage. Women operate farms with a significantly higher total acreage per farm than men in these states. In addition to specialty crop farms, women operate sizable cow-calf and mixed livestock farms. In Oklahoma beef sales accounted for more than fifty percent of total farm receipts in 2003. In com-paring farm performance, female-operated farms have lower levels of farm income but higher levels of off-farm income and smaller amounts of farm debt than those owned by men. These studies imply that women will continue to play a significant role in the agricultural production of the southern plains.[32]

The generations of women who have worked the land of the southern plains since 1930 have experienced hardships of biblical proportion: back-breaking toil, loss of children, hunger, privation, dust and sleet storms, drought, floods, economic depression, and discrimination. But they have also experienced pride in families raised, crops harvested, livestock herds enlarged, technological conveniences acquired, and neighbors welcomed. They know the beauty of the first sunlight on the fields and the satisfaction of rest after a day's work well done. They also understand the freedom of being in charge of their own time. Historian William W. Savage, Jr., commented in 1977, "Life in the country may be hard, but it offers subtle pleasures and meaningful re-wards, and it affirms the worth of the individual in ways that urban life cannot." Vivian McClaren assumed all of the farm work while her visually impaired husband raised the children when they started their cotton and grain farm twenty-eight years ago. Vicki Davis Patschke jokes about being a two-farm family. A fourth-generation farmer on land her great-grandfather bought from the state of Texas in 1903, she works her farm entirely independent of her husband's land. These are just a few of the women who choose life on the southern plains in the twenty-first century. Continuity, challenge, freedom, community, and beauty are choices southern plains women make instead of guaranteed prosperity.[33]

# Notes

## Introduction to the Collection

1. Walter Prescott Webb, *The Great Plains* (Boston: Ginn and Company, 1931), 506.
2. Noah Smithwick, *The Evolution of a State or Recollections of Old Texas Days* (Austin: University of Texas Press, 1983), 5. First published 1900. My thanks to Jean A. Stuntz for locating the exact quotation and reference; Webb, *The Great Plains.*
3. The Center for Great Plains Studies website link to Great Books of the Great Plains is an excellent starting point to begin researching current books on plains women's history (although it does not include books on Texas); accessed June 20, 2007, http://plainshumanities.unl.edu.
4. Don Mitchell, quoted in Michael Lansing, "Feminist Geography in US Western History," *Journal of Historical Geography* 29 (2003): 230.
5. See Lansing, 230–47, for an excellent discussion on applying the concept of personal experience, or "space," to the larger construction of region, or "place."
6. An example of earlier work, albeit more narrowly focused, can be found in Glenda Riley's *The Female Frontier: A Comparative View of Women on the Prairies and the Plains* (Lawrence: University Press of Kansas, 1988). The *Great Plains Quarterly* Spring 1988 issue specialized in women's issues.
7. See "Editor's Introduction," in *Writing the Range: Race, Class and Culture in the Women's West*, edited by Elizabeth Jameson and Susan Armitage (Norman: University of Oklahoma Press, 1997), 4.
8. David Johnson, ed., *Regionalism Reconsidered: New Approaches to the Field* (New York: Garland Publishing, 1994), ix. See also Edward L. Ayres, Patricia Nelson Limerick, Stephen Nissembaum, and Peter S. Onuf, *All Over the Map: Rethinking American Region* (Baltimore: Johns Hopkins University Press, 1996).
9. Thomas Bender, "Whole and Parts: The Need for Synthesis in American History," *The Journal of American History* 73, no. 1 (June 1986): 120–36.

10. Webb, 8.

11. According to Wishart, the Great Plains have been considered a distinct region ever since the explorers Zebulon Pike (1806) and Stephen Long (1820) traveled through the region and gave it the designation "The Great American Desert." David Wishart, *The Encyclopedia of the Great Plains* (Lincoln: University of Nebraska Press, 2004), xiii.

12. Wishart, xiii–xvi.

13. Elliot West, *The Way West: Essays on the Central Plains* (Albuquerque: University of New Mexico Press, 1995), 11.

## Sacagawea

1. Donna J. Kessler, *The Making of Sacagawea: A Euro-American Legend* (Tuscaloosa: University of Alabama Press, 1996); Donna Barbie, "Sacagawea: The Making of a Myth," in *Sifters: Native American Women's Lives*, ed. Theda Perdue (Oxford: Oxford University Press, 2001), 60–76.

2. Virginia Scharff, *Twenty Thousand Roads: Women, Movement, and the West* (Berkeley: University of California Press, 2003).

## Introduction to the Northern Plains

1. Kathleen Norris, *Dakota: A Spiritual Geography* (New York: Ticknor and Fields, 1993), 36.

2. David Wishart, *The Encyclopedia of the Great Plains* (Lincoln: University of Nebraska Press, 2004), xiii–xviii.

3. Norris, 156.

4. Alice B. Kehoe, "The Function of Ceremonial Sexual Intercourse Among the Northern Plains Indians," *Plains Anthropologists* 15 (1970): 99–104.

5. Olava Kornelia Holland Boesch, transcribed interview by Elaine Lindgren, October 18, 1983, Carrington, ND. Institute for Regional Studies, H. Elaine Lindgren Papers, MS 292, Box 3, Folder S4, Fargo, ND.

6. Georgina Binnie-Clark, *Wheat & Women* (Toronto: University of Toronto Press, 1979). First published in 1914.

7. H. Elaine Lindgren, *Land in Her Own Name: Women as Homesteaders in North Dakota* (Fargo: North Dakota Institute for Regional Studies, 1991; Norman: University of Oklahoma Press, 1996).

## Chapter 1

1. Because American Indians did not leave behind written records, utilizing oral history and archaeological evidence helps piece together an understanding of gender roles and cultural norms in this early precontact period.

2. Angela Cavender Wilson, "Grandmother to Granddaughter," in *Natives and Aca-*

*demics: Researching and Writing About American Indians*, ed. Devon A. Mihesuah, (Lincoln: University of Nebraska Press, 1998), 35.

3. Colin Calloway, *One Vast Winter Count: The Native American West Before Lewis and Clark* (Lincoln: University of Nebraska Press, 2003), 30.

4. The best early collection of anthropological research includes John Wesley Powell's researchers who, in the late nineteenth and early twentieth centuries, traveled throughout Indian reservations collecting information for publication in the Annual Reports to the Smithsonian Institution as part of the Bureau of American Ethnology. The purpose was to study Native American languages and cultures. For a complete listing of the tables of contents for all annual reports, see "Publications of the Bureau of American Ethnology," Native American Nations, www.nanations.com/bureau_ethnology.htm.

5. Peggy Sanday, quoted in Marla N. Powers, *Oglala Women: Myth, Ritual, and Reality* (Chicago: University of Chicago Press, 1986), 5.

6. George A. Dorsey, *Traditions of the Arikara* (Washington, DC: The Carnegie Institution of Washington, 1904), as found on www.trailtribes.org/kniferiver/whos-who.htm.

7. Preston Holder, quoted in Katherine M. Weist, "Plains Indian Women: An Assessment," in *Anthropology on the Great Plains*, ed. W. Raymond Wood and Margot Liberty (Lincoln: University of Nebraska Press, 1980), 260.

8. Calloway, 30.

9. Ibid.

10. "Order of Life and Death," in *Mythology of the Blackfoot Indians*, comp. and trans. Clark Wissler and D. C. Duvall (Lincoln: University of Nebraska Press, 1995), 19.

11. For an explanation of each of these ceremonies, see Black Elk, *The Sacred Pipe: Black Elk's Account of the Seven Rites of the Oglala Sioux*, ed. Joseph Epes Brown (Norman: University of Oklahoma Press, 1953; repr., New York: Penguin, 1971).

12. For a discussion on the more modern ramifications of White Buffalo Cow Woman, see Robert B. Pickering, *Seeing the White Buffalo* (Boulder, CO: Johnson Books, 1997).

13. Frank Bird Linderman, *Blackfeet Indians*, illus. Winold Reiss (New York: Gramercy Books, 1995); *American: The Life Story of a Great Indian, Plenty-coups, Chief of the Crows*, illus. H. M. Stoops (New York: The John Day Company, 1930); *Pretty-Shield: Medicine Woman of the Crow* (Lincoln: Bison Books, 2003); and *Indian Old-man Stories: More Sparks from a War Eagles Lodge-Fire*, illus. Charles M. Russell (New York: C. Scribner's Sons, 1920). See also Jesse Green, ed. and annot., *Cushing at Zuñi: The Correspondence and Journals of Frank Hamilton Cushing, 1879–1884* (Albuquerque: University of New Mexico Press, 1990). See the following by Frank Hamilton Cushing: *My Adventures in Zuñi*, with an introduction by Oakah L. Johns, Jr. (Palo Alto, CA: American West Publishing Company, 1970); *The Mythic World of the Zuñi*, ed. and illus. Barton Wright (Albuquerque: University of New Mexico Press, 1988); "Origin Myth from Oraibi," *American Journal of Folk-Lore* 36, no. 140 (April–June 1923): 163–70; and, *Zuñi Folk Tales*, foreword

by John Wesley Powell and introduction by Mary Austin (Tucson: University of Arizona Press, 1931). See also the following by George Bird Grinnell: *Blackfoot Lodge Tales: The Story of a Prairie People* (Williamstown, MA: Corner House Publishers, 1972); *By Cheyenne Campfires* (New Haven, CT: Yale University Press, 1926); *The Cheyenne Indians: Their History and Ways of Life*, 2 vols. (New Haven, CT: Yale University Press, 1924); *The Fighting Cheyennes* (Norman: University of Oklahoma Press, 1915); *Pawnee, Blackfoot, and Cheyenne: History and Folklore of the Plains*, from the writings of George Bird Grinnell, selected and with an introduction by Dee Brown (New York: C. Scribner's Sons, 1961); and *The Story of the Indian* (New York: D. Appleton, 1896).

14. Before the common era, or BCE, is the standard designation. Most researchers understand that using BC (before Christ) is an ethnocentric designation not recognized by all cultures.

15. Ron L. Morton and Carl Gawboy, *Talking Rocks: Geology and 10,000 Years of Native American Tradition in the Lake Superior Region* (St. Paul: University of Minnesota Press, 1999), 18, 23, 32, 45, and 86; and Alan J. Osborn, "Paleo-Indians," in *Encyclopedia of the Great Plains Indians*, ed. David J. Wishart (Lincoln: University of Nebraska Press, 2007), 104–7.

16. For more information, see Morton and Gawboy, *Talking Rocks.*

17. Some of those archaeologists include William Duncan Strong, "From History to Prehistory in the Northern Great Plains," in *Essays in Historical Anthropology of North America*, Smithsonian Miscellaneous Publications, vol. 100 (Washington, DC: Smithsonian Institution, 1940): 291–351; Waldo Wedel, "Cultural Consequences in the Central Great Plains," in ibid.; and William Mulloy, "The Northern Plains," in *Archaeology of the Eastern United States*, ed. James B. Griffin (Chicago: University of Chicago Press, 1952): 124–38, as found in Robert H. Lowie, *Indians of the Plains* (Lincoln: Bison Books, 1982), 184.

18. Calloway, 31–32. See also Barry Pritzer, *A Native American Encyclopedia: History, Culture, and Peoples* (Oxford: Oxford University Press, 2000).

19. George C. Frison, "Archaic Period Site," in Wishart, 24.

20. Warren R. DeBoer, "Of Dice and Women: Gambling and Exchange in Native North America," *Journal of Archeological Methods and Theory* 8, no. 3 (September 2001), 215–17.

21. DeBoer, 245.

22. Frison, 24.

23. Edwin Thompson Denig, *Five Indian Tribes of the Upper Missouri: Sioux, Arikaras, Assiniboines, Crees, and Crows*, ed. and introduction by John C. Ewers (Norman: University of Oklahoma Press, 1961), 50–54.

24. Regarding the kinship organization of early northern plains tribes, debate continues over the Blackfeet and the Gros Ventre, who seemed to choose their own tribal subdivisions. There is also some confusion over the Assiniboine and Dakota, as the earliest mentions of clans seemed to represent woodland clans. Lowie, *Indians of the Plains*, 89–97. For more on matrilineal and patrilineal systems, see Gibson, *The American Indian.*

25. Black Elk, 116–18.

26. Ibid.

27. Loretta Fowler, *The Columbia Guide to American Indians of the Great Plains* (New York: Columbia University Press, 2003), 14.

28. See Calloway; Fowler; and Wishart.

29. Alice B. Kehoe, "The Shackles of Tradition," in *The Hidden Half: Studies of Plains Indian Women*, ed. Patricia Albers and Beatrice Medicine (Lanham, MD: University Press of America, 1983), 69.

30. Denig, 10–13.

31. Quoted in Marla N. Powers, *Oglala Women: Myth, Ritual, and Reality* (Chicago: University of Chicago Press, 1986), 23.

32. Fowler, 6–7.

33. Ibid., 35.

34. Jeffery R. Hanson, "Introduction," in *Waheenee: An Indian Girl's Story Told by Herself to Gilbert L. Wilson, Ph.D.*, by Gilbert L. Wilson (Lincoln: University of Nebraska Press, 1981), vi.

35. Fowler, 35.

36. Janet D. Spector, "Male/Female Task Differentiation Among the Hidatsa: Toward the Development of an Archeological Approach to the Study of Gender," in Albers and Medicine, 82.

37. Michael Lansing, "Plains Indian Women and Interracial Marriage in the Upper Missouri Trade, 1804–1868," *The Western Historical Quarterly* 31, no. 4 (Winter 2000), 416.

38. F. V. Hayden, quoted in Katherine M. Weist, "Beasts of Burden and Menial Slaves: Nineteenth Century Observations of Northern Plains Indian Women," in Albers and Medicine, 42.

39. Lansing, 414.

40. Frank B. Linderman, *Pretty-Shield: Medicine Woman of the Crows* (Lincoln: University of Nebraska Press, 1974), 53–65. *Pretty-Shield* is one of the few books that shares information about childhood on the northern plains.

41. Linderman, 50.

42. Gilbert, L. Wilson, *Waheenee: An Indian Girl's Story Told by Herself to Gilbert L. Wilson, Ph.D.* (Lincoln: University of Nebraska Press, 1981), 60.

43. Ella Deloria's *Waterlily* provides a woman's perspective on child rearing. See also Powers, *Oglala Women*.

44. Weist, "Plains Indian Women," 257–58.

45. Ibid.

46. Ibid.

47. Ibid.

48. Weist, "Beasts of Burden," 44.

49. Lowie, *Indians of the Plains*, 78–83.

50. Wilson, 126.

51. See Lowie, *The Crow*, 44–61; and Lowie, *Indians of the Plains*, 78–83.

52. Raymond J. DeMallie, "Male and Female in Traditional Lakota Culture," in Albers

and Medicine, 42; Beatrice Medicine, "'Warrior Women': Sex Role Alternatives for Plains Indian Women," in Albers and Medicine, 267–77; Robert Anderson, "The Northern Cheyenne War Mothers," *Anthropological Quarterly* 29, no. 3 (July 1956): 82–90; and Ramona Ford, "Native American Women: Changing Statuses, Changing Interpretations," in *Writing the Range: Race, Class, and Culture in the Women's West*, ed. Elizabeth Jameson and Susan Armitage (Norman: University of Oklahoma Press, 1997).

53. Kehoe, "The Shackles of Tradition," 69.

54. Medicine, 268.

55. *Pretty-Shield*, 203.

56. Weist, "Plains Indian Women," 259.

57. Ibid., 258–59.

58. DeBoer, 227.

59. Devon A. Mihesuah, "Commonality of Difference: American Indian Women and History," *American Indian Quarterly* 20, no. 1, Special Issue: Writing About American Indians (Winter 1996): 20.

60. The final major battle between the Sioux and Ojibwa purportedly occurred at Strawberry Island at today's Lac du Flambeau Band of Lake Superior Ojibwa Indians Reservation in northern Wisconsin in 1745. Doug Etten, "Local Descendant Stakes Claim to Strawberry Island," *Lakeland Times*, June 16, 2008, www.lakeland-times.com. See also Elizabeth M. Tornes, ed., *Memories of Lac du Flambeau Elders* (Madison: University of Wisconsin Press, 2004).

61. See Sylvia Van Kirk, *Many Tender Ties: Women in the Fur-Trade Society, 1670–1870* (Norman: University of Oklahoma, 1980). The English Hudson Bay Company (HBC) arrived in Hudson Bay hoping to expand its trade network westward in the 1670s. The company challenged French dominance in the fur trade but had little success. While the HBC outlasted the French Empire in the north, its interaction with inhabitants and management style differed significantly from the French. The English did not adapt to Indian ways, move among tribes in the West establishing trading posts, nor did they intermarry into tribal communities. Therefore, the lasting impact of the English of the Hudson Bay Company on Native Americans remained virtually nonexistent and receives little attention in this chapter.

62. Perhaps the best source on the early French encounters remains the Jesuit Relations, a series of more than seventy volumes written by early French Jesuits who lived and worked among the Native Americans throughout the St. Lawrence and deep into the interior. For an online version, see www.puffin.creighton.edu/Jesuit/relations/.

63. Calloway, 229.

64. W. J. Eccles, *Essays on New France* (New York: Oxford University Press, 1987), 38–49. For more information on the shunning of Native women as potential mates, see Van Kirk, 35–37, 92–94, 114–16, 145–47, and 153–56.

65. See Sandra K. Mathews, *American Indians in the Early West* (Santa Barbara, CA: ABC-CLIO, 2008), 193–230; and Lansing, 417–19.

66. Calloway, 241–43.

67. Calloway, 243; and William J. Eccles, *The French in North America, 1500–1783* (Markham, ON: Fitzhenry and Whiteside Publishers, 1998), 93–99. See also Susan Sleeper-Smith, *Indian Women and French Men: Rethinking Cultural Encounter in the Western Great Lakes* (Amherst: University of Massachusetts Press, 2001); and Katherine E. Lawn and Claudio R. Salvucci, eds., *Women in New France: Extracts from the Jesuit Relations* (Bristol, PA: Evolution Publishing and Manufacturing, 2003). See the following by William J. Eccles: *The Canadian Frontier, 1534–1760* (Albuquerque: University of New Mexico Press, 1974); *Essays on New France* (Toronto: Oxford University Press, 1987); and *France in America* (New York: Harper and Row, 1972). See also the following by Allan Greer: *The People of New France* (Toronto: University of Toronto Press, 1997); *The Jesuit Relations: Natives and Missionaries in Seventeenth-Century North America* (Boston: Bedford/St. Martin's, 2000).

68. Sara Sue Kidwell, "Indian Women as Cultural Mediators," *Ethnohistory* 39, no. 2 (Spring 1992): 97. See also Alice B. Kehoe, "The Functioning of Ceremonial Sexual Intercourse Among the Northern Plains Indians," *Plains Anthropologists* 15 (1970): 99–103.

69. Lansing, 414.

70. Lansing, 420.

71. Mihesuah, 20.

72. Van Kirk, 9–52, 170–71.

73. Pekka Hämäläinen, "The Rise and Fall of Plains Indian Horse Culture," *The Journal of American History* 90, no. 3 (December 2003): 85.

74. Calloway, 272–73.

75. Alen M. Llein, "The Political-Economy of Gender: The 19th Century Plains Indian Case Study," in Albers and Medicine, 155–59.

76. Ibid., 153.

77. Weist, "Plains Indian Women," 264.

78. Ibid.

79. Linderman, 12–20.

80. Weist, "Beasts of Burden and Menial Slaves," 35.

81. See Harold P. Howard, *Sacagawea* (Norman: University of Oklahoma Press, 1979). For information on captive taking, see James F. Brooks, *Captives and Cousins: Slavery, Kinship, and Community in the Southwest Borderlands* (Chapel Hill: University of North Carolina Press, 2002); and Juliana Barr, "From Captive to Slave: Commodifying Indian Women on the Borderlands," *Journal of American History* 92, no. 1 (June 2005): 19–46.

82. Patricia Albers, "Introduction: New Perspectives on Plains Indian Women," in Albers and Medicine, 3.

83. Devon A. Mihesuah, "Commonality of Difference," in *Natives and Academics: Researching and Writing About American Indians*, ed. Devon A. Mihesuah (Lincoln: University of Nebraska Press, 1998), 45.

84. Anthony C. Wallace, *Jefferson and the Indians: The Tragic Fate of the First Americans* (Cambridge: Harvard University Press, 1999), 18.

85. For more information, see Gary E. Moulton, *The Journals of the Lewis & Clark Expedition*, vols. 1–13 (Lincoln: University of Nebraska Press, 1994).

86. Standing Bear, quoted in Powers, 18.

## Chapter 2

1. "Skull Bundle Myth Related by Mrs. White Duck," in Alfred W. Bowers, *Mandan Social and Ceremonial Organization* (Chicago: University of Chicago Press, 1950; repr., Moscow: University of Idaho Press, 1991), 196–97.

2. Bowers, *Mandan Social and Ceremonial Organization*, 1; Alfred W. Bowers, *Hidatsa Social and Ceremonial Organization* (Washington, DC: US Government Printing Office, 1963; repr., Lincoln: University of Nebraska Press, 1992), xxxix, xl–xlii.

3. US Bureau of the Census, "Census Schedules for the Fort Berthold Indian Reservation," 1891, Archives Series 31113, State Historical Society of North Dakota, Bismarck, ND. For Rattles Her Medicine's life story, written from the perspective of the Christian missionary at Fort Berthold, see Charles Hall, "Hopadi-Tsidiash, Mrs. Emma Whiteduck," n.d., MS 10286.00625, Box 6, Harold W. Case Collection (hereafter cited as Case Collection), State Historical Society of North Dakota, Bismarck, ND. Bowers, *Mandan Social and Ceremonial Organization*, 4–6, notes Mrs. White Duck's marriage with a Mandan as the basis of some of her knowledge about Mandan traditions.

4. See Virginia Bergman Peters, *Women of the Earth Lodges: Tribal Life on the Plains* (Norman: University of Oklahoma Press, 1995).

5. Ella Cara Deloria, *Waterlily* (Lincoln: University of Nebraska Press, 1988).

6. Rev. and Mrs. Harold W. Case, eds., *100 Years at Ft. Berthold: The History of Fort Berthold Indian Mission, 1876–1976* (Bismarck, ND: Bismarck Tribune, 1977), 3–7.

7. Charles Hall, "Getting a Living," 1932, RG 2497.AM S2F13, Box 22, Santee Normal Training School Collection (hereafter cited as SNTSC), Nebraska State Historical Society, Lincoln, NE.

8. Ibid.

9. Emma Hall, "In the Shadows," *The Word Carrier*, June 1881, Santee Normal Training School, 1873–1937, Nebraska State Historical Society, Lincoln, NE.

10. Bowers, *Mandan Social and Ceremonial Organization*, 69, 82, 84.

11. Bowers, *Hidatsa Social and Ceremonial Organization*, 451–55; and Bowers, *Mandan Social and Ceremonial Organization*, 315–23. See also Peters, 40–41.

12. Bowers, *Hidatsa Social and Ceremonial Organization*, 200; Peters, 56.

13. Bowers, xlii.

14. Bowers, *Mandan Social and Ceremonial Organization*, 65, 74, 173–74.

15. C. L. Hall, "Indian Spring," *The World Carrier*, May 1883.

16. Ibid.

17. Bowers, *Hidatsa Social and Ceremonial Organization*, 201–4; Peters, 57–58.

18. Bowers, *Hidatsa Social and Ceremonial Organization*, 204–7; Peters, 58–59; Bowers, *Mandan Social and Ceremonial Organization*, 183–85. For a description of the White Buffalo Cow Society's ceremonies, see Carolyn Gilman and Mary Jane Schneider, *The Way to Independence: Memories of a Hidatsa Indian Family, 1840–1920* (St. Paul: Minnesota Historical Society Press, 1987), 82–83.

19. Peters, 70; and Bowers, *Mandan Social and Ceremonial Organization*, 60–62.

20. See Bowers, *Mandan Social and Ceremonial Organization*, 74–80; Bowers, *Hidatsa Social and Ceremonial Organization*, 138–42; and Peters, 83.

21. Charles Hall, "Marriage," 1932–36, *The Story of Fort Berthold*, MS 10286.00707, Box 7, Case Collection, 48.

22. Ibid.

23. Mary Jane Schneider, *The Hidatsa*, Indians of North America, ed. Frank W. Porter III (New York: Chelsea House Publishers, 1989), 30; and Adrian R. Dunn, "A History of Old Fort Berthold," *North Dakota History* 30, no. 4 (October 1963); repr., Bismarck: State Historical Society of North Dakota, 1964.

24. James P. Ronda, *Lewis and Clark Among the Indians* (Lincoln: University of Nebraska Press, 1984, 2002), 3–4; Schneider, 34–35.

25. Paul VanDevelder, *Coyote Warrior: One Man, Three Tribes, and the Trial That Forged a Nation* (New York: Little, Brown and Company, 2004), 17, 59, 80; and Ronda, 77–78.

26. Ronda, 131.

27. Ibid., 131–32.

28. Annie Heloise Abel, introduction to *Chardon's Journal at Fort Clark, 1834–1839: Descriptive of Life on the Upper Missouri; of a Fur Trader's Experiences Among the Mandans, Gros Ventres, and Their Neighbors; of the Ravages of the Small-Pox Epidemic of 1837*, by Francis T. Chardon (Iowa City: Athens Press, 1932), xv, xvii, xix.

29. Ray H. Mattison, introduction to "Henry A. Boller: Missouri River Fur Trader," *North Dakota History* 33, nos. 3–4 (Spring and Summer 1966); repr., Bismarck: State Historical Society of North Dakota, 1966, 4–6. Fort Atkinson would eventually acquire the name Fort Berthold after being taken over by the American Fur Company (see Dunn, 33).

30. Abel, xxii. See also Katherine M. Weist, "Beasts of Burden and Menial Slaves: Nineteenth Century Observations of Northern Plains Indian Women," in *The Hidden Half: Studies of Plains Indian Women*, ed. Patricia Albers and Beatrice Medicine (Lanham: University Press of America, 1983), 31.

31. Sylvia Van Kirk, *Many Tender Ties: Women in Fur-Trade Society, 1670–1870* (Norman: University of Oklahoma Press, 1980), 6, 75.

32. Ibid., 78–79.

33. Jennifer S. H. Brown, *Strangers in Blood: Fur Trade Company Families in Indian Country* (Vancouver: University of British Columbia Press, 1980; repr., Norman: University of Oklahoma Press, 1996), 67; and Van Kirk, 24, 46.

34. Van Kirk, 4, 53, 54, 56–58, 61, 65.

35. Ibid., 18.

36. Ibid., 23, 25.

37. Ibid., 83.
38. Ibid., 6–7.
39. Ibid., 79–80, 83, 87.
40. Mattison, 6.
41. Henry A. Boller, *Among the Indians: Four Years on the Upper Missouri, 1858–1862,* ed. Milo Milton Quaife (Lincoln: University of Nebraska Press, 1972), 182–83; 199–200.
42. Ibid., 123–24.
43. Ibid.
44. Ibid., 125.
45. Ibid., 79–80.
46. Ibid., 81–85.
47. Ibid.
48. Ibid., 86–87.
49. Ibid., 152.
50. Ibid., 219, 222.
51. Ibid., 224.
52. Ibid., 226–27.
53. For European observations on polygyny, see Weist, 34; and Van Kirk, 24.
54. Boller, 201.
55. Ibid. For different scholarly viewpoints regarding whether the incidence of polygyny in a fur trade context entailed a loss or gain in status for Plains Indian women, see Alan M. Klein, "The Political-Economy of Gender: A 19th Century Plains Indian Case Study," in Albers and Medicine, 144, 154–57; and Martha Harroun Foster, "Of Baggage and Bondage: Gender and Status Among Hidatsa and Crow Women," *American Indian Culture and Research Journal* 17, no. 2 (1993), 129–31, 134.
56. Boller, 223. Van Kirk, 21, examines Europeans who constantly evaluated the "looks" of Native women.
57. Boller, 304.
58. Ibid., 285.
59. Ibid., 143.
60. Mattison, 71.
61. Ibid., 49.
62. Ibid.
63. Ibid.
64. For a similar observation of traders, see Michael Lansing, "Plains Indian Women and Interracial Marriage in the Upper Missouri Trade, 1804–1868," *Western Historical Quarterly* 31 (Winter 2000), 425. See also Van Kirk, 83.
65. Boller, 47.
66. Ibid., 89.
67. Ibid., 78.
68. Ibid., 49.
69. Chardon, 29, 112, 140, 149, 153, 178.

70. See Abel, xxi–xxii, for an account of Chardon's marriages.

71. See Chardon, 12, 37, 71, 98, 104, 165. Lansing, 413, discusses the "whipping" Chardon received from his Lakota wife and its implications.

72. Abel, xxi.

73. Chardon, 133.

74. Raymond J. DeMallie, "Afterword," in *Waterlily* by Ella Cara Deloria (Lincoln: University of Nebraska Press, 1988); and John Prater, "Ella Deloria: Varied Intercourse; Ella Deloria's Life and Work," *Wicazo Sa Review* 11, no. 2 (Autumn 1995), 43.

75. DeMallie, 234.

76. Deloria, 3, 5.

77. Ibid., 20.

78. Ibid., 59.

79. Ibid., 35.

80. Ibid., 61, 63, 66–67, 82–83, 86. See also Raymond J. DeMallie, "Male and Female in Traditional Lakota Culture," in Albers and Medicine, 238–40, 243.

81. Deloria, 136.

82. Ibid., 141, 153. See DeMallie, "Male and Female in Traditional Lakota Culture," 250; and Deloria, 13, 141, 220.

83. Deloria, 167.

84. Ibid., 169–70, 179.

85. Boller, 245–46.

## Chapter 3

1. Walker D. Wyman, ed., *Frontier Woman: The Life of a Woman Homesteader on the Dakota Frontier*, as retold from the original notes and letters of Grace Fairchild (River Falls: University of Wisconsin-River Falls Press, 1972), 7–8 and 13. Although Fairchild identifies the poetry as "by Benet" (perhaps Stephen Vincent Benet), the poem's source cannot be confirmed.

2. J. Sanford Rikoon, ed., *Rachel Calof's Story: Jewish Homesteader on the Northern Plains* (Bloomington and Indianapolis: Indiana University Press, 1995), 23.

3. Walter Prescott Webb, *The Great Plains* (New York: Grosset and Dunlap, 1931), 505–6; also quoted in Sandra L. Myres, *Westering Women and the Frontier Experience, 1800–1915* (Albuquerque: University of New Mexico Press, 1999), 286n36. For other discussions of women's so-called reluctance or eagerness to settle the plains, see also Glenda Riley, *The Female Frontier: A Comparative View of Women on the Prairie and the Plains* (Lawrence: University Press of Kansas, 1988).

4. So significant was European immigration to the settlement of North Dakota, for example, that Frederick Luebke has described the population of that state in 1890 as 42.7 percent "foreign-born." Frederick Luebke, ed., *European Immigrants in the American West: Community Histories* (Albuquerque: University of New Mexico Press, 1998), ix. For discussions of various ethnicities in northern plains

settlements, see essays in Luebke by Robert C. Ostergren and Royden K. Loewen. See also Frederick Luebke, *Ethnicity on the Great Plains* (Lincoln: University of Nebraska Press, 1980).

5. See Sandoz's famous work *Old Jules* (Boston: Little Brown and Co., 1935) and *Love Song to the Plains* (New York: Harper and Bros., 1961); see Cather's *Oh Pioneers!* (Boston and New York: Houghton Mifflin, 1913), *Song of the Lark* (Boston and New York: Houghton Mifflin, 1915), and *My Ántonia* (Boston and New York: Houghton Mifflin, 1918).

6. Randi Warne, introduction to *Purple Springs* by Nellie L. McClung (Toronto, ON: University of Toronto Press, 1992), x.

7. Nellie McClung, *Sowing Seeds in Danny* (New York: Grosset and Dunlap, 1908); *The Second Chance* (Toronto: William Briggs, 1910); and *Purple Springs* (Toronto: Thomas Allen, 1921).

8. Laura Ingalls Wilder, *By the Shores of Silver Lake* (New York: HarperCollins, 1939); *The Long Winter* (New York: HarperCollins, 1940); *Little Town on the Prairie* (New York: HarperCollins, 1941); *These Happy Golden Years* (New York: HarperCollins, 1943); and *The First Four Years* (New York: HarperCollins, 1971). Wilder's surviving child and literary collaborator, Rose Wilder Lane, was born on the South Dakota homestead in 1886.

9. For a study on the pervasive connection in women's prescriptive literature between domestic ideology and imperialism, see Mary P. Ryan, *Empire of the Mother: American Writing About Domesticity, 1830–1860* (New York: Institute for Research in History and Hawthorn Press, 1982).

10. Classic sources on the cult of true womanhood and domestic ideology include Barbara Welter, "The Cult of True Womanhood, 1820–1860," *American Quarterly* 18 (Summer 1966): 151–74; Gerda Lerner, "The Lady and the Mill Girl: Changes in the Status of Women in the Age of Jackson, 1800–1840," *Midcontinent American Studies Journal* 10 (Spring 1969): 5–14; Nancy F. Cott, *The Bonds of Womanhood: "Women's Sphere" in New England, 1780–1835* (New Haven, CT: Yale University Press, 1977); Kathryn Kish Sklar, *Catherine Beecher: A Study in American Domesticity* (New Haven, CT: Yale University Press, 1973); Carroll Smith-Rosenberg, "The Female World of Love and Ritual: Relations Between Women in Nineteenth-Century America," in *Disorderly Conduct: Visions of Gender in Victorian America* (New York: Alfred A. Knopf, 1985), 53–76. For more recent scholarship that focuses on the American West, see Amy Kaplan, "Manifest Domesticity," *American Literature* (September 1998): 581–606; Adrienne Caughfield, *True Women and Westward Expansion* (College Station: Texas A&M University Press, 2005); Brenda K. Jackson, *Domesticating the West: The Re-Creation of the 19th Century American Middle Class* (Lincoln: University of Nebraska Press, 2005).

11. Kaplan, 583.

12. Robert Griswold, "Anglo Women and Domestic Ideology in the American West in the Nineteenth and Early Twentieth Centuries," in *Western Women: Their Land, Their Lives*, ed. Lillian Schlissel, Vicki L. Ruiz, and Janice Monk (Albuquerque:

University of New Mexico Press, 1988), 15 and 18. While most historians have examined rural plains women in the domestication process, Paula M. Nelson has described a town-oriented domestication in "'Do Everything'—Women in Small Prairie Towns, 1870–1920," *Journal of the West* 36 (October 1997): 52–60.

13. Griswold, 18.

14. Kaplan, 581.

15. Andrea G. Radke, "Refining Rural Spaces: Women and Vernacular Gentility in the Great Plains, 1880–1920," *Great Plains Quarterly* 24 (Fall 2004): 227.

16. For more on domestication, see Radke, "Refining Rural Spaces"; Riley, *The Female Frontier*; and Myres, 3. See also Julie Roy Jeffrey, *Frontier Women: "Civilizing" the West? 1840–1880*, rev. ed. (New York: Hill and Wang, 1998).

17. Chad Montrie, "'Men Alone Cannot Settle a Country': Domesticating Nature in the Kansas-Nebraska Grasslands," *Great Plains Quarterly* 25 (Fall 2005): 246.

18. Griswold, 22.

19. Kaplan, 582.

20. Griswold, 22.

21. Susan C. Peterson, "A Widening Horizon: Catholic Sisterhoods on the Northern Plains, 1874–1910," *Great Plains Quarterly* 5 (Spring 1985): 125–32.

22. Kaplan, 582.

23. Suzanne H. Schrems, "Teaching School on the Western Frontier: Acceptable Occupation for Nineteenth Century Women," *Montana: The Magazine of Western History* 37 (Summer 1987): 54.

24. Ibid.

25. Mary Hurlbut Cordier, *Schoolwomen of the Prairies and Plains* (Albuquerque: University of New Mexico Press, 1992). See also Mary Hurlbut Cordier, "Prairie Schoolwomen, Mid-1850s to 1920s in Iowa, Kansas, and Nebraska," *Great Plains Quarterly* 8 (Spring 1988): 107.

26. The Federal Land Ordinance of 1785 designated section 16 of each township to be sold for the maintenance of public schools.

27. Wyman, 31.

28. Ronald Manzer, *Public Schools and Political Ideas: Canadian Educational Policy in Perspective* (Toronto: University of Toronto Press, 1994), 72–74; and E. Brian Titley and Peter J. Miller, *Education in Canada: An Interpretation* (Calgary, AB: Detselig Enterprises Limited, 1982), 14–25. For an examination of race and education, see Paul R. Carr and Darren E. Lund, *Great White North? Exploring Whiteness, Privilege, and Identity in Education* (New York: Sense Publishers, 2007).

29. Schrems, 56.

30. Courtney Ann Vaughn-Roberson, "Having a Purpose in Life: Western Women Teachers in the Twentieth Century," *Great Plains Quarterly* 5 (Spring 1985): 107.

31. See Andrea G. Radke-Moss, *Bright Epoch: Women and Coeducation in the American West* (Lincoln: University of Nebraska Press, 2008).

32. Montrie, 250.

33. Ruth B. Moynihan, Susan Armitage, and Christine Fischer Dichamp, *So Much to*

*Be Done: Women Settlers on the Mining and Ranching Frontier* (Lincoln: University of Nebraska Press, 1989), xvi.

34. H. Elaine Lindgren, *Land in Her Own Name: Women as Homesteaders in North Dakota* (Fargo: North Dakota State University Press, 1991), 51.

35. Mary Kinnear, *A Female Economy: Women's Work in a Prairie Province, 1870–1970* (Montreal and Kingston: McGill-Queen's University Press, 1998), 87, 89–93.

36. Donna M. Lucey, *Photographing Montana, 1894–1928: The Life and Work of Evelyn Cameron* (Missoula, MT: Mountain Press Publishing Co., 2001); Dan Aadland, *Women and Warriors of the Plains: The Pioneer Photography of Julia E. Tuell* (Missoula, MT: Mountain Press Publishing Co., 2000); John M. Duffy, "Dakota Images: Ada B. Caldwell," *South Dakota History* 30 (Summer 200): 248–49; and Joyce Litz, *The Montana Frontier: One Woman's West* (Albuquerque: University of New Mexico Press, 2004).

37. For histories of woman suffrage in the West, including the northern plains, see Susan B. Anthony and Ida Husted Harper, eds., *The History of Woman Suffrage* (Rochester, NY: Susan B. Anthony, 1902); Beverly Beeton, *Women Vote in the West: The Woman Suffrage Movement, 1869–1896* (New York: Garland Publishing, 1986); Beverly Beeton and G. Thomas Edwards, "Susan B. Anthony's Woman Suffrage Crusade in the American West," *Journal of the West* 21 (Summer 1982): 5–15; T. A. Larson, "Dolls, Vassals, and Drudge—Pioneer Women in the West," *Western Historical Quarterly* 3 (Spring 1970): 4–16; T. A. Larson, "Woman Suffrage in Western America," *Utah Historical Quarterly* 38 (Spring 1970): 7–19; Richard White, *"It's Your Misfortune and None of My Own": A New History of the American West* (Norman: University of Oklahoma Press, 1991).

38. Wyoming granted territorial woman suffrage in 1869, state suffrage in 1890; Kansas fought the first state woman suffrage referendum in 1867; full suffrage was finally achieved in 1912; Colorado led a famously unsuccessful referendum in 1877, but full suffrage passed in 1893. For histories of woman suffrage in the West, see Eleanor Flexner, *Century of Struggle: The Woman's Rights Movement in the United States*, rev. ed. (Cambridge and London: Belknap Press of Harvard University Press, 1975); Myres, 3.

39. Merry Helm, "Suffrage Bill," Dakota Datebook, January 23, 2004, State Historical Society of North Dakota and North Dakota Humanities Council, www.prairie-public.org/programs/datebook/bydate/04/0104/012304.jsp.

40. Ibid. Kansas women gained the right to school suffrage in 1861. See Flexner, 179.

41. White, 357–59; Flexner, 188–89.

42. Carrie Chapman Catt and Nettie Rogers Shuler, *Woman Suffrage and Politics* (New York: Charles Scribner's Sons, 1923), 193–94.

43. Flexner, 244. For more on the South Dakota suffrage campaign, see Patricia O'Keefe Easton, "Woman Suffrage in South Dakota: The Final Decade, 1911–1920," *South Dakota History* 13 (Fall 1983): 206–26; Mary Kay Jennings, "Lake County Woman Suffrage Campaign in 1890," *South Dakota History* 5 (Winter 1975): 390–409; Dennis A. Norlin, "The Suffrage Movement and South Dakota

Churches: Radicals and the Status Quo, 1890s," *South Dakota History* 14 (Winter 1984): 308–34; Cecilia M. Wittmayer, "The 1889–1890 Woman Suffrage Campaign: A Need to Organize," *South Dakota History* 11 (Fall 1981): 199–225; and Dorinda Riessen Reed, *The Woman Suffrage Movement in South Dakota*, 2nd ed. (Pierre, SD: Committee on the Status of Women, 1976).

44. Flexner, 229.

45. Ibid.

46. Ibid., 256, 277.

47. The Non-Partisan League was a Great Plains socialist organization founded in 1915 that advocated state ownership of mills, grain elevators, railroads, and banks.

48. Helm, "Suffrage Bill," January 23, 2004. For a specific discussion of the 1919 federal amendment's ratification in North and South Dakota, see Catt and Schuler, 361–62.

49. Catt and Schuler, 304.

50. Ibid., 362–63.

51. Ibid.

52. Warne, "Introduction," in McClung, *Purple Springs*, xx.

53. Chris Dooley, "The Suffrage Movement," "The Political Equality League," and "Nellie McClung," in *Timelinks* (Winnipeg: River East School District and the University of Manitoba, 1997), http://timelinks.merlin.mb.ca/referenc/subject. htm. For more on the Canadian woman suffrage movement, see also Catherine Cleverdon, *The Woman Suffrage Movement in Canada* (Toronto: University of Toronto Press, 1950).

54. Nellie McClung, *In Times Like These* (Toronto: McLeod and Allen, 1915); and *Purple Springs*.

55. Warne, "Introduction," xxiii–xxxi. For McClung's battles with the conservative Roblin government over suffrage, see her autobiography, *The Stream Runs Fast: My Own Story* (Toronto: Thomas Allen, 1945), reprinted in Veronica Strong-Boag and Michelle Lynn Rosa, eds., *Nellie McClung and the Complete Autobiography: A Clearing in the West and The Stream Runs Fast* (Peterborough, ON: Broadview Press, 2003); and Kinnear, *A Female Economy*.

56. Carrie Chapman Catt, "Why the Federal Amendment?" in *Woman Suffrage by Federal Constitutional Amendment*, comp. Carrie Chapman Catt (New York: National Woman Suffrage Publishing Co., 1917), www.blackmask.com/thatway/ books164c/suff.htm#1_0_3. Catt used the examples of the three prairie provinces granting woman suffrage in 1916 (along with a list of other nations and territories) as part of her reasons why the United States should pass a federal amendment: "Keeping Pace with Other Countries Demands It" (Catt, "Objections to the Federal Amendment," *Woman Suffrage by Federal Constitutional Amendment*).

57. The Saskatoon Women's Calendar Collective, "Suffrage: ' . . . not idiots nor imbeciles,'" *Herstory: An Exhibition,* from *Herstory: The Canadian Women's Calendar* (Saskatoon: University of Saskatchewan Libraries, 1995), http://library.usask.ca/

herstory/suffer.html.

58. Dooley, "Nellie McClung," in *Timelinks*, http://timelinks.merlin.mb.ca/referenc/subject.htm.

59. Caughfield, ix.

60. Rex Alan Smith, *Moon of Popping Trees: The Tragedy at Wounded Knee and the End of the Indian Wars* (Lincoln and London: University of Nebraska Press, 1977); and Dee Brown, *Bury My Heart at Wounded Knee* (New York: Bantam Books, 1970).

61. Caughfield, 8.

62. Ibid., 15.

63. Elizabeth B. Custer, *Following the Guidon*, introduction by Shirley A. Leckie (Lincoln and London: University of Nebraska Press, Bison Books Edition, 1994), 87. For another description of Plains Indian life by an officer's wife see Frances C. Carrington, *My Army Life and the Fort Phil Kearney Massacre*, with an introduction by Shannon Smith Calitri (Lincoln: University of Nebraska Press, 2004).

64. Elizabeth B. Custer, *"Boots and Saddles"; or, Life in Dakota with General Custer* (New York and London: Harper and Brothers, 1902), chaps. 22 and 25, http://web.archive.org/web/20050307015632/www.browzerbooks.com/advent/Boots/5.htm.

65. Kaplan, 591.

66. Ibid., 585.

67. South Dakota State Historical Society, "Mary C. Collins, 1846–1920," in *Dakota Profiles*, www.sdhistory.org/rp/dp/dp_collins.htm. See also "Dakota Images: Mary C. Collins," *South Dakota History* 7 (Winter 1976).

68. Susan Cummins Miller, ed., "Elaine Goodale Eastman (1893–1953)," in *A Sweet, Separate Intimacy: Women Writers of the American Frontier, 1800–1922* (Lubbock: Texas Tech University Press, 2007), 303–4. See also Theodore D. Sargent, *The Life of Elaine Goodale Eastman* (Lincoln: University of Nebraska Press, 2005).

69. Ruth Ann Alexander, "Gentle Evangelists: Women in Dakota Episcopal Missions, 1867–1900," *South Dakota History* 24 (Fall/Winter 1994): 174.

70. Margaret D. Jacobs, "Maternal Colonialism: White Women and Indigenous Child Removal in the American West and Australia, 1880–1940," *Western Historical Quarterly* 36 (Winter 2005): 454.

71. Jacobs, 455 and 466.

72. Zitkala-Sˆa (Gertrude Simmons Bonnin), from "Impressions of an Indian Childhood," "The School Days of an Indian Girl," and "An Indian Teacher Among Indians," *Atlantic Monthly* 85 (January, February, and March 1900): 45–47, 186–87, 386, reprinted in Linda K. Kerber and Jane Sherron De Hart, eds., *Women's America: Refocusing the Past*, 6th ed. (New York and Oxford: Oxford University Press, 2004).

73. Susan Cummins Miller, "Gertrude Simmons Bonnin (Zitkala-Sa)," in *A Sweet, Separate Intimacy*, 385.

74. Kerber and De Hart, "Zitkala-Sa," 282. For more on boarding school education, see Robert Trennert, "Educating Indian Girls at Nonreservation Boarding Schools, 1878–1920," *Western Historical Quarterly* 13 (July 1982): 271–90.

75. Lisa E. Emmerich, "Marguerite LaFlesche Diddock: Office of Indian Affairs Field Matron," *Great Plains Quarterly* 13 (Summer 1993): 162–71.
76. Valerie Sherer Mathes, "Susan LaFlesche Picotte, M.D.: Nineteenth-Century Physician and Reformer," *Great Plains Quarterly* 13 (Summer 1993): 172–86.
77. Kaplan, 582.
78. Frank B. Linderman, *Pretty-Shield: Medicine Woman of the Crows* (Lincoln and London: University of Nebraska Press, 1972).
79. Linderman, back cover. See also Aadland, 44.
80. Patricia Albers, "Sioux Women in Transition: A Study of Their Changing Status in Domestic and Capitalist Sectors of Production," in *The Hidden Half: Studies of Plains Indian Women*, ed. Patricia Albers and Beatrice Medicine (Washington, DC: University Press of America, 1983), cited in Sarah Carter, "First Nations Women of Prairie Canada in the Early Reserve Years, the 1870s to the 1920s: A Preliminary Inquiry," in *Women of the First Nations*, ed. Christine Miller and Patricia Chuchryk (Winnipeg: University of Manitoba Press, 1996), 53.
81. Carter, 52–57.
82. Ibid. 56.
83. Sylvia Van Kirk, *"Many Tender Ties": Women in Fur-Trade Society, 1670–1870* (Winnipeg, MB: Watson and Dwyer, 1980).
84. Métis National Council, www.metisnation.ca.
85. Maria Campbell, *Halfbreed* (Lincoln and London: University of Nebraska Press, 1973).
86. Diane P. Payment, "'*La vie en rose*'? Métis Women at Batoche, 1870–1920," in Miller and Chuchryk, 19–37. For more on the tension between marginalization and empowerment, see Carter, 51–75.
87. C. L. Higham, *Noble, Wretched, and Redeemable: Protestant Missionaries to the Indians in Canada and the United States, 1820–1900* (Albuquerque: University of New Mexico Press, 2000).

## Chapter 4

1. For a discussion on national interpretations of their respective wests, see Elizabeth Jameson and Jeremy Mouat, "Telling Differences: The Forty-Ninth Parallel and Historiographies of the West and Nation," *The Pacific Historical Review* 75, no. 2 (May 2006): 183–230; Era Bell Thompson, *American Daughter* (Chicago: University of Chicago Press, 1946); Cheryl Foggo, *Pourin' Down Rain* (Calgary, AB: Detselig Enterprises, 1990).
2. Thompson, 95.
3. The term *performative* describes an action that is deemed to have been performed by saying or writing something.
4. Arthur P. Davis, review of *Black Boy* by Richard Wright, *The Journal of Negro Education* 14, no. 1 (Autumn 1945), 589–90; N. T., review of *Black Boy* by Richard Wright, *Phylon (1940–1956)* 6, no. 2 (1945), 1850–86; Arthur P. Davis, review of

*American Daughter* by Era Bell Thompson, *The Journal of Negro Education* 15, no. 4 (1946), 647–48; Louise H. Elder, review of *American Daughter* by Era Bell Thompson, *Phylon (1940–1956)* 7, no. 3 (1946), 307; and Ralph Ellison, "Stepchild Fantasy," *The Saturday Review of Literature*, 29–23 (June 8, 1946), 25–26.

5. Joanne M. Braxton, *Black Women Writing Autobiography: A Tradition Within a Tradition* (Philadelphia, PA: Temple University Press, 1989), 144–80. Braxton argues that Thompson and other black women autobiographers of the 1940s tell stories of survival and self-sufficiency rather than write works of protest, as did their male counterparts. Braxton identifies *American Daughter* as a work of "isolation and transcendence" and argues that it is the precursor to the work of Maya Angelou, Ruby Lee Goodwin, and other works of social vision.

6. Davis, review of *Black Boy*, 589.

7. Michael Kimmel, *Manhood in America: A Cultural History* (New York: The Free Press, 1996), 230. Wright's 1940 novel *Native Son* and Ralph Ellison's 1952 *The Invisible Man* were other major literary contributors to emerging black masculinity that signaled the "anguished cry for full recognition of their [black] manhood." Kimmel, 241.

8. Ira De A. Reid, review of *American Daughter* by Era Bell Thompson, *Journal of Educational Sociology* 21, no. 6 (February 1948), 382; and Louise H. Elder, review of *American Daughter*, 307.

9. Ellison, "Stepchild Fantasy," 25–26.

10. Thompson, 16.

11. Michael K. Johnson, "'This Strange White World': Race and Place in Era Bell Thompson's *American Daughter*," *Great Plains Quarterly* 24 (Spring 2004): 101.

12. Glenda Riley, "American Daughters: Black Women in the West," *Montana* 38, no. 2 (Spring 1988), 18. The population of North Dakota in 1910 is recorded at 577,056 in US Bureau of the Census, *Thirteenth Census of the United States, 1910* (Washington, DC: US Government Printing Office, 1910).

13. Scholars Kevin L. Cole and Leah Weins investigate the issue of religious displacement in *American Daughter*, fleshing out the themes of geographic, racial, and familial displacement recognized by Braxton. See Cole and Weins, "Religions, Idealism, and African American Autobiography in the Northern Plains: Era Bell Thompson's *American Daughter*," *Great Plains Quarterly* 23, no. 4 (2003): 219–29.

14. Era Bell Thompson, "Bigotry Has No Boundaries, Once U Negro Student—Now Editor, Says," *Grand Forks Herald*, July 17, 1968, p. 18, quoted in Anderson, "Era Bell Thompson," 11.

15. Thompson, *American Daughter*, 137.

16. Ibid., 122.

17. Ibid., 141–42.

18. After the publication of *American Daughter* in 1946, Thompson worked for *Ebony* magazine. She wrote and edited for the magazine until 1964, when she was named international editor of Johnson Publishing Company. Her accomplishments have been recognized by North Dakota, which proudly claims her as a daughter of

the state. She was awarded an honorary doctorate from the University of North Dakota (UND) in 1969, was awarded the Roughrider Award in 1976, and lent her name to the Black Cultural Center at UND in 1979. *American Daughter* was reprinted in 1967 and 1986.

19. Foggo, *Pourin' Down Rain*, 107.

20. Ibid., 105.

21. Ibid., 112.

22. Ibid.

23. Cheryl Foggo, "Delicious Moments," in *Unsettled Pasts: Reconceiving the West Through Women's History*, ed. Sarah Carter, Lesley Erickson, Patricia Roome, and Char Smith (Calgary, AB: University of Calgary Press, 2006), 270.

24. Foggo, *Pourin' Down Rain*, 4.

25. Ibid.

26. Ibid.

27. Ibid., 17–18.

28. Ibid., 6.

29. Ibid., 67.

30. *Encyclopedia of the Great Plains*, 2004, s.v. "Settlement Patterns, Canada," by John Herd Thompson. On Ukrainian women in the northern plains, see Frances Swyripa, *Wedded to the Cause: Ukrainian-Canadian Women and Ethnic Identity, 1891–1991* (Toronto: University of Toronto Press, 1993).

31. Jenel Virden, *Good-bye Piccadilly: British War Brides in America* (Urbana: University of Illinois Press, 1996), 30.

32. Ibid., 11–12.

33. Elfrieda Berthiaume Shukert and Barbara Smith Scibetta, *War Brides of World War II* (Novato, CA: Presidio, 1988), 8.

34. Barbara Ladouceur and Phyllis Spence, *Blackouts to Bright Lights: Canadian War Bride Stories* (Vancouver: Ronsdale Press, 1995), xi. Scholarship on war brides who immigrated to Canada includes, among others, Joyce Hibbert, *The War Brides* (Toronto: PMA Books, 1978); Linda Granfield, *Brass Buttons and Silver Horseshoes: Stories from Canada's British War Brides* (Toronto: McClelland and Stewart, 2002); Ben Wicks, *Promise You'll Take Care of My Daughter: The Remarkable War Brides of World War II* (Toronto: Stoddart, 1992); Melynda Jarratt, *War Brides: The Stories of the Women Who Left Everything Behind to Follow the Men They Loved* (Stroud, UK: Tempus Publishing Group, 2007); Cynthia J Faryon, *A War Bride's Story: Risking It All for Love After World War II* (Canmore, AB: Altitude, 2004); Helen Hall Shewchuck, *If Kisses Were Roses: A 50th Anniversary Tribute to War Brides; Canada Remembers* (Naughton, ON: H.H. Shewchuck, 1996); Cheryl A Butler, "'Janey Canuck': Experiences of World War II British War Brides Who Emigrated to Canada" (master's thesis, University of Toronto, 1995); Beverley Tosh and Laura Brandon, *War Brides: One-Way Passage* (Moose Jaw, SK: Moose Jaw Museum and Art Gallery, 2008); and "The War Brides: From Romance to Reality," video (Ottawa: Kiss the Bride Productions, 2001). Not until the

Canada Act of 1982 did Canada sever its remaining dependence on Great Britain.

35. "War Brides of WWII," *Immigration Historical Notes* (Ottawa: Citizenship and Immigration Canada, 2003), n.p.

36. Suzanne Boyer, "Exhibition Features 80 Portraits of War Brides," *The Moose Jaw Times Herald*, September 6, 2008.

37. "16,000 Canadians Will Return with Brides," *Syracuse* (New York) *Herald Journal*, December 15, 1943.

38. "War Brides of WWII," n.p; "Canadian War Brides—60 Years," Veteran Affairs Canada, accessed October, 2008, www.vac-acc.gc.ca/remembers/sub. cfm?source=history/secondwar/warbrides.

39. The Canadian Department of National Defense assumed full control of war bride transportation to Canada in 1944. See "Transportation Statistics," *Canadian War Brides, The Authoritative Source of Information on the Canadian War Brides of WWII*, accessed October 2008, www.canadianwarbrides.com/cwbstats1.asp.

40. Joan Reichardt, "War Bride Recalls Trip to Canada," *The American War Bride Experience, GI Brides of World War II*, accessed October 2008, www.geocities.com/us_warbrides/bride_stories/canwb.html. See also accounts mentioning food on the ship in Ladouceur and Spence, 16, 22, 33, 66, 93, 109, 129–30, 158–59, 182, 221, 277, 286.

41. Ladouceur and Spence, xi. The cost to the Canadian government of transporting brides averaged $140.29 per bride. This cost included transportation in the United Kingdom, transportation by ship to Canada, meals during transport, train fares, hostel accommodations, and hospitalization en route. See "Transportation Statistics," *Canadian War Brides*.

42. Reichardt, "War Bride Recalls Trip to Canada."

43. Barbara Walsh, "It Was a Bit of a Shock When I Came to Canada," in Ladouceur and Spence, 159.

44. Joyce Anderson, quoted in Granfield, 12.

45. "Canadian War Brides—60 Years," Veteran Affairs Canada.

46. Nancy Pittet, "It's All an Adventure When You Think about It," in Ladouceur and Spence, 214.

47. Marguerite Feist, quoted in Granfield, 36.

48. Paul Manning, "English People Find em Wild," *Abilene* (Texas) *Reporter News*, October 24, 1941.

49. Connie Rust, "Mother Was Horrified, She Really Was," in Ladouceur and Spence, 16.

50. Ibid., 17.

51. Hilda Bradshaw, quoted in Granfield, 23.

52. Eileen Ironside, quoted in Granfield, 61.

53. Pittet, 215.

54. Barbara Friedman, *From the Battlefront to the Bridal Suite: Media Coverage of British War Brides, 1942–1946* (Columbia: University of Missouri Press, 2007), 68.

55. Ibid., 26.

56. Ibid., 28.

57. Ibid., 81.

58. Doreen Richard, interview by Sheena Kohl, June 26, 2002, Montana War Brides Oral History Project, Montana Historical Society Archives, Helena.

59. Ibid.

60. Ibid.

61. Ibid.

62. Elvia Stockton, interview by Sheena Kohl, July 17, 2001, Montana War Brides Oral History Project, Montana Historical Society Archives, Helena.

63. Ibid.

64. Ibid.

65. Scholarship on Mary Brave Bird includes Dana Poole, "The Role of Women in the Native American Civil Rights Movement" (master's thesis, Central Connecticut State University, 1998); Amy Washburn, "Where Have All the Women's Political Autobiographies Gone?: A Feminist Exploration of Women's Role(s) in the Anti-Racist and Anti-Capitalist Movement Era of the United States in Mary Brave Bird's *Lakota Woman*; Assata Shakur's *Assata: An Autobiography*; and Susan Stern's *With the Weathermen*" (master's thesis, State University of New York at New Paltz, 2005); and Kathleen U. Haven, "Women's Voices of the World: Daughters and Rebels" (master's thesis, Rollins College, 1995). On Anna Mae Pictou-Aquash, see Devon A. Mihesuah, "Anna Mae Pictou-Aquash: An American Indian Activist," in *Sifters*, ed. Theda Perdue (New York: Oxford University Press, 2001); Devon A. Mihesuah, *Indigenous American Women: Decolonization, Empowerment, Activism* (Lincoln: University of Nebraska Press, 2003); Joanna Brand, *The Life and Death of Anna Mae Aquash* (Toronto: Lorimer and Co., 1978); *The Spirit of Annie Mae*, DVD, directed by Catherine Anne Martin (National Film Board of Canada, 2002); Shirley Hill Witt, "The Brave-Hearted Women: The Struggle at Wounded Knee," *Civil Rights Digest* 8 (1976): 38–45; Peter Matthiessen, *In the Spirit of Crazy Horse* (New York: Viking Press, 1983); and Steve Hendricks, *The Unquiet Grave: The FBI and the Struggle for the Soul of Indian Country* (New York: Thunder's Mouth Press, 2006).

66. Mary Crow Dog, *Lakota Woman*, with Richard Erdoes (New York: Grove Weidenfeld, 1990; repr., New York: Harper Perennial, 1991).

67. Mary Brave Bird, *Ohitika Woman*, with Richard Erdoes (New York: Grove Press, 1993).

68. "A Conversation with Mary Brave Bird," *The American Indian Quarterly* 24, no. 3 (Summer 2000): 482–93.

69. On the problems particular to Native women's autobiography, see Kathleen Mullen Sands, "Native Women's Personal Narrative: Voices Past and Present," in *American Women's Autobiography: Fea(s)ts of Memory*, ed. Margo Culley (Madison: University of Wisconsin Press, 1992), 268–73.

70. Crow Dog, *Lakota Woman*, 67–68.

71. Patricia C. Albers, "Sioux Women in Transition," in *The Hidden Half: Studies of Plains Indian Women*, ed. Patricia Albers and Beatrice Medicine (Washington, DC:

University Press of America, 1983), 175.

72. Richard Erdoes, foreword to Brave Bird, *Ohitika Woman*, xii–xiii.

73. Anna Mae Pictou-Aquash, September 1975, in *The Spirit of Annie Mae*, DVD.

74. Liz Sonneborn, *A to Z of American Indian Women*, rev. ed., s.v. "Aquash, Anna Mae"; Mihesuah, *Indigenous American Women*, 116–17; and Crow Dog, *Lakota Woman*, 186–98.

75. Brand, 62–63.

76. The Trail of Broken Treaties began as a civil rights march in Washington, D.C., but lack of accommodations for protestors led to a riot at the Bureau of Indian Affairs building. AIM occupied the building and was paid $66,000 to transport protestors home. See *Encyclopedia of the Great Plains*, ed. David Wishart (Lincoln: University of Nebraska Press, 2004), s.v. "American Indian Movement," by Akim D. Reinhardt.

77. See works listed in note 38.

78. Mihesuah, "Anna Mae Pictou-Aquash," 208.

79. Sonneborn, "Aquash, Anna Mae." The mysteries surrounding her death were finally answered in February of 2004 when Arlo Looking Cloud, fellow AIM member, was convicted of her murder after only four hours of deliberation by the jury. For details of the trial, *U.S. v. Fritz Arlo Looking Cloud*, see Hendricks, 295–320.

80. Dennis Banks and Richard Erdoes, *Ojibwa Warrior: Dennis Banks and the Rise of the American Indian Movement* (Norman: University of Oklahoma Press, 2004).

81. Crow Dog, *Lakota Woman*, 131.

82. Mihesuah, "Anna Mae Pictou-Aquash," 208.

83. In *Lakota Woman*, Brave Bird articulates this sentiment when she writes, "Once our men had gotten their rights and their balls back, we might start arguing with them about who should do the dishes. But not before," 131.

84. Crow Dog, *Lakota Woman*, 14.

85. Ibid., 93.

86. For discussions on the difficulties of establishing tribal identity, see Eva Marie Garroutte, *Real Indians: Identity and the Survival of Native Americans* (Berkeley: University of California Press, 2003); and for Canada, Eugeen Roosens, *Creating Ethnicity: The Process of Ethnogenesis* (Newberry Park, CA: Sage, 1989).

87. Mihesuah, "Anna Mae Pictou-Aquash," 211.

88. Brave Bird, *Ohitika Woman*, 274.

## Mari Sandoz

1. Mari Sandoz, *These Were the Sioux* (New York: Hastings House, c. 1961; repr. Lincoln: University of Nebraska Press, 1985), 9.

## Introduction to the Central Plains

1. David Wishart, *The Encyclopedia of the Great Plains* (Lincoln: University of Nebraska Press, 2004), xiii.

2. Ibid., 613-18; 555–61.

3. Joan Jensen and Darlis Miller, "The Gentle Tamers Revisited: New Approaches to the History of Women in the American West," *The Pacific Historical Review* 49, no. 2 (May 1980), 173–213.

4. Wishart, 320.

5. Elliot West, *The Way to the West: Essays on the Central Plains* (Albuquerque: University of New Mexico Press, 1995), 85–125.

6. West, 125.

7. Wishart, *Encyclopedia*, s.v. "From Women to Gender," 321.

8. West, 125.

9. Wishart, 323.

## Chapter 5

1. Patricia J. O'Brien, "The Central Lowland Plains: An Overview, A.D. 500–1500," in *Plains Indians, A.D. 500–1500: The Archaeological Past of Historic Groups*. ed. Karl H. Schlesier (Norman: University of Oklahoma Press, 1994), 199.

2. Loretta Fowler, *The Columbia Guide to American Indians of the Great Plains* (New York: Columbia University Press, 2003), 31, 194.

3. Benson Tong, *Susan LaFlesche Picotte, M.D.: Omaha Leader and Reformer* (Norman: University of Oklahoma Press, 1999), 4.

4. Charles C. Mann, *1491: New Revelations of the Americas Before Columbus* (New York: Vintage Books, 2005), 28.

5. Tong, 4.

6. Daniel Maltz and JoAllyn Archambault, "Gender and Power in Native North America, Concluding Remarks," in *Women and Power in Native North America*, ed. Laura F. Klein and Lillian A. Ackerman (Norman: Oklahoma Press, 1995), 237.

7. Paula Gunn Allen, *The Sacred Hoop: Recovering the Feminine in American Indian Traditions* (Boston: Beacon Press, 1986), 13.

8. George A. Dorsey, *Mythology of the Wichita* (Norman: University of Oklahoma Press, 1995), 19.

9. Ibid.

10. Ibid.

11. George A. Dorsey, *The Pawnee Mythology* (Lincoln: University of Nebraska Press, 1997), 13–14.

12. Ibid.,15–16.

13. Mann, 218, 223.

14. Dorsey, *Mythology of the Wichita*, 25.

15. Robert H. Lowie, *Indians of the Plains* (New York: McGraw-Hill, 1982), 19–20.

16. H. N. Llewellyn and Huber Self, *The Cheyenne Way* (Norman: University of Oklahoma Press, 1941), 176–77.

17. Llewellyn and Self, 169–90; James H. Howard, *The Ponca Tribe* (Washington, DC: The Smithsonian Institution, 1965), 147.

18. Howard, 147.

19. Author Charles C. Mann focused on the North American cultures prior to Columbus's arrival in his acclaimed work *1491: New Revelations of the Americas Before Columbus*. He astutely wrote, "North America was a busy, talkative place. By 1000 A.D., trade relationships had covered the continent for more than a thousand years; mother-of-pearl from the Gulf of Mexico has been found in Manitoba, and Lake Superior copper in Louisiana." These goods most likely traveled through the central plains. Mann, 28.

20. Nancy Shoemaker, *Negotiators of Change: Historical Perspectives on Native American Women* (New York: Routledge, 1995), 5.

21. Archaeologist Jeffrey L. Eighmy describes movement on the plains between 1050 and 1500 as seasonal. He wrote, "[T]he seasonal hunting hypothesis needs to explain why Upper Republican hunters were coming hundreds of miles through 'some of the best buffalo country on the Plains' just so they could hunt places like Goshen Hole and Cedar Point" (p. 235). Jeffrey L. Eighmy, "The Central High Plains: A Cultural Historical Summary," in *Plains Indians, A.D. 500–1500: The Archaeological Past of Historic Groups*, ed. Karl H. Schlesier (Norman: University of Oklahoma Press, 1994), 234–35. In the same volume Patricia J. O'Brien delineates the spread of culture through the central lowland plains. Different archaeological phases demonstrated the movement both in people and in trade. Patricia J. O'Brien, "The Central Lowland Plains: An Overview A.D. 500–1500," in Schlesier, 199–216.

22. Mark Warhus, *Another America: Native American Maps and the History of Our Land* (New York: St. Martin's Griffin, 1997), 27.

23. Elizabeth A. H. John, "A Wichita Migration Tale," *American Indian Quarterly* 7, no. 4 (Fall 1983), 61.

24. Warhus, 27. See also David J. Wishart, *An Unspeakable Sadness: The Dispossession of the Nebraska Indians* (Lincoln: University of Nebraska Press, 1994), 27.

25. Berlin Basil Chapman, *The Otoes and Missourias: A Study of Indian Removal and the Legal Aftermath* (Oklahoma City: Times Journal Publishing Company, 1965), xiv.

26. Warhus, 27–28.

27. Lowie, 80.

28. Wishart, 19–20.

29. Ibid., 20–21.

30. Paul H. Carlson, *The Plains Indians* (College Station: Texas A&M University Press, 1998), 124.

31. Ibid.

32. Herbert Eugene Bolton, *Coronado: Knight of the Pueblos and Plains* (Albuquerque: University of New Mexico Press, 1964), 294.

33. Ibid., 124, 126–27.

34. Shoemaker, 11. See Tong for a brief description of women's roles in the buffalo

hunt. He stated, "Omaha women were responsible for processing the gains of the hunt, which included drying and jerking of the meat and dressing and tanning the skins." Tong, *Susan LaFlesche Picotte, M.D.,* 5.

35. Wishart, 19.
36. Carlson, 126–27. For overlapping Spanish and French exploration in present-day Kansas see Homer E. Socolofsky and Huber Self, *Historical Atlas of Kansas* (Norman: University of Oklahoma Press, 1972), map #8.
37. Wishart, 5.
38. Ibid., 23.
39. Ibid., 7.
40. Dorsey, *The Mythology of the Wichita,* 19.
41. The Spanish used the term *Quivira* for the plains area. According to Marc Simmons, "the name Quivira became attached to the remote plains lying northeast of New Mexico and centering upon the modern state of Kansas." Marc Simmons, *The Last Conquistador: Juan de Oñate and the Settling of the Far Southwest* (Norman: University of Oklahoma Press, 1991), 156.
42. Simmons, 162. See also Warhus, 27–28.
43. Wishart, 19.
44. Tong, 6–7.
45. Wishart, 3.
46. Klein and Ackerman, 3. For a discussion of power and reciprocity, see pages 12–14.

## Chapter 6

1. Edwin Thompson Denig, *Five Indian Tribes of the Upper Missouri: Sioux, Arickaras, Assiniboines, Crees, Crows,* ed. with an introduction by John C. Ewers (Norman: University of Oklahoma Press, 1961), 199.
2. For example, Will Roscoe, *Changing Ones: Third and Fourth Genders in Native North America* (New York: St. Martin's Griffin, 2000); Sabine Lang, *Men as Women, Women as Men: Changing Gender in Native American Culture,* trans. John L. Vantine (Austin: University of Texas Press, 1998); Sue-Ellen Jacobs, Wesley Thomas, and Sabine Lang, *Two-Spirit People: Native American Gender Identity, Sexuality, and Spirituality* (Urbana: University of Illinois Press, 1997); and Walter L. Williams, *The Spirit and the Flesh: Sexual Diversity in American Indian Culture* (Boston: Beacon Press, 1992).
3. Historians have demonstrated that at various times in American history, the dominant social group (i.e., usually white Americans, especially with northern and western European ancestry) associated various sexual crimes and other forms of "impropriety" with people considered to be of "lower" races. This was all part of the act of racializing and "othering" people. See, for example, Siobhan B. Sommerville, *Queering the Color Line: Race and the Invention of Homosexuality in American Culture* (Durham, NC: Duke University Press, 2000); and Peter

Boag, *Same-Sex Affairs: Constructing and Controlling Homosexuality in the Pacific Northwest* (Berkeley: University of California Press, 2003), 45–73, 125–53.

4. Vern L. Bullough, "Transgenderism and the Concept of Gender," *The International Journal of Transgenderism* 4, no. 3 (2000), accessed June 2, 2005, www.symposium. com/ijt/gilbert/bullough.htm; Joanne Meyerowitz, "Sex Change and the Popular Press," *GLQ* 4, no. 2 (1998), 160–61; and Gordene Olga MacKenzie, *Transgender Nation* (Bowling Green, OH: Bowling Green State University Popular Press, 1994).

5. For example, as recently as 2002 two authorities on women who dressed as men and fought in the American Civil War made the astonishing claim that homosexuality is a "negative" generalization about historic cross-dressers. *An inaccurate* rather than a *negative* generalization would not only be a more appropriate assessment, but also more objective. See DeAnne Blanton and Lauren M. Cook, *They Fought Like Demons: Women Soldiers in the American Civil War* (Baton Rouge: Louisiana State University Press, 2002), 198.

6. I recognize that the term *transgender* was coined in the latter part of the twentieth century and has, therefore, a specific historical meaning that cannot be imposed on the period and place that this essay considers. I use the term in a very loose and simple sense to refer to Anglos, African Americans, and Mexicans, all of whom appear in this history, who crossed gender and sex boundaries and took on identities and personas of individuals associated by their cultures with the genders and sexes of their biological opposites.

7. "A Female Pike's Peaker in Trousers," *Rocky Mountain News Weekly* (Denver, Colorado), September 10, 1859, 2.

8. E. J. Guerin, *Mountain Charley, or the Adventures of Mrs. E. J. Guerin, Who Was Thirteen Years in Male Attire; An Autobiography Comprising a Period of Thirteen Years Life in the States, California, and Pike's Peak*, with an introduction by Fred W. Mazzulla and William Kostka (Norman: University of Oklahoma Press, 1968), viii, 37–55; quotation is on page 37.

9. Albert D. Richardson, *Beyond the Mississippi: Life and Adventure on the Prairies, Mountains, and Pacific Coast* (Hartford, CT: American Publishing Company, 1867), 200.

10. Ibid.

11. Ibid.

12. "A Female Pike's Peaker in Trousers," *Rocky Mountain News Weekly* (Denver, Colorado), September 10,1859, 2.

13. Horace Greeley, *An Overland Journey, from New York to San Francisco, in the Summer of 1859* (New York: C.M. Saxton, Barker and Company, 1860), 85.

14. Guerin, x, xi; G. W., "Mountain Charley: Colorado Story of Love, Lunacy and Revenge," reproduced in Guerin, 72 (quoted), 73 (quoted), 74, 75, 112 (quoted).

15. Gilbert Allen, "The Woman Express Rider," *The Frontier: The Great Western Magazine* 4, no. 12 (June 1906): 14–15.

16. "Frontier Tales," *Denver Field and Farm*, September 1, 1894, 6.

17. *Lewiston* (Idaho) *Morning Tribune*, March 8, 1909, clipping in "Jo Monahan"

Vertical File, Idaho State Historical Society, Boise, ID; *Lewiston* (Idaho) *Morning Tribune*, March 9, 1904, 5; "Cowboy Jo—Was a Woman!" *American-Journal-Examiner*, 1904, photocopy in "Jo Monahan" Vertical File. Also see Peter Boag, "Go West Young Man, Go East Young Woman: Searching for the *Trans* in Western Gender History," *Western Historical Quarterly* 36, no. 4 (2005): 495, 496.

18. See Boag, "Go West Young Man, Go East Young Woman."

19. On this subject, see, for example, Jonathan Ned Katz, *The Invention of Homosexuality* (New York: Plume, 1996); and Lillian Faderman, *Odd Girls and Twilight Lovers: A History of Lesbian Life in Twentieth-Century America* (New York: Penguin, 1992). It need be pointed out, however, that people in the mid-nineteenth century, even on the western frontier, sometimes did use the term *hermaphrodite* to refer to individuals who seemingly behaved in ways consonant with both genders or with a gender that did not fit their apparent biological sex. This did not, however, automatically mean that such individuals engaged in or even desired sexual activities with members of their own biological sex. A good example of this is Edwin Thompson Denig, who included in his *Five Indian Tribes of the Upper Missouri* a section entitled "Crow Hermaphrodites." He explained that one such male who dressed and behaved like a woman was nonetheless married to a woman, which "presents the anomaly of husband and wife in the same dress attending to the same domestic duties." See Denig, 187–88. Historian Susan Lee Johnson found that one Euro-American man involved in the California gold rush in 1852 referred in his diary to "a Chileno *hermaphrodite*." Likewise, according to Johnson, "no one . . . seemed especially troubled about h/er presence." See Susan Lee Johnson, *Roaring Camp: The Social World of the California Gold Rush* (New York: W.W. Norton, 2000), 171. But also see Patricia Crawford and Sara Mendelson, "Sexual Identities in Early Modern England: The Marriage of Two Women in 1680," *Gender & History* 7, no. 3 (1995): 367; Emma Donoghue, *Passions Between Women: British Lesbian Culture, 1668–1801* (New York: HarperCollins, 1993), 26–27; and Elizabeth Reis, "Impossible Hermaphrodites: Intersex in America, 1620–1960," *Journal of American History* 92, no. 1 (2005): 411–41.

20. Richardson, 200. The late-nineteenth-century emergence of modern notions of heterosexuality and homosexuality and accompanying alterations in notions of gender are well treated in Jonathan Ned Katz, *The Invention of Heterosexuality* (New York: Dutton, 1995).

21. G. W., "Mountain Charley," 24, 72; Allen, 14, 15; *Denver Field and Farm*, September 1, 1894, 6; "Cowboy Jo—Was a Woman!"

22. Guerin, 20, 22, 29–30. Other examples of this transformation in western female-to-male cross-dressers are contained in Boag, "Go West Young Man, Go East Young Woman," 486.

23. See particularly Marjorie Garber, *Vested Interests: Cross Dressing & Cultural Anxiety* (New York: Routledge, 1992). For the most part, what limited scholarship that exists on women who dressed as men in the American West also explains this phenomenon by means of the progress narrative. See, for example, Evelyn A.

Schlatter, "Drag's a Life: Women, Gender, and Cross-Dressing in the Nineteenth-Century West," in *Writing the Range: Race, Class, and Culture in the Women's West*, ed. Elizabeth Jameson and Susan Armitage (Norman: University of Oklahoma Press, 1997), 334–48; DeAnne Blanton, "Cathy Williams: Black Woman Soldier, 1866–1868," *Minerva* 10 (1992): 1–12; Phillip Thomas Tucker, *Cathy Williams: From Slave to Female Buffalo Soldier* (Mechanicsburg, PA: Stackpole Books, 2002); and Sally Zanjani, *A Mine of Her Own: Women Prospectors in the American West, 1850–1950* (Lincoln: University of Nebraska Press, 1997), 85–120.

24. Tucker, 88, 180, 223 (quoted).

25. Elizabeth B. Custer, *"Boots and Saddles"; or, Life in Dakota with General Custer* (New York: Harper and Brothers, 1885), 202 (quoted); Katherine Gibson Fougera, *With Custer's Cavalry* (Caldwell, ID: Caxton Printers, 1940); Gwendolin Damon Wagner, *Old Neutriment* (Boston: Ruth Hill Publisher, 1934; repr., Lincoln: University of Nebraska Press, 1989).

26. Custer, 199, 202 (quoted).

27. Angel Kwolek-Folland, "Customers and Neighbors: Women in the Economy of Lawrence, Kansas, 1870–1885," *Business and Economic History* 27, no. 1 (1998): 133, 134; Margaret F. Walker, "A Woman's Work Is Never Done; Or, The Dirt on Men and Their Laundry," *Overland Journal* 16, no. 2 (1998): 6; Cynthia A. Wood, "Army Laundresses and Civilization on the Western Frontier," *Journal of the West* 41, no. 3 (2002): 27; Vickie Wendel, "Getting Those Clothes Clean," *Civil War Times Illustrated* 38, no. 4 (1999): 36; Vickie Wendel, "Washer Women," *Civil War Times Illustrated* 38, no. 4 (1999): 34–35.

28. Robert M. Utley, *Frontier Regulars, 1866–1891: The United States Army and the Indian* (New York: Macmillan Publishing, 1973), 22; Don Rickey, Jr., *Forty Miles a Day on Beans and Hay: The Enlisted Soldier Fighting the Indian Wars* (Norman: University of Oklahoma Press, 1963), 126; Alice D. Holmes, "'And I Was Always with Him': The Life of Jane Thorpy, Army Laundress," *Journal of Arizona History* 38, no. 2 (1997): 178, 179; Patricia Y. Stallard, *Glittering Misery: Dependents of the Indian Fighting Army* (San Rafael, CA: Presidio Press and Fort Collins, CO: The Old Army Press, 1978), 59; Anne Bruner Eales, *Army Wives on the American Frontier: Living by the Bugles* (Boulder, CO: Johnson Books, 1996), 138; Wendel, "Washer Women," 35; Miller J. Stewart, "Army Laundresses: Ladies of the 'Soap Suds Row,'" *Nebraska History* 6, no. 4 (1980): 424. Wendel and Stewart give somewhat lower figures; it appears they did not multiply the wage over nineteen men.

29. Custer, 71, 195, 196, 198 (quoted); Fougera, 191.

30. Wagner, 112; Fougera, 191; John Duffy, "Medicine in the West: An Historical Overview," *Journal of the West* 21, no. 3 (1982): 5, 7, 11, 12; Custer, 198; Charles R. King, "The Woman's Experience of Childbirth on the Western Frontier," *Journal of the West* 29, no. 1 (1999): 79.

31. Stewart, 430; Anne M. Butler, *Daughters of Joy, Sisters of Misery: Prostitutes in the American West, 1865–90* (Urbana: University of Illinois Press, 1985), 143; Custer, 201.

32. Custer, 201 (quoted). On Mexican midwifery, see Fran Leeper Buss, *La Partera: Story of a Midwife* (Ann Arbor: University of Michigan Press, 1980), 5, 6; Margarita A. Kay, "Mexican, Mexican American, and Chicana Childbirth," in *Twice a Minority: Mexican American Women*, ed. Margarita B. Melville (St. Louis, MO: C.V. Mosby Company, 1980), 53; Grace Granger Keyes, "Mexican-American and Anglo Midwifery in San Antonio, Texas," (Ph.D. diss., University of Wisconsin-Milwaukee, 1985), 33, 34, 36, 136, 141, 142. On various midwifery chores, see Judy Barrett Litoff, "Forgotten Women: American Midwives at the Turn of the Twentieth Century," *Historian* 40, no. 2 (1978): 237; Custer, 201. On midwifery in the nineteenth-century trans-Mississippi West, see Duffy, 13; and King, 80–83.

33. Utley, 24, 25; Rickey, 17; Eales, 138; Butler, 142; Tucker, 119; Walker, 10; Paul Ong, "Chinese Laundries as an Urban Occupation in Nineteenth-Century California," *The Annals of the Chinese Historical Society of the Pacific Northwest* (1983): 72; Kwolek-Folland, 133; Nupur Chaudhuri, "'We All Seem Like Brothers and Sisters': The African-American Community in Manhattan, Kansas, 1865–1940," *Kansas History* 14, no. 4 (1991–92): 286, 287.

34. Stewart, 421; Wendel, 33; Walker, 5; Eales, 138; Stallard, 13; Holmes, 178; Butler, 144.

35. Utley, 85; Rickey, 116, 117, 119, 135; Tucker, 119. See also Walker, 10, 11; Johnson, 30–31, 119–20; Custer, 199; Fougera, 223.

36. Custer, 106, 200; Paul Hutton, "Noonan's Last Stand: 'We was flabbergasted,'" *True West* 52, no. 10 (2005): 118 and 48; Utley, 73, 74; Rickey, 34–35 and 123.

37. Hutton, 119; Fougera, 191, 223–24; Custer, 199 (quoted), 200.

38. Butler, 144–45.

39. Stallard, 13, 55; Wood, 27; Stewart, 422; Holmes, 184; Custer, 200 (quoted); Fougera, 193 (quoted).

40. Joan Wang, "Gender, Race and Civilization: The Competition Between American Power Laundries and Chinese Steam Laundries, 1870s–1920s," *American Studies International* 40, no. 1 (2002): 52 (quoted), 57, 74; Walker, 4, 5, 6, 7; Ong, 69, 72, 74; Johnson, 31, 125, 137.

41. Fougera, 223, 224.

42. Custer, 199.

43. On borderland kidnapping and captives, see James F. Brooks, *Captives & Cousins: Slavery, Kinship, and Community in the Southwest Borderlands* (Chapel Hill: University of North Carolina Press, 2002); J. J. Methvin, *Andele: The Mexican-Kiowa Captive; A Story of Real Life Among the Indians* (Albuquerque: University of New Mexico Press, 1996). On transgenderism among Native peoples of the borderlands, see Roscoe, 224, 236; Williams, 39; Claire R. Farrer, "A 'Berdache' by any Other Name . . . Is a Brother, Friend, Lover, Spouse: Reflections on a Mescalero Apache Singer of Ceremonies," in Jacobs, Thomas, and Lang, 236–51; Wesley Thomas, "Navajo Cultural Constructions of Gender and Sexuality," in Jacobs, Thomas, and Lang, 156–73; Carolyn Epple, "A Navajo Worldview and *Nádleehí*: Implications for Western Categories," in Jacobs, Thomas, and Lang, 174–91.

44. "Straight Through the Heart," *Bismarck* (Dakota Territory) *Tribune*, December 2,1878, 1; also see Wagner, *Old Neutriment*, 113–15, for suggestive material on this issue.
45. On male-male sexuality in the late-nineteenth-century West, Boag, *Same-Sex Affairs*; Williams, 152–74; D. Michael Quinn, *Same-Sex Dynamics Among Nineteenth-Century Americans: A Mormon Example* (Urbana: University of Illinois Press, 1996); in the army, Thomas Lowry, *The Story the Soldiers Wouldn't Tell: Sex in the Civil War* (Mechanicsburg, PA: Stackpole Books, 1994), 109–14. On male homosexual subculture in nineteenth-century Mexico, Victor Manuel Macías-González, "A Note on Homosexuality in Porfirian and Postrevolutionary Northern Mexico," *Journal of the Southwest* 43, no. 4 (2001): 543–48; Martin Nesvig, "The Lure of the Perverse: Moral Negotiation of Pederasty in Porfirian Mexico," *Mexican Studies/ Estudios Mexicanos* 16, no. 1 (2000): 1–37; Robert McKee Irwin, Edward J. McCaughan, and Michelle Rocío Nasser, *The Famous 41: Sexuality and Social Control in Mexico, 1901* (New York: Palgrave Macmillan, 2003). On Old Nash's death, Fougera, 222; Hutton, 119.
46. Custer, 201, 202.

## Chapter 7

1. Mary Parker Richards, diary entry, April 29, 1846, in *Winter Quarters: The 1846–1848 Life Writings of Mary Haskin Parker Richards*, ed. Maurine Carr Ward (Logan: Utah State University Press, 1996), 121 (hereafter cited as Richards, *Diary and Letters*).
2. Richard Bennett, *Mormons at the Missouri, 1846–1852: 'And We Should Die'* (Norman: University of Oklahoma Press, 1987), 1–25, 68–90. See also Wallace Stegner, *The Gathering of Zion: The Story of the Mormon Trail* (London: Eyre and Spottiswoode, 1966), 1–13.
3. Patricia Nelson Limerick, "Peace Initiative: Using the Mormons to Rethink Culture and Ethnicity in American History," in *Something in the Soil: Legacies and Reckonings in the New West* (New York: W.W. Norton, 2000), 235–55.
4. Lawrence Coates, "Cultural Conflict: Mormons and Indians in Nebraska," *Brigham Young University Studies* 24, no. 3 (1984): 275–300, 284; Bennett, 73; Elliott West, "Land," in *The Way to the West: Essays on the Central Plains* (Albuquerque: University of New Mexico Press, 1997): 13–50, 21.
5. Bennett, 113–28, 168–83; Stegner, 73–108.
6. Heber C. Kimball, quoted by William Clayton in entry of December 21, 1845, in George Smith, "Nauvoo Roots of Mormon Polygamy, 1841–1846: A Preliminary Demographic Report," *Dialogue* 27, no. 1 (1994): 1–36, 23.
7. Ibid., 23.
8. Ibid.
9. Stanley Kimball, "Mormon Trail Network in Nebraska, 1846–1868: A New Look," *Brigham Young University Studies* 24, no. 3 (1984): 321–36; Stegner, 73–89.

10. For a map of Mormon encampments on the road to Winter Quarters, see Bennett, 34–35; diseases at Winter Quarters, 131–41; housing and population at Winter Quarters, 76–77, 80–81. See also A. R. Mortensen, "Mormons, Nebraska, and the Way West," *Nebraska History* 46, no. 4 (1965): 259–71, 264–65.

11. Bennett, 199–214; Kimball, "Mormon Trail Network," 321–36; Maureen Ursenbach Beecher, "Women's Work on the Mormon Frontier," *Utah Historical Quarterly* 49, no. 3 (1981): 276–90; Maurine Carr Ward, "The Fabric of Life: An Introduction," in *Winter Quarters; The 1846–1848 Life Writings of Mary Haskin Parker Richards* (Logan: Utah State University Press, 1996), 28.

12. Loren Horton, "'The Worst That I Had Yet Witnessed'; Mormon Diarists Cross Iowa in 1846," *Iowa Heritage Illustrated* 77, no. 2 (1996): 70–73; Conrey Bryson, *Winter Quarters* (Salt Lake City: Deseret Books, 1986); "Pioneer Margaretta Lemon King, Sketch Prepared by Lillian King Brown, Her Daughter," Film 920, Reel 51, p.1, L. Tom Perry Special Collections, Harold B. Lee Library, Brigham Young University (hereafter cited as BYU Archives); "Susan A. Noble," MS 525, p. 11, BYU Archives; "Nancy Tracy," MS 2198, Folder 4, p. 42, BYU Archives; Elizabeth Staker, "A Brief History of Our Grandfather Alma Staker and a Continuation of Our Grandmother Elizabeth Young Staker," MS 1271, pp. 2–3, BYU Archives; Sina Chipman, "Biography of Niels Nielson and Karen Pedersen Nielsen," Film 920, Reel 51, p. 2, BYU Archives; Nora Lund, "History of Jane Terry Young," Film 920, Reel 5, pp. 96–97, BYU Archives; "Biography of Elizabeth Terry Howard," Film 920, Reel 5, p. 74, BYU Archives; "Biographical Sketch of the Life of Elizabeth Cunningham Kelly," Film 920, Reel 51, p. 132, BYU Archives; "Biography of Mary Thornton," Film 920, Reel 52, p. 3, BYU Archives.

13. Maureen Ursenbach Beecher, "A Growling Grumbling, Devilish, Sickly Time," *The Personal Writings of Eliza Roxcy Snow* (Salt lake City: University of Utah Press, 1995), 111–12 (hereafter cited as Snow Diary); Bennett, 175–79, 179 (quoted). Bennett adds that women's exercise of powers of the priesthood are "unheard of and discouraged in the church today," 179. See also Kenneth Godfrey, Audrey Godfrey, and Jill Mulvay Derr, *Women's Voices: An Untold History of the Latter-day Saints, 1830–1900* (Salt Lake City: Deseret Book Co., 1982), 19. Godfrey et al. explain that during the first decade of the Mormon Church's existence, Joseph Smith supported the expression of spiritual powers among men and women alike, including the laying on of hands, speaking in tongues, and giving blessings. However, by 1839, Smith reversed this position, as prayer meetings became chaotic with enthused converts of both sexes speaking in tongues.

14. Elizabeth Willis, "Voice in the Wilderness: The Diaries of Patty Sessions," *Journal of American Folklore* 101 (1988): 37–47, 38 (quoted).

15. Smith, "Nauvoo Roots of Polygamy," 35.

16. Ibid., 9–11.

17. Ibid., 9.

18. Ibid., 10–11.

19. Ibid.

20. Godfrey et al., 50–51; Smith, "Nauvoo Roots of Polygamy," 27; Beecher, "Growling, Grumbling Time," 109–10.

21. Smith, "Nauvoo Roots of Polygamy," 10–11; see tables, 37–68.

22. Ibid., 17–19.

23. Snow Diary, 113–71; "Narrative of Eliza P. Lyman," MS 1217, 8–30, BYU Archives. Lyman, for example, refers to "Father Tanner" (p. 8) ; "Father Huntington" (p. 13); "Father Allred" (p. 17); "Father Tubbs" (p. 20); and "Father Lott" (p. 20).

24. Stephen Pratt, "Parley Pratt in Winter Quarters and the Trail West," *Brigham Young University Studies* 24, no. 3 (1984): 373–88, 382. See also Beecher, "Growling, Grumbling Time," 110.

25. Maureen Ursenbach Beecher, ed., *Mormon Midwife: The 1846–1888 Diaries of Patty Bartlett Sessions* (Logan: Utah State University Press, 2001), 20–23 (hereafter cited as Sessions Diary). For records of plural marriages "by proxy," see Smith, "Nauvoo Roots of Polygamy," 69–72.

26. Gordon Irving, "The Law of Adoption: One Phase of the Development of the Mormon Concept of Salvation, 1836–1900," *Brigham Young University Studies* 14 (Spring 1974): 291–314; see esp. 295–302.

27. Bennett, 187–93, 191 (quoted). See also Pratt, 383.

28. Sessions Diary, 57–97. From July 1846 to June 1847, Patty Sessions attended forty-seven births at Winter Quarters.

29. Willis, 46.

30. Sessions Diary, 62–7.

31. Richards, *Diary and Letters*, 111. On February 15, 1847, Mary Richards recorded a conversation she had with one of the Mormon apostles, Heber Kimball. Richards commented to Kimball on how even-tempered his first wife was toward sister-wives. Kimball replied that he was aware of his first wife's anguish over his subsequent marriages and that he "loved her the more" for her forbearance. In James Allen's biography of William Clayton, *Trials of Discipleship: The Story of William Clayton, A Mormon* (Urbana: University of Illinois Press, 1987), the author reconstructs from Clayton's diary his perceptions about plural marriage. Clayton noted one of his wives' initial distress over living in a polygamous household, but within three months assumed she had reconciled herself to it. His initial comments about the depth of her "bitterness," however, belie his sanguine assumptions about her later. He seems to have simply absorbed the church fathers' confidence that wives can adjust to plural marriage. See pp. 188–220.

32. Sessions Diary, October 24, 1846, 64.

33. Ibid.

34. Ibid., 65.

35. Ibid., 66.

36. Ibid., 66–67.

37. Lawrence Foster, "Polygamy and the Frontier: Mormon Women in Early Utah," *Utah Historical Quarterly* 50, no. 3 (Summer 1982): 268–89. Foster's statistics encompass the period 1832 to 1932.

38. Ward, 1–6, 11–13, 29–30. See also Richards, *Diary and Letters*, 89, 100, 103–4.

39. Richards, *Diary and Letters*, 71, 72, 73, 74.

40. Ward, 30.

41. Richards, *Diary and Letters*, 78.

42. Ibid.

43. Richards, *Diary and Letters*, 109.

44. Ibid., 131.

45. Ibid., 193.

46. Ibid., 103.

47. Sessions Diary, 75. For more examples of Sessions laying on hands to heal the sick, see 71, 73, 77, and 78.

48. Ibid., 79.

49. Ibid., 72. See also 79, 81, and 82 for additional examples of women's prayer meetings.

50. Ibid., 83.

51. Ibid. For the five meetings in the week before they left Winter Quarters, see 82–84. See also Snow Diary, 151, 170. For infrequent prayer meetings on the trail west, see 85–94.

52. Sessions Diary, 82.

53. Lucy Meserve Smith narrative, MS 432, Folder 1, p. 8, BYU Archives.

54. Ibid., 8–9.

55. Irving, 299.

56. Bennett, 74.

57. Ibid., 193. Stegner also commented on the class differences between wealthy church leaders and ordinary Mormon folk, in *The Gathering of Zion*, 120–21.

58. Beecher, "Growling, Grumbling Time," 109–10; Snow Diary, 143–44 (mid-September 1846).

59. Snow Diary, 117.

60. Ibid.

61. Ibid., 126.

62. Ibid.

63. Ibid.

64. Ibid., 136.

65. Ibid., 154. Historian Gordon Irving described the advantages of claiming fictive kinship with an apostle through adoption and the jealousies this caused. See Irving, 298–302.

66. Snow Diary, see poems on pp. 114, 115, 116, 122, 125, 145, 161–63, 167–69. Snow earned renown within the Mormon community for her literary praises to the Mormon mission.

67. Elizabeth Gilbert to Brigham Young, letter dated August 18, 1846, Brigham Young Papers; quoted in Bennett, 81n65.

68. Irving, 291–93; Beecher, "Introduction," *Mormon Midwife*, 20–22.

69. Richards, *Diary and Letters*, 119.

70. Ibid., 124.

71. Ibid.

72. Ibid.


## Chapter 8

1. Pamela Riney-Kehrberg, *Waiting on the Bounty: The Dust Bowl Diary of Mary Knackstedt Dyck* (Iowa City: University of Iowa Press, 1999), 33.

2. For the purposes of this essay, the term *rural* is used to designate people involved in agriculture or in agricultural communities.

3. Mary Neth, *Preserving the Family Farm: Women, Community, and the Foundations of Agribusiness in the Midwest, 1900–1940* (Baltimore: Johns Hopkins University Press, 1995), 97.

4. Henry Nash Smith, "Rain Follows the Plow: The Notion of Increased Rainfall for the Great Plains, 1844–1880," *The Huntington Library Quarterly* (February 1947): 174. Nash's classic essay traces the evolution of the "Rain Follows the Plow" theory. He credits Charles Dana Wilber with building on Hayden's earlier theory and for coining the pithy phrase: "And with a gift of phrase much grater than that of [Samuel G.] Aughey, he [Charles Dana Wilber] condensed the whole theory into the maxim, 'Rain Follows the Plow.'" See also Charles Dana Wilber, *The Great Valleys and Prairies of Nebraska and the Northwest* (Omaha, NE: Daily Republic Print, 1881), 69.

5. Nash, 174.

6. See Walter Prescott Webb's classic study, *The Great Plains* (Boston: Ginn and Company, 1931), for an analysis of the agricultural baggage frontier farmers from eastern regions brought with them; Gen. 1:27–28.

7. Julie Roy Jeffries, "'There Is Some Splendid Scenery': Women's Responses to the Great Plains Landscape," *Great Plains Quarterly* 8 (Spring 1988): 69. See also Jeffries's book, *Frontier Women: the Trans-Mississippi West, 1840–1890* (New York: Hill and Wang, 1979).

8. Riney-Kehrberg, 2.

9. John Steinbeck, *The Grapes of Wrath* (New York: Viking, 1989).

10. US Department of Commerce, Bureau of the Census, *The Growth of Metropolitan Districts in the United States: 1900–1940* (Washington, DC: US Government Printing Office, 1947), 8.

11. Dorothy Schwieder and Deborah Fink, "Plains Women: Rural Life in the 1930s," *Great Plains Quarterly* 8 (Spring 1988): 79–88.

12. Viola B., quoted in Katherine Jellison, *Entitled to Power: Farm Women and Technology, 1913–1963* (Chapel Hill: University of North Carolina Press, 1993), 75–76.

13. Caroline Henderson, *Letters from the Dust Bowl*, ed. Alvin O. Turner (Norman: University of Oklahoma Press, 2001), 156.

14. Ibid, 82–84. See also Riney-Kehrberg for discussions on women finding ways to stay on the farm, especially using federal money.

15. Henderson, 118.

16. Report of the Great Plains Committee, "The Future of the Great Plains (Washington, DC: US Government Printing Office, 1936), 5.

17. Ibid., 6.

18. Walter Fuhriman, "Federal Aid to Irrigation Development," *Journal of Farm Economics* 31, no. 4 (November 1949): 966: "As early as 1888, [federal funds were] appropriated for the purpose of investigating the extent to which arid regions could be reverted by irrigation. . . . [I]n 1902 the Federal Government, by passing the Reclamation Act, entered the field of direct promotion of irrigated agriculture."

19. Sixteenth Census of the United States: 1940; Irrigation of Agricultural Lands, Specific Irrigation Census Statistics (Washington, DC: US Government Printing Office, 1943), 29–30; Donald Woster, *Dust Bowl: The Southern Plains in the 1930s* (Oxford: Oxford University Press, 1979), 234.

20. Jenny Barker Devine notes that women in Iowa took the lead in identifying themselves as agricultural activists with interests beyond family and home. See "Quite a Ripple but No Revolution: The Changing Roles of Women in the Iowa Farm Bureau Federation, 1921–1951," *The Annals of Iowa* 64 (Winter 2005): 1–36.

21. Carolyn Sachs, *Gendered Fields: Rural Women, Agriculture, and Environment* (Boulder, CO: Westview Press, 1996), 6.

22. Ibid., 9.

23. University of California Sustainable Agriculture Research and Education Program, accessed August 23, 2006, www.sarep.ucdavis.edu/concept.htm.

24. "A woman in Oregon," quoted in Sachs, 62.

25. Sachs, 27–8.

26. Jane Green and Deb Rood, "Mission and Vision," About Nebraska WIA, University of Nebraska-Lincoln, accessed January 8, 2006, http://wia.unl.edu/index.htm. See also Wava G. Haney and Lorna Clancy Miller, "US Farm Women, Politics, and Policy," *Journal of Rural Studies* 7, nos. 1–2 (1991): 115–21.

27. Nebraska Women in Agriculture, History of Nebraska WIA, University of Nebraska-Lincoln, accessed August 23, 2006, http://wia.unl.edu/index.html.

28. Denise O'Brian, "Remarks upon Induction to the Iowa Hall of Fame," *Women, Food, and Agriculture Network* 3, no. 3 (September 2000): 6; Denise O'Brian, "How We Started," *Women, Food, and Agriculture Network* 1, no. 1 (February 1998): 1–4; and Ruth Chantry, Outreach Coordinator for Nebraska Sustainable Agriculture Society, telephone interview with author, May 18, 2005.

29. Chantry, interview.

30. Annette Dubas, personal correspondence with author, June 1, 2005. In possession of the author.

31. Ibid.

32. Chantry, interview.

33. Sachs, 138.

34. Chantry, interview.

35. Sachs, 62; Jessica Rochester, "Does Gender Influence CSAs?" *Women, Food, and Agriculture Network* 4, no. 2 (March 2001): 5.

36. Off-farm employment often provides medical insurance, an increasing concern among farm families.

37. Lawrence C. Kelly, *The Assault on Assimilation: John Collier and the Origins of Indian Policy Reform* (Albuquerque: University of New Mexico Press, 1983), xiii.

38. Lisa E. Emmerich, "'Right in the Midst of My Own People': Native American Women and the Field Matron Program," *American Indian Quarterly* 15, no. 2 (Spring 1991): 202.

39. Ibid., 202.

40. Loretta Fowler, *The Columbia Guide to American Indians of the Great Plains* (New York: Columbia University Press, 2003), 115–16. Central plains tribes that accepted the IRA include the Omahas, Northern Poncas, Santee Sioux, and the Tongue River Cheyenne.

41. Wynona Caramony, interview by author, August 23, 2005, tape recording, Macy, NE.

42. Ibid.

43. See Theodore D. Sargent, *The Life of Elaine Goodale Eastman* (Lincoln: Nebraska University Press, 2005) for a biography of a white woman activist for on-reservation elementary schools for Native American children.

44. Fowler, 115. For a political history of the Arts and Crafts policy, see Robert Fay Schrader, *The Indian Arts and Crafts Board: As Aspect of New Deal Indian Policy* (Albuquerque: University of New Mexico Press, 1983).

45. Caramony, interview; Sarah Deutsch, *No Separate Refuge: Culture, Class, and Gender on an Anglo-Hispanic Frontier in the American Southwest, 1880–1940* (New York: Oxford University Press, 1987), 194.

46. Deutsch, 196.

47. Caramony, interview.

48. Fowler, 124; Clyde Ellis, *A Dancing People: Powwow Culture on the Southern Plains* (Lawrence: University Press of Kansas, 2003), 24.

49. See Donald Fixico, *Termination and Relocation: Federal Indian Policy, 1945–1960* (Albuquerque: University of New Mexico Press, 1986). See also Kenneth R. Phillip, *Termination Revisited: American Indians on the Trail to Self-Determination, 1933–1953* (Lincoln: Nebraska University Press, 1999).

50. Ponca reservation terminated in 1966.

51. Donna Highton Langston, "American Indian Women's Activism in the 1960s and 1970s," *Hypatia* 18, no. 2 (2003): 116.

52. Jere Franco, "Empowering the World War II Native American Veteran: Postwar Civil Rights" *Wicazo Sa Review* 9 (Spring 1993): 32–37.

53. Helen L. Peterson, "American Indian Political Participation," *The Annals of the American Academy of Political and Social Science*, 311, no. 1 (1957):116–26. See also Thomas W. Cowger, *National Congress of American Indians: The Founding Years* (Lincoln: University of Nebraska Press, 1999).

54. Peterson, 125.
55. Langston, 115.
56. Ibid., 128.
57. Jane Lawrence, The Indian Health Service and the Sterilization of Native American Women," *American Indian Quarterly* 24, no. 3 (Summer 2000), 400–419.
58. See also Devon Abbott Mihesuan, "Finding a Modern American Female Identity," in *Indigenous American Women: Decolonization, Empowerment, Activism* (Lincoln: University of Nebraska Press, 2003).
59. David Wishart, *An Unspeakable Sadness: The Dispossession of the Nebraska Indians* (Lincoln: University of Nebraska Press, 1994), 245.
60. Caramony, interview.
61. Ibid.
62. Ibid.
63. John Garber, Sharon Garber, Jeff Vincent, and Darcy Boellstorff, "An Analysis of Refugee Resettlement Patterns in the Great Plains," *Great Plains Research* 14 (Fall 2004): 166–67.
64. Kate Nguyen, interview by author, August 14, 2006, tape recording, Hastings, NE.
65. Ibid. The composition of the family had been determined by a resettlement regulation that allowed either a nuclear family or an extended family to move to the United States. Defining themselves as an extended family, the women moved to the United States with the hope that Kate's mother would attain citizenship and sponsor her husband. The process took ten years.
66. Ibid.
67. Ibid.
68. Ibid.
69. Vign Ngo, interview by author, June 29, 2005, Hastings, NE.
70. Garber et. al, 165–84.
71. Ngo, interview.
72. Nguyen, interview.
73. Guntamanee (Ead) Mattley, interview by author, September 16, 2005, tape recording, Hastings, NE.
74. Ibid.
75. Cinthia Garcia, interview by author, July 22, 2005, Hastings, NE.
76. Ana Garcia, interview by author, July 22, 2005, Hastings, NE.
77. Ibid.
78. Deutsch, 60–62.
79. Louis Bloch, "Facts About Mexican Immigration Before and Since the Quota Restrictions," *Journal of the American Statistical Association* 24, no. 165 (March 1929): 50.
80. See Vicki Ruiz's *Cannery Women, Cannery Lives: Mexican Women, Unionization, and the California Food Processing Industry, 1930–1950* (Albuquerque: University of New Mexico Press, 1987) for a groundbreaking work on Hispanic women's activism.

81. Gary Gerstile, "Liberty, Coercion, and the Making of America," *Journal of American History* 84, no. 2 (1997): 525. The United States had a population of only 76 million in 1900; John Higham, *Send These to Me: Immigrants in Urban America* (Baltimore: Johns Hopkins University Press, 1984), 43.

82. Jorge Durand, Douglas S. Massey, and Emilio A. Parrado, "The New Era of Mexican Migration to the United States," *Journal of American History* 86, no. 2 (1999): 518–536.

83. Matthew Frye Jacobson, *Whiteness of a Different Color: European Immigrants and the Alchemy of Race* (Cambridge, MA: Harvard University Press, 1999).

84. Mattley, interview.

## Introduction to the Southern Plains

1. Elizabeth Jameson and Susan Armitage, *Writing the Range: Race, Class, and Culture in the Women's West* (Norman: University of Oklahoma Press, 1997), 4.

2. Antonia I. Castañeda, "Women of Color and the Rewriting of Western History: The Discourse, Politics, and Decolonization of History," *Pacific Historical Review* 61, no. 4 (November 1992): 514.

3. Jameson and Armitage, 5.

4. Ibid., 9.

5. David Wishart, *The Encyclopedia of the Great Plains* (Lincoln: University of Nebraska Press, 2004), 613–18.

6. Ibid., 862.

7. Ibid., 31–32.

8. Castañeda, 533.

## Chapter 9

1. Many works deal with the settlement of the northern frontier and the lifestyles and legal rights of those who moved north: Roberto Villaseñor E., *El Coronel Don José Escandón y la conquista del Nuevo Santander* (Mexico City: Boletín del Archivo General de la Nación, 1979); Lawrence F. Hill, *José de Escandón and the Founding of Nuevo Santander* (Columbus: Ohio State University Press, 1926); Juan Fidel Zorrilla, *Historia de Tamaulipas* (Ciudad Victoria, Tamaulipas: Dirección General de Educación y Cultura, 1987); Oakah Jones, *Los Paisanos: Spanish Settlers on the Northern Frontier of New Spain* (Norman: University of Oklahoma Press, 1979); Julia Coopwood, "History of the La Bahía Settlement During the Administration of Captain Manuel Ramirez de la Piscina, 1750–1767" (master's thesis, University of Texas at Austin, 1938); Jean A. Stuntz, *Hers, His and Theirs: Community Property Law in Spain and Early Texas* (Lubbock: Texas Tech University Press, 2005); Charles R. Cutter, *The Legal Culture of Northern New Spain, 1700–1810* (Albuquerque: University of New Mexico Press, 1998); Antonio Dominguez Ortiz, *Ciclos y temas de la historia de España: clases privilegiadas en el Antiguo Régimen*

(Madrid: Ediciones ISTMO, 1979); Kathryn Stoner O'Connor, *The Presidio La Bahía del Espíritu Santo de Zuñiga, 1721–1846* (Austin, TX: Van Boeckmann-Jones, 1966); Francisco de Solano, *Cedulario de tierras: compilación de legislación agrarian colonial (1497–1820)* (Mexico City: Universidad Nacional Autónoma de México, 1984); Clara Elena Suárez Argüello, *Camino real y carrera larga: la arriería en la Nueva España durante el siglo XVIII* (Mexico City: Centro de Investigaciones y Estudios Superiores en Antropologia Social, 1996).

2. Patricia Osante, *Orígenes del Nuevo Santander (1748–1772)* (Mexico City: Universidad Nacional Autónoma de México, Universidad Nacional Autonoma de Tamaulipas, 1997), 100–120, 220; Armando Alonso, *Tejano Legacy: Rancheros and Settlers in South Texas, 1734–1900* (Albuquerque: University of New Mexico Press, 1998), 27–29; A. B. J. Hammett, *The Empresario: Don Martín de León (The Richest Man in Texas)* (Kerrville, TX: Braswell Printing Co., 1971), 10; Manuel Barrera, *Then the Gringos Came: The Story of Martín de León and the Texas Revolution* (Laredo, TX: Barrera Publications, 1992), 11.

3. Hammett, 8–9; Barrera, 10–11.

4. Asunción Lavrin and Edith Couturier, "Dowries and Wills: A View of Women's Socioeconomic Role in Colonial Guadalajara and Puebla, 1640–1790," *Hispanic American Historical Review* 59, no. 2 (May 1979): 293.

5. Inventory of goods of Patricia de la Garza signed at Presas del Rey, January 1, 1801, vol. 1, p. 34, Index to Deed Records, Victoria County Clerk's Office, Victoria County Courthouse, Victoria, TX (hereafter cited as VCCO); Patricia de la Garza to P. B. Cocke, Deed, January 24, 1837, vol. 1, p. 34, Index to Deed Records, VCCO; Lavrin and Couturier, 288–95; Hammett, 8–9, 20–25; Barrera, 10–11; Victor M. Rose, *Some Historical Facts in Regard to the Settlement of Victoria, Texas* (Laredo, TX: Daily Times Print, 1883), 104–5; William H. Oberste, *Texas Irish Empresarios and Their Colonies*, 2nd ed. (Austin, TX: Von Boeckmann-Jones, 1973), 68.

6. "Libro formado por el Capitán de Milicias y primer Alcalde Constitucional de La Bahía del Espíritu Santo," Archivo General de la Nación, Mexico City, Mexico; Census of Santa Margarita Ranch, Sergeant José de Jesús Aldrete, November 10, 1811, Spanish Archives, San Antonio, also in Bexar Archives; Martín de León to Salcedo, Petition to Ferdinand VII, 1800, Martín de León Papers, O'Connor Room, Victoria County Public Library, Victoria, Texas (hereafter cited as OCR/VC); Alonso de León, "Relación del descubrimiento, población y pacificación de este nuevo reno de León: Temperatmento y calidad de la tierra," in *Documentos inéditos o muy raros para la historia de México*, ed. Genaro García (Mexico City: Editorial Porrúa, 1975), 15; Israel Cavazos Garza, *El General Alonso de León, descubridor de Texas* (Monterrey, Mexico: Real Ayuntamiento de Monterrey, 1993), 14–15; Osante, *Orígenes del Nuevo Santander (1748–1772)*; Zorrilla, *Historia de Tamaulipas*; and Villaseñor, *El Coronel Don José Escandón*.

7. Martín de León to Salcedo, Petition to Ferdinand VII, 1800, Martín de León Papers, OCR/VC.

8. Robinson, 126; Solano, Law Number 226 , 537–39; Davenport, 4–6; D. A. Brading, "Government and Elite in Late Colonial Mexico," *Hispanic American Historical Review* 53, no. 3 (August 1973): 392; Hammett, 11–12; Barrera, 20–22.

9. Martín de León to Salcedo, Petition to Ferdinand VII, 1800, Martín de León Papers, OCR/VC; Nettie Lee Benson, "Bishop Marín de Porras and Texas," *Southwestern Historical Quarterly* 51 (July 1947): 26–29.

10. Jesús F. de la Teja, *San Antonio de Béxar: A Community on New Spain's Northern Frontier* (Albuquerque: University of New Mexico Press, 1995), 117. The Spanish Archives at the General Land Office, Austin, Texas, do not show a recorded title for the Santa Margarita Ranch, although de León's request for the land is on file. That the de León family did take up residence on the ranch is indicated by the census records for 1811, which list their names and those of their family, the ranch hands, and the teacher.

11. Petition, Martín de León to the King, #42, copy in Martín de León Papers, OCR/VC; Moorehead, 72–73, 92–93, 172, 224; Julia Kathryn Garrett, *Green Flag Over Texas: A Story of the Last Years of Spain in Texas* (Austin, TX: Jenkins Publishing Co. and New York: The Pemberton Press, 1969), 11–14; Odie B. Faulk, *Last Years of Spanish Texas* (The Hague: Mouton, 1964), 120–23; Jones, 55; Gerald Ashford, *Spanish Texas: Yesterday and Today* (Austin, TX: Jenkins Publishing, 1971), 191–93.

12. Lavrin and Couturier, 285–87; Paul Horgan, *Great River: The Rio Grande in North American History* (New York: Rinehart, 1954; repr., Austin: Texas Monthly Press, 1984), 353–54; Henry F. Brown, *Baptism Through the Centuries* (Mountain Valley, CA: Pacific Press, 1965), 16–24, 29–30; James W. Bruner, *Christian Doctrine* (Dallas, TX: Baptist General Convention of Texas, 1944), 57–59.

13. Hammett, 13; Barrera, 31.

14. Josefina Zoraida Vázquez, "Los Primeros Tropiezos," in *Compendio de la Historia General de México*, vol. 3, ed. Nicolas León (Mexico City: El Colegio de México, 1976), 5; William Edward Syers, *Texas: The Beginning, 1519–1839* (Waco, TX: The Texian Press, 1978), 136, 137; Jones, 21; Nettie Lee Benson, "Texas as Viewed from Mexico," *Southwestern Historical Quarterly*, 90 (January 1987): 219; Chipman, 236–38, 238–39.

15. Some authors, including Jane Long, his wife, suggest that Long was killed at the instigation of Texas governor José Félix Trespalacios. Jones, 21; Benson, "Texas as Viewed from Mexico," 219; Chipman, 238–39.

16. Michael P. Costeloe, *La primera república federal de México (1824–1835): un estudio de los partidos politicos en el México independiente*, trans. Manuel Fernández Gasalla (Mexico City: Fondo de Cultura Económica, 1975), 24. Roy Grimes, in *300 Years in Victoria County* (Victoria, TX: Victoria Advocate Publishing Co., 1968; repr., Austin, TX: Nortex Press, 1985), suggests that the name Victoria was left out "perhaps by oversight." Martín de León's original petition in the General Land Office does not mention Victoria and there was little reason to suppose that de León had anything more than religion in mind when he suggested the name.

Guadalupe Victoria, at the time, was not yet president of the republic, and only one of a triumvirate. Victor M. Rose, in *Some Historical Facts in Regard to the Settlement of Victoria, Texas*, 10–11, claims that Guadalupe Victoria was de León's "warm personal friend." This supposition, which is unsubstantiated, is highly unlikely since Guadalupe Victoria was never in Texas nor is there any evidence of Martín de León ever going to Mexico City. A more logical conclusion is that the Provincial Deputation, trying to ingratiate itself with the ruling triumvirate, added Victoria after discussion with de León.

17. Hammett, 10–11; Barrera, 70–71; Family Group Records prepared from La Bahía and Victoria census data, Gloria Candelaria, Victoria County Genealogical Society, Victoria, TX (hereafter cited as VCGS.)

18. Hammett, 10–12; Family Record Group of Placido Benavides, Candelaria, VCGS.

19. Eugene C. Barker, *The Life of Stephen F. Austin, Founder of Texas, 1793–1836: A Chapter in the Westward Movement of the Anglo-American People* (Austin: University of Texas Press, 1985), 369; William R. Hogan, *The Texas Republic: A Social and Economic History* (Austin: University of Texas Press, 1986), 229, 234; Mary Virginia Henderson, "Minor Empresario Contracts for the Colonization of Texas, 1825–1834," *Southwestern Historical Quarterly* 32 (July 1928), 1:11; Patrick Ireland Nixon, *The Medical Story of Early Texas, 1528–1853* (Lancaster, PA: Mollie Bennett Lupe Memorial Fund, 1946), 138; Hogan, 228; Family Group Records of Placido Benavides, Candelaria, VCGS.

20. Grimes, 76–77.

21. Stephen L. Hardin, *Texian Iliad: A Military History of the Texas Revolution, 1835–1836* (Austin: University of Texas Press, 1994), 42–43; Hobart Huson, *Refugio, A Comprehensive History of Refugio County: From Aboriginal Times to 1953*, 2 vols. (Woodsboro, TX: Rooke Foundation, 1953–1955), 212; Abel Rubio, *Stolen Heritage: A Mexican-American's Rediscovery of His Family's Lost Land Grant*, ed. Thomas H. Krenecke (Austin, TX: Eakin Press, 1986), 178–79.

22. J. J. Linn, *Reminiscences of Fifty Years in Texas* (New York: D&J Sadlier and Co., 1883), 259; Grimes, 88, 135; Rose, 190–91.

23. Grimes, 129, 135; Huson, 213; Castañeda, *Our Catholic Heritage*, 6:284.

24. Grimes, 88.

25. Linn, 248; Grimes, 86.

26. Linn, 248; Grimes, 85–86.

27. Patricia de la Garza to T. Rusk, May 15, 1836, Rusk Papers, State Archives, Austin, TX; P. Dimmitt to T. Rusk, July, 1836, Rusk Papers, State Archives, Austin, TX; Passenger lists of Vessels Arriving in New Orleans, July 18, 1836, M259–14, Microfilm at New Orleans Public Library, New Orleans, LA. Grimes, in his book *300 Years in Victoria County*, maintains that the family "assembled at Linville and took ship for New Orleans" (p. 135). From the passenger lists of arriving ships in New Orleans, it is evident that the many families who left in June left from Matagorda, not Linnville. In Paul Lack, *Texas Revolutionary Experience* (College Station: Texas A&M University Press, 1992), 206, the Rusk Papers indicate that Rusk put the families aboard the *Durango* at Matagorda. That may have been Rusk's intent, but

they did not arrive at New Orleans on the *Durango*.

28. Fernando de León to Patricia de la Garza, June 11, 1835, vol. 2, p. 205 (new vol. 1, p. 404), VCCO; Patricia de la Garza de León by attorney José María Carvajal to Alexander G. Cochran, December 8, 1836, vol. 2, p. 208, VCCO; Patricia de la Garza to P. B. Cocke, Deed, January 24, 1837, vol. 1, p. 34, Deed Records, VCCO; Pleasant Branch Cocke of New Orleans to James H. Sheppherd of New Orleans, attorney for Isaac Franklin, also of New Orleans, Deed, July 5, 1837, vol. 2, p. 87, Deed Records, VCCO; María de Jesús de León to Pleasant B. Cocke, Transfer, September 1, 1854, vol. 6, p. 64, original sale January 23, 1837, in Louisiana, Deed Records, VCCO; P. B. Cocke to Robert Ruffin Barrow of Freebone, LA, November 16, 1841, vol. 1, p. 507 (new vol. 2, p. 728), Deed Records, VCCO.

29. Hammett, 80–81; Tax rolls for 1839, 1841, 1844, VCCO.

30. See family letters, Matiana Benavides to Patricio de León, in de León archives, Victoria County Public Library, Victoria, TX; marriage of Librada Benavides and Juan de Hoyos, 1860, and birth of their first child with Luz Escalera as godmother. Gerald E. Poyo and Gilberto Hinojosa, "Spanish Texas and Borderlands Historiography in Transition," *Journal of American History* 75 no. 2 (September 1988): 393–416; Hugo G. Nutini, *San Bernardino Contla: Marriage and Family Structure in a Tlaxcalan Municipio* (Pittsburgh: University of Pittsburgh Press, 1968), 19; William A. Vega et al., "Cohesion and Adaptability in Mexican-American and Anglo Families," *Journal of Marriage and the Family* 48 (November 1986): 857, 865; Elizabeth Anne Kuznesof, "The History of the Family in Latin America: A Critique of Recent Work," *Latin American Research Review* 24, no. 2 (1989): 168, 175; Ernest L. Schusky, *Variation in Kinship* (New York: Holt, Rinehart and Winston, 1974), 3.

31. Jesús F. de la Teja, "Pleasing and Fertile Desert: Land Grants in the San Antonio River Valley, 1718–1836," *South Texas Studies* (Spring 2000): 130–38.

32. Ibid., 103; *Ramon Musquiz v. M. M. Blake and others*, 24 Texas 461, VCCO.

33. Huson, 232.

34. *Patricia de la Garza v. Robert Carlisle and Bridget Quinn*, Case #24, Fall term 1849, settled Fall term 1851, 25–A District Clerk's Misc. Records, Civil Court Docket, Archives, Victoria College/University of Houston, Victoria, TX.

35. Petition of Patricia de la Garza, May term, 1847, filed for record December 29, 1848, vol. 1, p. 527, VCCO.

36. Final Record of Guardian, May 1847, vol. 1, p. 527, Probate Records, VCCO; Fernando de León to William Dally, Lease, February 16, 1847, vol. 3, p. 131, and Fernando de León to Alva Fitzpatrick, January 13, 1847, vol. 3, p. 105, Deed Records, VCCO; Patricia de la Garza from R. Carlisle and Bridget Quinn, Mortgage, September 23, 1838, vol. 1, p. 32, Deed Records, VCCO; Will of Patricia de la Garza, Probate Records, VCCO.

37. Ibid.

38. Will of Patricio [*sic*] Garza de León, October 17, 1850, vol. 2, p. 591, Probate Records, VCCO.

39. Marriage Records for Fernando de León and Luz Escalera de León, St. Mary's Church records, Catholic Archives, Austin, TX; Adoption records, Francisco Santiago de León, August 1850, VCCO.

40. Will of Patricio [*sic*] Garza de León, VCCO.

41. Ibid. Gilbert G. González and Raúl Fernández, "Chicano History: Transcending Cultural Models," *Pacific Historical Review* 63, no. 4 (November 1994): 480–81. The Aldretes of Refugio had retained large quantities of land since José Miguel Aldrete, as a Mexican government official, had acquired far more than his original league and labor. The Aldretes remained powerful landowners in Refugio until the 1880s; see Huson, 212–15.

## Chapter 10

1. Dramatization based on Etta D. Mason, Field Worker, "Interview with Nancy Fulsom Cox," Choctaw Freedman, Atoka, Oklahoma, in *Indian Pioneer History Collection*, Oklahoma Historical Society, Oklahoma City, IPH I, vol. II, nos. 309–10.

2. "Indian Territory" refers to the land area that is today the state of Oklahoma. From 1830 to 1906 it was the land of indigenous peoples from all over the United States who were dispossessed from their homelands and forced into permanent exile. The Choctaw Nation was the portion of Indian Territory owned by the Choctaws. From 1830 until 1866, Choctaw Nation included the southern half of what became the state of Oklahoma. After the Civil War, the United States confiscated the western half of Choctaw Nation as war reparations, since the Choctaws sided with the Confederacy.

3. John Swanton, *Source Material for the Social and Ceremonial Life of the Choctaw Indians*, Smithsonian Institution Bureau of Ethnology, Bulletin 103, reprinted and with an introduction by Virginia Pounds Brown (Birmingham, AL: Birmingham Public Library Press, 1993), 239–41; John Swanton, "An Early Account of the Choctaw Indians," *Memoirs of the American Anthropological Association* 5, no. 2 (1909): 64; H. B. Cushman, *History of the Choctaw, Chickasaw, and Natchez Indians*, ed. Angie Debo (Greenville, TX: Headlight Printing House, 1899), 60, 230–31, 258, 367–68; George P. Folsom, *The Vindicator* (New Boggy, Choctaw Nation), December 8, 1875; Adam Hodgson, *Letters from North America, Written During a Tour of the United States and Canada* (London: Hurst, Robinson and Co., 1824), 214–15; David I. Bushnell, *The Choctaw of Bayou Lacomb St. Tammany Parish, Louisiana*, Bureau of American Ethnology, Bulletin 48 (Washington, DC: US Government Printing Office, 1909), 23; Charles Hudson, *The Southeastern Indians* (Nashville: University of Tennessee Press, 1976), 363–64; Angie Debo, *The Rise and Fall of the Choctaw Republic*, The Civilization of the American Indian Series (Norman: University of Oklahoma Press, 1923, 1961), 7, 22, 45–46, 177; Donna L. Akers, *Living in the Land of Death: The Choctaw Nation, 1830–1860* (Lansing: Michigan State University Press, 2004), 27–28, 64.

4. For more information on Oklahoma's African American towns, see Hannibal Johnson, *Acres of Aspiration: The All Black Towns in Oklahoma* (Austin, TX: Eakin

Press, 2002), 7–15; and Murray R. Wickett, *Whites, Native Americans, and African Americans in Oklahoma, 1865–1907* (Baton Rouge: Louisiana State University Press, 2000), 85. For information on Robert M. Jones, see Michael L. Bruce, "Our Best Men Are Fast Leaving Us': The Life and Times of Robert M. Jones," *The Chronicles of Oklahoma* 66, no. 1 (1988): 294–305.

5. Henry Benson, *Life Among the Choctaw Indians* (New York: Johnson Reprint Company, 1970), 33–34; and *Annual Report of the Commissioner of Indian Affairs* (Washington, DC: US Government Printing Office, 1836), 391; 1837, 541–42; 1843, 336; 1852, 412; *Senate Documents*, 23rd Cong., 1st Sess., No. 512, III, 149, show that in 1831, a census of the Choctaw Nation conducted by the United States government recorded 19,554 Choctaws, 97 white citizens, and 248 African slaves.

6. Tiya Miles, *Ties That Bind: The Story of an Afro-Cherokee Family in Slavery and Freedom* (Berkeley: University of California Press, 2005), 41–43; and Theda Perdue, *Slavery and the Evolution of Cherokee Society* (Knoxville: University of Tennessee Press, 1979), 57–58.

7. "Interview of Polly Colbert," *The WPA Oklahoma Slave Narratives*, ed. T. Linsay Baker and Julie P. Baker (Norman: University of Oklahoma Press, 1996), 86–88; "Interview of Phyllis Petite," 317, 320; "Interview of Matilda Poe," 324–26; and "Interview of Morris Sheppard," 375–82.

8. Swanton, *Source Material*, 163; Perdue, *Slavery*, 4–8.

9. Perdue, 50–51.

10. See Carolyn Johnson, *Cherokee Women in Crisis: Trail of Tears, Civil War, and Allotment: 1838–1907* (Tuscaloosa: University of Alabama Press, 2003), for a discussion of the question of the declension of women's power in Cherokee society.

11. Johnson, 4–5.

12. Albert Memmi, *The Colonizer and the Colonized* (New York: Orion Press, 1965), 71.

13. "Interview of Betty Robertson," *WPA Oklahoma Slave Narratives*, 355.

14. Lucinda Davis, *WPA Oklahoma Slave Narratives*, 108.

15. Miles, 29.

16. "Treaty with the Cherokee, 1866," *Indian Affairs, Laws and Treaties*, vol. 2, ed. Charles J. Kappler (Washington, DC: US Government Printing Office, 1904), 934; "Treaty with the Choctaw and Chickasaw," 919–20; "Treaty with the Creeks, 1866," 932–33; "Treaty with the Seminoles, 1866," 911.

17. *Report of the Commissioner of Indian Affairs*, 1865, 318–19.

18. Reginald Horsman, *Race and Manifest Destiny: The Origins of American Racial Anglo-Saxonism* (Cambridge, MA: Harvard University Press, 1981), 75–81; *Report of the Commissioner of Indian Affairs* 1865, 306; Israel Folsom to Peter P. Pitchlynn, February 23, 1848, Peter P. Pitchlynn Collection, Box 2, File 2, Western History Collection, University of Oklahoma, Norman, OK (hereafter cited as Pitchlynn Collection); Solomon to Master, December 11, 1857, Box 3, File 3, Pitchlynn Collection; Memmi 120.

19. Memmi, 120.

20. *U.S. Statutes at Large*, 14:769; Kappler, *Laws and Treaties*, 2:918–31; and Debo, *The Rise and Fall*, 100–105.

21. Mason, "Interview with Nancy Fulsom Cox."

22. Cushman, 386–87.

23. Edmond Folsom to Peter P. Pitchlynn, August 12, 1832, Box 1, File 30, Pitchlynn Collection; Israel Folsom to Peter P. Pitchlynn, September 24, 1841, and December 7, 1841, Box 1, Files 68 and 71, Pitchlynn Collection; David Folsom to Peter P. Pitchlynn, January 16, 1846, Box 1, File 100, Pitchlynn Collection; and Jacob Folsom to Peter P. Pitchlynn, January 19, 1858, Box 3, File 11, Pitchlynn Collection. By the mid- to late nineteenth century, there were many Folsom families, some of whom were prosperous slave-holding plantation owners. Cushman, 325–327; and Sampson Folsom to Peter P. Pitchlynn, February 12, 1860, Box 3, File 61, Pitchlynn Collection.

24. Hudson, 328, 355, 363; Debo, *History*, 46–47.

25. *Niles Register*, 37 (1829), 181.

26. Potipher Tembo, "Suspected Witches Find Refuge in Kaleni Hills," *The Times of Zambia*, July 7, 2005, www.globalaging.org/elderrights/world/2005/witches.htm.

27. William G. McLoughlin, *Cherokee Renascence in the New Republic* (Princeton, NJ: Princeton University Press, 1986), 13–14; Raymond D. Fogelson, "An Analysis of Cherokee Sorcery and Witchcraft," in *Four Centuries of Southeastern Indians*, ed. Charles Hudson (Athens: University of Georgia Press, 1875), 117, 127.

28. Joel Martin, *Sacred Revolt: The Muskogees' Struggle for a New World* (Boston: Beacon Press, 1991), 177–82; and Hudson, 175, 177–82.

29. Marie-Helene Huet, "Deadly Fears: Dom Augustin Calmet's Vampires and the Rule Over Death," *Eighteenth-Century Life* 21 (May 1997): 222.

30. Mason, "Interview with Nancy Fulsom Cox," 310.

## Chapter 11

1. Loretta Fowler, *The Columbia Guide to American Indians of the Great Plains* (New York: Columbia University Press, 2003), 11.

2. Ibid., 10–11.

3. Ibid., 19, 17.

4. Ibid., 28.

5. Pekka Hämäläinen, *Comanche Empire* (New Haven, CT: Yale University Press, 2008), 239.

6. Quoted in Hämäläinen, 248.

7. Hämäläinen, 248.

8. Carol Lipscomb, "Comanche Indians," in *The New Handbook of Texas*, 6 vols., ed. Ron Tyler, (Austin: The Texas State Historical Association, 1996), 2:242–45; Randolph B. Campbell, *Gone to Texas: A History of the Lone Star State* (New York: Oxford University Press, 2003), 63.

9. Morris W. Foster, *Being Comanche: A Social History of an American Indian Community* (Tucson: University of Arizona Press, 1991), 65, 183.

10. Fowler, 146, 152–53.

11. Foster, 284–90.

12. Barbara A. Hail, ed., *Gifts of Pride and Love: Kiowa and Comanche Cradles* (Providence, RI: Brown University, Haffenreffer Museum of Anthropology, 2000), 63.

13. Hämäläinen, 255. For more information on Sarah Ann Horn, see also Michael Tate, "Comanche Captives: People Between Two Worlds," *The Chronicles of Oklahoma* 72, no. 3 (1994): 228–63.

14. Hämäläinen, 250.

15. Ibid., 253.

16. Ibid., 248–49.

17. Ibid., 224.

18. William Chebahtah and Nancy McGown Minor, *Chevato: The Story of the Apache Warrior Who Captured Herman Lehmann* (Lincoln: University of Nebraska Press, 2007), 98. Adopting into the kinship structure appears to be uncommon among the Wichitas, as opposed to the Comanches. According to Juliana Barr in *Peace Came in the Form of a Woman: Indians and Spaniards in the Texas Borderlands* (Chapel Hill: University of North Carolina Press, 2007), the Wichitas maintained distinctions between captives and tribal members. They did not "marry many captive women or adopt many children, particularly Spanish captives, into their families" (p. 250). For an early essay on the role of Plains Indian women in raids, see Valerie Shier Mathes, "A New Look at the Role of Women in Indian Society," *American Indian Quarterly* 2, no. 2 (Summer 1975): 131–39. Although covering an earlier era, see also James Brook, "'This Evil Extends Especially . . . to the Feminine Sex': Negotiating Captivity in the New Mexico Borderlands," *Feminist Studies* 22, no. 2 (Summer 1996): 279–309.

19. Chebahtah and Minor, 100–101.

20. Ibid., 103.

21. Hämäläinen, 255.

22. Fowler, 24.

23. Barr, 247–48.

24. Barr, 277.

25. Chebahtah and Minor, 174.

26. Elliot West, "Trails and Footprints: The Past of the Future Southern Plains," in *The Future of the Southern Plains*, ed. Sherry Smith (Norman: University of Oklahoma Press, 2001), 27–30; and Margaret Schmidt Hacker, "Parker, Cynthia Ann," in Tyler, *The New Handbook of Texas*, 5:57–58. See also Tate, 22–263.

27. Hämäläinen, 326.

28. Ibid.

29. Campbell, 291–95.

30. Hämäläinen, 254.

31. Merial Dorchester, quoted in Rebecca Herring, "Their Work Was Never Done: Women Missionaries on the Kiowa-Comanche Reservation," *The Chronicles of*

*Oklahoma*, no. 1 (Spring 1986), 70.

32. David E. Jones, *Sanapia: Comanche Medicine Woman* (New York: Holt, Rinehart and Winston, 1972), 22. See also the section on Sanapia in Helen Jaskoski, "'My Heart Will Go Out': Healing Songs of Native American Women," *International Journal of Women's Studies* 4, no. 2 (1989): 118–43.

33. Hail, 67.

34. Ibid., 68.

35. Deena Gonzalez, *Refusing the Favor: The Spanish-Mexican Women of Santa Fe, 1820–1880* (Oxford: Oxford University Press, 1999), 5.

36. H. Allen Anderson, "Romero, Casimero," *Handbook of Texas Online*, accessed July 29, 2008, www.tshaonline.org/handbook/online/articles/RR/froaq.html.

37. Sarah Deutsch, "Women and Intercultural Relations: The Case of Hispanic New Mexico and Colorado," *Signs* 12, no. 4 (1978): 722.

38. Ibid., 723–24.

39. Virginia Scharff, *Twenty Thousand Roads: Women, Movement and the West* (Berkeley: University of California Press, 2003), 45.

40. Ibid.

41. Gonzalez, 10.

42. William Robbins, *Colony and Empire: The Transformation of the American West* (Lawrence: University of Kansas Press, 1994), 29.

43. Gonzalez, 10.

44. Vicki L. Ruiz, *From Out of the Shadows: Mexican Women in Twentieth-Century America* (New York: Oxford University Press, 1998), 6.

45. Gonzalez, 104.

46. Ruiz, 73.

47. Sara Estela Ramírez, quoted in Ruiz, 99.

48. Ruiz, 99.

49. Soledad Peña, quoted in Ruiz, 99.

50. Ruiz, 7–8.

51. Ibid., 3.

52. Ibid., 11–12.

53. David Gutiérrez, quoted in Ruiz, 6.

54. Frank Van Nuys, *Americanizing the West: Race, Immigrants, and Citizenship, 1890–1930* (Lawrence: University Press of Kansas, 2002), 1.

55. Ibid., 28.

56. Deutsch, 736; Van Nuys, 123.

57. Van Nuys, 27. For further discussion, see David G. Gutierrez, *Walls and Mirrors: Mexican Americans, Mexican Immigrants, and the Politics of Ethnicity* (Berkeley: University of California Press, 1995).

58. Deutsch, 737.

59. For a discussion on the gendered politics of the League of United Latin American Citizens, established in Corpus Christi, Texas, in 1929, see Cynthia E. Orozco's essay, "Alice Dickerson Montemayor: Feminism and Mexican American Politics in the 1930s," in *Writing the Range: Race, Class, and Culture in the Women's West*, ed.

Elizabeth Jameson and Susan Armitage (Norman: University of Oklahoma Press, 1997), 435–56.

60. Scharff, 37.

61. Richard White, *"It's Your Misfortune and None of My Own": A New History of the American West* (Norman: University of Oklahoma Press, 1993), 220–22.

62. T. C. Richardson and Harwood P. Hinton, "Ranching," in Tyler, 5:429–33.

63. William Robbins, *Colony and Empire*, 71.

64. Francis, B. Vick, "Cornelia Wadsworth Ritchie Adair," in *Texas Women on the Cattle Trails*, ed. Sarah R. Massey (College Station: Texas A&M Press, 2006), 151–52.

65. Cornelia Wadsworth Adair, quoted in Massey, 153.

66. H. Allen Anderson, "Goodnight, Charles," in Tyler, 3:240–43; H. Allen Anderson, "Adair, John George," in Tyler, 1:23.

67. Vick, 154.

68. Ibid.

69. Nancy Baker Jones, "Adair, Cornelia Wadsworth," in Tyler, 1:22–23.

70. Michael Thurgood Haynes, "Mary Ann (Molly) Dryer Goodnight," in Massey, 135–36.

71. Joyce Gibson Roach, "Goodnight, Mary Ann Dyer [Molly]," in Tyler, 3:243–44; Mrs. Clyde W. Warwick, ed., *The Randall County Story* (Hereford, TX: Pioneer Book Publishers, 1969), 15.

72. Jones, 1:22–23.

73. William O. Stillman, "Prevention of Cruelty to Animals," *Proceedings of the Academy of Political Science in the City of New York* 2, no. 4, Organization for Social Work (July 1912): 155. The first Society for the Prevention of Cruelty to Animals was established in London in 1834; the first chapter in the United States was established in New York in 1866.

74. Haynes, 142.

75. Warwick, 33; Dolly Thompson Taylor to Wilma Hixon, interview, July 18 and 27, 1936, Panhandle-Plains Historical Museum Research Center (hereafter cited as PPHMRC).

76. Memoirs of Mrs. John Wesley Hough, given to Hellen Heath, July 6, 1936, PPHMRC.

77. Sandra Gail Teichmann, ed., *Woman of the Plains: The Journals and Stories of Nellie M. Perry* (College Station: Texas A&M University Press, 2000), 21–22, 27.

78. Pauline Durrett Robertson and R. L. Robertson, "Mystery Woman of Old Tascosa: The Legend of Frenchy McCormick, 1852–1941," in *Panhandle Pilgrimage: Illustrated Tales Tracing History in the Texas Panhandle*, ed. Pauline Durrett Robertson and R. L. Robertson (Amarillo, TX: Paramount Publishing Co., 1977), 3–25. Much later Tascosa became famous as Cal Farley's Boys Ranch; Ernest R. Archambeau, *Old Tascosa, 1886–1888* (Canyon, TX: Panhandle-Plains Historical Society, 1966), 7–8, 20.

79. Della Tyler Key, *In the Cattle Country: History of Potter County* (Amarillo, TX: Tyler–Berkley Company, 1961), 254–65.

80. C. Robert Haywood, *Victorian West: Class and Culture in Kansas Cattle Towns*

(Lawrence: University Press of Kansas, 1991), 34.

81. Key, 107–17. For a concise essay that describes changes brought about by technology for white and black women in Texas, see Angela Boswell, "From Farm to Future: Women's Journey Through Twentieth-Century Texas," in *Twentieth-Century Texas*, ed. John W. Storey and Mary L. Kelley (Denton: University of North Texas Press, 2008), 105–31.

82. Warwick, 70–80.

83. Merton L. Dillon, "Religion in Lubbock," in *A History of Lubbock*, ed. Lawrence L. Graves (Lubbock: West Texas Museum Association, 1963), 455–60.

84. H. Allen Andersen, "Mercy Academy," in Tyler, 4:632; J. P. Reynolds, "Goodnight College," in Tyler, 3:244; Colby D. Hall, "Hereford Christian College," in Tyler, 3:569; H. Allen Andersen, "Clarendon College," in Tyler, 2:130–31. For a concise history on education in Oklahoma, see Bobby H. Johnson, "From Sod House to Lyceum: Education in the Oklahoma Territory, 1889–1906," in *The American West: Essays in Honor of W. Eugene Hollon*, ed. Ronald Lora (Toledo, OH: University of Toledo, 1980), 231–49.

85. James D. Hamlin, "Amarillo College," in Tyler, 1:143–44; Nancy Beck Young, "West Texas A&M University," in Tyler, 6:901–2; Lawrence L. Graves, "Texas Tech University," in Tyler, 6:436.

86. Lawrence L. Graves, "Economic, Social, and Cultural Developments," in Graves, 214–15; Lawrence L. Graves, "Education, Welfare, and Recreation," in Graves, 541–42.

87. Key, 229–31, 234.

88. Ibid., 236–37, 239–42.

89. Warwick, 225, 262, 285, 292; The (Canyon City, TX) *Stayer*, 1896–1903, and *The Canyon City* (Texas) *News*, 1903–1920; H. Allen Anderson, "Hereford, TX," in Tyler, 3:568–69; and H. Allen Anderson, "Ochiltree, TX," in Tyler, 4:1103.

## Chapter 12

1. *The Oklahoman*, January 15, 2006. See also "NOAA Warns New Year Will Bring Serious Threat of Wildfires," Environmental News/Science News, Community Dispatch.com, accessed January 13, 2006, http://community dispatch.com/artman/publish/article_3285.shtml; "Wildfires Ravage Southern Plains," CBS News, accessed January 13, 2006, www.cbsnews.com/stories/2005/12/28/nationa/main1166988_page2.shtml; R. L. Tortorelli, "Floods and Droughts: Oklahoma, National Water Summary, 1988–89: TS Geological Survey," USGS Water Resources of Oklahoma, accessed April 25, 2005, http://ok.water.usgs.gov/drought/drought.paper.html; and Donald Worster, *Dust Bowl: The Southern Plains in the 1930s* (New York: Oxford University Press, 1979), 26. For a collection of essays on twentieth-century social, economic, and political history of the southern Great Plains, see Sherry L. Smith, ed., *The Future of the Southern Great Plains* (Norman: University of Oklahoma Press, 2003).

2. John Steinbeck, *The Grapes of Wrath* (New York: Viking Press, 1939). Sources on

the "Okie" migration are James N. Gregory, *American Exodus: The Dust Bowl Migration and Okie Culture in California* (New York: Oxford University Press, 1991); Marsha Weisiger, *Land of Plenty: Oklahomans in the Cotton Fields of Arizona, 1933–1942* (Norman: University of Oklahoma Press, 1995); William Howarth, "The Okies Beyond the Dust Bowl," *National Geographic* 166 (September 1984), 323–48; and Fabiola Cabeza de Baca, *We Fed Them Cactus* (Albuquerque: University of New Mexico Press, 1954), 178.

3. Cabeza de Baca, x, 11, 171–78. See also Sarah Deutsch, *No Separate Refuge: Culture, Class, and Gender on an Anglo-Hispanic Frontier in the American Southwest, 1880–1940* (New York: Oxford University Press, 1987).

4. Joan M. Jensen, "New Mexico Farm Women, 1900–1940," *Promise to the Land: Essays on Rural Women* (Albuquerque: University of New Mexico Press, 1991), 84, 83–96.

5. Joan M. Jensen, "Crossing Ethnic Barriers in the Southwest: Women's Agricultural Extension Education, 1914–1940," in *Promise to the Land*, 221–30; Joan M. Jensen, "'I've Worked, I'm Not Afraid of Work': Farm Women in New Mexico, 1920–1940," and "Canning Comes to New Mexico: Women and the Agricultural Extension Service, 1914–1919," in *New Mexico Women, Intercultural Perspectives*, ed. Joan M. Jensen and Darlis Miller (Albuquerque: University of New Mexico Press, 1986), 227–55, 201–26.

6. Virginia C. Purdy, "'Dust to Eat': A Document from the Dust Bowl," *The Chronicles of Oklahoma* 58 (1980): 440–54; Caroline Henderson, *Letters from the Dust Bowl*, ed. Alvin O. Turner (Norman: University of Oklahoma Press, 2001), 142. The historiography of the Dust Bowl is extensive, and nearly all sources rely to some extent on firsthand accounts. Major works include Donald Worster's previously cited *Dust Bowl: The Southern Plains in the 1930s*; Paul Bonnifield, *The Dust Bowl: Men, Dirt, and Depression* (Albuquerque: University of New Mexico Press, 1979); R. Douglas Hurt, *Dust Bowl* (Chicago: Nelson-Hall, 1981); John R. Wunder, Frances W. Kaye, and Vernon Carstensen, eds., *Americans View Their Dust Bowl Experience* (Boulder: University Press of Colorado, 1999); Timothy Egan, *The Worst Hard Time: The Untold Story of Those Who Survived the Great American Dust Bowl* (Boston: Houghton Mifflin Company, 2006).

7. Turner, 20, 149–50.

8. Ibid., 3–29, 210–13.

9. Under the sharecropping system, poor families contracted annually with landowners to work the fields for a portion of the crop. The landowner provided them with housing and supplies. At harvest the family sold its crop and paid its debts to the landowner. The system created a continual cycle of poverty. Etta Carroll, quoted in Rebecca Sharpless, *Fertile Ground, Narrow Choices: Women on Texas Cotton Farms, 1900–1940* (Chapel Hill: University of North Carolina Press, 1999), 247.

10. Rebecca Sharpless, "Hester Calvert, Farm Wife," in *The Human Tradition in Texas*, ed. Ty Cashion and Jesus F. de la Teja (Wilmington, DE: Scholarly Resources Inc., 2001), 115–27.

11. Ibid., 124. See also Martha Mitten Allen, "Women on the Land," in *Texas Country: The Changing Rural Scene*, ed. Glen E. Lich and Dona B. Reeves-Marquardt (College Station: Texas A&M University Press, 1986), 119–33; Jeane Westin, *Making Do: How Women Survived the '30s* (Chicago: Follett Publishing Company, 1976); Marilyn Irvin Holt, *Linoleum, Better Babies & The Modern Farm Woman, 1890–1930* (Albuquerque: University of New Mexico Press, 1995); Katherine Jellison, *Entitled to Power: Farm Women and Technology, 1913–1963* (Chapel Hill: University of North Carolina Press, 1993).

12. Turner, 199, 215–16, 28. A thorough examination of the *Brown v. Board of Education* Supreme Court case that ended segregation in public schools is available at www.lib.umich.edu/exhibits/brownarchive.

13. Deutsch, 163, 163–67.

14. Ibid., 177, 181.

15. Myrtle Calvert Dodd, quoted in Sharpless, *Fertile Ground, Narrow Choices*, 12–15, 148.

16. Ibid., 159–167.

17. Eddie Stimpson, quoted in Sharpless, *Fertile Ground, Narrow Choices*, 70–71, 180–86. On the Orville and Naomi Williams tenant farm in McClain County, Oklahoma, this system continued into the 1950s. Itinerant black pickers were expected to leave at the end of each day after they collected their pay: one dollar per hundredweight. Personal communication with author, Oklahoma City, OK, 1983.

18. "Okies on Record Ask Roosevelt to Remedy Plight," Voices from the Dust Bowl Scrapbook, Library of Congress, accessed May 5, 2006, http://memory.loc.gov/cgibin/ampage?collId=afcts&fileNam=sb001.db&recNum=18.

19. Henry Wallace, quoted in Jellison, "A Chance to Live as the City Sisters," *The Great Depression and the New Deal*, 98–99, 67–105; Helen Catlettt, quoted in Allen, 129.

20. John C. Belcher, "Fertility of the Village Residents of Oklahoma," *Social Forces* 24 (March 1946): 328–31; Robert T. McMillan, "Old-Age Dependency in Oklahoma," *Social Forces* 26 (October 1947): 50–57; Johnston Murray, "Oklahoma is in a Mess!" *Saturday Evening Post* (April 30, 1955): 19.

21. R. Douglas Hurt, "Return of the Dust Bowl: The Filthy Fifties," *Journal of the West* 18 (October 1979): 87, 85–93; Arthur H. Doerr, "Dry Conditions in Oklahoma in the 1930s and 1950s as Delimited by the Original Thornthwaite Climatic Classification," *Great Plains Journal* 2 (Spring 1963): 67–76.

22. Jane Adams, "The *Farm Journal*'s Discourse of Farm Women's Femininity," *Anthropology and Humanism* 29, no. 1 (2004): 45–62.

23. Ruth Sayre, quoted in Adams, 51; Gertrude Dieken, quoted in Adams, 51; Frances Bolton, quoted in Adams, 52.

24. Adams, 52–57.

25. Delois Alexander, "From Microwaves to Module Builders, Women in Farming Are Able to Adapt," *Commentator* (Spring 2002): 7, accessed March 8, 2006, www.pcca.com/Publications/Commentator/2002/Spring/page03.asp; Delores

Marie Wilmot, quoted in Brad Lookingbill, "'A God-Forsaken Place': Folk Escha-
tology and the Dust Bowl'" in Wunder et al., 163, 151–69.

26. Etta Carroll, quoted in Sharpless, *Fertile Ground, Narrow Choices*, 215, 200–17.
27. Alice Owens Caulfield, quoted in Sharpless, *Fertile Ground, Narrow Choices*,
215–16.
28. William W. Savage, Jr., "Rural Images, Rural Values, and American Culture: A
Comment," in *Rural Oklahoma*, ed. Donald E. Green (Oklahoma City: Oklahoma
Historical Society, 1977), 118–20.
29. Warren Cohen, "The Drought of 1996," *U.S. News and World Report* 120 (June 10,
1996): 35; Paul Gray and Nancy Harbert, "Bone Dry," *Time* 147 (June 10, 1996):
44; "Summer Sizzle Continues in Texas, Southern Plains," CNN.com, August 3,
1998, accessed January 12, 2006, www.cnn.com/US/9808/03/heat.wave.o2; and
James N. Thurman, "Oklahoma in the Grip of New Dust Bowl," *Christian Science
Monitor* 90 (August 24, 1998): 1.
30. Most of the off-farm jobs held by women are within driving distance, allowing
them to live at home. This, of course, prolongs their workday. Jill L. Findeis and
Hema Swaminathan, "Gender and Intergenerational Transfer of the Farm: Its
Influence on Multiple Job-Holding and On-Farm Decision-Making Among U.S.
Farm Women," Working Paper 03–06 (Department of Agricultural Economics
and Rural Sociology, Pennsylvania State University, 2003), 1–13; William Sander,
"The Economics of Divorce in the Farm Sector," *North Central Journal of Agricul-
tural Economics* 8 (January 1986): 1–6. See also Sandra Shackel, "Ranch and Farm
Women in the Contemporary American West," in *Western Women's Lives: Conti-
nuity and Change in the Twentieth Century*, ed. Sandra K. Shackel (Albuquerque:
University of New Mexico Press, 2003).
31. Findeis and Swaminathan, 1–13.
32. Kimberly A. Zeuli and Robert P. King, "Gender Difference in Farm Management,"
*Review of Agricultural Economics* 20 (Autumn-Winter 1998): 513–29; Economic
Research Service, Unites States Department of Agriculture, "State Fact Sheets:
Oklahoma," accessed April 25, 2005, www.ers.usda.gov/State Facts/OK.htm;
"Increase Reported in Women-Run Farms," *Herald Democrat Online*, accessed
April 1, 2005, www.heralddemocrat.com/articles/2005/03/18/life agriculture/
iq_1776917.txt.
33. Savage, 115; "Voices of American Farm Women," Mathematical Association of
America, accessed May 5, 2006, www.maa.org/exhi_usa/exhibitions/farm woman/
pg_farmwomen.pdf; and "From Microwaves to Module Builders," *Commentator*,
accessed March 8, 2006, www.pcca.com/Publications/Commentator/2001/Winter/
page04.asp.

# Bibliography

## Introduction

Ayres, Edward L., Patricia Nelson Limerick, Stephen Nissembaum, and Peter S. Onuf. *All Over the Map: Rethinking American Region.* Baltimore: Johns Hopkins University Press, 1996.

Bender, Thomas. "Whole and Parts: The Need for Synthesis in American History." *The Journal of American History* 73, no. 1 (June 1986): 120–36.

"Great Books of the Great Plains," Plains Humanities Alliance, The Center for Great Plains. Accessed June 20, 2007, http://plainshumanities.unl.edu.

Jameson, Betsy, and Susan Armitage. *Writing the Range: Race, Class and Culture in the Women's West.* Norman: University of Oklahoma Press, 1997.

Johnson, David, ed. *Regionalism Reconsidered: New Approaches to the Field.* New York: Garland Publishing, 1994.

Lansing, Michael. "Feminist Geography in US Western History." *Journal of Historical Geography* 29 (2003): 230–47.

Riley, Glenda. *The Female Frontier: A Comparative View of Women on the Prairies and the Plains.* Lawrence: University Press of Kansas, 1988.

Smithwick, Noah. *The Evolution of a State or Recollections of Old Texas Days.* Austin: University of Texas Press, 1983. First published Austin, TX: Gammel Book Company, 1900.

Webb, Walter Prescott. *The Great Plains.* Boston: Ginn and Company, 1931.

West, Elliot. *The Way West: Essays on the Central Plains.* Albuquerque: University of New Mexico Press, 1995.

Wishart, David. *Encyclopedia of the Great Plains.* Lincoln: University of Nebraska Press, 2004.

## Northern Plains Essays

"16,000 Canadians Will Return with Brides." *Syracuse* (New York) *Herald Journal,* December 15, 1943.

"A Conversation with Mary Brave Bird." *The American Indian Quarterly* 24 (Summer 2000): 182–93.

Aadland, Dan. *Women and Warriors of the Plains: The Pioneer Photography of Julia E. Tuell.* Missoula, MT: Mountain Press Publishing Co., 2000.

Albers, Patricia. "Introduction: New Perspectives on Plains Indian Women." In Albers and Medicine, *The Hidden Half,* 1–26.

———. "Sioux Women in Transition: A Study of Their Changing Status in Domestic and Capitalist Sectors of Production." In Albers and Medicine, *The Hidden Half,* 175–236.

Albers, Patricia, and Beatrice Medicine. *The Hidden Half: Studies of Plains Indian Women.* Lanham, MD: University Press of America, 1983.

Alexander, Ruth Ann. "Gentle Evangelists: Women in Dakota Episcopal Missions, 1867–1900." *South Dakota History* 24 (Fall/Winter 1994): 174–93.

Anderson, Kathie Ryckman. "Era Bell Thompson: A North Dakota Daughter." *North Dakota History* 49 (Fall 1982): 11–18.

Anderson, Robert. "The Northern Cheyenne War Mothers." *Anthropological Quarterly* 29, no. 3 (July 1956): 82–90.

Anthony, Susan B., and Ida Husted Harper, eds. *The History of Woman Suffrage.* Rochester, NY: Susan B. Anthony, 1902.

Barbie, Donna. "Sacagawea: The Making of a Myth." In *Sifters: Native American Women's Lives,* edited by Theda Perdue, 60–76. Oxford: Oxford University Press, 2001.

Barr, Juliana. *Peace Came in the Form of a Woman: Indians and Spaniards in the Texas Borderlands.* Chapel Hill: University of North Carolina Press, 2007.

———. "From Captive to Slave: Commodifying Indian Women on the Borderlands." *Journal of American History* 92, no. 1 (June 2005): 19–46.

Beeton, Beverly. *Women Vote in the West: The Woman Suffrage Movement, 1869–1896.* New York: Garland Publishing, 1986.

Beeton, Beverly, and G. Thomas Edwards. "Susan B. Anthony's Woman Suffrage Crusade in the American West." *Journal of the West* 21 (Summer 1982): 5–15.

Binnie-Clark, Georgina. *Wheat & Women.* Toronto: University of Toronto Press, 1979.

Board, John C. "The Lady from Montana." *Montana* 17, no. 3 (Summer 1967): 2–17.

Boesch, Olava Kornelia Holland. Transcribed interview by Elaine Lindgren, October 18, 1983. Carrington, ND. Institute for Regional Studies, H. Elaine Lindgren Papers, MS 292, Box 3, Folder S4. Fargo, ND.

Boller, Henry A. *Among the Indians: Four Years on the Upper Missouri, 1858–1862.* Edited by Milo Milton Quaife. Lincoln: University of Nebraska Press, 1972.

———. "Henry A. Boller: Missouri River Fur Trader." *North Dakota History* 33, nos. 3 and 4 (Spring and Summer 1966). Reprint, Bismarck, ND: The State Historical Society of North Dakota, 1966.

Bolton, Herbert Eugene. *Coronado, Knight of Pueblos and Plains*. With an introduction by John L. Kessell. Albuquerque: University of New Mexico Press, 1990.

Bowers, Alfred W. *Hidatsa Social and Ceremonial Organization*. Washington, DC: US Government Printing Office, 1963. Reprint, Lincoln: University of Nebraska Press, 1992.

———. *Mandan Social and Ceremonial Organization*. Chicago: University of Chicago Press, 1950. Reprint, Moscow: University of Idaho Press, 1991.

Boyer, Suzanne. "Exhibition Features 80 Portraits of War Brides." *The Moose Jaw Times Herald*, September 6, 2008.

Brave Bird, Mary, and Richard Erdoes. *Ohitika Woman*. New York: Grove Press, 1993.

Braxton, Joanne M. *Black Women Writing Autobiography: A Tradition Within a Tradition*. Philadelphia: Temple University Press, 1989.

Brooks, James F. *Captives and Cousins: Slavery, Kinship, and Community in the Southwest Borderlands*. Chapel Hill: University of North Carolina Press, 2002.

Brown, Dee. *Bury My Heart at Wounded Knee*. New York: Bantam Books, 1970.

Brown, Jennifer. *Strangers in Blood: Fur Trade Company Families in Indian Country*. Vancouver: University of British Columbia Press, 1980.

Butler, Cheryl A. "'Janey Canuck': Experiences of World War II British War Brides Who Emigrated to Canada." Master's thesis, University of Toronto, 1995.

Calloway, Collin G. *One Vast Winter Count: The Native American West Before Lewis and Clark*. Lincoln: University of Nebraska Press, 2003.

Campbell, Maria. *Halfbreed*. Lincoln and London: University of Nebraska Press, 1973.

"Canadian War Brides—60 Years." Veteran Affairs Canada. Accessed March 1, 2010, www.vac-acc.gc.ca/remembers/sub.cfm?source=history/secondwar/warbrides.

Carter, Sarah, Lesley Erickson, Patricia Roome, and Char Smith, eds. *Unsettled Pasts: Reconceiving the West Through Women's History*. Calgary, AB: University of Calgary Press, 2006.

———. "First Nations Women of Prairie Canada in the Early Reserve Years, the 1870s to the 1920s: A Preliminary Inquiry." In *Women of the First Nations*, edited by Christine Miller and Patricia Chuchryk, 51–75. Winnipeg: University of Manitoba Press, 1996.

Carr, Paul R., and Darren E. Lund. *Great White North? Exploring Whiteness, Privilege, and Identity in Education*. New York: Sense Publishers, 2007.

Carrington, Frances C. *My Army Life and the Fort Phil Kearney Massacre*. With an introduction by Shannon Smith Calitri. Lincoln: University of Nebraska Press, 2004.

Cather, Willa. *My Ántonia*. Boston and New York: Houghton Mifflin, 1918.

———. *Oh Pioneers!* Boston and New York: Houghton Mifflin, 1913.

———. *Song of the Lark*. Boston and New York: Houghton Mifflin, 1915.

Catt, Carrie Chapman, and Nettie Rogers Shuler. *Woman Suffrage and Politics*. New York: Charles Scribner's Sons, 1923.

———. *Woman Suffrage by Federal Constitutional Amendment*. New York: National Woman Suffrage Publishing Co., 1917.

Caughfield, Adrienne. *True Women and Westward Expansion.* College Station: Texas A&M University Press, 2005.

Chardon, Francis T. *Chardon's Journal at Fort Clark, 1834–1839: Descriptive of Life on the Upper Missouri; of a Fur Trader's Experiences Among the Mandans, Gros Ventres, and Their Neighbors; of the Ravages of the Small-Pox Epidemic of 1837.* Edited with Historical Introduction and Notes by Annie Heloise Abel. Iowa City: Athens Press, 1932.

Cleverdon, Catherine. *The Woman Suffrage Movement in Canada.* Toronto: University of Toronto Press, 1950.

Cole, Kevin L., and Leah Weins. "Religion, Idealism, and African American Autobiography in the Northern Plains: Era Bell Thompson's American Daughter." *Great Plains Quarterly* 12 (Fall 2003): 219–29.

Cordier, Mary Hurlbut. "Prairie Schoolwomen, Mid-1850s to 1920s in Iowa, Kansas, and Nebraska." *Great Plains Quarterly* 8 (Spring 1988): 102–19.

———. *Schoolwomen of the Prairies and Plains.* Albuquerque: University of New Mexico Press, 1992.

Cott, Nancy F. *The Bonds of Womanhood: "Women's Sphere" in New England, 1780–1835.* New Haven: Yale University Press, 1977.

Crow Dog, Mary. "Two Cut Off Hands." In Crow Dog and Erdoes, *Lakota Woman,* 186–98.

Crow Dog, Mary, and Richard Erdoes. *Lakota Woman.* New York: Grove Press, 1990. Reprint, New York: Harper Perennial, 1991.

Cushing, Frank Hamilton. *My Adventures in Zuñi.* With an introduction by Oakah L. Jones, Jr. Palo Alto, CA: American West Publishing Co., 1970.

———. *The Mythic World of the Zuñi.* Edited and illustrated by Barton Wright. Albuquerque: University of New Mexico Press, 1988.

———. "Origin Myth from Oraibi." *American Journal of Folk-Lore* 36, no. 140 (April-June 1923): 163–70.

———. *Zuñi Folk Tales.* Foreword by John Wesley Powell. Introduction by Mary Austin. Tucson: University of Arizona Press, 1931.

Custer, Elizabeth B. *"Boots and Saddles"; or, Life in Dakota with General Custer.* New York and London: Harper and Brothers, 1902.

———. *Following the Guidon.* With an introduction by Shirley Leckie. Lincoln and London: University of Nebraska Press, 1994.

Davidson, Sue. *A Heart in Politics: Jeannette Rankin and Patsy T. Mink.* Seattle, WA: Seal Press, 1994.

DeBoer, Warren R. "Of Dice and Women: Gambling and Exchange in Native North America." *Journal of Archeological Methods and Theory* 8, no. 3 (September 2001): 215–68.

Deloria, Ella Cara. *Dakota Texts.* New York: G.E. Stechert, 1932.

———. *Speaking of Indians.* New York: Friendship Press, 1944.

———. *Waterlily.* With an afterword by Raymond J. DeMallie. Lincoln and London: University of Nebraska Press, 1988.

Deloria, Ella Cara, and Frank Boas. *Dakota Grammar*. Washington, DC: US Government Printing Office, 1941.

DeMallie, Raymond J. "Male and Female in Traditional Lakota Culture." In Albers and Medicine, *The Hidden Half*, 237–266.

Dillehay, Thomas D. *The Settlement of the Americas: A New Prehistory*. New York: Basic Books, 2000.

Dooley, Chris. "The Suffrage Movement," "The Political Equality League," and "Nellie McClung," in *Timelinks*. Winnipeg: River East School District and the University of Manitoba, 1997. http://timelinks.merlin.mb.ca/referenc/subject.htm.

Dorsey, George A. *Traditions of the Arikara*. Washington, DC: Carnegie Institution of Washington, 1904.

Duffy, John M. "Dakota Images: Ada B. Caldwell." *South Dakota History* 30 (Summer 2000): 248–49.

Dunn, Adrian R. "A History of Old Fort Berthold." *North Dakota History* 30, no. 4 (October 1963). Reprint, Bismarck: State Historical Society of North Dakota, 1964.

Easton, Patricia O'Keefe. "Woman Suffrage in South Dakota: The Final Decade, 1911–1920." *South Dakota History* 13 (Fall 1983): 206–26.

Eccles, William J. *The French in North America, 1500–1783*. Markham, ON: Fitzhenry and Whitside Publishers, 1998.

———. *The Canadian Frontier, 1534–1760*. Albuquerque: University of New Mexico Press, 1974.

———. *Essays on New France*. Toronto: Oxford University Press, 1987.

———. *France in America*. New York: Harper and Row, 1972.

Emmerich, Lisa E. "Marguerite LaFlesche Diddock: Office of Indian Affairs Field Matron." *Great Plains Quarterly* 13 (Summer 1993): 162–71.

Fagan, Brian M. *Ancient North America: The Archaeology of a Continent*, 3rd ed. London: Thames and Hudson, 2000.

Faragher, John Mack. "The Custom of the Country: Cross-Cultural Marriage in the Far Western Fur Trade." In *Western Women: Their Land, Their Lives*, edited by Lillian Schlissel, Vicki L. Ruiz, and Janice Monk, 199–225. Albuquerque: University of New Mexico Press, 1988.

Faryon, Cynthia J. *A War Bride's Story: Risking It All for Love After World War II*. Canmore, AB: Altitude Publishing, 2004.

Flexner, Eleanor. *Century of Struggle: The Woman's Rights Movement in the United States*, rev. ed. Cambridge and London: Belknap Press of Harvard University Press, 1975.

Foggo, Cheryl. "Delicious Moments." In Carter, Erickson, Roome, and Smith, *Unsettled Pasts*, 267–76.

———. *Pourin' Down Rain*. Calgary, AB: Detselig Enterprises, 1990.

Ford, Ramona. "Native American Women: Changing Statuses, Changing Interpretations." In Jameson and Armitage, *Writing the Range*, 42–68.

Foster, Martha Harroun. "Of Bondage and Baggage: Gender and Status Among Hidatsa and Crow Women." *American Indian Culture and Research Journal* 17, no. 2 (1993): 121–52.

Fowler, Loretta. *The Columbia Guide to American Indians of the Great Plains.* New York: Columbia University Press, 2003.

Friedman, Barbara. *From the Battlefront to the Bridal Suite: Media Coverage of British War Brides, 1942–1946.* Columbia: University of Missouri Press, 2007.

Frison, George C. "Archaic Period Site." In *Encyclopedia of the Great Plains Indians*, edited by David Wishart, 24. Lincoln: University of Nebraska Press, 2007.

Garroutte, Eva Marie. *Real Indians: Identity and the Survival of Native Americans.* Berkeley: University of California Press, 2003.

Gibson, Arrell Morgan. *The American Indian: Prehistory to the Present.* Lexington, MA: D.C. Heath and Company, 1980.

Giles, Kevin S. *Flight of the Dove: The Story of Jeannette Rankin.* Beaverton, OR: Touchstone Press, 1980.

Gilman, Carolyn, and Mary Jane Schneider. *The Way to Independence: Memories of a Hidatsa Indian Family, 1840–1920.* St. Paul: Minnesota Historical Society Press, 1987.

Granfield, Linda. *Brass Buttons and Silver Horseshoes: Stories from Canada's British War Brides.* Toronto: McClelland & Stewart, 2002.

Green, Jesse, ed. and annot. *Cushing at Zuñi: The Correspondence and Journals of Frank Hamilton Cushing, 1879–1884.* Albuquerque: University of New Mexico Press, 1990.

Greer, Allan. *The People of New France.* Toronto: University of Toronto Press, 1997.

———. *The Jesuit Relations: Natives and Missionaries in Seventeenth-Century North America.* Boston: Bedford/St. Martin's, 2000.

Grinnell, George Bird. *Blackfoot Lodge Tales: The Story of a Prairie People.* Williamstown, MA: Corner House Publishers, 1972.

———. *By Cheyenne Campfires.* With photographs by Elizabeth C. Grinnell. New Haven, CT: Yale University Press, 1926.

———. *The Cheyenne Indians: Their History and Ways of Life.* 2 vols. New Haven, CT: Yale University Press, 1924.

———. *The Fighting Cheyennes.* Norman: University of Oklahoma Press, 1915.

———. *Pawnee, Blackfoot, and Cheyenne: History and Folklore of the Plains, from the writings of George Bird Grinnell.* Selected and with an introduction by Dee Brown. New York: C. Scribner's Sons, 1961.

———. *The Story of the Indian.* New York: D. Appleton, 1896.

Griswold, Robert. "Anglo Women and Domestic Ideology in the American West in the Nineteenth and Early Twentieth Centuries." In *Western Women: Their Land, Their Lives*, edited by Lillian Schlissel, Vicki L. Ruiz, and Janice Monk, 15–46. Albuquerque: University of New Mexico Press, 1988.

Hämäläinen, Pekka. *Comanche Empire.* New Haven, CT: Yale University Press, 2008.

Hanson, Jeffery R. Introduction to *Waheenee: An Indian girl's Story Told by Herself to Gilbert L. Wilson, Ph.D.* Lincoln: University of Nebraska Press, 1981.

Hardaway, Roger D. "Jeannette Rankin: The Early Years." *North Dakota Quarterly* 48 (Spring 1980): 62–68.

Harvey, Mark W. T. "James J. Hill, Jeannette Rankin, and John Muir: The American West in the Progressive Era, 1890 to 1920." In *Western Lives : A Biographical History of the American West*, edited by Richard W. Etulain, chap. 11. Albuquerque: University of New Mexico Press, 2004.

Harris, Ted. *Jeannette Rankin : Suffragist, First Woman Elected to Congress, and Pacifist.* New York: Arno Press, 1982.

Haven, Kathleen U. "Women's Voices of the World: Daughters and Rebels." Master's thesis, Rollins College, 1995.

Helm, Merry. "Suffrage Bill." Dakota Datebook, January 23, 2004, State Historical Society of North Dakota and North Dakota Humanities Council. www.prairiepublic.org/programs/datebook/bydate/04/0104/012304.jsp.

Hendricks, Steve. *The Unquiet Grave: The FBI and the Struggle for the Soul of Indian Country.* New York: Thunder's Mouth Press, 2006.

Higham, C. L. *Noble, Wretched, and Redeemable: Protestant Missionaries to the Indians in Canada and the United States, 1820–1900.* Albuquerque: University of New Mexico Press, 2000.

Hibbert, Joyce. *The War Brides.* Toronto: PMA Books, 1978.

Jackson, Brenda K. *Domesticating the West: The Re-Creation of the 19th Century American Middle Class.* Lincoln: University of Nebraska Press, 2005.

Jacobs, Margaret D. "Maternal Colonialism: White Women and Indigenous Child Removal in the American West and Australia, 1880–1940." *Western Historical Quarterly* 36 (Winter 2005): 453–476.

Jameson, Elizabeth, and Jeremy Mouat. "Telling Differences: The Forty-Ninth Parallel and Historiographies of the West and Nation." *The Pacific Historical Review* 75, no. 2 (May 2006):183–230.

Jarratt, Melynda. *War Brides: The Stories of the Women Who Left Everything Behind to Follow the Men They Loved.* Stroud: Tempus, 2007.

Jeffrey, Julie Roy. *Frontier Women: "Civilizing" the West? 1840–1880*, rev. ed. New York: Hill and Wang, 1998.

Jennings, Mary Kay. "Lake County Woman Suffrage Campaign in 1890." *South Dakota History* 5 (Winter 1975): 390–409.

Johnson, Michael K. "'This Strange White World': Race and Place in Era Bell Thompson's *American Daughter*." *Great Plains Quarterly* 24 (Spring 2004): 101–11.

Josephson, Hannah. *Jeannette Rankin: First Lady in Congress—A Biography.* Indianapolis: Bobbs-Merrill Co., Inc., 1974.

Kaplan, Amy. "Manifest Domesticity." *American Literature* (Sept 1998): 581–606.

Kehoe, Alice B. "The Shackles of Tradition." In Albers and Medicine, *The Hidden Half*, 53–73.

———. "The Function of Ceremonial Sexual Intercourse Among the Northern Plains Indians." *Plains Anthropologists* 15 (1970): 99–104.

Kerber, Linda K., and Jane Sherron De Hart, eds. *Women's America: Refocusing the Past*, 6th ed. New York and Oxford: Oxford University Press, 2004.

Kessell, John L. *Spain in the Southwest: A Narrative History of Colonial New Mexico, Arizona, Texas, and California.* Norman: University of Oklahoma Press, 2002.

Kessler, Donna J. *The Making of Sacagawea: A Euro-American Legend.* Tuscaloosa: University of Alabama Press, 1996.

Kidwell, Sara Sue. "Indian Women as Cultural Mediators." *Ethnohistory* 39, no. 2 (Spring 1992): 97–107.

Kinnear, Mary. *A Female Economy: Women's Work in a Prairie Province, 1870–1970.* Montreal and Kingston: McGill-Queen's University Press, 1998.

Ladouceur, Barbara, and Phyllis Spence. *Blackouts to Bright Lights: Canadian War Bride Stories.* Vancouver: Ronsdale Press, 1995.

Lansing, Michael. "Plains Indian Women and Interracial Marriage in the Upper Missouri Trade, 1804–1868." *Western Historical Quarterly* 31, no. 4 (Winter 2000): 413–33.

Larson, T. A. "Dolls, Vassals, and Drudge—Pioneer Women in the West." *Western Historical Quarterly* 3 (Spring 1970): 4–16.

———. "Montana Women and the Battle for the Ballot." *Montana: The Magazine of Western History* 23 (Winter 1973): 25–41.

———. "Woman Suffrage in Western America." *Utah Historical Quarterly* 38 (Spring 1970): 7–19.

Lawn, Katherine E., and Claudio R. Salvucci, eds. *Women in New France: Extracts from The Jesuit Relations.* Merchantville, NJ: Evolution Publishing and Manufacturing, 2003.

Lee, Jo-Anne. "'Living in Dream': Oral Narratives of Three Recent Immigrant Women." In *"Other" Voices: Historical Essays on Saskatchewan Women*, edited by David De Brou and Aileen Moffatt, 144–59. Regina: Canadian Plains Research Center, 1995.

Lerner, Gerda. "The Lady and the Mill Girl: Changes in the Status of Women in the Age of Jackson, 1800–1840." *Midcontinent American Studies Journal* 10 (Spring 1969): 5–14.

Linderman, Frank B. *Pretty-Shield: Medicine Woman of the Crows.* Lincoln and London: University of Nebraska Press, 1932; 1972.

———. *Blackfeet Indians.* Illustrated by Winold Reiss. New York: Gramercy Books, 1995.

———. *American: The Life Story of a Great Indian, Plenty-coups, Chief of the Crows.* Illustrated by H. M. Stoops. New York: The John Day Company, 1930.

———. *Indian Old-Man Stories: More Sparks from War Eagle's Lodge-Fire.* Illustrated by Charles M. Russell. New York: C. Scribner's Sons, 1920.

Lindgren, H. Elaine. *Land in Her Own Name: Women as Homesteaders in North Dakota.* Fargo: North Dakota State University Press, 1991.

Litz, Joyce. *The Montana Frontier: One Woman's West.* Albuquerque: University of New Mexico Press, 2004.

Llein, Alen M. "The Political-Economy of Gender: The 19th Century Plains Indian Case Study." In Albers and Medicine, *The Hidden Half,* 143–173.

Looking Horse, Chief Arvol. "Special Message from Arvol Looking Horse, 19th Generation Keeper of the Sacred White Buffalo Calf Pipe." Manataka American Indian Council. Accessed December 29, 2007, www.manataka.org/page108.thml.

Lopach, James J., and Jean A. Luckowski. *Jeannette Rankin: A Political Woman.* Boulder: University of Colorado Press, 2005.

Lowie, Robert H. *Indians of the Plains.* Foreword by Raymond J. DeMallie. Lincoln: University of Nebraska Press, 1954.

———. *The Crow Indians.* Introduction by Phenocia Bauerle. Lincoln: Bison Books, 2004.

Lucey, Donna M. *Photographing Montana, 1894–1928: The Life and Work of Evelyn Cameron.* Missoula, MT: Mountain Press Publishing Co., 2001.

Luebke, Frederick, ed. *European Immigrants in the American West: Community Histories.* Albuquerque: University of New Mexico Press, 1998.

———. *Ethnicity on the Great Plains.* Lincoln: University of Nebraska Press, 1980.

Manning, Paul. "English People Find em Wild." *Abilene* (Texas) *Reporter News,* October 24, 1941.

Manzer, Ronald. *Public Schools and Political Ideas: Canadian Educational Policy in Perspective.* Toronto: University of Toronto Press, 1994.

Mathes, Valerie Sherer. "Susan LaFlesche Picotte, M.D.: Nineteenth-Century Physician and Reformer." *Great Plains Quarterly* 13 (Summer 1993): 172–86.

Mathews, Sandra K. *American Indians in the Early West.* Santa Barbara, CA: ABC-CLIO, 2008.

Matthiessen, Peter. *In the Spirit of Crazy Horse.* New York: Viking Press, 1983.

Means, Bill. "The Legend of White Buffalo Calf Woman." YouTube video. Accessed January 3, 2008, www.youtube.com/watch?v=ezNKgRbnVPY

Medicine, Beatrice. " 'Warrior Women': Sex Role Alternatives for Plains Indian Women." In Albers and Medicine, *The Hidden Half,* 267–80.

Melzer, Richard, Robert Torrez, and Sandra Mathews. "New Mexico." Unpublished manuscript, author collection.

Moynihan, Ruth B., Susan Armitage, and Christine Fischer Dichamp. *So Much to Be Done: Women Settlers on the Mining and Ranching Frontier.* Lincoln: University of Nebraska Press, 1989.

Myres, Sandra L. *Westering Women and the Frontier Experience, 1800–1915.* Albuquerque: University of New Mexico Press, 1999.

McClung, Nellie. *In Times Like These.* Toronto: McLeod and Allen, 1915.

———. *Purple Springs.* With an introduction by Randi Warne. Toronto and London: University of Toronto Press, 1992.

———. *Purple Springs.* Toronto: Thomas Allen, 1921.

———. *The Second Chance.* Toronto: William Briggs, 1910.

———. *Sowing Seeds in Danny.* New York: Grosset and Dunlap, 1908.

———. *The Stream Runs Fast: My Own Story.* Toronto: Thomas Allen, 1945.

Miller, Susan Cummins, ed. *A Sweet, Separate Intimacy: Women Writers of the American Frontier, 1800–1922.* Lubbock: Texas Tech University Press, 2007.

Mihesuah, Devon A. *Indigenous American Women: Decolonization, Empowerment, Activism.* Lincoln: University of Nebraska Press, 2003.

——. "Anna Mae Pictou-Aquash: An American Indian Activist." In *Sifters: Native American Women's Lives,* edited by Theda Perdue, 204–22. New York: Oxford University Press, 2001.

——. "Commonality of Difference." In *Natives and Academics: Researching and Writing About American Indians,* edited by Devon Mihesuah, 37–54. Lincoln: University of Nebraska Press, 1998.

——. "Commonality of Difference: American Indian Women and History." Special issue: Writing about American Indians. *American Indian Quarterly* 20, no.1 (Winter 1996): 15–27.

Montrie, Chad. "'Men Alone Cannot Settle a Country': Domesticating Nature in the Kansas-Nebraska Grasslands." *Great Plains Quarterly* 25 (Fall 2005): 245–58.

Morton, Ron, and Carl Gawboy. *Talking Rocks: Geology and 10,000 Years of Native American Tradition in the Lake Superior Region.* St. Paul: University of Minnesota Press, 2003.

Moulton, Gary E. *The Journals of the Lewis & Clark Expedition,* vols. 1–13. Lincoln: University of Nebraska Press, 2001.

Mulford, Karen. *Trailblazers: Twenty Amazing Western Women.* Flagstaff, AZ: Northland Press, 2001.

Mulloy, William. "The Northern Plains." In *Archaeology of the Eastern United States,* edited by James B. Griffin, 124–38. Chicago: University of Chicago Press, 1952.

Myres, Sandra L. *Westering Women and the Frontier Experience, 1800–1915.* Albuquerque: University of New Mexico Press, 1999.

*Mythology of the Blackfoot Indians.* Compiled and translated by Clark Wissler and D. C. Duvall. Lincoln: University of Nebraska Press, 1995.

National Park Service. "Beringia." Accessed December 30, 2007, www.nps.gov/akso/beringia.index.htm.

Nelson, Paula M. "'Do Everything'—Women in Small Prairie Towns, 1870–1920." *Journal of the West* 36 (October 1997): 52–60.

Norlin, Dennis A. "The Suffrage Movement and South Dakota Churches: Radicals and the Status Quo, 1890s." *South Dakota History* 14 (Winter 1984): 308–34.

Norris, Kathleen. *Dakota: A Spiritual Geography.* New York: Ticknor and Fields, 1993.

Payment, Diane P. "'*La vie en rose*'? Métis Women at Batoche, 1870–1920." In *Women of the First Nations,* edited by Christine Miller and Patricia Chuchryk, 19–37. Winnipeg: University of Manitoba Press, 1996.

Peterson, Susan. "A Widening Horizon: Catholic Sisterhoods on the Northern Plains, 1874–1910." *Great Plains Quarterly* 5 (Spring 1985): 125–32.

Peters, Virginia Bergman. *Women of the Earth Lodges: Tribal Life on the Plains.* Norman: University of Oklahoma Press, 1995.

Petrik, Paula. *No Step Backward: Women and Family on the Rocky Mountain Mining Frontier, Helena, Montana, 1865–1900.* Helena: Montana Historical Society Press, 1987.

Pickering, Robert B. *Seeing the White Buffalo.* Boulder, CO: Johnson Books, 1997.

Poole, Dana. "The Role of Women in the Native American Civil Rights Movement." Master's thesis, Central Connecticut State University, 1998.

Powers, Marla N. *Oglala Women: Myth, Ritual, and Reality.* Chicago: University of Chicago Press, 1986.

Pritzer, Barry M. *A Native American Encyclopedia: History, Culture, and Peoples.* Oxford: Oxford University Press, 2000.

Radke, Andrea. "Refining Rural Spaces: Women and Vernacular Gentility in the Great Plains, 1880–1920." *Great Plains Quarterly* 24 (Fall 2004): 227–48.

———. "Women in the Fur Trade." In Wishart, *Encyclopedia of the Great Plains,* 341.

Radke-Moss, Andrea. *Bright Epoch: Women and Coeducation in the American West.* Lincoln: University of Nebraska Press, 2008.

Reed, Dorinda Riessen. *The Woman Suffrage Movement in South Dakota,* 2nd ed. Pierre, SD: Committee on the Status of Women, 1976.

Reichardt, Joan. "War Bride Recalls Trip to Canada." The American War Bride Experience, GI Brides of World War II. Accessed June 22, 2009, www.geocities.com/us_warbrides/bride_stories/canwb.html.

Rice, Julian. *Deer Women and Elk Men: The Lakota Narratives of Ella Deloria.* Albuquerque: University of New Mexico Press, 1992.

Richard, Doreen. Interview by Sheena Kohl, June 26, 2002. Montana War Brides Oral History Project. Montana Historical Society Archives, Helena.

Richey, Elinor. *Eminent Women of the West: Jeanette Rankin, Woman of Commitment.* Berkeley, CA: Howell-North Books, 1975.

Rikoon, J. Sanford, ed. *Rachel Calof's Story: Jewish Homesteader on the Northern Plains.* Bloomington and Indianapolis: Indiana University Press, 1995.

Riley, Glenda. "American Daughters: Black Women in the West." *Montana: The Magazine of Western History* 38 (Spring 1988): 14–39.

———. *The Female Frontier: A Comparative View of Women on the Prairie and the Plains.* Lawrence: University Press of Kansas, 1988.

Ronda, James P. *Lewis and Clark Among the Indians.* Lincoln: University of Nebraska Press, 1984. Reprint, Lincoln: University of Nebraska Press, 2002.

Roosens, Eugeen. *Creating Ethnicity: The Process of Ethnogenesis.* Newberry Park, CA: Sage, 1989.

Sandoz, Mari. *Love Song to the Plains.* New York: Harper and Bros., 1961.

———. *Old Jules.* Boston: Little Brown and Co., 1935.

Sargent, Theodore D. *The Life of Elaine Goodale Eastman.* Lincoln: University of Nebraska Press, 2005.

Saskatoon Women's Calendar Collective. "Suffrage: ' . . . not idiots nor imbeciles.'" *Herstory: An Exhibition, from Herstory: The Canadian Women's Calendar.* Saskatoon: University of Saskatchewan Libraries, 1995. http://library.usask.ca/herstory/suffer.html.

Schaffer, Ronald. "The Montana Woman Suffrage Campaign: 1911–14." *Pacific Northwest Quarterly* 55 (Spring 1964): 9–15.

Scharff, Virginia. *Twenty Thousand Roads: Women, Movement and the West*. Berkeley: University of California Press, 2003.

Schrems, Suzanne H. "Teaching School on the Western Frontier: Acceptable Occupation for Nineteenth Century Women." *Montana: The Magazine of Western History* 37 (Summer 1987): 54–63.

Shewchuck, Helen Hall. *If Kisses Were Roses: A 50th Anniversary Tribute to War Brides: Canada Remembers*. Naughton, ON: H.H. Shewchuck, 1996.

Shukert, Elfrieda Berthiaume, and Barbara Smith Scibetta. *War Brides of World War II*. Novato, CA: Presidio, 1988.

Sklar, Kathryn Kish. *Catherine Beecher: A Study in American Domesticity*. New Haven, CT: Yale University Press, 1973.

Sleeper-Smith, Susan. *Indian Women and French Men: Rethinking Cultural Encounter in the Western Great Lakes*. Amherst: University of Massachusetts Press, 2001.

Smith, Norma. *Jeannette Rankin, America's Conscience*. Helena: Montana Historical Society Press, 2002.

Smith, Rex Alan. *Moon of Popping Trees: The Tragedy at Wounded Knee and the End of the Indian Wars*. Lincoln and London: University of Nebraska Press, 1977.

Smith-Rosenberg, Carroll. *Disorderly Conduct: Visions of Gender in Victorian America*. New York: Alfred A. Knopf, 1985.

Sonneborn, Liz. *A to Z of American Indian Women*, rev. ed., s.v. "Aquash, Anna Mae," *The Spirit of Annie Mae*. DVD. Directed by Catherine Anne Martin. National Film Board of Canada, 2002.

Spector, Janet D. "Male/Female Task Differentiation Among the Hidatsa: Toward the Development of an Archeological Approach to the Study of Gender." In Albers and Medicine, *The Hidden Half*, 77–97.

Stockton, Elvia. Interviewed by Sheena Kohl, July 17, 2001. Montana War Brides Oral History Project. Montana Historical Society Archives, Helena.

Strong, William Duncan. "From History to Prehistory in the Northern Great Plains." In *Essays in Historical Anthropology of North America*. Smithsonian Miscellaneous Publications, Vol. 100. Washington, DC: Smithsonian Institution, 1940.

Strong-Boag, Veronica, and Michelle Lynn Rosa, eds. *Nellie McClung and the Complete Autobiography: A Clearing in the West and The Stream Runs Fast*. Peterborough, ON: Broadview Press, 2003.

Swyripa, Frances. *Wedded to the Cause: Ukrainian-Canadian Women and Ethnic Identity, 1891–1991*. Toronto: University of Toronto Press, 1993.

Thompson, Era Bell. *American Daughter*. Chicago: University of Chicago Press, 1946.

Titley, E. Brian, and Peter J. Miller. *Education in Canada: An Interpretation*. Calgary, AB: Detselig Enterprises Limited, 1982.

Tosh, Beverley, and Laura Brandon. *War Brides: One-Way Passage*. Moose Jaw, SK: Moose Jaw Museum and Art Gallery, 2008.

Trennert, Robert. "Educating Indian Girls at Nonreservation Boarding Schools, 1878–1920." *Western Historical Quarterly* 13 (July 1982): 271–90.

Van Kirk, Sylvia. *"Many Tender Ties"*: *Women in Fur-Trade Society, 1670–1870*. Winnipeg, MB: Watson and Dwyer, 1980.

Vaughn-Roberson, Courtney Ann. "Having a Purpose in Life: Western Women Teachers in the Twentieth Century." *Great Plains Quarterly* 5 (Spring 1985): 107–24.

Virden, Jenel. *Good-Bye Piccadilly: British War Brides in America*. Urbana: University of Illinois Press, 1996.

Wallace, Anthony C. *Jefferson and the Indians: The Tragic Fate of the First Americans*. Cambridge, MA: Harvard University Press, 1999.

"The War Brides: From Romance to Reality." Video. Ottawa: Kiss the Bride Productions, 2001.

"War Brides of WWII." Immigration Historical Notes. Ottawa: Citizenship and Immigration Canada, 2003.

Webb, Walter Prescott. *The Great Plains*. New York: Grosset and Dunlap, 1931.

Weber, David J. *The Spanish Frontier in North America*. New Haven, CT: Yale University Press, 1994.

Wedel, Waldo R. "Cultural Consequences in the Central Great Plains." In *Essays in Historical Anthropology of North America*. Miscellaneous Publications, Vol. 100. Washington, DC: Smithsonian Institution, 1940.

Weist, Katherine M. "Beasts of Burden and Menial Slaves: Nineteenth-Century Observations of Northern Plains Indian Women." In Albers and Medicine, *The Hidden Half*, 29–52.

———."Plains Indian Women: An Assessment." In *Anthropology on the Great Plains*, edited by W. Raymond Wood and Margot Liberty, 255–71. Lincoln: University of Nebraska Press, 1980.

Welter, Barbara. "The Cult of True Womanhood, 1820–1860." *American Quarterly* 18 (Summer 1966): 151–74.

Wheeler, Leslie. "Woman Suffrage's Gray-Bearded Champion Comes to Montana, 1889." *Montana: The Magazine of Western History* 31 (Fall 1981): 2–13.

White, Richard. *"It's Your Misfortune and None of My Own"*: *A New History of the American West*. Norman: University of Oklahoma Press, 1991.

Wicks, Ben. *Promise You'll Take Care of My Daughter: The Remarkable War Brides of World War II*. Toronto: Stoddart, 1992.

Wilder, Laura Ingalls. *By the Shores of Silver Lake*. New York: HarperCollins, 1939.

———. *The First Four Years*. New York: HarperCollins, 1971.

———. *Little Town on the Prairie*. New York: HarperCollins, 1941.

———. *The Long Winter*. New York: HarperCollins, 1940.

———. *These Happy Golden Years*. New York: HarperCollins, 1943.

Wilson, Angela Cavender. "Grandmother to Granddaughter." In *Natives and Academics: Researching and Writing About American Indians*, edited by Devon A. Mihesuah, 27–36. Lincoln: University of Nebraska Press, 1998.

Wilson, Gilbert L. *Waheenee: An Indian Girl's Story Told by Herself to Gilbert L. Wilson*. St. Paul, MN: Webb Publishing Company, 1927. Reprinted with an introduction by Jeffery R. Hanson. Lincoln: University of Nebraska Press, 1981.

Winestine, Belle Fligelman. "Mother Was Shocked." *Montana: The Magazine of Western History* 24 (Fall 1973): 70–78.

Wingreen, Amy Eleanor, and Mary Brave Bird. *From the Ridiculous to the Sublime.* Columbia: University of Missouri, 1993.

Wishart, David J., ed. *Encyclopedia of the Great Plains.* Lincoln: University of Nebraska Press, 2004.

———. *Encyclopedia of the Great Plains Indians.* Lincoln: Bison Books, 2007.

Witt, Shirley Hill. "The Brave-Hearted Women: The Struggle at Wounded Knee." *Civil Rights Digest* 8 (1976): 38–45.

Wittmayer, Cecilia M. "The 1889–1890 Woman Suffrage Campaign: A Need to Organize." *South Dakota History* 11 (Fall 1981): 199–225.

Wyman, Walker D., ed. *Frontier Woman: The Life of a Woman Homesteader on the Dakota Frontier.* As retold from the original notes and letters of Grace Fairchild. River Falls: University of Wisconsin-River Falls Press, 1972.

## Central Plains Essays

Allen, Gilbert. "The Woman Express Rider." *The Frontier: The Great Western Magazine* 4, no. 12 (June 1906): 14–15.

Allen, James. *Trials of Discipleship: The Story of William Clayton, A Mormon.* Urbana: University of Illinois Press, 1987.

Allen, Paula Gunn. *The Sacred Hoop: Recovering the Feminine in American Indian Traditions.* Boston: Beacon Press, 1986.

Beecher, Maureen Ursenbach, ed. *Mormon Midwife: The 1846–1888 Diaries of Patty Bartlett Sessions.* Logan: Utah State University Press, 2001.

———. *The Personal Writings of Eliza Roxcy Snow.* Salt Lake City: University of Utah Press, 1995.

———. "Women's Work on the Mormon Frontier." *Utah Historical Quarterly* 49, no. 3 (1981): 276–90.

Bennett, Richard. *Mormons at the Missouri, 1846–1852: "And We Should Die."* Norman: University of Oklahoma Press, 1987.

Blanton, De Anne. "Cathy Williams: Black Woman Soldier, 1866–1868." *Minerva* 10 (1992): 1–12.

Blanton, DeAnne, and Lauren M. Cook. *They Fought Like Demons: Women Soldiers in the American Civil War.* Baton Rouge: Louisiana State University Press, 2002.

Bloch, Louis. "Facts About Mexican Immigration Before and Since the Quota Restrictions." *Journal of the American Statistical Association* 24, no. 165 (March 1929): 50–60.

Boag, Peter. "Go West Young Man, Go East Young Woman: Searching for the *Trans* in Western Gender History." *Western Historical Quarterly* 36, no. 4 (2005): 477–97.

———. *Same-Sex Affairs: Constructing and Controlling Homosexuality in the Pacific Northwest.* Berkeley: University of California Press, 2003.

Bolton, Herbert Eugene. *Coronado: Knight of the Pueblos and Plains.* Albuquerque: University of New Mexico Press, 1964.

Brooks, James F. *Captives & Cousins: Slavery, Kinship, and Community in the Southwest Borderlands.* Chapel Hill: University of North Carolina Press, 2002.

Bryson, Conrey. *Winter Quarters.* Salt Lake City: Deseret Books, 1986.

Bullough, Vern L. "Transgenderism and the Concept of Gender." *International Journal of Transgenderism* 4, no. 3 (2000). Accessed June 2, 2005, http://www.symposium.com/ijt/gilbert/bullough.htm.

Buss, Fran Leeper. *La Partera: Story of a Midwife.* Ann Arbor: University of Michigan Press, 1980.

Butler, Anne M. *Daughters of Joy, Sisters of Misery: Prostitutes in the American West, 1865–90.* Urbana: University of Illinois Press, 1985.

Caramony, Wynona. Interview by author. Tape recording. August 23, 2005. Macy, NE.

Carlson, Paul H. *The Plains Indians.* College Station: Texas A&M University Press, 1998.

Chantry, Ruth. Telephone interview by author. May 18, 2005.

Chapman, Berlin Basil. *The Otoes and Missourias: A Study of Indian Removal and the Legal Aftermath.* Oklahoma City: Times Journal Publishing Company, 1965.

Chaudhuri, Nupur. "'We All Seem Like Brothers and Sisters': The African-American Community in Manhattan, Kansas, 1865–1940." *Kansas History* 14, no. 4 (1991–92): 270–88.

Cowger, Thomas W. *National Congress of American Indians: The Founding Years.* Lincoln: University of Nebraska Press, 1999.

Crawford, Patricia, and Sara Mendelson. "Sexual Identities in Early Modern England: The Marriage of Two Women in 1680." *Gender & History* 7, no. 3 (1995): 362–77.

Custer, Elizabeth B. *"Boots and Saddles"; or, Life in Dakota with General Custer.* New York: Harper and Brothers, 1885.

Denig, Edwin Thompson. *Five Indian Tribes of the Upper Missouri: Sioux, Arickaras, Assiniboines, Crees, Crows.* Edited with an introduction by John C. Ewers. Norman: University of Oklahoma Press, 1961.

Derr, Jill Mulvay, Audrey Godfrey, and Kenneth Godfrey, eds. *Women's Voices: An Untold History of the Latter-day Saints, 1830–1900.* Salt Lake City: Deseret Book Co., 1982.

Deutsch, Sarah. *No Separate Refuge: Culture, Class, and Gender on an Anglo-Hispanic Frontier in the American Southwest, 1880–1940.* New York: Oxford University Press, 1987.

Devine, Jenny Barker. "Quite a Ripple but No Revolution: The Changing Roles of Women in the Iowa Farm Bureau Federation, 1921–1951." *The Annals of Iowa* 64 (Winter 2005): 1–36.

Donoghue, Emma. *Passions Between Women: British Lesbian Culture, 1668–1801.* New York: Harper Collins, 1993.

Dorsey, George A. *Mythology of the Wichita.* Norman: University of Oklahoma Press, 1995.

———. *The Pawnee Mythology.* Lincoln: University of Nebraska Press, 1997.

Dubas, Annette. Personal correspondence with author. June 1, 2005. In possession of the author.

Duffy, John. "Medicine in the West: An Historical Overview." *Journal of the West* 21, no. 3 (1982): 5–14.

Durand, Jorge, Douglas S. Massey, and Emilio A. Parrado. "The New Era of Mexican Migration to the United States." *Journal of American History* 86, no. 2 (1999): 518–36.

Eales, Anne Bruner. *Army Wives on the American Frontier: Living by the Bugles.* Boulder, CO: Johnson Books, 1996.

Eighmy, Jeffrey L. "The Central High Plains: A Cultural Historical Summary." In Schlesier, *Plains Indians*, 224–38.

Ellis, Clyde. *A Dancing People: Powwow Culture on the Southern Plains.* Lawrence: University Press of Kansas, 2003.

Embry, Jessie. *Mormon Polygamous Families: Life in the Principle.* Salt Lake City: University of Utah Press, 1987.

Emmerich, Lisa E. "'Right in the Midst of My Own People': Native American Women and the Field Matron Program." *American Indian Quarterly* 15, no. 2 (Spring 1991): 201–16.

Epple, Carolyn. "A Navajo Worldview and *Nádleehí*: Implications for Western Categories." In Jacobs, Thomas, and Lang, *Two-Spirit People*, 174–91.

Faderman, Lillian. *Odd Girls and Twilight Lovers: A History of Lesbian Life in Twentieth-Century America.* New York: Penguin, 1992.

Farrer, Claire R. "A 'Berdache' by Any Other Name . . . Is a Brother, Friend, Lover, Spouse: Reflections on a Mescalero Apache Singer of Ceremonies." In Jacobs, Thomas, and Lang, *Two-Spirit People*, 236–51.

Fixico, Donald. *Termination and Relocation: Federal Indian Policy, 1945–1960.* Albuquerque: University of New Mexico Press, 1986.

Foster, Lawrence. "Polygamy and the Frontier: Mormon Women in Early Utah." *Utah Historical Quarterly* 50, no. 3 (Summer 1982): 268–89.

Fougera, Katherine Gibson. *With Custer's Cavalry.* Caldwell, ID: Caxton Printers, 1940.

"Frontier Tales." *Denver Field and Farm*, September 1, 1894.

Fowler, Loretta. *The Columbia Guide to American Indians of the Great Plains.* New York: Columbia University Press, 2003.

Franco, Jere. "Empowering the World War II Native American Veteran: Postwar Civil Rights." *Wicazo Sa Review* 9 (Spring 1993): 32–37.

Fuhriman, Walter. "Federal Aid to Irrigation Development." *Journal of Farm Economics* 31, no. 4 (November 1949): 965–75.

Garber, John, Sharon Garber, Jeff Vincent, and Darcy Boellstorff. "An Analysis of Refugee Resettlement Patterns in the Great Plains." *Great Plains Research* 14 (Fall 2004): 163–83.

Garber, Marjorie. *Vested Interests: Cross Dressing & Cultural Anxiety.* New York: Routledge, 1992.

Garcia, Ana. Interview by author. July 22, 2005. Hastings, NE.

Garcia, Cinthia. Interview by author. July 22, 2005. Hastings, NE.

Gerstile, Gary. "Liberty, Coercion, and the Making of Americans." *Journal of American History* 84, no. 2 (1997): 524–58.

Greeley, Horace. *An Overland Journey, from New York to San Francisco, in the Summer of 1859.* New York: C.M. Saxton, Barker and Company, 1860.

Guerin, E. J. *Mountain Charley, or the Adventures of Mrs. E. J. Guerin, Who Was Thirteen Years in Male Attire; An Autobiography Comprising a Period of Thirteen Years Life in the States, California, and Pike's Peak.* With an introduction by Fred W. Mazzulla and William Kostka. Norman: University of Oklahoma Press, 1968.

Haney, Wava G., and Lorna Clancy Miller. "US Farm Women, Politics, and Policy." Journal of Rural Studies 7, nos. 1–2 (1991): 115–121.

Henderson, Caroline. *Letters from the Dust Bowl.* Edited by Alvin O. Turner. Norman: University of Oklahoma Press, 2001.

Higham, John. *Send These to Me: Immigrants in Urban America.* Baltimore: Johns Hopkins University Press, 1984.

Holmes, Alice D. "'And I Was Always with Him': The Life of Jane Thorpy, Army Laundress." *Journal of Arizona History* 38, no. 2 (1997): 177–90.

Horton, Loren. "'The Worst That I Had Yet Witnessed': Mormon Diarists Cross Iowa in 1846." *Iowa Heritage Illustrated* 77, no. 2 (1996): 70–73.

Howard, James H. *The Ponca Tribe.* Washington, DC: The Smithsonian Institution, 1965.

Hutton, Paul. "Noonan's Last Stand: 'We Was Flabbergasted.'" *True West* 52, no. 10 (2005): 118–19.

Irving, Gordon. "The Law of Adoption: One Phase of the Development of the Mormon Concept of Salvation, 1836–1900." *Brigham Young University Studies* 14 (Spring 1974): 291–314.

Irwin, Robert McKee, Edward J. McCaughan, and Michelle Rocío Nasser. *The Famous 41: Sexuality and Social Control in Mexico, 1901.* New York: Palgrave Macmillan, 2003.

Jacobs, Sue Ellen, Wesley Thomas, and Sabine Lang. *Two-Spirit People: Native American Gender Identity, Sexuality, and Spirituality.* Urbana: University of Illinois Press, 1997.

Jacobson, Matthew Frye. *Whiteness of a Different Color: European Immigrants and the Alchemy of Race.* Cambridge, MA: Harvard University Press, 1999.

Jeffries, Julie Roy. *Frontier Women: The Trans-Mississippi West, 1840–1890.* New York: Hill and Wang, 1979.

———. "'There Is Some Splendid Scenery': Women's Responses to the Great Plains Landscape." *Great Plains Quarterly* 8 (Spring 1988): 69–78.

Jellison, Katherine. *Entitled to Power: Farm Women and Technology, 1913–1963.* Chapel Hill: University of North Carolina Press, 1993.

Jensen, Joan, and Darlis Miller. "The Gentle Tamers Revisited: New Approaches to the History of Women in the American West." *The Pacific Historical Review* 49, no. 2 (May 1980): 173–213.

"Jo Monahan" Vertical File. Unpublished source. Idaho State Historical Society, Boise, ID.

John, Elizabeth A. H. "A Wichita Migration Tale." *American Indian Quarterly* 7, no. 4 (Fall 1983): 57–63.

Johnson, Susan Lee. *Roaring Camp: The Social World of the California Gold Rush.* New York: W.W. Norton, 2000.

Katz, Jonathan Ned. *The Invention of Homosexuality.* New York: Plume, 1996.

Kay, Margarita A. "Mexican, Mexican American, and Chicana Childbirth." In *Twice a Minority: Mexican American Women,* edited by Margarita B. Melville, 52–65. St. Louis, MO: C.V. Mosby Company, 1980.

Kelly, Lawrence C. *The Assault on Assimilation: John Collier and the Origins of Indian Policy Reform.* Albuquerque: University of New Mexico Press, 1983.

Keyes, Grace Granger. "Mexican-American and Anglo Midwifery in San Antonio, Texas." Ph.D. diss., University of Wisconsin-Milwaukee, 1985.

Kimball, Stanley. "Mormon Trail Network in Nebraska, 1846–1868: A New Look." *Brigham Young University Studies* 24, no. 3 (1984): 321–36.

King, Charles R. "The Woman's Experience of Childbirth on the Western Frontier." *Journal of the West* 29, no. 1 (1999): 76–84.

Kwolek-Folland, Angel. "Customers and Neighbors: Women in the Economy of Lawrence, Kansas, 1870–1885." *Business and Economic History* 27, no. 1 (1998): 129–39.

L. Tom Perry Special Collections, Harold B. Lee Library, Brigham Young University, Provo, UT:

"Pioneer Margaretta Lemon King, Sketch Prepared by Lillian King Brown, Her Daughter," Film 920, Reel 51.

"Susan A. Noble," MS 525.

"Nancy Tracy," MS 2198, Folder 4.

Staker, Elizabeth. "A Brief History of Our Grandfather Alma Staker and a Continuation of Our Grandmother Elizabeth Young Staker," MS 1271.

Chipman, Sina. "Biography of Niels Nielson and Karen Pedersen Nielsen," Film 920, Reel 51.

"History of Jane Terry Young," Film 920, Reel 5.

"Biography of Elizabeth Terry Howard," Film 920, Reel 5.

"Biographical Sketch of the Life of Elizabeth Cunningham Kelly," Film 920, Reel 51.

"Biography of Mary Thornton," Film 920, Reel 52.

"Narrative of Eliza P. Lyman," MS 1217.

"Lucy Meserve Smith," MS 432, Folder 1.

Lang, Sabine. *Men as Women, Women as Men: Changing Gender in Native American Culture.* Translated by John L. Vantine. Austin: University of Texas Press, 1998.

Langston, Donna Highton. "American Indian Women's Activism in the 1960s and 1970s." *Hypatia* 18, no. 2 (2003): 114–32.

Lawrence, Jane. "The Indian Health Service and the Sterilization of Native American

Women." *American Indian Quarterly* 24, no. 3 (Summer 2000): 400–419.

Litoff, Judy Barrett. "Forgotten Women: American Midwives at the Turn of the Twentieth Century." *Historian* 40, no. 2 (1978): 235–51.

Llewellyn, H. N., and Huber Self. *The Cheyenne Way*. Norman: University of Oklahoma Press, 1941.

Lowie, Robert H. *Indians of the Plains*. New York: McGraw-Hill, 1954.

Lowry, Thomas. *The Story the Soldiers Wouldn't Tell: Sex in the Civil War*. Mechanicsburg, PA: Stackpole Books, 1994.

Lund, Jennifer, "'Pleasing to the Eyes of an Exile': The Latter-day Saint Sojourn at Winter Quarters, 1846–1848." *Brigham Young University Studies* 39, no. 2 (2000): 112–43.

Macías-González, Victor Manuel. "A Note on Homosexuality in Porfirian and Postrevolutionary Northern Mexico." *Journal of the Southwest* 43, no. 4 (2001): 543–48.

MacKenzie, Gordene Olga. *Transgender Nation*. Bowling Green, OH: Bowling Green State University Popular Press, 1994.

Maltz, Daniel, and JoAllyn Archambault. "Gender and Power in Native North America, Concluding Remarks." In *Women and Power in Native North America*, edited by Laura F. Klein and Lillian A. Ackerman, 230–250. Norman: University of Oklahoma Press, 1995.

Mann, Charles C. *1491: New Revelations of the Americas Before Columbus*. New York: Vintage Books, 2005.

Mattley, Guntamanee (Ead). Interview by author. Tape recording. September 16, 2005. Hastings, NE.

Methvin, J. J. *Andele: The Mexican-Kiowa Captive: A Story of Real Life Among the Indians*. Albuquerque: University of New Mexico Press, 1996.

Meyerowitz, Joanne. "Sex Change and the Popular Press: Historical Notes on Transsexuality in the United States, 1930–1955." *GLQ* 4, no. 2 (1998): 159–87.

Mihesuah, Devon Abbott. "Finding a Modern American Female Identity." In *Indigenous American Women: Decolonization, Empowerment, Activism*. Lincoln: University of Nebraska Press, 2003.

Mortensen, A. R. "Mormons, Nebraska, and the Way West." *Nebraska History* 46, no. 4 (1965): 259–71.

Nebraska Women in Agriculture. University of Nebraska-Lincoln. Accessed August 23, 2006, http://wia.unl.edu/index.html.

Nesvig, Martin. "The Lure of the Perverse: Moral Negotiation of Pederasty in Porfirian Mexico." *Mexican Studies/Estudios Mexicanos* 16, no. 1 (2000): 1–37.

Neth, Mary. *Preserving the Family Farm: Women, Community, and the Foundations of Agribusiness in the Midwest, 1900–1940*. Baltimore: Johns Hopkins University Press, 1995.

Ngo, Vygn. Interview by author. June 29, 2005. Hastings, NE.

Nguyen, Kate. Interview by author. Tape recording. August 14, 2005. Hastings, NE.

O'Brian, Denise. "Remarks upon Induction to the Iowa Hall of Fame." *Women, Food, and Agriculture Network* 3, no. 3 (September 2000): 1–4.

———. "How We Started." *Women, Food, and Agriculture Network* 1, no. 1 (February 1998): 1–4.

O'Brien, Patricia J. "The Central Lowland Plains: An Overview, A.D. 500–1500." In Schlesier, *Plains Indians*, 199–223.

Ong, Paul. "Chinese Laundries as an Urban Occupation in Nineteenth-Century California." *The Annals of the Chinese Historical Society of the Pacific Northwest* (1983): 68–85.

Peterson, Helen L. "American Indian Political Participation." *Annals of the American Academy of Political and Social Science.* American Indians and American Life 311 (May 1957): 116–26.

Phillip, Kenneth R. *Termination Revisited: American Indians on the Trail to Self-Determination, 1933–1953.* Lincoln: Nebraska University Press, 1999.

Pratt, Stephen. "Parley Pratt in Winter Quarters and the Trail West," *Brigham Young University Studies* 24, no. 3 (1984): 373–88.

Quinn, D. Michael. *Same-Sex Dynamics Among Nineteenth–Century Americans: A Mormon Example.* Urbana: University of Illinois Press, 1996.

Reis, Elizabeth. "Impossible Hermaphrodites: Intersex in America, 1620–1960." *Journal of American History* 92, no. 1 (2005): 411–41.

Report of the Great Plains Committee. "The Future of the Great Plains." Washington, DC: US Government Printing Office, 1936.

Richardson, Albert D. *Beyond the Mississippi: Life and Adventure on the Prairies, Mountains, and Pacific Coast.* Hartford, CT: American Publishing Company, 1867.

Rickey, Don, Jr. *Forty Miles a Day on Beans and Hay: The Enlisted Soldier Fighting the Indian Wars.* Norman: University of Oklahoma Press, 1963.

Riney-Kehrberg, Pamela. *Waiting on the Bounty: The Dust Bowl Diary of Mary Knackstedt Dyck.* Iowa City: University of Iowa Press, 1999.

———. *Rooted in Dust: Surviving Drought and Depression in Southwest Kansas.* Lawrence: University Press of Kansas, 1994.

Rochester, Jessica. "Does Gender Influence CSAs?" *Women, Food, and Agriculture Network* 4, no. 1 (March 2001): 5.

Roscoe, Will. *Changing Ones: Third and Fourth Genders in Native North America.* New York: St. Martin's Griffin, 2000.

Ruiz, Vicki. *Cannery Women, Cannery Lives: Mexican Women, Unionization, and the California Food Processing Industry, 1930–1950.* Albuquerque: University of New Mexico Press, 1987.

Sandoz, Mari. *These Were the Sioux.* New York: Hastings House, c. 1961. Reprint, Lincoln: University of Nebraska Press, 1985.

Sachs, Carolyn. *Gendered Fields: Rural Women, Agriculture, and Environment.* Boulder, CO: Westview Press, 1996.

Schlatter, Evelyn A. "Drag's a Life: Women, Gender, and Cross-Dressing in the Nineteenth-Century West." In *Writing the Range: Race, Class, and Culture in the Women's West*, edited by Elizabeth Jameson and Susan Armitage, 334–48. Norman: University of Oklahoma Press, 1997.

Schlesier, Karl H., ed. *Plains Indians, A.D. 500–1500: The Archaeological Past of Historic Groups.* Norman: University of Oklahoma Press, 1994.

Schrader, Robert Fay. *The Indian Arts and Crafts Board: As Aspect of New Deal Indian Policy.* Albuquerque: University of New Mexico Press, 1983.

Schwieder, Dorothy, and Deborah Fink. "Plains Women: Rural Life in the 1930s." *Great Plains Quarterly* 8 (Spring 1988): 79–88.

Shelby, H. E. "The Importance of Irrigation in the Economy of the West." *Journal of Farm Economics* 31, no. 4 (November 1949): 955–46.

Shoemaker, Nancy. *Negotiators of Change: Historical Perspectives on Native American Women.* New York: Routledge, 1995.

Simmons, Marc. *The Last Conquistador: Juan de Oñate and the Settling of the Far Southwest.* Norman: University of Oklahoma Press, 1991.

Smith, George. "Nauvoo Roots of Mormon Polygamy, 1841–1846: A Preliminary Demographic Report," *Dialogue* 27, no. 1 (1994): 1–36.

Smith, Henry Nash. "Rain Follows the Plow: The Notion of Increased Rainfall for the Great Plains, 1844–1880." *The Huntington Library Quarterly* (February 1947): 174.

Socolofsky, Homer E., and Huber Self. *Historical Atlas of Kansas.* Norman: University of Oklahoma Press, 1972.

Sommerville, Siobhan B. *Queering the Color Line: Race and the Invention of Homosexuality in American Culture.* Durham, NC: Duke University Press, 2000.

Stallard, Patricia Y. *Glittering Misery: Dependents of the Indian Fighting Army.* San Rafael, CA: Presidio Press and Fort Collins, CO: The Old Army Press, 1978.

Stegner, Wallace. *The Gathering of Zion: The Story of the Mormon Trail.* London: Eyre and Spottiswoode, 1966.

Steinbeck, John. *The Grapes of Wrath.* New York: Viking, 1989.

Stewart, Miller J. "Army Laundresses: Ladies of the 'Soap Suds Row.'" *Nebraska History* 6, no. 4 (1980): 421–36.

Thomas, Wesley. "Navajo Cultural Constructions of Gender and Sexuality." In Jacobs, Thomas, and Lang, *Two-Spirit People,* 156–73.

Tong, Benson. *Susan LaFlesche Picotte, M.D.: Omaha Leader and Reformer.* Norman: University of Oklahoma Press, 1999.

Tucker, Phillip Thomas. *Cathy Williams: From Slave to Female Buffalo Soldier.* Mechanicsburg, PA: Stackpole Books, 2002.

US Bureau of the Census. *1940; Irrigation of Agricultural Lands, Specific Irrigation Census Statistics.* Printed in the Sixteenth Census of the United States. Washington, DC: US Government Printing Office, 1943.

US Department of Commerce, Bureau of the Census. *The Growth of Metropolitan Districts in the United States: 1900–1940.* Washington, DC: US Government Printing Office, 1947.

University of California Sustainable Agriculture Research and Education Program. Accessed August 23, 2006, www.sarep.ucdavis.edu/concept.htm.

Utley, Robert M. *Frontier Regulars, 1866–1891: The United States Army and the Indian.* New York: Macmillian Publishing, 1973.

Van Wagoner, Richard. *Mormon Polygamy: A History.* Salt Lake City: Signature Books, 1989.

Wagner, Gwendolin Damon. *Old Neutriment.* Boston: Ruth Hill Publisher, 1934. Reprint, Lincoln: University of Nebraska Press, 1989.

Walker, Margaret F. "A Woman's Work Is Never Done; Or, The Dirt on Men and Their Laundry." *Overland Journal* 16, no. 2 (1998): 4–13.

Wang, Joan. "Gender, Race and Civilization: The Competition Between American Power Laundries and Chinese Steam Laundries, 1870s–1920s." *American Studies International* 40, no. 1 (2002): 52–73.

Ward, Maurine Carr, ed. *Winter Quarters: The 1846–1848 Life Writings of Mary Haskin Parker Richards.* Logan: Utah State University Press, 1996.

Warhus, Mark. *Another America: Native American Maps and the History of Our Land.* New York: St. Martin's Griffin, 1997.

Webb, Walter Prescott. *The Great Plains.* Boston: Ginn and Company, 1931.

Wendel, Vickie. "Getting Those Clothes Clean." *Civil War Times Illustrated* 38, no. 4 (1999): 36.

———. "Washer Women." *Civil War Times Illustrated* 38, no. 4 (1999): 30–36.

West, Elliot. *The Way to the West: Essays on the Central Plains.* Albuquerque: University of New Mexico Press, 1995.

Williams, Walter L. *The Spirit and the Flesh: Sexual Diversity in American Indian Culture.* Boston: Beacon Press, 1992.

Willis, Elizabeth. "Voice in the Wilderness: The Diaries of Patty Sessions." *Journal of American Folklore* 101 (1988): 37–47.

Wishart, David. *An Unspeakable Sadness: The Dispossession of the Nebraska Indians.* Lincoln: University of Nebraska Press, 1994.

Wood, Cynthia A. "Army Laundresses and Civilization on the Western Frontier." *Journal of the West* 41, no. 3 (2002): 26–34.

Woster, Donald. *Dust Bowl: The Southern Plains in the 1930s.* Oxford: Oxford University Press, 1979.

Zanjani, Sally. *A Mine of Her Own: Women Prospectors in the American West, 1850–1950.* Lincoln: University of Nebraska Press, 1997.

## Southern Plains Essays

Adams, Jane. "The *Farm Journal's* Discourse of Farm Women's Femininity." *Anthropology and Humanism* 29, no. 1 (2004): 45–62.

Akers, Donna L. *Living in the Land of Death: The Choctaw Nation, 1830–1860.* Lansing: Michigan State University Press, 2004.

Alonso, Armando. *Tejano Legacy: Rancheros and Settlers in South Texas, 1734–1900.* Albuquerque: University of New Mexico Press, 1998.

*Annual Report of the Commissioner of Indian Affairs.* Washington, DC: US Government Printing Office, 1836, 1837, 1843, 1852.

Archambeau, Ernest R. *Old Tascosa, 1886–1888.* Canyon, TX: Panhandle-Plains Historical Society, 1966.

Argüello, Clara Elena Suárez. *Camino real y carrera larga: la arriería en la Nueva España durante el siglo XVIII.* Mexico City: Centro de Investigaciones y Estudios Superiores en Antropologia Social, 1996.

Ashford, Gerald. *Spanish Texas: Yesterday and Today.* Austin, TX: Jenkins Publishing, 1971.

Baker, T. Linsay, and Julie P. Baker, eds. *The WPA Oklahoma Slave Narratives.* Norman: University of Oklahoma Press, 1996.

Barker, Eugene C. *The Life of Stephen F. Austin, Founder of Texas, 1793–1836: A Chapter in the Westward Movement of the Anglo-American People.* Austin: University of Texas Press, 1985.

Barr, Juliana. *Peace Came in the Form of a Woman: Indians and Spaniards in the Texas Borderlands.* Chapel Hill: University of North Carolina Press, 2007.

Barrera, Manuel. *Then the Gringos Came: The Story of Martín de León and the Texas Revolution.* Laredo, TX: Barrera Publications.

Belcher, John C. "Fertility of the Village Residents of Oklahoma." *Social Forces* 24 (March 1946): 328–31.

Benson, Henry. *Life Among the Choctaw Indians.* New York: Johnson Reprint Company, 1970.

Benson, Nettie Lee. "Bishop Marín de Porras and Texas." *Southwestern Historical Quarterly* 51 (July 1947): 26–29.

———. "Texas as Viewed from Mexico." *Southwestern Historical Quarterly* 90 (January 1987): 219–91.

Bonnifield, Paul. *The Dust Bowl: Men, Dirt, and Depression.* Albuquerque: University of New Mexico Press, 1979.

Boswell, Angela. "From Farm to Future: Women's Journey Through Twentieth-Century Texas." In *Twentieth-Century Texas,* edited by John W. Storey and Mary L. Kelley, 105–31. Denton: University of North Texas Press, 2008.

Brading, D. A. "Government and Elite in Late Colonial Mexico." *Hispanic American Historical Review* 53, no. 3 (August 1973): 389–414.

*Brown v. Board of Education.* Accessed August 1, 2006, www.lib.umich.edu/exhibits/brownarchive.

Brooks, James F. "'This Evil Extends Especially . . . to the Feminine Sex': Negotiating Captivity in the New Mexico Borderlands." *Feminist Studies* 22, no. 2 (Summer 1996): 279–309.

Brown, Henry F. *Baptism Through the Centuries.* Mountain View, CA: Pacific Press, 1965.

Bruce, Michael L. "Our Best Men Are Leaving Us Fast." *Chronicles of Oklahoma* 66, no. 1 (1988): 294.

Brunner, Emil. *The Christian Doctrine of God.* Translated by Olive Wyon. Philadelphia: Westminster Press, 1950–1979.

Bushnell, David I. "The Choctaw of Bayou Lacomb, St. Tammany Parish, Louisiana." *Bureau of American Ethnology,* Bulletin 48 (1909): 23.

Cabeza de Baca, Fabiola. *We Fed Them Cactus.* Albuquerque: University of New Mexico Press, 1954.

Campbell, Randolph B. *Gone to Texas: A History of the Lone Star State.* New York: Oxford University Press, 2003.

Candelaria, Gloria, Genealogical Records, Family Group Records, prepared from Victoria County census records by Gloria Candelaria, Victoria Hispanic Genealogical and Historical Society of Texas, Victoria.

Cashion, Ty, and Jesus F. De La Teja, eds. *The Human Tradition in Texas.* Wilmington, DE: Scholarly Resources Inc., 2001.

Castañeda, Antonia I. "Women of Color and the Rewriting of Western History: The Discourse, Politics, and Decolonization of History." *Pacific Historical Review* 61, no. 4 (November 1992): 501–33.

Castañeda, Carlos E. *Our Catholic Heritage in Texas, 1519–1936.* Vol. 6, *The Transition Period: The Fight for Freedom, 1810–1836.* Austin, TX: Von Boeckmann-Homes, 1950.

Census of Santa Margarita Ranch, Sergeant José de Jesús Aldrete, November 10, 1811, Spanish Archives, San Antonio; also in Bexar Archives.

Chebahtah, William, and Nancy McGown Minor. *Chevato: The Story of the Apache Warrior Who Captured Herman Lehmann.* Lincoln: University of Nebraska Press, 2007.

Chipman, Donald E. *Spanish Texas, 1519–1821.* Austin: University of Texas Press, 1992.

Cohen, Warren. "The Drought of 1996." *U.S. News and World Report* 120 (June 10, 1996): 35.

Coopwood, Julia. "History of the La Bahía Settlement During the Administration of Captain Manuel Ramirez de la Piscina, 1750–1767." Master's thesis, University of Texas at Austin, 1938.

Costeloe, Michael P. *La Primera República Federal de México (1824–1835): un studio de los partidos politicos en el México independiente.* Translated by Manuel Fernández Gasalla. Mexico City: Fondo de Cultura Económica, 1975.

Cushman, H. B. *History of the Choctaw, Chickasaw, and Natchez Indians.* Edited by Angie Debo. Greenville, TX: Headlight Printing House, 1899.

Cutter, Charles R. *The Legal Culture of Northern New Spain, 1700–1810.* Albuquerque: University of New Mexico Press, 1998.

Debo, Angie. *The Rise and Fall of the Choctaw Nation.* 2nd ed. Norman: University of Oklahoma Press, 1961.

de la Garza de León, Patricia. Deed Records, Victoria County Clerk's Office, Victoria, TX:

Fernando de León to Alva Fitzpatrick, January 13, 1847, vol. 3, p. 105.

Fernando de León to William Dally, Lease, February 16, 1847, vol. 3, p. 131.

María de Jesús de León to Pleasant B. Cocke, Transfer, September 1, 1854, vol. 6, p. 64. Original sale January 23, 1837, in Louisiana.

P. B. Cocke to Robert Ruffin Barrow of Freebone, LA, November 16, 1841, vol. 1, p. 507 (new vol. 2, p. 728) .

Pleasant Branch Cocke of New Orleans to James H. Sheppherd of New Orleans, attorney for Isaac Franklin, also of New Orleans, Deed, July 5, 1837, vol. 2, p. 87.

Patricia de la Garza. Inventory of goods signed at Presas del Rey, January 1, 1801, vol. 1, p. 34, Index to Deed Records.

Patricia de la Garza from R. Carlisle and Bridget Quinn, Mortgage, September 23, 1838, vol. 1, p. 32.

Patricia de la Garza to P. B. Cocke, Deed, January 24, 1837, vol. 1, p. 34.

Patricia de la Garza de León by attorney José María Carvajal to Alexander G. Cochran, vol. 2, p. 208, December 8, 1836.

Deutsch, Sarah. *No Separate Refuge: Culture, Class, and Gender on an Anglo-Hispanic Frontier in the American Southwest, 1880–1940.* New York: Oxford University Press, 1987.

———. "Women and Intercultural Relations: The Case of Hispanic New Mexico and Colorado." *Signs* 12, no. 4 (Summer 1987): 719–739.

Doerr, Arthur H. "Dry Conditions in Oklahoma in the 1930s and 1950s as Delimited by the Original Thornthwaite Climatic Classification." *Great Plains Journal* 2 (Spring 1963): 67–76.

Economic Research Service, US Department of Agriculture. "State Fact Sheets: Oklahoma." Accessed April 25, 2005, www.ers.usda.gov/State Facts/OK.htm.

Egan, Timothy. *The Worst Hard Time: The Untold Story of Those Who Survived the Great American Dust Bowl.* Boston: Houghton Mifflin Company, 2006.

Fairchild, Louis. *The Lonesome Plains: Death and Revival on an American Frontier.* College Station: Texas A&M University Press, 2002.

Faulk, Odie B. *The Last Years of Spanish Texas, 1778–1821.* The Hague: Mouton and Co., 1964.

Final Record of Guardian, May 1847, vol. 1, p. 527, Probate Records, Victoria County Clerk's Office, Victoria, TX.

Findeis, Jill L., and Hema Swaminathan. "Gender and Intergenerational Transfer of the Farm: Its Influence on Multiple Job-Holding and On-Farm Decision-Making Among U.S. Farm Women." Working Paper 03–06, Department of Agricultural Economics and Rural Sociology, The Pennsylvania State University, 2003: 1–13.

Fogelson, Raymond D. "An Analysis of Cherokee Sorcery and Witchcraft." In *Four Centuries of Southeastern Indians,* edited by Charles M. Hudson, 117. Athens University of Georgia Press, 1975.

Folsom, George. *New Boggy.* Choctaw Nation: J. H. Moore, 1875.

Folsom, Joseph. *Constitution and Laws of the Choctaw Nation, 1855, 1865, and 1866.* Wilmington, DE: Scholarly Resources, 1869. Reprinted 1973.

Foster, Morris W. *Being Comanche: A Social History of an American Indian Community.* Tucson: University of Arizona Press, 1991.

Fowler, Loretta. *The Columbia Guide to American Indians of the Great Plains.* New York: Columbia University Press, 2003.

"From Microwaves to Module Builders, Women in Farming Are Able to Adapt." *Commentator* (Spring 2002): 7. Accessed March 8, 2006, www.pcca.com/Publications/Commentator/2002/Spring/page03.asp.

García, Genaro, ed. *Documentos Inéditos o Muy Raros Para la Historia de México.* Mexico City: Editorial Porrúa, 1975.

Garrett, Julia Kathryn. *Green Flag Over Texas: A Story of the Last Years of Spain in Texas.* Austin, TX: Jenkins Publishing Co. and New York: The Pemberton Press, 1969.

Garza, Israel Cavazos. *El General Alonso de León, Descubridor de Texas.* Monterrey, Mexico: Real Ayuntamiento de Monterrey, 1993.

George, Louise Carroll, ed. *Some of My Heroes Are Ladies: Women, Ages 85 to 101, Tell About Life in the Texas Panhandle.* Baltimore: Gateway Press, 2003.

Goodell, William. *The American Slave Code in Theory and Practice: Its Distinctive Features Shown by Its Statutes, Judicial Decisions, and Illustrative Facts.* New York: American and Foreign Anti-Slavery Society, 1853.

Gonzalez, Deena. *Refusing the Favor: The Spanish-Mexican Women of Santa Fe, 1820–1880.* Oxford: Oxford University Press, 1999.

González, Gilbert G., and Raúl Fernández. "Chicano History: Transcending Cultural Models." *Pacific Historical Review* 63, no. 4 (November 1994): 480–81.

Graves, Lawrence L., ed. *A History of Lubbock.* Lubbock: West Texas Museum Association, 1963.

Gray, Paul, and Nancy Harbert. "Bone Dry." *Time* 147 (June 10, 1996): 44.

Green, Donald E., ed. *Rural Oklahoma.* Oklahoma City: Oklahoma Historical Society, 1977.

Grimes, Roy, ed. *300 Years in Victoria County.* Victoria, TX: Victoria Advocate Publishing Co., 1968. Reprint, Austin, TX: Nortex Press, 1985.

Gregory, James N. *American Exodus: The Dust Bowl Migration and Okie Culture in California.* New York: Oxford University Press, 1991.

Hail, Barbara A., ed. *Gifts of Pride and Love: Kiowa and Comanche Cradles.* Providence, RI: Brown University, Haffenreffer Museum of Anthropology, 2000.

Hämäläinen, Pekka. *Comanche Empire.* New Haven, CT: Yale University Press, 2008.

Hammett, A. B. J. *The Empresario: Don Martín de León (The Richest Man in Texas).* Kerrville, TX: Braswell Printing Co., 1971.

Hardin, Stephen L. *Texian Iliad: A Military History of the Texas Revolution, 1835–1836.* Austin: University of Texas Press, 1994.

Haynes, Michael Thurgood. "Mary Ann (Molly) Dyer Goodnight." In Massey, *Texas Women on the Cattle Trails*, 133–47.

Haywood, C. Robert. *Victorian West: Class and Culture in Kansas Cattle Towns.* Lawrence: University Press of Kansas, 1991.

Henderson, Caroline. *Letters from the Dust Bowl.* Edited by Alvin O. Turner. Norman: University of Oklahoma Press, 2001.

Henderson, Mary Virginia. "Minor Empresario Contracts for the Colonization of Texas, 1825–1834." *Southwestern Historical Quarterly* 31 (April 1928): 295–324; and 32 (July 1928): 1–28.

Herring, Rebecca. "Their Work Was Never Done: Women Missionaries on the Kiowa-Comanche Reservation." *The Chronicles of Oklahoma* 64, no. 1 (Spring 1986): 69–83.

Hicks, J. Kent. "Pastores Presence on the Southern High Plains of Texas." *Historical Archeology* 34 (2004): 46–60.

Hill, Lawrence F. *José de Escandón and the Founding of Nuevo Santander.* Columbus: Ohio State University Press, 1926.

Hill, Luther. *History of the State of Oklahoma.* New York: Lewis Publishing Co., 1908.

Hodgson, Adam. *Letters from North America, Written During a Tour in the United States and Canada.* London: Hurst, Robinson, and Co., 1824.

Hogan, William R. *The Texas Republic: A Social and Economic History.* Austin: University of Texas Press, 1986.

Horgan, Paul. *Great River: The Rio Grande in North American History.* New York: Rinehart, 1954. Reprint, Austin: Texas Monthly Press, 1984.

Holt, Marilyn Irvin. *Linoleum, Better Babies & the Modern Farm Woman, 1890–1930.* Albuquerque: University of New Mexico Press, 1995.

Horsman, Reginald. *Race and Manifest Destiny: The Origins of American Racial Anglo-Saxonism.* Cambridge, MA: Harvard University Press, 1981.

Hough, Mrs. John Wesley. Memoirs given to Hellen Heath July 6, 1936. Panhandle-Plains Historical Museum Research Center, Canyon, TX.

Howarth, William. "The Okies Beyond the Dust Bowl." *National Geographic* 166 (September 1984): 323–48.

Hudson, Charles. *The Southeastern Indians.* Nashville: University of Tennessee Press, 1976.

Huet, Marie-Helene. "Deadly Fears: Dom Augustin Calmet's Vampires and the Rule Over Death." *Eighteenth Century Life* 21 (May 1997): 222.

Hurt, R. Douglas. *Dust Bowl.* Chicago: Nelson-Hall, 1981.

———. "Return of the Dust Bowl: The Filthy Fifties." *Journal of the West* 18 (October 1979): 85–93.

Huson, Hobart. *Refugio, A Comprehensive History of Refugio County: From Aboriginal Times to 1953.* 2 vols. Woodsboro, TX: Rooke Foundation, 1953–1955.

"Increase Reported in Women-Run Farms." *Herald Democrat Online.* Accessed August 10, 2006, www.heralddemocrat.com/articles/2005/03/18/lifeagriculture/iq_1776917.txt.

*Interview with Nancy Fulsom Cox, Choctaw Freedman.* Edited by Grant Foreman. Works Progress Administration oral history project. Oklahoma: Oklahoma Historical Society, 1936.

Jameson, Elizabeth, and Susan Armitage, eds. *Writing the Range: Race, Class, and Culture in the Women's West.* Norman: University of Oklahoma Press, 1997.

Jaskoski, Helen. "'My Heart Will Go Out': Healing Songs of Native American Women." *International Journal of Women's Studies* 4, no. 2 (1989): 118–43.

Jellison, Katherine. *Entitled to Power: Farm Women and Technology, 1913–1963.* Chapel Hill: University of North Carolina Press, 1993.

Jensen, Joan M. *Promise to the Land: Essays on Rural Women.* Albuquerque: University of New Mexico Press, 1991.

Jensen, Joan M., and Darlis Miller, eds. *New Mexico Women: Intercultural Perspectives.* Albuquerque: University of New Mexico Press, 1986.

Johnson, Bobby H. "From Sod House to Lyceum: Education in the Oklahoma Territory, 1889–1906." In *The American West: Essays in Honor of W. Eugene Hollon*, edited by Ronald Lora, 231–49. Toledo, OH: University of Toledo, 1980.

Johnson, Carolyn. *Cherokee Women in Crisis: Trail of Tears, Civil War, and Allotment, 1838–1907*. Tuscaloosa: University of Alabama Press, 2003.

Johnson, Hannibal. *Acres of Aspiration: The All Black Towns in Oklahoma*. Austin, TX: Eakin Press, 2002.

Jones, David E. *Sanapia: Comanche Medicine Woman*. New York: Holt, Rinehart and Winston, 1972.

Jones, Oakah L., Jr. *Los Paisanos: Spanish Settlers on the Northern Frontier of New Spain*. Norman: University of Oklahoma Press, 1979.

Kappler, Charles. "Indian Affairs: Laws and Treaties." OSU Library Digital Publications. Stillwater, OK. Accessed April 3, 2009, http://digital.library.okstate.edu/kappler.

Key, Della Tyler. *In the Cattle Country: History of Potter County*. Amarillo, TX: Tyler-Berkley Company, 1961.

Kuznesof, Elizabeth Anne. "The History of the Family in Latin America: A Critique of Recent Work." *Latin American Research Review* 24, no. 2 (1989): 168–86.

Lavrin, Asunción, and Edith Couturier. "Dowries and Wills: A View of Women's Socio-economic Role in Colonial Guadalajara and Puebla, 1640–1790." *Hispanic American Historical Review* 9, no. 2 (May 1979): 280–304.

León, Alonso de. "Relación del Descubrimiento, Población y Pacificación de Este Nuevo Reno de León: Temperatmento y Calidad de la Tierra." In García, *Documentos Inéditos o Muy Raros Para la Historia de México*, 719–39.

León, Fernando de, and Luz Escalera de León. Marriage records. St. Mary's Church records, Catholic Archives, Austin, TX.

León, Francisco Santiago de. Adoption records, August 1850, Victoria County Clerk's Office, Victoria, TX.

León, Martín de. Petition to the King, #42, copy in Martín de León Papers, O'Connor Room, Victoria County Public Library, Victoria, TX.

León, Martín de, to Salcedo, Petition to Ferdinand VII, 1800, Martín de León Papers, O'Connor Room, Victoria County Public Library, Victoria, TX.

León, Fernando de, to Patricia de la Garza. June 11, 1835, vol. 2, p. 205 (new vol. 1, p. 404).

"Libro formado por el Capitán de Milicias y primer Alcalde Constitucional de La Bahía del Espíritu Santo," Archivo General de la Nación, Mexico City, Mexico.

Lich, Glen E., and Dona B. Reeves-Marquardt, eds. *Texas Country: The Changing Rural Scene*. College Station: Texas A&M University Press, 1986.

Linn, J. J. *Reminiscences of Fifty Years in Texas*. New York: D&J Sadlier and Co., 1883.

Martin, Joel. *Sacred Revolt: The Muskogee's Struggle for a New World*. Boston: Beacon Press, 1991.

Massey, Sarah R., ed. *Texas Women on the Cattle Trails*. College Station: Texas A&M Press, 2006.

McLoughlin, William G. *Cherokee Renascence in the New Republic*. Princeton, NJ: Princeton University Press, 1986.

McMillan, Robert T. "Old-Age Dependency in Oklahoma." *Social Forces* 26 (October 1947): 50–57.

Memmi, Albert. *The Colonizer and the Colonized.* New York: Orion Press, 1965.

Miles, Tiya. *Ties That Bind: The Story of an Afro-Cherokee Family in Slavery and Freedom.* Berkeley: University of California Press, 2005.

Moorehead, Max L. *The Presidio: Bastion of the Spanish Borderlands.* Norman: University of Oklahoma Press, 1975.

Murray, Johnston. "Oklahoma is in a Mess!" *Saturday Evening Post* (April 30, 1955): 19.

Nixon, Patrick Ireland. *The Medical Story of Early Texas, 1528–1853.* Lancaster, PA: Mollie Bennett Lupe Memorial Fund, 1946.

"NOAA Warns New Year Will Bring Serious Threat of Wildfires." Environmental News/Science News, Community Dispatch.com. Accessed January 13, 2006, http://community dispatch.com/artman/publish/article_3285.shtml.

Nutini, Hugo G. *San Bernardino Contla: Marriage and Family Structure in a Tlaxcalan Municipio.* Pittsburgh: University of Pittsburgh Press, 1968.

Oberste, William H. *Texas Irish Empresarios and Their Colonies.* 2nd ed. Austin, TX: Von Boeckmann-Jones, 1973.

O'Connor, Kathryn Stoner. *The Presidio La Bahía del Espíritu Santo de Zuñiga, 1721–1846.* Austin, TX: Van Boeckmann-Jones, 1966.

"Okies on Record Ask Roosevelt to Remedy Plight." *Voices From the Dust Bowl Scrapbook.* The Library of Congress. Accessed May 5, 2006, http://memory.loc.gov/cgi-bin/ampage?collId=afcts&fileNam=sb001.db&recNum=18.

Ortiz, Antonio Dominguez. *Ciclos y temas de la historia de España: clases privilegiadas en el Antiguo Régimen.* Madrid: Ediciones ISTMO, 1979.

Osante, Patricia. *Orígenes del Nuevo Santander (1748–1772).* Mexico City: Universidad Nacional Autónoma de México, Universidad Autónoma de Tamaulipas, 1997.

Passenger lists of Vessels Arriving in New Orleans, July 18, 1836, M259–14, Microfilm at New Orleans Public Library, New Orleans, LA.

Patricia de la Garza to T. Rusk, May 15, 1836. Rusk Papers, State Archives, Austin, TX.

Patricia de la Garza, Will, Probate Records, vol. 1. Victoria County Clerk's Office, Victoria, TX.

P. Dimmitt to T. Rusk, July, 1836. Rusk Papers, State Archives, Austin, TX.

Peter P. Pitchlynn Collection. Papers ed. University of Oklahoma Libraries, Western History Collections, Norman, OK.

Perdue, Theda. *Slavery and the Evolution of Cherokee Society.* Knoxville: University of Tennessee Press, 1979.

Petty, J. W., Jr. *Victor Rose's History of Victoria.* Victoria, TX: Book Mart, 1961.

Poyo, Gerald E., and Gilberto Hinojosa. "Spanish Texas and Borderlands Historiography in Transition." *Journal of American History* 75, no. 2 (September 1988): 393–416.

Purdy, Virginia C. "'Dust to Eat': A Document from the Dust Bowl." *The Chronicles of Oklahoma* 58, no. 4 (1980): 440–54.

Robertson, Pauline Durrett, and R. L. Robertson. *Panhandle Pilgrimage: Illustrated*

*Tales Tracing History in the Texas Panhandle.* Amarillo, TX: Paramount Publishing, 1977.

Robinson, Willard B. "Colonial Ranch Architecture in the Spanish-Mexican Tradition." *Southwestern Historical Quarterly* 83 (October 1979): 123–50.

Robbins, William. *Colony and Empire: The Transformation of the American West.* Lawrence: University of Kansas Press, 1994.

Rose, Victor M. *Some Historical Facts in Regard to the Settlement of Victoria, Texas.* Laredo, TX: Daily Times Print, 1883. Reprinted as *Victor Rose's History of Victoria,* edited by J. W. Petty, Jr. Victoria, TX: Book Mart, 1961.

Rubio, Abel. *Stolen Heritage: A Mexican-American's Rediscovery of His Family's Lost Land Grant.* Edited by Thomas H. Krenecke. Austin, TX: Eakin Press, 1986.

Ruiz, Vicki L. *From Out of the Shadows: Mexican Women in Twentieth-Century America.* New York: Oxford University Press, 1998.

Sander, William. "The Economics of Divorce in the Farm Sector." *North Central Journal of Agricultural Economics* 8 (January 1986): 1–6.

Shackel, Sandra K. *Western Women's Lives: Continuity and Change in the Twentieth Century.* Albuquerque: University of New Mexico Press, 2003.

Scharff, Virginia. *Twenty Thousand Roads: Women, Movement, and the West.* Berkeley: University of California Press, 2003.

Schusky, Ernest L. *Variation in Kinship.* New York: Holt, Rinehart and Winston, 1974.

Sharpless, Rebecca. *Fertile Ground, Narrow Choices: Women on Texas Cotton Farms, 1900–1940.* Chapel Hill: University of North Carolina Press, 1999.

Smith, Sherry L., ed. *The Future of the Southern Great Plains.* Norman: University of Oklahoma Press, 2003.

Solano, Francisco. *Cedulario de tierras: Compilación de legislación agraria colonial (1497–1820),* Law Number 226. Mexico City: Universidad Nacional Autónoma de México, 1984.

Steinbeck, John. *The Grapes of Wrath.* New York: Viking Press, 1939.

Stillman, William O. "Prevention of Cruelty to Animals." *Proceedings of the Academy of Political Science in the City of New York,* Organization for Social Work 2, no. 4 (July 1912): 150–58.

Stuntz, Jean A. *Hers, His, and Theirs: Community Property Law in Spain and Early Texas.* Lubbock: Texas Tech University Press, 2005.

"Summer Sizzle Continues in Texas, Southern Plains." CNN.com, August 3,1998. Accessed January 13, 2006, www.cnn.com/US/9808/03/heat.wave.o2.

Swanton, John. "An Early Account of the Choctaw Indians." *Memoirs of the American Anthropological Association* 5, no. 2 (1918): 64.

———. *Source Material for the Social and Ceremonial Life of the Choctaw Indians.* Birmingham, AL: Birmingham Public Library Press, 1993.

Syers, William Edward. *Texas: The Beginning, 1519–1839.* Waco, TX: The Texian Press, 1978.

Tate, Michael L. "Comanche Captives: People Between Two Worlds." *Chronicles of Oklahoma* 72, no. 3 (1994): 228–63.

Tax rolls for 1839, 1841, 1844, Victoria County Clerk's Office, Victoria, TX.

Taylor, Dolly Thompson. Interview by Wilma Hixon, July 18 and 27, 1936. Panhandle-Plains Historical Museum Research Center, Canyon, TX.

Teichmann, Sandra Gail, ed., *Woman of the Plains: The Journals and Stories of Nellie M. Perry.* College Station: Texas A&M University Press, 2000.

Teja, Jesús F. de la. "'Pleasing and Fertile Desert': Land Grants in the San Antonio River Valley, 1718–1836." *South Texas Studies*, Spring 2000.

———. *San Antonio de Béxar: A Community on New Spain's Northern Frontier.* Albuquerque: University of New Mexico Press, 1995.

"The Handbook of Texas Online." Texas State Historical Association. Accessed July 29, 2008, www.tsha.utexas.edu/handbook/online.

Thurman, James N. "Oklahoma in the Grip of New Dust Bowl." *Christian Science Monitor* 90 (August 24, 1998): 1.

Tortorelli, R. L. "Floods and Droughts: Oklahoma, National Water Summary, 1988–89: TS. Geological Survey." USGS Water Resources of Oklahoma. Accessed April 25, 2005, http://ok.water.usgs.gov/drought/drought.paper.html.

US Census Bureau. US Census 1880, 1890, 1900, 1910, 1920, 1930. Washington, DC: US Government Printing Office.

Van Nuys, Frank. *Americanizing the West: Race, Immigrants, and Citizenship, 1890–1930.* Lawrence: University Press of Kansas, 2002.

Vázquez, Josefina Zoraida. "Los Primeros Tropiezos." In *Historia General de México.* Vol. 3. Mexico City: El Colegio de México, 1976.

Vega, William A., et al. "Cohesion and Adaptability in Mexican-American and Anglo Families." *Journal of Marriage and the Family* 48 (November 1986): 857–65.

Vick, Francis B. "Cornelia Wadsworth Ritchie Adair." In Massey, *Texas Women on the Cattle Trails*, 148–64.

Villaseñor, Roberto E. *El Coronel Don José Escandón y la conquista del Nuevo Santander.* Mexico D. F.: Boletín del Archivo General de la Nación, 1979.

"Voices of American Farm Women." Voices of American Farm Women Educational Programming Guide. Exhibition made possible by Valmont Industrial Exhibits USA, a national program of Mid-America Arts Alliance. Accessed May 5, 2006, www.maa.org/exhi_usa/exhibitions/farm woman/pg_farmwomen.pdf.

Warwick, Mrs. Clyde W., ed. *The Randall County Story.* Hereford, TX: Pioneer Book Publishers, 1969.

Weisiger, Marsha. *Land of Plenty: Oklahomans in the Cotton Fields of Arizona, 1933–1942.* Norman: University of Oklahoma Press, 1995.

Westin, Jeane. *Making Do: How Women Survived the 30s.* Chicago: Follett, 1976.

Wickett, Murray R. *Whites, Native Americans, and African Americans in Oklahoma.* Baton Rouge: Louisiana State University Press, 2000.

"Wildfires Ravage Southern Plains," CBS News, Accessed January 13, 2006, www.cbsnews.com/stories/2005/12/28/nationa/main1166988_page2.shtml.

White, Richard. *"It's Your Misfortune and None of My Own": A New History of the American West.* Norman: University of Oklahoma Press, 1993.

Worster, Donald. *Dust Bowl: The Southern Plains in the 1930s.* New York: Oxford University Press, 1979.

Wunder, John R., Frances W. Kaye, and Vernon Carstensen, eds. *Americans View Their Dust Bowl Experience.* Boulder: University Press of Colorado, 1999.

Zeuli, Kimberly A., and Robert P. King. "Gender Difference in Farm Management." *Review of Agricultural Economics* 20 (Autumn-Winter 1998): 513–29.

Zorrilla, Juan Fidel. *Historia de Tamaulipas.* Ciudad Victoria, Tamaulipas: Dirección General de Educación y Cultura, 1987.

# Contributors

**Donna L. Akers,** citizen of the Choctaw Nation of Oklahoma, is associate professor at the University of Nebraska, specializing in Indigenous and Native American decolonization studies.

**Gretchen A. Albers** is a PhD candidate at the University of Calgary, specializing in North American western history, women's history, and Aboriginal history.

**Rebecca Bales** is assistant professor of Native American studies and history at California State University, Monterey Bay, specializing in women's studies, California history, and US race relations.

**Peter Boag,** Columbia Chair in the History of the American West at Washington State University, specializes in gender, sexuality, and the modern United States.

**Caroline Castillo Crimm** is professor of history at Sam Houston State University in Huntsville, Texas, specializing in Latin America, nineteenth-century Texas, and the borderlands.

**Roger Davis,** professor of history at the University of Nebraska at Kearney, specializes in the history of the Gilded Age and nineteenth-century Latin America.

**Dee Garceau** is a filmmaker and associate professor of history at Rhodes College in Memphis, Tennessee, specializing in gender in the American West and North American Indian history.

**Joan M. Jensen,** professor emerita of American history at New Mexico State University, specializes in rural and western women's history.

**Renee M. Laegreid**, associate professor of history at Hastings College in Nebraska, specializes in women's and gender history in the American West.

**Elaine Lindgren**, professor emerita of sociology at North Dakota State University, specializes in social change, sociology of work, and gender.

**Sandra K. Mathews** is professor of history at Nebraska Wesleyan University, specializing in the American West, comparative borderlands, and American Indian history.

**Sandra J. McBride**, instructor of English at Nebraska Wesleyan University, specializes in composition and gender studies.

**Sarah R. Payne**, historical consultant, specializes in environmental history, comparative gender, and the history of the American West.

**Andrea G. Radke-Moss**, professor of history at Brigham Young University–Idaho, specializes in the American West and women's history.

**Linda W. Reese**, retired associate professor at East Central University in Oklahoma, specializes in the American West, women's history, and Oklahoma history.

**Sandra Scofield** is an award-winning author, editor, and mentor of other writers. Experiences and memories growing up in Texas have strongly influenced her writing and landscape painting.

**Shannon D. Smith** is associate director of teaching, learning, and professional development at EDUCAUSE in Boulder, Colorado, and online adjunct instructor at Oglala Lakota College.

**Jean Stuntz**, associate professor of history at West Texas A&M University, specializes in western women's history, and history of Texas and the borderlands.

# Index TK

AAA (Agricultural Adjustment Administration), 232–33
abuse, 22, 101, 193, 208
Ackerman, Lillian A., 109
activism: of Hispanic women, 213–14; introduction to, 148–49; Native women and, 80–85, 154–59; rural farm women and, 149–54
Adair, Cornelia, 217–18
Adair, John, 217–18
Adams, Jane, 235, 236
"adoption, law of," 135, 143–45
African Americans: Choctaw Nation and, 196–99; cotton farming and, 231–32, 293n17; literature of, 260n5, 260n7; on northern plains, 69–74
Agricultural Adjustment Administration (AAA), 232–33
agriculture: ceremonial cycles and, 100; in Choctaw Nation, 193; early Native tribes and, 18–19; education and activism in, 149–54; farm women and, 231–35; Native women and, 39–40, 93–94, 100–101, 193; in origin stories, 29, 96; tradition and innovation in, 174; women homesteaders and, 49–50, 55–56; Women in Agriculture program, 153

AIM (American Indian Movement), 81, 83–84, 157–58, 264n76
Albers, Patricia, 27, 65
Aldrete, José Miguel, 181, 188, 285n41
Alexander, Delois, 236
Alexander, Ruth Ann, 62–63
Allen, Gilbert, 114–15, 117–18
Allen, Paula Gunn, 98
Amarillo, Texas, xvii–xviii, 220–23
*American Daughter* (Thompson), 69–72, 260n5
American Indian Movement (AIM), 81, 83–84, 157–58, 264n76
Americanization Movement, 215
Anderson, Joyce, 76
Anthony, Susan B., 58
Aquash, Nogeeshik, 83
archaeology, 14–15, 32, 246n15, 246n17, 266n21
Archaic era, 16
Archambault, JoAllyn, 97
Armitage, Susan, 171
Armstrong, William, 195
arts, Indian, xix–xx, 156
Asian immigrants, 160–63
assimilation: of *coureurs des bois*, 24–25; gender roles and, 155, 196; of Hispanic immigrants, 215–16; immi-

O'Brien, Patricia J., 96, 266n21
Ohitika Woman (Brave Bird), 81, 82
Oklahoma homesteaders, 224–28,
    233–34, 238, 240
Old Nash, 94, 119–26
de Oñate, Juan, 102, 107–8, 207
origin stories, 10–14, 29–30, 96–100
owl, in children's tale, 19–20

Packineau, Frank, 30
Parker, Cynthia Ann, 210
Parker, Mary Haskin. See Richards, Mary
    Parker
Parker, Quanah, 210, 211
patriarchal oppression, 192–93, 195–96
patrilineal kinship system, 16
Patschke, Vicki Davis, 241
Peña, Soledad, 214
Penn State University Department of
    Agricultural Economics and Rural
    Sociology study, 239
Perdue, Theda, 191, 193
Perry, George, 220
Perry, Nellie, 220
Peters, Anastasius, 221
Peterson, Helen, 157
Philharmonic Club, 223
photography, 56
Picotte, Susan LaFlesche, 64, 97
Pictou-Aquash, Anna Mae, 80–85,
    264n79
Pike, Zebulon Montgomery, xxv, 180,
    244n11
Pitchlynn, Peter, 193–95
Pittet, Nancy, 76–77, 78
place: gender and ethnicity and, 9,
    69–74; Native civil rights and, 80–85;
    war brides and, 74–80
Plumber, Rachel, 209
plural marriage, 132–33, 135–40, 208–9,
    274n31
Pocahontas, 27
Political Equality League (PEL), 60
polygamy, 132–33, 135–40, 208–9,
    274n31
polygyny, 26, 34, 42

Pourin' Down Rain (Foggo), 72–74
Powell, John Wesley, 245n4
Pretty-Shield, 22, 64
priesthood authority, Mormon women's
    use of, 131–32, 141–46, 273n13
El Primer Congreso Mexicanista, 214
progress narrative, 119–26
prohibition, 57, 58, 59
by proxy ceremonies, Mormon, 134–35,
    145–46
Pyle, Mary Shields "Mamie," 58

quilting, xix–xx
Quinn, Bridget, 186
Quivira, 108, 267n41

race: gender and culture and, 9, 69–74,
    190–205; war brides and, 74–80. See
    also ethnicity
racism, 194–98, 213–14, 229–31, 267n3
Radisson, Pierre-Esprit, 23
Ramirez, Sara Estela, 213–14
Rancho de Santa Margarita, 178–81
Randall County, 221
rape, 81, 101
Rattles Her Medicine, 30–31, 33
REA (Rural Electrification Administra-
    tion), 233
Red River Rebellion, 65–66
Reel, Estelle, 63
Reese, Linda W., 164, 174
Reeves, Margaret, 230–31
regionalism, xxiv
Reichardt, Joan, 76
religion, 220–21, 236–38
relocation, 157
reservations, 64–65
Richard, Doreen, 78–79
Richards, Jane Snyder, 141, 145–46
Richards, Mary Parker, 128, 134, 137–41,
    145–47, 274n31
Richards, Phineas, 140
Richards, Samuel, 138–40
Richardson, Albert, 112, 113, 117
Rickert, Ester, 165
Riel, Louis, 65–66